MUSTER ROLLS
OF THE
SOLDIERS OF THE WAR OF 1812
Detached from the Militia
of
NORTH CAROLINA
in 1812 and 1814

*Published Under the Direction
of the Adjutant General*

With an Added Index
By MAURICE S. TOLER

Southern Historical Press, Inc.
Greenville, South Carolina

Originally Published 1851

SOUTHERN HISTORICAL PRESS, INC.
PO BOX 1267
Greenville, SC   29601

ISBN #978-1-63914-086-2

Printed in the United States of America

MUSTER ROLLS

OF THE

SOLDIERS OF THE WAR OF 1812:

DETACHED FROM

THE MILITIA OF NORTH CAROLINA,

IN 1812 AND 1814.

PUBLISHED IN PURSUANCE OF THE RESOLUTIONS OF THE GENERAL ASSEMBLY OF JANUARY 21, 1851,

UNDER THE DIRECTION OF THE ADJUTANT GENERAL.

RALEIGH:

PRINTED BY CH. C. RABOTEAU, AT THE TIMES OFFICE.

1851.

Reprinted 1926 By
The Barber Printing Company, Inc.
Winston-Salem, N. C.

RESOLUTIONS directing the Adjutant General to publish copies of the Muster Rolls of the Soldiers of the war of 1812.

Resolved, That the Adjutant General be and is hereby directed to have published a hundred copies, duly certified, of the Muster Rolls of the Soldiers of the war of 1812, which are on file in his Department; and that one copy be sent to the Clerk of the county court in each county of this State.

Resolved further, That when it shall be made to appear to the Treasurer, that the requirements of the above Resolution have been complied with, he shall pay to the Adjutant General, as a compensation for his services, out of any money not otherwise appropriated, the sum of one hundred dollars.

Read three times and ratified in General Assembly, this 28th day of January, A. D. 1851.

J. C. DOBBIN, S. H. C.
W. N. EDWARDS, S. S.

MUSTER ROLL

Of the Infantry detached from the Militia of North Carolina, in pursuance of a Requisition of the President of the United States in virtue of an Act of Congress of the 10th of April, 1812.

DIVISION,

Thomas Brown, Major General, Commanding.

FIRST BRIGADE, detached from the 1st, 13th, 2d, 3d, 12th, 5th, 4th and 14th Brigades of the Organized Militia of the State—Thomas Davis, Brigader General, Commanding.

FIRST REGIMENT, detached from the 1st and 13th Brigade of Ditto.
Josiah Flowers, Lieutenant Colonel Commandant,
Caleb Etheridge, First Major,
John M. Cotter, Second Major.

First Company of the First Regiment, detached from the Currituck Regiment

1 John Ship, *Captain*
2 Cornelius Jones, 1st *Lieut.*
3 Amburrus Walston, 2d *do.*
4 Gideon Bonney, *Ensign*
5 Joshua White, *Private*
6 Samuel Beasley
7 Dennis Capts
8 John Smith
9 Jacob Wichel
10 John White jr
11 Malachi Dudley
12 Levan Dudley
13 Jacob Williams
14 William Beasley
15 Caleb Wilson
16 Augustus Linton
17 James Northam
18 Merrit Ballance
19 Thomas Etheridge
20 Nicholas Elydon
21 William Garrett
22 Ivy Halstead
23 Joseph Sawyer
24 Charles Sawyer
25 William Bray jr
26 Thomas Mitchel
27 William Bunnell
28 Joseph Poyner
29 Jonathan Wright
30 Richard Decker
31 Jesse Parr
32 Thomas Archland
33 Merese Jarvis
34 Henry Spence
35 Arthur Spence
36 John Boswell
37 James Fentus
38 Bartlett Burton
39 Charles Fulford
40 Joseph Fulford
41 John Gregory
42 Andrew Heath
43 James Whitheral, jr
44 James Nicholson
45 William Snider
46 William Perkins
47 Henry Doxey
48 Mitchel Gregory
49 John Baker
50 John Mayo
51 William Halstead
52 James Banks
53 James Gregory
54 John Gray
55 Josiah Taylor
56 Thomas McMooney
57 Hollowell Sawyer
58 Joel Poyner
59 Frederick White
60 George Fisher
61 Benjamin Taylor
62 Shadrack Kallum
63 William Thompson

Second Company, detached from the Currituck Regiment.

1 Hillary Bell, *Capt.*
2 Joshua Baxter, *Lieut.*
5 Michel Orneal, *Private,*
6 James Parker
7 William Spry
8 Thomas Gregory
9 Jesse Robeson
10 William Devout
11 Jeremiah Gorden
12 Thomas Whitehall
13 Thomas Writentt
14 Elijah Hunnings
15 John Griffin
16 Thomas Mercer
17 Caleb Harress
18 James Sawyer
19 Cornelius Mecoy
20 Jasper Gibson
21 Thomas B. Jarvis
22 Ishum Hunt
23 Thomas Allen
24 John Demdtund
25 Josiah Beals
26 Noah Hobbs
27 Uriah Simpson
28 Mark Harris
29 Jonathan Chapter
30 Trininger Sandler
31 William Greves

32 Nathan Shannon
33 Peter M Gray
34 Thomas Curls
35 Joseph Sanderson
36 Matthias Davis
37 Isaac Dowdy
38 William Leimpoon
39 Thomas Parker
40 Thomas Daniel
41 David Daniel
42 Baley Daniel
43 Avra Daniel
44 John Daniel
45 John Shannon
46 John Credworth
47 Joseph Baglen
48 John Barnett
49 Daniel Stow
50 Valentine Waite
51 Joseph Quidley
52 Thomas Scarborough
53 Wallis Stirran
54 Zachariah Burrus
55 William Gray
56 Benjamin Stow
57 John Quidley
58 Moses Auston
59 Cornelius Auston
60 Bartlett Quidley

Third Company, detached from the Camden Regiment.

1 James S Garling, *Captain*
2 Baley Barco, *First Lieutenant*
3 Willis Wilson, *Second do*
4 Wilson Webster, *Ensign*
5 James Forbes, *First Sergeant*
6 John W. Harrison, *Second do*
7 James Godfrey, *Third do*
8 Edward Pugh, *Fourth do*
9 William Godfrey, *First corporal*
10 Simon Jones, *Second do*
11 Jeremiah Jones, *Third do*
12 Isaac Berry, *Fourth do*
13 Robert Boushel, *Private*
14 John Gallup
15 Edward Curlin
16 Phillip Morissett
17 Timothy Berry
18 Nathan Gregory
19 Frederick Gregory
20 Etheridge Standley
21 William Berry
22 Joseph McCoy
23 Jesse Dowdy
24 Roding Mercer
25 Dempsey Wilson

26 John Shorter
27 James Willis
28 Caleb Jarvis
29 Elias McKoy
30 Henry Gregory
31 William Dowdy
32 Peter Seymore
33 Abner Sanderlin
34 Jonathan Gregory
35 Caleb Woodard
36 Wilson Sikes
37 Samuel Gregory
38 John Lewis
39 Isaac Avery
40 Jabez Garlington
41 Edmond Gregory sen
42 Miles Berry
43 Shipperd Foster
44 Tully Morrissett
45 John Mitchell
46 David Dunken
47 James Garret
48 Jacob James
49 Abner Sikes
50 Abner Cooper

51 Lemuel Gregory
52 James Huit
53 Cornelius Bryon
54 Nathaniel Hughes
55 Owen W Harrison
56 Edmund Gregory, jr
57 Thomas Portlock
58 Joshua Gallup
59 Henry W Harrison
60 Wilson W Nash
61 Josiah Nash
62 Archibald Sawyer

63 Markum Stafford
64 Joshua Smisson
65 Joseph Bray
66 Thomas Gregory
67 William Proctor
68 Wilson Duncan
69 Dempsey J Burgess
70 Moses Brock
71 Bradley Smith
72 Zebulin Dunkin
73 Benjamin Carter

Fourth Company, detached from the Pasquotank Regiment.

1 William Spence, *Captain*
2 Richard Muse, *Lieutenant*
3 Joseph Sutton, *Ensign*
4 John Graves, *Private*
5 Jesse Bray
6 Edward Greves
7 Thaddeus Snowden
8 Peter William
9 David Griffin
10 John Low
11 Holowell Vardell
12 Thomas Denby
13 John Keel
14 Benjamin Lowry
15 Samuel Overman
16 Urias Turner
17 Samuel Spelman
18 Thomas Woodley
19 Joshua Benton
20 Charles Hunt
21 Jesse Jordan
22 William Hite
23 Elijah Munden
24 Isaac Gallop
25 Caleb Bundy
26 Nathan Bundy
27 Jonathan Garrett
28 William Turner
29 Nixon Low
30 Jesse Bundy
31 William Munden
32 Noah Perry
33 Benjamin Brothers
34 Josiah Mackey
35 Henry Cox
36 Enoch Pritchard
37 Joseph Harrell
38 Miles Turner
39 Arthur Gordon
40 Henry Raper
41 Daniel White
42 Lemuel Cambell

43 Richard Clark
44 Christopher Cartwright
45 Samuel Dozier
46 Stephen Scott
47 Adam Deal
48 Jordan Gray
49 Thomas Humphis
50 Samuel Jones
51 Enoch Sawyer
52 Britton Temple
53 Isaac Williams
54 William Cartwright
55 Benjamin Gilbert
56 Lot Fentress
57 Richard Clayton
58 John F Markum
59 John Lowry
60 William Nichilson
61 Cornelius Scott
62 Lemuel Barrington
63 Frederick Davis
64 Michel Phillips
65 Alexander Whitehouse
66 Thomas Cartwright
67 Joshua Cartwright
68 John Harris
69 James Davis
70 William Carter
71 James Jackson
72 Joshua Jackson
73 Robert Spence
74 David Nichols
75 Edward Scott
76 Julian D Belinger
77 James Leonard
78 John Casa
79 Thomas Allen
80 Jacob Simpson
81 John Cartwright
82 Stephen Chaney
83 George White
84 Davis Spelman

Fifth Company, detached from Perquimans Regiment.

1 Thomas Myers, *Captain*
2 Matthew Jordan, *Lieutenant*
3 Willis Roberts, *Ensign*
4 Charles Clay, *Private*
5 Exum Nuby
6 Reuben Overman
7 Lemuel Tucker
8 Benjamin Maudlin
9 Abel Rogerson
10 Elisha Harreld
11 Elisha Farles
12 Henry Garrett
13 William Standen
14 Joseph Bagley
15 Phillip Mason
16 William Tweddy
17 William Colleson
18 Harrison Turner
19 James Turner, jr
20 James Turner, sen
21 George P Whidbee
22 Stephen Twiddy
23 Jonathan Bogue
24 Tully Williams
25 Myles Turner
26 Thomas Allen
27 William Hatfield
28 Joseph Arrenton
29 Joshua McCoy
30 Thomas Jones
31 Thomas Arrenton
32 Jonathan Smith
33 Joseph Jackson
34 Reuben Hobbs
35 Lemuel Bateman
36 John Jackson
37 Francis Wills
38 Hardy Bateman
39 Thomas Woodley
40 Obadiah Reddick
41 Reddick Hallswell
42 Lemuel Lain
43 Tully Moss
44 Joseph Pike
45 Samuel Maudlin
46 Isaac Twiddy
47 Thomas Allen
48 Sassel McCoy
49 Benjamin Bateman
50 Griffin Brinkly
51 Joshua Talton
52 Elisha Eliott
53 John Moss
54 Asa Lymons
55 Nathan Bagley
56 Moses Webb
57 Delight Nixon
58 William Burnham
59 Abraham Green
60 Aaron Green
61 Thomas Hudson
62 Tully Laden
63 Jesse Ward
64 Samuel Barclipt
65 James Stanton
66 Saphem Elliott
67 Benjamin Shinner
68 Samuel Weeks
69 Thomas Hendricks
70 William Barker
71 Isaac Wilson
72 Henry Hobbs
73 John Sylvester
74 Benjamin Munden
75 Edward Saunders
76 Joseph Arrenton
77 Edward Arrenton
78 Nathan Nichilson
79 Exum Newby
80 John Hardle.

Sixth Company, detached from Chowan Regiment.

1 John Meguire, *Captain*
2 Thomas Tapping, *Lieutenant*
3 Welch Fullerton, *Ensign*
4 Thomas Tarlton, *First Sergeant*
5 Abram Holloway, *Second do*
6 Luke Holloway, *Third do*
7 Green Meredith, *Fourth do*
8 Job Perkins, *First Corporal*
9 Julius Bunch, *Second do*
10 Neil Sherwood, *Third do*
11 Joseph Pain, *Fourth do*
12 David Welch, *Private*
13 James Ward
14 Dachim Mansfield
15 Charles Miller
16 Reddick Wood
17 Elisha Hurdle
18 Archibald Leath
19 William Flury
20 Samuel Fitt
21 Thomas Webb
22 Abraham Pettigor
23 Charles Stewart
24 John Bond
25 Salter Bunch
26 John Standing
27 Nimrod West
28 Caleb Ganot

29 Peter Markell
30 John McGlaughlin
31 Henry Morris
32 John Bysam
33 James Braughton
34 James Crery
35 William Wingate
36 Josiah Bogue
37 Felston Cotten
38 Nathaniel Bunch
39 James Robertson
49 Hana Jorden
41 Miles Halsey
42 Noah Smith
43 Demsey Trotman

44 Miles Elliott
45 John Ward
46 John Watson
47 William Walton
48 Micajah Ward
49 Daniel Harris
50 Jacob Perry
51 Abner Goodwin
52 George Webb
53 Levi Persons
54 James Swan
55 Elisha Parker
56 John Middleton
57 Daniel Liverman

Seventh Company, detached from the Gates Regiment.

1 Thomas Freeman, *Captain*
2 Robert Reddick, *Lieutenant*
3 Simon Stallings, *Ensign*
4 Edwin Ballard, *First Sergeant*
5 Lemuel Goodman, *Second do*
6 Lemuel Reddick, *Third do*
7 Richard H Lee, *Fourth do*
8 Henry Brinkley, *First Corporal*
9 Abbey Benton, *Second do*
10 David Benton, *Third do*
11 John Hare, *Fourth do*
12 William Lunding, *Private*
13 Jacob Benton
14 John Blanchard
15 Ransom Phillips
16 Aaron Harrell
17 Abner Green
18 Elisha Robertson
19 Isaac Hiott
20 Kader Bereman
21 Dempsey Blanchard
22 William Green
23 Henry King
24 Timothy Robertson
25 William Spright
26 Moses Spivey
27 John Alphin
28 Luke Parker
29 Willis Figg
30 Kader Hurdle
31 Joseph Phillips
32 Moses Davis
33 John Saunders
34 James Jordan
35 John Spright
36 William Matthews

37 Elisha Matthias
38 Kader Reddick
39 Luke Freling
40 Harman Hays
41 Abram Parker
42 William Sumner
43 Benjamin Morgain
44 James Spright
45 Jethro Briggs
46 Thomas Brown
47 Jesse Carter
48 William Haffler
49 Arthur Boyett
50 Frederick Alphin
51 Jacob P Jones
52 John Fanney
53 Elisha Peel
54 William Benton
55 Jesse Down
56 John Outlaw
57 Richard P Curl
58 Miles Parker
59 Barnard Marsh
60 John Felton
61 Stephen Eure
62 Kinchin Phillips
63 Benjamin Cross
64 Cypron Eure
65 Vinson H Jones
66 Robert Parker
67 Josiah Ellis
68 Reddick Peel
69 Jethro Benton
70 Henry H Benton
71 John Arnold
72 Frederick Simpson

Eighth Company, detached from the Hertford Regiment.

1 Irwin Jenkins, *Captain*
2 Everard Garrett, *Lieutenant*
3 Benjamin Hill, *Ensign*

4 Andrew Oliver, *Cadet*
5 James Spires, *do*
6 William Walton, *First Sergeant*

7 Hardy Banks, *Second Sergeant*
8 Josiah Battle, *Third do*
9 John Scott, *Fourth do*
10 Arthur Booth, *First Corporal*
11 Elisha Horton, *Second do*
12 Charles Jenkins, *Third do*
13 James Witherington, *Fourth do*
14 John Manning, *Drummer*
15 Wiley Brown, *Fifer*
16 James Early, *Private*
17 Lemuel Holloman
18 James Hayes
19 Thomas Britton
20 Luke McGlaulum
21 Nathan Baker
22 Cornelius H Goodwin
23 Anthony Brown
24 Anthony Williams
25 Noah Evans
26 Jacob Sewell
27 Jethro Sewell
28 Jacob Hare
29 John Baker
30 John Scull
31 Thomas Holland
32 Henry D Jenkins
33 John Curl
34 John Denton
35 William Ballester
36 Thomas Clark
37 Josiah I Askins
38 Lewis Carter
39 Jonas Atkins
40 Henry Brantly
41 William Williams
42 Henry Wiggins
43 Miles Hobbs
44 John Everitt
45 Alexander Booth
46 Levi Crecy

47 Thomas Thorne
48 Zachariah Brown
49 Edward Crump
50 Anthony B Lee
51 John Benthall
52 Robert Brantley
53 Thomas Neale
54 Alexander Smith
55 William Brown
56 Isaac Pearce
57 George Asken
58 Edward Brantley
59 Henry Eure
60 Joseph G Rea
61 William Wynns
62 Thomas Weston
63 Allen L Ramsey
64 Elisha Mints
65 James Parker
66 Benjamin Ezell
67 Britton Sikes
68 William Andrews
69 Isaac Foster
70 John C Montgomery
71 Reuben Clark
72 Lewis Boon
73 Josiah Robbins
74 Elijah Archer
75 Ephraim King
76 Samuel Boon
77 Mathuel Archer
78 James Raleigh
79 John Weaver
80 James B Jones
81 Hardy Davis
82 Mills Walters
83 Abram Boon
84 West Boon
85 John Bizzett

Ninth Company, detached from Washington Regiment.

1 Henry Garret, *Captain*
2 Andrew Armstrong, *Lieutenant*
3 John Rogers, *Ensign*
4 Zachariah Sutton
5 Joseph Snyder
6 Benjamin Cullipher
7 Eliakim Norman
8 Isaac Cullipher
9 Davis Biggs
10 Zebedee Tarkinton
11 Jehu Ambrose
12 Enos Tarkinton
13 Reuben Clifton
14 Levi Ambrose
15 Roger Snell
16 Nathan I Swain

17 Edward Nar
18 Isaac Rawson
19 Samuel Jones
20 Isaac Skittlethrop
21 Edmund Skittlethrop
22 Joseph Spruill
23 William Forlan
24 Enoch Steely
25 John Simpson
26 John Airs
27 Jesse Collins
28 William Woodley
29 Miles Hopkins
30 Andrew Spruill
31 Arthur Skittlethrop
32 Isham Pearce

33 Bethuel Murray
34 William Allen
35 Ezekiel Blount
36 Thomas Smith
37 Hiram Snell
38 Frederick B Jennings
39 Charles Morse

40 Edward Parish
41 Simeon Swain
42 James F James
43 Joseph Sax
44 Starkey Tarkinton
45 Thomas Gilbert
46 Enoch Bundy

Tenth Company, detached from the Tyrrell Regiment.

1 William Alexander, *Captain*
2 Richard Howell, *Lieutenant*
3 James Haysell, *Ensign*
4 Benjamin Brickhouse
5 James Davenport
6 Uriah Spruill
7 Emri Spruill
8 Uzzell Brickhouse
9 Benjamin Clayton
10 James McAlsten
11 William Brickhouse
12 Harman Alexander
13 Ricardo Rudd
14 William Steatman
15 Elisha Stirum
16 Solomon Creed
17 John West
18 William Swain
19 Isaac West
20 Benjamin Hassell
21 Spencer Midgitt
22 Isaac Liverman
23 James Sivels
24 Harry Charles
25 Stephen Powell
26 Joshua Swain
27 Ozias Roughton
28 Zadoch Hassell
29 James Whitbee

30 Maxy Davis
31 Selby Patrick
32 Asa Barratt
33 William White
34 Thomas Sawyer
35 Peleg Simmons
36 Selby Armstrong
37 Bartlett Jones
38 Ebenezer Cohoon
39 William Russ
40 John Banks
41 Azariah Hutson
42 Thomas Clayton
43 William Ward
44 Mitchel Paine
45 Joseph Mason
46 Joseph Man
47 Hiram Hooker
48 John Mydgett
49 Robert Holmes
50 Michael Hadok
51 Hezekiah Mariner
52 John Wynn
53 Jeremiah Phillip
54 Noah Dowers
55 Enoch Davenport
56 Charles Phillips
57 Silby Powers

SECOND REGIMENT

Detached from the 2d, 12th and 3d Brigades.

Simon Bruton, Lieutenant Colonel Commandant.
Nathan Tisdale, First Major,
John A Lillington, Second Major.

First Company, detached from Hyde Regiment.

1 Beverly Rew, *Captain*
2 Joshua Bell, *Lieutenant*
3 James Cheves, *Ensign*
4 Moses Windley
5 Jasper Smith
6 Enoch Flinn, jr
7 Joshua Freeman
8 John Peartree

9 Christopher Matison
10 Maurice Jones
11 Benjamin Slade
12 James Daniels
13 Winfield Davis
14 Oden Wilkinson
15 Joshua Muse
16 John Winfield

B

17 Benjamin Smith
18 Selden Henderson
19 William Banks
20 John Fortiscue
21 John Russell Fortiscue
22 Jeremiah Warner
23 Burrige Selby
24 Thomas Winfield
25 Jacob Caffee
26 Hugh Foddree
27 Richard Migett
28 James Owens
29 Jordan Carrow
30 Thomas Simons
31 Edward Fuller
32 Levi O'Neale

33 William Berry
34 Thomas Daniels
35 Clement Daniels
36 William Bunn
37 Shadrick Daniels
38 Benjamin Bunn
39 Zephaniah Sawyer
40 William Cohoon
41 Jeremiah Hall
42 Joy Sanderson
43 Robert Hopkins
44 Robert Jennett
45 Selby Spencer
46 Solomon Thornton
47 William Casons.

Second Company, detached from Beaufort Regiment.

1 Frederick Brooks, *Captain*
2 Richard Barner, *Lieutenant*
3 John Vines, *Ensign*
4 Will Grist
5 John Booner
6 Richard Bonner
7 John Langley
8 Thomas Heures
9 George C Burbage
10 William Loveland
11 David C Clark
12 Samuel Campbell
13 George Congleton
14 James Howard
15 Jonathan Wallace
16 Jonathan Waters
17 Frederick Waters
18 Charles Waters
19 Eleazer Jackson
20 William Archibald
21 Absalom Price
22 James M Mahow
23 James Boyd
24 James Eborn
25 Alfred Lanir
26 James Cowper
27 Abram Cox
28 Moses Evett
29 Jonathan Giddins
30 Thomas Morris

31 Jesse Evett
32 John Jones, sen.
33 Samuel Vines
34 Gibbin Dickson
35 Thomas Vines
36 William M Moreland
37 Meshart McReel
38 John Barrow
39 Arnett Latham
40 Henry Woodard
41 William Albird
42 Talbing Equals
43 John Barnett
44 Humphrey Cherry
45 Benjamin Cherry
46 James Brown
47 Zachariah Ferrell
48 Alfred Latham
49 Gideon Fannet
50 James Wood
51 William Rawts
52 Ephraim Dickson
53 Jesse Robeson
54 Samuel Philpot
55 Rowland Mayo
56 John Grist
57 Henry Harding
58 Cannon Smith
56 Bryan Archlin

Third Company, detached from Pitt Regiment.

1 Reading Shipp, *Captain*
2 Henry Smith, *Lieutenant*
3 John Smith, *Ensign*
4 William Browning
5 Eliphlet King
6 Sampson Wauley
7 David Smith

8 Elisha Holloman
9 Robert Thomas
10 Kinyan Downs
11 William H Griffin
12 Henry Wright
13 Jepthah May
14 John Pumphrey

15 Newman Dunn
16 Allen Chance
17 Edward Arnold
18 Major Boid
19 William Mumford
20 Joshua Robertson
21 Lewis Burney
22 Jesse Boyd
23 Joseph Sanders
24 Edward Browning
25 James Spivey
26 Absalam Cox
27 Abram Smith
28 Frederick Litchworth
29 Samuel Smith
30 John Cannon
31 William Mooring
32 John Hardee
33 Dennis Cannon
34 Freeman McDowell
35 William Chance
36 Henry Cannon
37 Grove Corbett
38 Frederick Mills
39 Allen Smith
40 Asa Starks
41 Samuel Corbett
42 Samuel Knight

43 Cannon Chaner
44 Samuel Venters
45 Zachariah Cox
46 Kennedy Smith
47 Willie Smith
48 Palmer Cannon
49 Redding Peters
50 Obed Roundtree
51 Benjamin Bently
52 Isaac Robertson
53 Levi Stocks
54 John Roy
55 Nehemiah Dixon
56 Samuel Merrell
57 Stephen Right
58 Cannon Stocks
59 John Mattocks
60 Fred Mills, jr
61 John Vanpelt
62 Cullen Tripp
63 Warren Andrews
64 Witham Casson
65 Simon Barney
66 William Parkes
67 George Bland
68 Edward T Salter
69 Richard F Macklewam

Fourth Company, detached from Craven Regiment.

1 Horatio Dade, *Captain*
2 David Murdock, *Lieutenant*
3 Abner Neale, *second do*
4 Daniel McBean, *Ensign*
5 William H Ives
6 Thomas Leath, *Corporal*
7 James Delamar
8 William Caraway
9 Jeremiah Bateman
10 James Carney, sr
11 Vine Allen
12 George Washington
13 John Gettig
14 Thomas Skidmore
15 James Lewis, *First Sergeant*
16 Jonathan Perkins
17 Darius Amyett
18 Ephraim Simpkins
19 Hardy L Jones
20 Silas Miller
21 Jesse Vendrich
22 James Tingle
23 Major Tingle
24 Iredell Burnett
25 John Rice
26 Thomas Green
27 William Butler
28 Reuben Clark

29 Jeremiah Washington
30 Nathan Slade
31 John Dowdy
32 Smith Jones
33 William Shines, *Corporal*
34 Cornelius Bateman
35 Seldon Delamar
36 Jesse Broadway
37 Barney Wadsworth
38 William J. Loftin
39 Henry Carrow
40 Equilla Pollard
41 Hardy Willis
42 Radford Ernell
43 Allen Ernell
44 Alexander Prichard
45 Alderson Thomas
46 Lewis McKoy
47 Zadock Woods
48 James White
49 Daniel Humphrey
50 Lewis Humphrey
51 Fred Jones
52 Samuel Smith
53 Asa Purify
54 John Everington
55 John Forns
56 Charles Nelson

57 Joseph Polyard
58 William Taylor, 2d *sergeant*
59 William Ward
60 John Parks
61 John Parker
62 Joseph Fulshire
63 Paul Berbank
64 Jesse Barrington
65 Jedediah Dixon
66 James Sewell
67 Thomas Purify
68 William Stableford
69 Frederick Powers
70 Joseph Wiggins
71 Reuben Hobbs

72 Abner Cooper
73 Southey Weatherington
74 William Williams
75 James Atherly
76 Matthew Williams, *Drummer*
77 David Lewis
78 Moses Nichols, 3d *Sergeant*
79 David Russell
80 Tolson Ryal
81 Robert Carney, 4th *Sergeant*
82 Abner Whitehead
83 John T Baily
84 James Lovick
85 Sylvester Brown
86 William Edgar, *corporal*

Fifth Company, detached from Lenoir Regiment.

1 Francis Kilpatrick, *captain*
2 Nathan Bird, 1st *lieutenant*
3 Benjamin Britton, 2d *do*
4 Gabriel Parker, 1st *sergeant*
5 James Uzzell, 2d *do*
6 John Wooten, 3d *do*
7 Francis Bright, 4th *do*
8 James Walford, 1st *corporal*
9 William *Mullin, 2d *do*
   *Miller in one return.
10 Spencer Phillips, 3d *do*
11 Robert Murray, 4th *do*
12 Joshua Bird, *drummer*
13 Isaac Walters, *fifer*
14 Henry Parker
15 Peter Phillips
16 William Kittral
17 John Wiggins
18 Curtis Phillips
19 John Byrd
20 James Davis
21 James B Miller
22 William Mosely
23 William Wayne
24 Samuel Abbot
25 Richard Jones
26 Zachariah Pate
27 Thomas Brown
28 Lewis Falkner
29 Francis Benton
30 John Goodman
31 John Whitfield
32 Henry Pickle
33 James Davis
34 Richard Pickle

35 Cornelius Harper
36 Alexander Thompson
37 William Carter
38 Ashael Herring
39 William Gray
40 Jacob Jackson
41 John Andrews
42 John Gray
43 William Miller
44 William Herring
45 Edwin Taylor
46 Francis Brown
47 William Gray
48 John Ritter
49 Francis Benton
50 Martin Hill
51 Richard Hill
52 Robert Mitchell
53 Nathaniel Walters
54 Joshua Mosely
55 George P Lorrik
56 Kinnon Taylor
57 Selathiel Potts
58 John B Hartsfield
59 Blount Coleman
60 Benjamin Hearing
61 Robert Wiggins
62 Nathaniel Hearing
63 Vinsten Andrews
64 Walter Allen
65 Rayman Surls
66 Joseph Henson
67 William Campbell
68 Shadrick Campbell

Sixth Company, detached from Wayne Regiment.

1 David *Watson, *captain*
   *Wasdon in one return
2 Needham Whitfield, 1st *Lieu't*

3 William Killegrew, 2d *do*
4 Hatch Whitfield, *ensign*
5 John Ammonds, *cadet*

6 Alexander Hines
7 Burwell Rowse
8 John Howell
9 David Jennigan
10 Bryan Barfield
11 Rophael Bird
12 Frinifold Manly
13 Amer McCullen
14 Henry Phillips
15 William Adam
16 David McDaniel
17 Need Pipkin
18 Joseph Pipkin
19 Morris Wyse
20 Thomas Fowler
21 Thomas Coor jr
22 William Rose jr
23 George Collins
24 Elias Harrell
25 Enos Toler
26 Charles Bendon
27 John Motton
28 Law Jackson
29 Joel Harrell
30 Needham Grantum
31 Daniel Bennett
32 John Musgrove
33 William Pipkin
34 William Bass
35 Aaron Lean
36 James Strilling
37 John Brogdon
38 Jesse Floid
39 Josiah Brown
40 John Casey
41 Samuel Flowers
42 Stephen Reeves
43 William Jones
44 Jesse Bass
45 Richard Falkim

46 Wiben Lewis
47 Ully Lewis
48 John Giddins
49 William Measles
50 Jehabud Herring
51 Abner Wiggs
52 Barna Cotten
53 James Johnston
54 William Wilson
55 Robert Jones
56 Levi Skipper
57 William Johnston
58 Edward Holmes
59 John Thompson
60 Phillip Hooks
61 Job Rooks
62 Mathew Daniel
63 George Mitchel
64 Thomas Pindar
65 Enos Holland
66 Joseph Fulghum
67 Joseph Taylor
68 Peter Rice
69 David Thompson
70 Jesse Harper
71 John Harrel
72 John Dean
73 William Hooks
74 Jacob Newsom
75 Joseph Newsom
76 John Britt
77 Wright Smith
78 Woodard Howell
79 Jason Macbau
80 Dawson Smith
81 Curtis Daniel
82 John Sasser
83 Giles Ham
84 Oliver Donell

Seventh Company, detached from Green Regiment.

1 Hymerisk Hooker, *captain*
2 Thomas Hooker, *lieutenant*
3 William Hooper, *first sergeant*
4 John Harper, *second do*
5 William Doughty, *third do*
6 John H Albritton, *fourth do*
7 Joseph J House, *first corporal*
8 Lemuel Speight, *second do*
9 Patrick Dickson, *third do*
10 Absalom Tyler, *fourth do*
11 Readin Jones
12 Joseph Harrell
13 Wiley Dale
14 Caleb Spivy
15 John Jackson
16 Calvin Mage

17 Right Canady
18 Rinchen Hollowday
19 Simeon Albritton
20 James Armond
21 Person Tutton
22 Benjamin Scaborough
23 John Minshew
24 Peter Eppes
25 Jesse Pope
26 Thomas Edwards
27 Stephen Cooke
28 James Hooker
29 Bryant Kilpatrick
30 Michel Coward
31 John Brand
32 Alfred Hart

33	James Butts	56	Gabriel Sherod
34	John Craft	57	Giles Smith
35	George Belcher	58	Elijah Smith
36	Henry Barfield	59	William Hamm
37	Samuel Hay	60	Haywood Hamm
38	Kinchen P Epes	61	Noah Peacock
39	Jesse Coward	62	John Peacock
40	Stephen Johnston	63	James Aycock
41	John Burord	64	Silus Lamb
42	Alexander Williams	65	Jesse Peacock
43	Stephen Chester	66	Elisha Davis
44	Abner Cox	67	Cullen Haywell
45	Elijah Newsom	68	John Peacock
46	John Mayton	69	Nathan Turrell
47	Robert Hinson	70	Edwin Holswell
48	Robert Hall	71	Hezekiah Smith
49	Winston Garland	72	Joseph Hollowell
50	Crewry Rogers	73	William Loveing
51	Hardy Dain	74	Harrison Love
52	Kinchen Faircloth	75	Daniel Ellis
53	Gideon Britt	76	William King
54	Samuel Whitby	77	James Woodard
55	James Elmore	78	Peter Wooten

Eighth Company, detached from Johnston Regiment.

1	Thomas Folsome, *captain*	34	Joseph Farmer
2	Jarrat M Jelks, *first lieutenant*	35	Benjamin Sellers
3	Henry Guy, *second do*	36	Jones Davis
4	John C Guy, *ensign*	37	Benjamin Johnston
5	Allen S Ballenger, *first sergeant*	38	Bryan Adams, jr.
6	Willis Hinton, *second do*	39	Hardy Adams
7	Nicholas Lynch, *third do*	40	Ridly Porter
8	Newit Bridges, *fourth do*	41	Absalom Woodall
9	Mabry Richison, *first corporal*	42	Reeves Joy
10	Jesse Wellons, *second do*	43	Myrick Joy
11	Stephen Hicks, *third do*	44	John Barber
12	Reddick Hews, *fourth do*	45	Brittain Barber
13	Thaddeus Duck, *drummer*	46	Bright Bird
14	James Jordan, *fifer*	47	Jeremiah Blackman
15	Braswell Bridges	48	Mathew Hinton
16	Jacob Avera	49	John Filgo
17	Needham Lambert	50	David Filgo
18	Samuel Frost	51	Nathaniel Johnston
19	Stephen Brown	52	John Killingworth, jr
20	Stephen Makins	53	Richard Rollins
21	Josiah Hinnant	54	Thomas Simpkins
22	Lewis Godwin	55	Edward Lee, sen.
23	Amos Batten	56	John Brunt
24	Hardy Batten	57	Bold Robin Hood
25	William Batten	58	Samuel Engram
26	Micajah Wilkinson	59	Nathan Bryan
27	Elam Smith	60	Noah Barefoot, jr
28	Jacob Walker	61	Benjamin Simpkins
29	Etheldred Bagly	62	Burnel Cole
30	Reuben Pope	63	Francis Harrell
31	John Allen	64	John Kean
32	Kedar Farmer	65	John Sellers
33	Joshua Daniel	66	Henry Lee

67 Frederick Biggener
68 Oliver Raines, jr.
69 William Holt
70 Hervey Raines, sen
71 Amos Peden
72 John Peden
73 Willis Woodard
74 Benjamin Bridges
75 Thomas Hollowell
76 Malichi Humphrey
77 Reuben Perry
78 John Lee
79 Nathan Stancel
80 David Bailey
81 Jonathan Fuller
82 Frederick Oneal
83 John Pender
84 Martin Hall
85 Drury Baley
86 Bud Price
87 William Green
88 Jacob Adams
89 Micajah Woodard
90 William Richardson

91 Thomas Gerald
92 Thomas Taylor
93 Jonathan Hinnant
94 Hardy Hinnant
95 Loverd Pearce
96 Bannister Grissel
97 Tobias Goodwin
98 Levi Richardson
99 William Pender
100 John Richardson
101 Lewis Hayly
102 Reddin Green
103 Nathan Stansill
104 Benjamin Martin
105 James Stevenson
106 Richard Whittington
107 George Mainard
108 Silas Goodwin
109 Brittain Honecut
110 Brittain Johnston
111 Bartley Stevens
112 Reuben Grower
113 James Johnston
114 Kiah Copeland

Ninth Company, detached from Duplin Regiment.

1 Bryan Glissen, *captain*
2 Stephen Williams, *lieutenant*
3 Samuel Cherry, *ensign*
4 James Grimes
5 James Sullivan
6 Joseph Osburn
7 Jonathan Jones
8 Richard Bradley
9 William Frederick
10 Thomas Bennett
11 Charles Gibbs
12 John Denmark
13 Buk Jernigan
14 John Blanchard
15 David Rouse
16 Abram Connegay
17 David Carr
18 John Greer
19 Moses Manchy
20 James M Cam
21 Elijah Mallard
22 George Bray
23 Felix Candy
24 Robert Sand
25 Owen Lanier
26 David Brooks
27 John Hankin
28 Elijah Tucker
29 William Best
30 Lewis Bowen
31 John Bowen
32 Nathan South

33 Andrew Wallace
34 James Evans
35 Richard Sellers
36 Thomas Lee
37 John Lanier
38 Henry Matthews
39 Richard Rusley
40 James Matthews
41 Samuel Sumner,
42 Isaac Weston
43 Stephen Grimes
44 John Peale
45 Isaac Phips
46 Robert Williams
47 John Grimes
48 Joseph Dickson
49 James Gaylor
50 Stephen Duncan
51 Warren Blount
52 Reuben Blanchard
53 Jacob Harrell
54 David Allen
55 Amos Walder
56 Daniel Jernigan
57 Jacob Gillmore
58 Jesse Outlaw
59 James Carter
60 Zachariah Carter
61 Lott Batts
62 Owen Hale
63 Stephen Herring
64 John Glisson

65 Harget Kornegay	73 Fountain Brown
66 James Flannigan	74 Daniel Kethly
67 Stephen Carmon	75 David Collins
68 James Brown	76 William Sellers
69 William West	77 Joshua Murett
70 Isaac Powell	78 William Smith
71 Jacob Powell	79 David Noles
72 John Manor	

Tenth Company, detached from Jones Regiment.

1 Anthony Hatch, *captain*	38 William Simmons
2 James Huston, *lieutenant*	39 George Koonce
3 Donald C Burkly, *ensign*	40 John Morris
4 Zadock Cox	41 Edward Bryan
5 Hall Bags	42 Samuel Hatch
6 James Rhodes, jr	43 James Wood
7 John Jones	44 Rigden Hewit
8 John Saunders, jr	45 Edmund Jones
9 Urban Williamson	46 George Smith
10 James Williamson	48 William Hubbard Houston
11 Thomas Hay	49 Theophilus Best
12 George Hay	50 Masbum Raimer
13 Joseph Hay	51 David King
14 William Wise	52 Theophilus Willians
15 Simeon Simons	53 William Richerson
16 Barge Gooding	54 Abraham Spencer
17 Asa Fasene	55 David Jones
18 John Stanly	56 Asa Sumner
19 Benjamin Miller	57 Bryan Smith
20 Peter Elliot	58 Lewis Smith
21 David Jones	59 Benjamin Brittain
22 Joshua Davis	60 Felix Jones
23 James McDaniel	61 Andrew Adams
24 David Ketchum	62 James Sandline
25 James Frazier	63 Lewis Mariner
26 James Masburn	64 James Daffin
27 William Hop	65 Jordan Moore
28 Hardy Saunders	66 William Lewis
29 John McKenny	67 Joshua Shepperd
30 William Giles	68 Isaac Coverton
31 John Pitman	69 Benjamin Wooten
32 Stephen Conaway	70 William Mason
33 David Berry	71 William Anderson
34 James Perry	72 Isaac James Jones
35 Jesse Lee	73 John Rue
36 Westly Davis	74 Sherwood Faulk
37 Edmund Howard	75 Benjamin Gause

Eleventh Company, detached from Onslow Regiment.

1 Jacob Galden, *captain*	9 Washington Hamnor
2 William Mitchel, *lieutenant*	10 Jacob Hufman
3 Hardy Pitts, *ensign*	11 Nathan Thompson
4 Benjamin Scott	12 Robert Wallace
5 Isaac Scott	13 James White
6 David Scott	14 Hardy Wood
7 James Wade	15 Jess Gregory
8 Aron Fox	16 Bryant Williams

17 Ebrey Sanding
18 Henry Shepherd
19 James Saunders
20 Elijah Hardeson
21 Neal Grisson
22 Burney Humphrey
23 Samuel Jones
24 Bray Harrell
25 Lewis Stenkman
26 Ephraim King
27 Thomas Alphin
28 Micajah King
29 Thomas Garnto
30 James McCullok
31 Benjamin Barrow
32 William Phillips
33 Abner Anders
34 Isaac Henderson
35 Beverly Simmons
36 Isaac Huggins
37 Henry Henderson
38 Hillory Henderson
39 Joseph Simmons
40 Hardy Newton
41 Elijah Russel
42 Alexander Nelson
43 Thomas Ennett
44 Joshua Mc Donald
45 William Williams
46 Francis Venters
47 Whitehurst Ennett
48 Edward Pearson

49 Stephen Hawkins
50 Benjamin Ward
51 Aldridge Hicks
52 Humphrey Marshall
53 Seth Hadnok
54 William Howard
55 John Milson
56 Ezekiel Askins
57 Edward Fonville
58 Demsy Wilson
59 Calvin Howard
60 John Wills
61 John Grant
62 William Grant
63 John Stephenson
64 Isaac Gilbert
65 Bazzel Grant
66 Isaac Riggs
67 John Crane
68 Aquila R Hill
69 Walter Hellen
70 Hill Williams
71 William Humphrey
72 Lewis Oliver
73 Moses Cox
74 Samuel Davis
75 William Ennett
76 John Hawkins
77 Malachi Wilder
78 Nichodemus Gargamy
79 Daniel Mitchell
80 Abram Burnett

Twelfth Company, detached from New Hanover Regiment.

1 John Mitchel, *Captain*
2 John Watson, *lieutenant*
3 D W Griffith, *ensign*
4 Collin Blue
5 Levi Chace
6 Henry Farrand
7 John Holmes
8 Jacob Levy
9 Ezekiel Trussel
10 James Marshall
11 Ezra Peck
12 Niel Robeson
13 Peleg Pierce
14 Jesse Wingate
15 John M Wright
16 John McFarland
17 William Branch
18 Jesse Saunders
19 Frederick George
20 William Larkins
21 James Stanly
22 Josiah Piner
23 Joseph Clifford
24 John Howell

25 John Hulett
26 Hardy Micks
27 Jacob Caston
28 Frederick Quinby
29 Henry Quinby
30 Oliver Caston
31 William Smith
32 Joseph Quinby
33 William Parmer
34 Alexander Mc Alister
35 Walter Simpson
36 Samuel Moore, jr
37 Joseph Simpson
38 William Berring
39 William Moore
40 Thomas Sharpless
41 James Goff
42 James Pinner
43 William Hand
44 Ambrose Smith
45 Luke Townly
46 Jeremiah Sutherland
47 Henry Williams
48 John Filyaw

49 Abram Hall
50 Lewis Hall
51 William Pegford
52 Nathaniel Wheeler
53 Angus Kurr
54 George Corbett
55 William Jones
56 James Fennell
57 Bennet Fellows
58 Arthur Evans
59 William Hawsley
60 William New
61 Zachariah F Burfield
62 Joseph Picket
63 Israel C Burdeaux

64 Hiram Brocket
65 James Price
66 John St. George
67 Kinchen Nichols
68 John Messick
69 Lean Messick
70 Owen Hansley
71 Woodham Shepherd
72 William Jones Larkins
73 James Walker
74 Swinson Gurgarmus
75 Moses Moore
76 Cornelius Murphy
77 James L White
78 Abijah Hanson

THIRD REGIMENT

Detached from the 5th Brigade.

Jeremiah Slade, Lieutenant Colonel Commandant.
James J Hill, First Major,
Andrew Joyner, Second Major.

First Company, detached from first Halifax Regiment.

1 James Overstreet, *captain*
2 Wilson C Whitaker, *lieutenant*
3 William Brickle, 2d *do*
4 John Vaughan
5 William Crowell
6 John Riks
7 James Whitaker
8 Thomas Applewhite
9 Moses Grimmer, *fifer*
10 Wallis Nicholson
11 Timothy Connell
12 Samuel Simmons
13 John Parker
14 John Scott
15 James Gaskins
16 Henry Bradford
17 Thomas Bradford
18 William Willey
19 John Bradford
20 George Goodwin
21 Willie Watson
22 Thomas B Parker
23 David Douglass
24 Wilson Brantly
25 John Glover
26 Hall Hudson
27 John W Branch
28 John Knight
29 James Merrit

30 Washington Turner
31 Samuel Brickle
32 John Shields
33 James Youngs
34 John Bryant
35 James Brantly
36 James Lawrence
37 Benjamin Pearce
38 John Matthews
39 Hansel Horne
40 Cullen Grimmer
41 Jethro Parker
42 Miles Cross
43 Willis Shelton
44 Robert Saunders
45 Patrick Mc Daniel
46 Wilson W Carter
47 John Scott
48 John Clark
49 Edward King
50 Hiram King
51 Jesse A Brooks
52 Blake Baker
53 Lewis Lewis
54 Joseph Pully
55 Rinchen Harriss
56 Jacob Bartholomew
57 James Abington

Second Company, detached from Second Halifax Regiment.

1 Isham Matthews, *captain*
2 Thomas Nichilson, *lieutenant*
3 John Alston, *ensign*
4 Zachariah Sullivan
5 Francis Anderson
6 Halvin Ash
7 William Brown
8 James Ash
9 William H Ballance
10 Robert Brinkley
11 Jesse Blackburn
12 Asa Blackburn
13 William J Bradie
14 John Cooley
15 John Curling
16 Jesse Christie
17 Samuel Carter
18 Gideon Dameron
19 William R Daniel
20 Rhoderick Easley
21 Allen Easley
22 Eaton F Allen
23 Allen Flood
24 Willson Green
25 Thomas Green
26 William Gurly
27 Thomas Y Grimsted
28 Benjamin Green
29 Jesse Hamblet
30 Miley Harbin
31 David Harriss
32 Jesse Harlow
33 Gabriel Hawkins
34 John Hawes
35 Hansel Hathcock
36 Edmund Jackson
37 Beverlv Jackson
38 Robert Jones
39 John Jordan
40 John King
41 Solomon Locklear
42 Exum Low
43 Samuel Locklear
44 John Lee jr
45 John A Losset
46 Jesse Moore
47 Alfred Moore
48 John Moore jr
49 William Montford
50 William Moore
51 John Mann
52 James Mason
53 Arthur Manly
54 Guilford Nicholson
55 Thomas H Green
56 William Onions
57 Eaton Powell
58 Rica Pullin
59 John Pugh
60 Ransom Powell
61 Frederick Pully
62 John Porter
63 Allen Powell
64 Michael Rand
65 Joseph Studivant
66 Abner Spear
67 Thomas Sammons
68 Benjamin Saunders
69 Peter Ship
70 Whiles Studivant
71 Arthur Spear
72 John Thrower
73 Lemuel Wilkins
74 John Wright sr
75 Caleb Woodard
76 Thomas Ward

Third Company, detached from Northampton Regiment.

1 James C Harrison, *captain**
2
3 Sterling Milton, *lieutenant*
4 Whitmel Rulland, *ensign**
*2 Captains and 2 ensigns ret'nd
5
6 William Erwin
7 Willis Jasey
8 Samuel Bryan
9 John M Williams
10 James Slightfoot
11 John Bryan
12 Obadiah Bowing
13 Elisha Boon
14 David Boon
15 James Vaughan
16 Willis Edge
17 Kinchen Murrell
18 John Sandefur jr
19 Cullen Mitchell
20 Bynum Harriss
21 John Woodruff
22 John Jones
23 Charles Love
24 Zachariah Allen
25 Solomon Holmes
26 John Norworthy
27 John Warwick
28 Randolph Newsum
29 John Simons

30 John Umphreys	72 Hermon Rowell
31 Williby Hastey	73 William Boon
32 George Garris	74 James Griffin
33 Henry Smith	75 Gilbert Griffin
34 Barnaba Bunn	76 Shadrack Grant
35 John Benton	77 Lewis Boon
36 Jiles Jewter	78 Stephen Wimborne
37 Abel Gay	79 Henry Evans
38 Nathan Pope	80 Joiner Boon
39 Newit Morgan	81 Austin Kindrik
40 Richard Pilano	82 Henry E Simons
41 Lewis Short	83 Joel Price
42 Alexander McGridor	84 Stott Watson
43 William Friear	85 Jep Boon
44 Thomas Norworthy	86 Cordal Newson
45 Reuben Scott	87 John Newson
46 Elisha Ryno	88 Seamore Newsom
47 Cullen Artis	89 Kinchen Artis
48 Robert Burnett	90 Herbert Scott
49 Thomas Williams	91 Whitfield Cross
50 Calson Futtrell	92 Aaron Fly
51 Robert Warren	93 Warren Bridges
52 Morris Parker	94 Brittain Lassiter
53 James W Davis	95 Daniel Futrell
54 Nehemiah Vinson	96 Samuel Parker
55 Rhodes Gary	97 Micajah Futrell
56 Drury Britt	98 Moab Underwood
57 Francis Parker	99 Benjamin Vaughan
58 Drew Walden	100 Isham Curl
59 Hardy Hart	101 Sterling Dupree
60 Henry Gilham	102 Arthur Tyner
61 Riggan Newsom	103 Robert Thompson
62 James Valentine	104 James Love
63 Willie Wilkinson	105 James Smith
64 Edmund Thompson	106 Richard Harrison
65 Benjamin Newsom	107 Lemuel Vaughan
66 Barnes Bridges	108 James Morriss
67 James Warwik	109 Jones Glover
68 Benjamin Griffin	110 John Richards
69 John James	111 Benjamin Edwards
70 Dennis O'Conner	112 William Collier
71 Thomas Norman	113 Littleton Tooke

Fourth Company, detached from Edgecombe Regiment.

1 David Barnes, *captain*	15 Bythel Staton
2 John B Walten, *lieutenant*	16 John Garrett
3 Josiah Wood, 2d *do*	17 Thomas Edmondson
4 James Knight, *ensign*	18 James Knight
5 Paul Randolph, *first sergeant*	19 William Savage
6 Alexander Cotten, *second do*	20 Thomas Baton
7 John L Southerlin, *third do*	21 Noah Cushing
8 Littleberry Barfield *fourth do*	22 Lawrence Mayo
9 Pelasky Dudley, *first corporal*	23 John Rhodes
10 Jonathan Bailey, *second do*	24 Whitmell Hardy
11 Etheldred Gray, *third do*	25 James Alsobrook
12 Joshua Warren, *fourth do*	26 Spear Bradley
13 Jonathan Thigpen, *drummer*	27 Kader Hales
14 Pitman Worsley, *fifer*	28 Bartholomew Bryan

29 Theophilus Parker
30 John Parker
31 Samuel Parker
32 Stephen Harper
33 Benjamin Portis
34 Samuel Portis
35 Joseph Portis
36 Charles Cobb
37 Abner Eason
38 David Rayner
39 Rading Sugg
40 Bartholomew Bowers
41 Andrew Clark
42 Wilie Cotton
43 David Dancy
44 Gideon Jolley
45 James Bilberry
46 Samuel Wood
47 Gray Thigpen
48 James Thigpen, jr
49 Howell Thigpen
50 John Nowell
51 James Cobb

52 John Blackburn
53 David Tennison
54 Benjamin Barfield
55 Michel Parker
56 David Morris
57 Brittain Pitman
58 Reuben Pitman
59 James Teat
60 Kalib Warren
61 Isaac Horne
62 Jacob Brake
63 Henry Horne
64 Theophilus Thomas
65 David Brake
66 Elisha Thomas
67 Thomas Price
68 Thomas Haughton
69 Lott Stalling
70 Josiah Crocker
71 Noah Davis
72 William Morgan
73 Eli Vann
74 John Hines

Fifth Company, detached from Martin Regiment.

1 Durham Davis, *captain*
2 James Reddick, *lieutenant*
3 James Howell, *ensign*
4 John C Williams *first sergeant*
5 George Harrison, *second do*
6 Luke Bennett, *third do*
7 Jesse Lolly, *fourth do*
8 Hosea Lanier, *first corporal*
9 James Hardeson, *second do*
10 Selathiel Sherod, *third do*
11 Jehu Pearce, *fourth do*
12 Jesse Hardeson, *drummer*
13 Samuel Robeson, *fifer*
14 James Garrott
15 William Bultry
16 Thomas Lassiter
17 John Amis
18 William Applin
19 Harmon Girkin
20 John Smithwick
21 Joshua Hardeson
22 Silas Wollard
23 Nathaniel Wollard
24 James Cottram
25 Timothy Brogden
26 Westley Floid
27 Edmond Rogers
28 Seth Meazel
29 Aaron Meazel
30 Jesse Meazel
31 John Rogerson
32 James Ward
33 Benjamin Futrell

34 John Rowbuck
35 William Everitt
36 David Roberson
37 Nathan Morris
38 Darling Cherry
39 William Beach
40 James Caraway
41 Whitmel Pierce
42 Richard Airs
43 Henry Best
44 William Rogers
45 Raleigh Rowbuck
46 Newton Coburn
47 Arden Taylor
48 Perry Brewer
49 Solomon Kelly
50 John Hawkins
51 James Stalls
52 Balentine Page
53 William Smith
54 Henry Smith
55 Willie Hoard
56 Thomas Ross
57 Chancey Davenport
58 William Correl
59 William James
60 William Whorton
61 Jonathan Calloway
62 John Wheatley
63 William Hines
64 Moses Weaver
65 Lawrence Hyman
66 Thomas Bryan

67 Elias Bryan
68 Nicholas Lord
69 Augustus Wood
70 Benjamin Aims
71 David Baston
72 Jesse Peal
73 David Cooper
74 David Rogerson
75 Micajah Perry

76 Thomas Cary
77 John Manning
78 Robert Daniel
79 Noah Robeson
80 James Hynes
81 Daniel Medford
82 Reuben Griffin
83 John Beach
84 Henry Robeson

Sixth Company, detached from Nash Regiment.

1 Francis Drake, *captain*
2 Isaac Watkins, *first lieutenant*
3 David Daniel, *second do*
4 Willoughby Manning, *ensign*
5 Samuel Sorsby, *first sergeant*
6 William Lepford, *second do*
7 Samuel Williams, *third do*
8 Alfred Bunn, *fourth do*
9 Henry Bridgers, *first corporal*
10 Archibald Wheless, *second do*
11 Joseph Whitehead, *third do*
12 Thomas Beckwith, *fourth do*
13 Guilford Whitfield, *drummer*
14 Green Henry, *fifer*
15 Thomas Davis
16 Levi C Arrington
17 Richard Carlisle
18 Jinnes Hackney
19 Joseph Green
20 William Griffin
21 Nathan Evans
22 Edward White
23 John Evans
24 Henry Hunt
25 Bennett Jones
26 George Evans
27 Wilson Hammons
28 Nathan Sikes
29 Thomas Bryant
30 Woody Tucker
31 David Wall
32 Cader Bass
33 Loody Ferrell
34 Thomas Lloyd
35 Hutchins Ferrell
36 Burton Ferrell

37 Henry Morgan
38 James Ferrell
39 Gillum Cone
40 Archibald Lemon
41 Clalon Mann
42 Samuel Davis
43 Edward Crowell
44 Benjamin Gloveyer
45 James B Crowell
46 Thomas Brown
47 Eli Tisdale
48 Jacob Atkins
49 Richard Triggler
50 John Poulan
51 Daniel Bachelor
52 Joseph Tucker
53 John Williams
54 Jacob Row
55 Elijah Wiggins
56 Elen Mecome
57 Edwin Brantly
58 Harrell Horn
59 Richard Stallings
60 Alston Gandy
61 Sampson Sikes
62 John Gandy
63 Thomas Valentine
64 Griffin Ganday
65 Solomon Thomas
66 Peter Gray
67 Amor Beckwith
68 Newit Edwards
69 John Hawks
70 William Richards
71 Jorden Barrow

Seventh Company, detached from Warren Regiment

1 Charles Allen, *captain*
2 Thomas Stackhouse, *lieutenant*
3 John Motholand
4 Micajah T Hawkins
5 Nathan Turner
6 Amos P Sledge
7 Doct M Robertson
8 Samuel Dowtin

9 Wilmot E Egerton
10 Owen F Myrick
11 Richard Ward
12 Thomas Davis
13 Ivy Allen
14 William Breadlove
15 Phlemon Perdue
16 William Oliver

17 William Turner
18 Arthur Tussell
19 Ransom Stroud
20 Lemuel Mitchel
21 Thomas Harton
22 Joseph Wren
23 William Powell
24 Allen Wren
25 Wiles Person
26 James C Bennet
27 Joshua Harper
28 Ransom Acock
29 Cudburth Neal
30 Henry Pearson
31 Richard Davis
32 James Powell
33 Peter Randolph
34 John Robertson
35 William Sherrin
36 Charles Stoddard
37 Lewis Sherrin
38 Kinchen Williamson
39 George Hazlewood
40 Jasper Capps
41 Thomas Walker
42 Elisha Sherod
43 Buck Robertson
44 Jiles Carter
45 Joshua Davis

46 Benjamin Davis
47 Thomas Newman
48 Pleasant Ellington
49 John Allen
50 Daniel A Perdne
51 Charles Bennet
52 Joel Ellington
53 James Thompson
54 D G Williams
55 Anderson Peebles
56 James Alston
57 Solomon Jenkins
58 Hardoway Davis
59 William Pertilla
60 Edward Pertilla
61 Richard Beach
62 Joel Tally
63 Miles Ellis
64 James Tally
65 Thomas Tally
66 Simes Ellis
67 Claton Lambert
68 John Hawks
69 Henry James
70 Daniel White
71 Obadiah Ellis
72 James Smith
73 Leonard King

Eighth Company, detached from Franklin Regiment.

1 Marmaduke N Jeffreys, *captain*
2 Benjamin Stewart, *lieutenant*
3 Nathaniel Hunt, *second do*
4 James Harrison, *ensign*
5 Richard Wright
6 Winson Cook
7
8 Newsome Bridges
9 Stephen Davis
10 Nathaniel Hayes
11 Thomas Tharington
12 William D Jones
13 Dabney M Duke
14 William T Dent
15 Izekiah Stephens
16 Benjamin G Richards
17 William Baker
18 Martin Murphray
19 James Bridges
20 John C Perry
21 Benjamin Lanicr
22 Duncan McLean
23 William Bird
25 Reddick Nellsmall, 1st *sergeant*
25 Kinchen Boon
26 Thomas B Arendel
27 Elijah Izzard

28 Julius Hill
29 Robert Thomas
30 John Baker
31 James Murphy
32 Willie Hight
33 Green D House
34 John Prince
35 Breedlove Pippen
36 John Mullins
37 Reddick Haswell
38 Thomas Haswell
39 Ignatius Goldsberry
40 Albert Perry
41 John M Sherod
42 Willie O Davis
43 Thomas Davis
44 Jesse Collins
45 David Collins
46 John Hill
47 Guilford Lewis
48 James Nelms
49 Willis Cook
50 Joseph Stevens
51 James Barrow
52 Henry Thomas
53 Joseph C Harris
54 Alexander Carson

55 James Vincent	67 William Simmons
56 Guilford Bass	68 Macomb Alfred
55 Bennett Perry	69 William C Perry
58 Miles Cary	70 Julius Alford
59 Joseph B Flemming	71 James Hunt
60 John Wichidht	72 Hugh Hayes
61 Green Wood	73 John J Lancaster
62 Simeon Jenkins	74 Drury Denton
63 Eaton Freeman	75 John Jones
64 Mathew Walker	76 William Alford
65 Alsey Young	77 William Debnam
66 John Young	78 Dilworth Sledge

FOURTH REGIMENT,

Detached from 4th and 14th Brigades.

Alfred Rowland, Lieutenant Colonel Commandant.
John A Cameron, First Major.
David Gillespie, Second Major.

First Company, detached from Bladen Regiment.

1 John Nicholson, *captain*	26 David White
2 James C Cumming, 1st *lieutenant*	27 James McLelland
3 Robert McKee, *second do*	28 Sampson Davis
4 James Campbell, *ensign*	29 Arthur Butler
5 Alexander McIver, *first sergeant*	30 Patrick Murphy
6 Thomas Smith, *second do*	31 William Davis, jr
7 Neil McMillan	32 William Davis, sen
8 Thomas Clardy	33 William McKay
9 Turpin Cheshire	34 Thomas Brown
10 Colin Shaw	35 John B Cowen
11 Anguish McMillan	36 George B Thomas
12 Evan Rice	37 Archibald Pattison
13 David Davis	38 Samuel Plumber
14 Julias High	39 Dennis Kelleham
15 Mercer Grimes	40 John Kelleham
16 William C Singletary	41 Pierce Kelleham
17 David Singletary	42 John Taylor
18 Jasper Hester	43 James Stredy
19 Daniel Gooden	44 John McFalten
20 Thomas Averit	45 Dugald McKitchen
21 Abel Burney	46 John Savage
22 Wilie Adkison	47 James Salter
23 Edward Pemberton	48 Alexander Lamer
24 James Kelley	49 Barnabas Brown
25 John Campbell	50 Joseph Hester

Second Company, detached from First Cumberland Regiment.

1 Arch'd McCraine, *captain*	7 Jesse Betha
2 Daniel Shaw, *first lieutenant*	8 Owen Boon
3 John Shaw, *second do*	9 James Sorrel
4 John Hodges, *ensign*	10 William Hodges
5 Robert Shaw	11 Neil McNeil
6 John Steele	12 William McKinsie

13 John Gordon
14 John McLelland
15 Ebenezer Folsome
16 Murdoc McRae
17 Hector McAuthur
18 Benjamin Morrison
19 Samuel Searsey
20 Rowland Fauekner
21 Aron Searcy
22 Peter Munro
23 Angus Ray
24 John McKellar
25 Neel Munro
26 Theophillus Denny
27 Cornelius Cofield
28 John McDougal
29 John Wilkinson
30 Hector McNeil
31 Richard Cade
32 Richard Wilkinson
33 Absalom Hammonds
34 James Norris
35 David Bone
36 Richard Bone
37 John Jackson
38 Thomas Gill
39 Joshua Jesop
40 Samuel Reeves
41 John Taylor
42 Robert Harwell
43 Francis Hobby

44 Thomas Paine
45 Drury Massey
46 Frederick Yarborough
47 Wilson Ray
48 Darius Cox
49 Murdock Campbell
50 Elisha Brown
51 Jesse Northington
52 Alexander Mckellan
53 Sion Tedder
54 Allen Campbell
55 Neil Bowie
56 Malcolm Pattison
57 William Lathom
58 Needham Moore
59 Horatio Griffin
60 Lewis Moore
61 Benjamin Moore
62 James Stephens
63 Allen Northington
64 Neil McNeil
65 Bogle Ferrand
66 Thomas H Massey
67 Joshua Carman
68 Aurthur Core
69 Shadrack Johnson
70 William Daniel
71 John Lewis
72 John Johnston
73 John Moore

Third Company, detached from Cumberland Regiment.

1 David Evans, *captain*
2 George Jones, *first lieutenant*
3 John Leonard
4 John Evans
5 James Rush
6 Phillip Horton
7 Samuel Salmon
8 Etheldred Syke
9 Thomas McMurray
10 Phillip McRae
11 Council McCullin
12 Pitkin McCullin
13 John Carver
14 Sion Horne
15 Waddel Cade
16 Mathew Hayes
17 Gilbert McColl
18 William Taylor
19 William Nunnery
20 John Bryan
21 Robert Olery
22 William Anderson
23 John Thagard
24 Samuel Reeves
25 James McDaniel

26 Zachariah Butler
27 Norman McNeil
28 John McKinzie
29 Samuel Butler
30 John Langdon
31 John Shaw
32 Douglass McLaughlan
33 James Denton
34 Hugh McGuire
35 Thomas Bowen
36 Jonathan Evans
37 John Ray
38 James Kirkpatrick
39 Murdock Orchillred
40 William Tillingast
41 Jesse Anson
42 Thomas Evans
43 Murwin Carrington
44 James Stevens
45 John B Smith
46 Murcock McLeod
47 German Seawell
48 George Holmes
49 William Horn
50 Thomas Cole

D

51 Jacob Seawell	62 Thomas Richardson
52 John Burgess	63 John Everitt
53 Jonathan Hare	64 Malcomb Patterson
54 Dugald McIntyre	65 Allen Dudley
55 John Johnston	66 John Law
56 Duncan Pharis	67 Isaac T Cushing
57 Jacob Faircloth	68 Samuel Smith
58 Daniel Everitt	69 John B Troy
59 Joshua Edwards	70 William Adkinson
60 Mathew Freeman	71 Thomas Wilkinson
61 Richard Everitt	

Fourth Company, detached from Sampson Regiment.

1 George Lassiter, *captain*	33 John House
2 Robert Lassiter, *first lieutenant*	34 Robin Pope
3 Josias Lee, *Second do*	35 James Harden
4 Abram Nailor, *ensign*	36 Jonathan Edge
5 Pharo Lee, *first sergeant*	37 David Ryold
6 Sion Danfoot, *second do*	38 Elias Two
7 Starling Otary	39 Jacob Stanly
8 Jacob Mannels	40 Thomas Jacobs
9 George Warwick	41 Edmond Goodwin
10 Joseph Two	42 Reddick Jones
11 Granbury Goodwin	43 Owen Ryold
12 John Warwick	44 Daniel Two
13 James Jones	45 Laban Williams
14 Gardner Keen	46 Stephen Maner
15 Isaac Manner	47 Hardy Stephens
16 Bryant Flowers	48 William Turner
17 Jesse Mannor	49 Joshua Bell
18 Hugh Burke	50 Samuel Robeson
19 Whiting Ryolds	51 Arthur Hare
20 Lewis Johnston	52 Joseph Herrin
21 Jesse Ezzel	53 Stephen Herrin
22 John Bird	54 Phelix Chesnut
23 Herrin Gregory	55 Samuel Gavin
24 Landen Two	56 Edmund Manuel
25 Daniel Hall	57 Nathaniel Boyet
26 Samuel Gavin	58 Elias Whilly
27 Owen Shorton	59 Jonas Quinby
28 Samuel Standly	60 Warren Jackson
29 John White	61 James Hobbs
30 Nathan Young	62 Raiford Faircloth
31 William Lee	63 Henry Lee
32 Joab Whiley	64 Joel M Lamb

Fifth Company, detached from Sampson Regiment.

1 Thomas Boykin, *captain*	11 Simon Reynolds
2 James Williamson, *lieutenant*	12 John Porter
3 Timothy Williamson, *second do*	13 Michel Porter
4 Lavis Spell, *ensign*	14 Core Cooper
5 Reyney McIlwines	15 Thomas Stephens
6 Laban Morgan, *second sergeant*	16 William Ryon
7 Hartwell Porter, *third do*	17 Henry Pope
8 Peter Ryon, *drummer*	18 Solomon Boykin
9 John Boykin	19 Edward Broy
10 Daniel Cooper	20 Allen Parker

21 John Ammonds
22 David Underwood
23 Zachariah Williams
24 Rayford Cooper
25 Willis Royal
26 Angus Johnston
27 Lewis Pope
28 Israel Tarlington
29 Henry Hart
30 Joshua Herring
31 John Pope
32 Hardy Royall
33 James Porter
34 Owen Crumpler
35 Jesse Strickland
36
37 John Blackwell
38 William Turner
39 William Pope
40 Neil Campbell
41 James Frazier
42 John Simonds

43 Rayford Grist
44 Noah Faircloth
45 Aaron Cummings
46 William Miller
47 Thomas Frazier
48 Sander Fisher
49 Sutton Grist
50 John Manor
51 John Orion
52 Blackman Tews
53 Samuel Revells
54 John Carter
55 Aron Peterson
56 Abram Sellers
57 Thomas Green
58 Luke Parker
59 David Whitney
60 Mathew Hall
61 Isaac Carter
62 Charles Butler
63 Henry Hall
64 John Blount

Sixth Company, detached from the Moore Regiment.

1 Nathaniel Tucker, *captain*
2 Neil Morrison, *first lieutenant*
3 Hugh McDaniel, *second do*
4 John Garner, *ensign*
5 Dougald Mathews
6 Robert Kennedy
7 Erwin Stephens
8 John Tyson
9 Alexander Black
10 William Goings
11 William Jackson
12 Stephen Berryman
13 Edward Goings
14 Neil Thompson
15 David Jones
16 George Anderson
17 John Myrick
18 Andrew Anderson
19 Malcolm McGilvery
20 William Wilson
21 Charles Smith
22 John Phillips
23 Drury Richardson
24 Raiford Phillips
25 Joab Cheek
26 John McLeod
27 Benjamin Pope
28 William Page
29 George Carlton
30 John Laughon
31 Elisha Rogers
32 Sampson Muse
33 Malcolm McDuffy

34 John Medlin
35 John White
36 William Gillmore
37 Alexander Medlin
38 John McDonald
39 John Spicer
40 Isom Sowell
41 Everitt Sheffield
42 Daniel Hollin
43 Simon Lewis
44 James Morgan
45 Jacob Gargle
46 Fredrick Antry
47 James Owen
48 Aben Brown
49 James Garner
50 Edward Moore
51 Bralley Garner
52 Angus McAuley
53 John Bird
54 John Martin
55 John Graham
56 John Patterson
57 Donald Mclean
58 Argus Morrison
59 John Richardson
60 John McLeod
61 William Williamson
62 Lauchlan McKinnon
63 Daniel Love
64 Duncan Blue
65 John Blue
66 Malcolm McNeil

67 Duncan McLean
68 Hugh Cameron
69 Edward Patterson
70 Archibald Blue
71 Neil McLeon
72 Nathan Maples
73 Thomas Maples
74 John Maples
75 James Maples
76 John Cole
77 John Johnston
78 William Sterling
79 William Koy
80 Thomas Rhodes
81 Joseph Stephens
82 Duncan Smith
83 Benjamin Morris

84 Robert Tapley
85 Benjamin Bushup
86 Malcolm Fulsum
87 Mathew Wicker
88 Charles Crawford
89 Benjamin Huckaby
90 John Bushup
91 Josiah Hogwood
92 William Oliver
93 John Underwood
94 John Baker
95 John Bledsoe
96 William Dalrymple
97 Benjamin C Bennett
98 William Murchinson
99 Archibald Bue
100 Benjamin Wicker

Seventh Company, detached from Columbus Regiment

1 Caleb Stephens, *captain*
2 John White, *first lieutenant*
3 Alexander Taylor, *ensign*
4 James Smith, *first sergeant*
5 Thomas B Wooten, *sec'nd do*
6 Michel High
7 David Baldwin
8 Prosper forma Duval
9 Thomas Hobbs
10 Amos Allen
11 James Baldwin jr
12 Elijah Reynols
13 John Reynols
14 William Hooks
15 Daniel Fowler
16 Richard Reynols
17 Anthony Cribb
18 Elijah Warley
19 Richard Folk
20 John Carteret

21 Frederick Door
22 Archibald Bogleman
23 Aron Floid
24 Robert Carlisle
25 John Gore
26 Richard Fowler
27 Isaiah Smith
28 Thomas Cribb
29 Hardy Duncan
30 Moses Duncan
31 Isaiah Sessions
32 Willis Lamberton
33 John Folks
34 Frederick Sasser
35 Josiah Powell
36 Archibald Taylor
37 Allen Barfield
38 Eli Nichols
39 Isaac Nichols
40 Amos Tyson

Eighth Company, detached from Anson Regiment

1 Frederick Staton, *captain*
2 Solomon Trull, *first lieutenant*
3 Henry James, *second do*
4 James White, *ensign*
5 James King
6 Thomas Ward
7 William Anderson
8 John Walden
9 Benjamin Williams
10 Francis Mullis
11 Isaac Watson
12 William James
13 Newbern Williams
14 Richard Manes
15 Mathew Rumage
16 David James

17 Elisha Griffin
18 Hosea James
19 Balis Carr
20 John Hagler
21 Asa Baggott
22 Robert Preston
23 John Fornberton
24 Moses Thomas
25 Reuben Vinson
26 William Gurley
27 Jasse Lcay
28 Needham Gurley
29 Jesse Barnett
30 Alsey Hyatt
31
32 John Winetuster

33 Abram Wimberly
34 James Perkins
35 James Morris
36 Lewis Collins
37 John Brown
38 Asa Rushing
39 David Hendrick
40
41 Arris Roser

42 Micajah Taylor
43 Absalom Stegall
44 Moses Pearce
45 Ason Pearce
46 William Sikes
47 William Pearce
48 William Mulder
49 George Mulder
50 William Oniel

Ninth Company, detached from Anson Regiment.

1 James Tindall, *captain*
2 Boggan Cash, *first lieutenant*
3 Malach Goulde, *second do*
4 Hezekiah Billingsby, *ensign*
5 William Jasper
6 John Goodwin
7 Thomas C Threadgill
8 Austin Fort
9 William German
10 John German
11 Lemuel Ingram
12 John Ingram
13 John Rushing
14 John Jones
15 Charles Strother
16 James Copeland
17 John Webb
18 Benjamin Sinclair
19 Orrin Sinclair
20 Jacob Phillips
21 Jesse Turner
22 William West
23 Stephen Nash
24 Westly Wortrind
25 Booky Dickson
26 Isham Ingram
27 William Worhine
28 Howell Threadgill
29 Nathaniel Davis
30 William Dabbs
31 Mathew Bushnell
32 Jeremiah Gullidge
33 Mills Ballie
34 John Moore
35 Matthew Hubbard
36 William Fielding
37 Jesse Cox

38 Christopher McRae
39 John Julding
40 James Brooks
41 Benjamin Teal
42 Harman Adams
43 Jurguhard McRae
44 Isaac Little
45 John Chewning
46 John Ross
47 Thomas Tyson
48 Bennet Williams
49 William Lewis
50 William Julke
51 Thomas Slay
52 Jesse Ratiff
53 Francis Downer
54 James Capel
55 William Wood
56 Handy May
57 James Miller
58 James Martin
59 Thomas Handcock
60 John Barber
61 John Williams
62 James Briley
63 Henry Adcock
64 William Scott
65 Thomas Jones
66 Neel McBride
67 Samuel Ratliff
68 Daniel McLeran
69 John Russon
70 John Short
71 James Mersham
72 Neil McLeran
73 Benjamin Hanley
74 Hezekiah Ingram

Tenth Company, detached from Richmond Regiment.

1 John Blue, *captain*
2 John McAlston
3 Daniel McAuley
4 Alexander Brown
5 James Torry
6 James Watkins
7 Fenly McSween

8 William Wakins
9 John James
10 Alexander McLeod, sen
11 Amos Corbett
12 Luke Barnett
13 Elisha Crowson
14 Lorick Stephens

15 Alexander McRae
16 Dempsey Pitman
17 James Williams
18 John Bostwick
19 William Harris
20 Stephen Jones
21 Angus McLoud
22 John McSween
23 Charles Hawley
24 Donald Mc Sween
25 Kenneth McInnis
26 David Britt
27 James Dawson
28 Cannor Weaver
29 Edward Gantlin
30 Martin James
31 Luke Woodle
32 James Smith
33 Berry Norton
34 Elias Pate
35 Hanly Snead
36 Henry Covington
37 William Robeson
38 Isaac Vaughan
39 James Brown
40 Alexander McDonald
41 Daniel McNair
42 Daniel Carmichel
43 John McRae
44 John McMillan
45 John McEwen
46 Peter Patterson
47 William Bringman

48 Alexander Shaw
49 Duncan Buie
50 James McDonald
51 Daniel Watson
52 Archibald McLeod
53 Josiah Bozeman
54 Gilbert McEachin
55 Roderick Campbell
56 Alexander McPherson
57 Malcom Shaw
58 Mathew Rainwater
59 John Chase
60 James Molton
61 John Migginson
62 Daniel Williams
63 James Mask
64 Sammuel Mallock
65 John Black
66 Wader Shepherd
67 Josiah Shepherd
68 John McDonald
69 Archibald McDonald
70 Donald McDonald
71 Lochlin McLennan
72 Jess Williams
73 Benjamin Thomas
74 Kennith McKinsie
75 Moody Ingram
76 John McLeod
77 Isaac Mason
78 Calloway Stephens
79 Eli Northam
80 John Stogner

Eleventh Company, detached from Robeson Regiment.

1 Isaac Sullivan, *captain*
2 William Brown, *first lieutenant*
3 Benjamin Blount, *second do*
4 Elias Thomas, *ensign*
5 John Stewart
6 John McMillan
7 Archibald Stewart
8 Charles Campbell
9 Jesse Musslewhite
10 Spencer Porter
11 William Council
12 John Wilkerson
13 Allen Buie
14 Stephen Banley
15 Charles Oxendine
16 Thomas Locklier
17 Silas Strickland
18 John McNeil
19 Daniel Chrisholm
20 Alexander Chrisholm
21 William Edward
22 Ralph Revells
23 Isaac Streeter

24 Hugh Locklier
25 Joseph Walters
26 James Ivey
27 William Davis
28 William Bodiford
29 Harman Cox
30 William Britt
31 Charles Storm
32 John Cox
33 Hardy Cox
34 Nathaniel Hawthorn
35 Daniel Pate
36 Duncan Baker
37 Isham Ivey
38 John Wilkins
39 John McKellar
40 Martin Lewis
41 Lemuel Thompson
42 John Drake
43 Peter McCormick
44 Daniel Stewart
45 Smith Dease
46 Amos Taylor

47 James McKay
48 Hardy Pope
49 Josiah Ratley
50 John Walters
51 John Drinkwater
52 Thomas Pope
53 Thomas Lowe
54 Jacob Pitman
55 William Walters
56 Dawson Walters
57 Moses Bass
58 Daniel McPhallair
59 Raiford S Witherell
60 Francis F Varnum
61 William Purvis
62 John Thompson
63 William Bullard

64 Reading Blount
65 Solomon Thomas
66 James Reeves
67 Charles Ivey, sen
68 Elijah Hammons
69 Joseph Blount
70 Duncan McMillan
71 Roderick Sutherland
72 Angus McCulland, sen
73 Angus McQueen
74 Alexander McKay
75 Hector McLeon
76 John McKay
77 Angus McCullum
78 Archibald Morrison
79 Daniel Nichilson
80 Daniel McRae

SECOND BRIGADE,

Detached from the 6th and 16th, 7th and 11th, 8th, 9th, 10th, and 15th Brigades of the organized Militia of the State.

EPHRAIM DAVIDSON, Brigadier General.

FIFTH REGIMENT,

Detached from the 6th and 16th Brigades.

Richard Atkinson, Lieutenant Colonel Commandant.
Simpson Shaw, First Major,
Benjamin Elliott, Second Major.

First Company of the Fifth Regiment, detached from the First Orange Regiment.

1 Hugh Munhollon, *captain*
2 James Latta, *lieutenant*
3 James Smith, *ensign*
4 John Munhollon, *first sergeant*
5 George Mebane, *second do*
6 Thomas Bradford, *third do*
7 George Tate, *fourth do*
8 Joseph Bradford
9 James Bird
10 Joseph Bird
11 William Reddin
12 John Wilson
13 Robert Barnhill
14 Nathaniel Beane
15 Joseph Hodge
16 James Wilson
17 John Warren
18 Lewis Simpson
19 William Smith
20 William Glinn

21 William Cherenhall
22 James Browning
23 Royal Willis
24 Elisha Glenn
25 James Wood
26 Samuel Willis
27 Lewis Durning
28 John Sikes
29 Joel Parish
30 Bird Lean
31 Miles Jones
32 Richard Howard
33 Francis Crocker
34 John O'neal
35 Moses Atwater
36 Gardner Ballard
37 Benjamin Bridges
38 James Chambers
39 George Smith
40 Charles Canley

41 William Bishop
42 John Curthington
43 Benjamin Price
44 Abner Jackson
45 Bradley Collins
46 William Jacobs
47 William Clemons
48 Scearly Docherty
49 James Lindsey
50 Theophilus Thompson
51 John Crabtree
52 Uriah Crabtree
53 William Mebane

54 John Jones
55 Thomas Thomas
56 Richard Wilson
57 Joseph Wilkinson
58 Martin Liggett
59 James White
60 Richard Jones sen
61 William R Tate
62 John Wood
63 Alexander Patten
64 Elijah Hart
65 William Price
66 Gabriel Finn

Second Company, detached from First Orange Regiment.

1 Robert Thompson, *captain*
2 Samuel Strahorn, *lieutenant*
3 William Bradshaw, *ensign*
4 William Kirkland
5 Davis Davis
6 Asa Couch
7 William Herndon
8 Isaac D Dollar
9 John Horn
10 Robert Allen
11 John Turner
12 William Allen
13 James Dollar
14 John Ivy
15 William Harris
16 John Hunt
17 William Lingo
18 Thomas Patterson
19 Thornton McFarlin
20 Francis Roberts
21 Levin Ellis
22 Harrison Parker
23 Henry Newton
24 Andrew Gray
25 Amos Nichols
26 John Horner
27 John Nichols
28 George Riggs
29 Wilson Ball
30 Isaac Morris

31 Mathew Durham
32 Edward Howington
33 Thomas F Cardwell
34 Henry Shepherd
35 Pleasant Herndon
36 Nathan Marcomb
37 James Ashley
38 Henry Trill
39 William Lyhn
40 John Hart
41 William Kirland
42 William McDaid
43 Alfred Hill
44 William Woods
45 Fisher Clendenning
46 Archibald Pugh
47 John Thompson
48 Jacob Green
49 James Ray jr
50 Samuel Stuart
51 Thomas Lynch
52 Robert Jeffries
53 Hugh Wood
54 John D Covington
55 Thomas Cate
56 Adam Douglass
57 James Lindsey
58
59 William Ragans

Third Company, detached from Second Orange, or Haw River Regiment.

1 John Stockard, *captain*
2 John Albright, *lieutenant*
3 Jacob Efland, *ensign*
4 John Proxter
5 Jacob Jackson
6 Henry Loy
7 Thomas Steel
8 Matthew Baswell
9 Edward Baswell
10 Hugh Baglas

11 Thomas Moore, *second sergeant*
12 Joseph Cable
13 Drewry Ballard
14 John Ireland
15 William Moore
16 David Barber
17 Peaton Wilson
18 Ziah Horniday
19 John Foust
20 James Upsom

21 Thomas Bevers
22 Joseph Murray
24 Alexander Filmar
23 Ned Heathcock
25 Palmer Freeman
26 William Hughs
27 Abraham Hawey
28 Henry Hurdle
29 John Wallis
30 Joel Tate
31 John Lewis
32 James Burrage
32 Lemuel Thompson
34 James Grimes
35 Osborn James
36 Daniel Criscow
37 Elisha Willis
38 Phillip Hodge

39 Charles Shanks
40 John Wilson
41 John Cable
42 Nehemiah Thomas
43 John Cook
44 Adam Long
45 Boston Graves
46 Daniel Thomas
47 David Spoon
48 John Hornaday
49 Nathaniel Robeson
50 William Holt
51 James Turner
52 Joel Albright
53 Alexander Taddis
54 John Long
55 Isaac McAdams
56 Michel Ryke

Fourth Company, detached from Randolph Regiment.

1 Joshua Craven, *captain*
2 Adam Winningham, *lieutenant*
3 Jacob Worthington, *ensign*
4 Raley Spinks, *first sergeant*
5 Peter Kivet, *second do*
6 Marmaduke Swean, *third do*
7 Frederick Brown, *fourth do*
8 Absalom Harper, *first corporal*
9 William Patterson, *second do*
10 Daniel Jackson, *third do*
11 Henry Johnston, *fourth do*
12 James McMasters, *drummer*
13 James Cude, *fifer*
14 Lewis Martin, *private*
15 Robert Haskin
16 Abel Winningham
17 Silas Davison
18 Isaac Vinson
19 Solomon Luther
20 Asa Peacock
21 Jacob Lassiter
22 Isham Harris
23 William Jackson
24 Thomas Shaw
25 Hezekiah Andrew
26 Lewis Scarlet
27 Henry Boss
28 James Wade
29 Martin Chandler
30 Archibald Dunbar
31 Thomas Nelson
32 Seth Wade
33 Duncan Harvey
34 William Brown
35 Campbell Powell
36 John Ferguson
37 William Cole
38 Isaac Miller

39 Frederick Fentress
40 Alexander Robins
41 Alexander Cunnigan
42 Frederick Steed
43 John Steed
44 Elijah Williams
45 John Malone
46 Stephen Hervey
47 John Smitherman
48 Alexander Dockery
49 Isham Steed
50 John Reid
51 John Pierce
52 Garrat Spinks
53 Joseph Argoe
54 James Harris
55 Lewis Garner
56 Thomas Bray
57 Ezekiel Mills
58 William Conner
59 West Hicks
60 Jacob Briles
61 Rhudolph Weymire
62 Ezra Bukerdite
63 Will Acborn
64 Abram Elliott
65 James Sweany
66 Henry Lamm
67 Samuel Beson
68 Dum Lamm
69 Henry Burton
70 James Barker
71 Michel Jackson
72 Jeremiah Barkerr
73 George Wilson
74 John Chaplain
75 Enoch Williams
76 John Wood

E

77 William Maples	87 Thomas Alexander
78 Henry Underwood	88 Larkin Curtis
79 Henry Kivett	89 Henry Curtis
80 Miles Stephens	90 William Gay
81 James Savage	91 George Black
82 John Burgess	92 John Brown
83 William Nelson	93 Abijah Moore
84 Anderson Roach	94 John Johnston
85 Nathan York	95 George Lean
86 William Howe	96 John Bryan

Fifth Company, detached from Chatham Regiment.

1 Carney Cotton, *captain*	46 Daniel Nevin
2 Daniel Smith, *first lieutenant*	47 Stephen Upchurch
3 John M Gee, *second do*	48 Matt Jinks
4 Riddick Burns, *ensign*	49 Jesse Patridge
5 Jonathan Rickets	50 Alexander Moore
6 William Sloan	51 William Spivey
7 George McDaniel	52 Moses Archer
8 John Coley	53 James Perry
9 James Burns jr	54 John Noblet
10 Aron Bryan sr	55 John Eastbridge
11 Benjamin Dowdy sen	56 John Whitehead
12 Frederick Phillips	57 Leonard Johnston
13 Elisha Jackson	58 Duty Dorset
14 Michel Welch	59 John Craton
15 Robert Barker	60 Henry Harris
16 Lemuel Underwood	61 John Evans
17 John Bray	62 Joseph Alston
18 John Lawler	63 Josiah Tomison
19 Thomas Mullins	64 Milliner Burk
20 Edom Edwards	65 Reuben May
21 John Purvis	66 David Blacklock
22 Joab Brooks	67 Isaac Field
23 Benjamin Emmerson	68 Willim aStedman
24 George Smith	69 James McMath jr
25 James Eastis	70 Edward Buckner
26 Ezekiel Mazey	71 John Taylor
27 William Mathews	72 John Gear
28 William Jordan	73 Isaac Richison
29 Guilford Gardner	74 Benjamin Curl
30 Elisha Kurby	75 Jesse Davis
31 Isaiah Cole	76 John Carton
32 George Merrett	77 Matthew Hogan
33 Samuel Harris	78 John Boon
34 Larkin Straughn	79 Banston Chaves
35 James Edwards	80 Benjamin Pytent
36 Josiah Kurby	81 Armstead Haynes
37 Cornelius Myrick	82 James Tidder
38 Wm F Richardson	83 Richard Evans
39 Joseph Elliott	84 Charles Evans
40 Joseph Hart	85 John Cullerson
41 James Myrick	86 David Fox, jr.
42 Azel Myrick	87 Aron Stout
43 James Dixon	88 David Vestal
44 James Wamble	89 Barnell Fox
45 Johnson Barber	90 John Davis

Sixth Company, detached from the Wake Regiment.

1 William McCullers, *captain*
2 John Walton, *lieutenant*
3 Britton Sanders, *ensign*
4 Littleton Houston
5 Burtess Upchurch
6 Nathaniel Ward
7 John Scott
8 John Pride
9 William Harwood
10 Little John Utley
11 Whitmill Hunter
12 Alvin Utley
13 Jyre Parish
14 Wiley Womak
15 John Watson
16 John Rand
17 Darling Jones
18 Giles B Bledsoe
19 Miller Sexton
20 Anthony Pilkinton
21 Isma Kellum
22 Noel Norris
23 William Holland
24 Peter Angel
25 Arthur Reves

Seventh Company, detached from Wake Regiment.

1 John T. C. Wistt, *captain*
2 Lewis Muse, *first lieutenant*
3 Nicholas Sheffield, *ensign*
4 Samuel Combs, *first sergeant*
5 Thomas Rice, *second do*
6 Samuel Pearson, *third do*
7 Dawson Atkinson, *fourth do*
8 David A Knott, *first corporal*
9 John R Kart, *second do*
10 John Carney, *third do*
11 Abraham H Boylan, *fourth do*
12 Preston Pearson
13 Ilie Nunn
14 William W Seaton
15 Mark Cook
16 Robert Harrison
17 Alfred Jones
18 Jonathan Busbee
19 Willis Parker
20 Martin Adams
21 James B Ruth
22 John Rice
23 Thomas Powers
24 Edmond R Pitt
25 William Brown
26 Robert Calum
27 James G Mitchel
28 William Harrison
29 Littleberry Williams
30 Nelson Andrews
31 William Davis
32 Allen Parks
33 John Olive
34 James Olive
35 Elias Gay
36 Allen Griffin
37 Thomas Bowden
38 Jesse Gibbs
39 John Dodd
40 Oran Vincent
41 Samuel Bake
42 William W Bell
43 William Brantley
44 Christopher Woodard
45 Joseph Woodard
46 William Bell
47 Shadrack Haywood
48 Jeremiah Bell
49 Willis Nelms
50 Josiah Davis
51 Cader Nutt
52 Robert Rutherford
53 James Morris
54 Wiley Roberts
55 John George
56 Wylie Carpenter
57 John Burges
58 Daniel George
59 John Lynn
60 James Thorn
61 Brittain Stephenson
62 Willis Holderfield
63 James Head
64 Little John Utley
65 William Harwood
66 John Pride
67 John Scott
68 Nathaniel Ward
69 Bentess Upchurch
70 Littleton Huston

Eighth Company, detached from Granville Regiment.

1 Willis Johnston, *captain*
2 William G Brown, *lieutenant*
3 William Dolby, *ensign*
4 Willie M Spears
5 Green B Walker
6 Tandy Walker

7 James G Tate
8 John Bass
9 Richard Wood
10 Francis Clark
11 Wiat Johnston
12 John Barnett, jr.
13 John Barnett
14 Solmon Hayes
15 Kinchen Higgs
16 Kinchen Bynum
17 Thomas Cole
18 James Mayson
19 William W Ananias
20 Valentine Mayfield
21 John Davis
22 Kade Kittrell
23 William Parks
24 John Roberts
25 Abram Lawrence
26 George Lienter
27 John Lyod
28 John Paskill
29 James Allen
30 James Gill
31 Moses Winston
32 Wiat Kennedy
33 Newman Robertson
34 Jehu Spear
35 Benjamin Huffman
36 Arthur Fuller
37 Lain Moore
38 Thomas Lile

39 Henry Morris
40 Fletcher Taylor
41 John Sherril
42 Asa Green
43 James Sewit
44 David Byers
45 William Bock
46 Henry Avery
47 Lazarus Minor
48 George Byers
49 William White
50 Wiat Cazart
51 Samuel Clemons
52 James Medders
53 Michel Christon
54 John Stephenson
55 Jesse Acock
56 Benjamin H Wortham
57 Henry Chambles
58 Samuel Persyth
59 Henry Jones
60 Mertin Freeman
61 Payton Madison
62 Merkle Tom Kithrell
63 Egreppy Nance
64 Edward Weathers
65 Henry Hendley
66 William Adcock
67 Arthur Fuller
68 Asa Green
69 Nicholas Green
70 John Mitchell

Ninth Company, detached from Granville Regiment.

1 Lestly Gilliam, *captain*
2 William Gilliam, *lieutenant*
3 Thomas Hunt, *ensign*
4 Thomas Howard, *first sergeant*
5 John Downey, *second do*
6 Thomas Downey, *third do*
7 Moses Pettiford, *fourth do*
8 Lioratia Bass, *first corporal*
9 Charles Pratt, *second do*
10 Bejamin Ward, *third do*
11 William Oakley, *fourth do*
12 Peyton Hayes, *private*
13 William Terry, *do*
14 Charles Duncan
15 Scarlet Anderson
16 Ransom Hester
17 Solomon Satterswhite
18 William Daniel
19 Overton Haines
20 Thomas Daniel
21 Phillip P Pool
22 Charles Smith
23 Meredith Lampkin
24 William Blanks

25 Elkshel Ellis
26 Robert Wilson
27 Robert Jenkins
28 William Hargrove
29 William Collins
30 John Norwood
31 Reuben Hawkins
32 William Barnes
33 Pleasant Mangum
34 Rowland Perdue
35 John Daniels
36 John Montague
37 Robert Stamper
38 John Chavis
39 Thomas Evans
40 William Evans
41 Jeremiah Anderson
42 Lemuel Tyler
43 Meredith Lampkins
44 William Griffin
45 Thomas Lewis
46 William Seares
47 Benjamin Grissom
48 Reuben Parish

40 Zachariah Mitchel	64 Barnett Higgs
50 William Johnston	65 Edward Setton
51 Robert Elliston	66 Payton Madison
52 Robert Gordon	67 Simuel Persithe
53 Robert Longmire	68 Miston Freeman
54 David Jones	69 Henry Jones
55 Thompson Hedgepith	70 Henry Chambles
56 Bewdie Howard	71 Benjamin H Wortham
57 William Gordon	72 Jese Adcock
58 James G Tate	73 John Stephenson
59 Lervey Pettiford	74 Michael Christian
60 John T Peace	75 James Meddows
61 Thomas House	76 Samuel Clement
62 Ransom Harris	77 Wyat Cazart
63 Willie Grissom	78 William White

Tenth Company, detached from Person Regiment. *No. 2Returns.*

1 Sampson Glenn, *captain*	34 John Ingram
2 John Glenn, *lieutenant*	35 John Pullum
3 Robert Williams, *second do*	36 John Atkinson
4 Solomon Pain, *ensign*	37 James Branch, *fourth sergeant*
5 Gabriel Davey, *first sergeant*	38 John Stanfield
6 Edmond Dixson, *second do*	39 Duncan Rose
7 Hosea Fuller, *third do*	40 Bird Walker
8 Lewis Ramsay	41 Thomas Gordan
9 Phillip Singleton	42 Thomas Dancey
10 Alexander Elixor	43 Edmond Mitchel
11 Asa Hudgins	44 David Nellum
12 William Nelums	45 Aron Chrisenberg
14 Phillip Day	46 William Pope
14 Phillip Day	47 William Singleton
15 John Cooper	48 Jeremiah Blanchard
16 Joseph Rogers	49 Thomas Halley Burton
17 Isaac Vanhook	50 John Carton
18 William W Chambers	51 James Mann
19 John Mann	52 Jeremiah Rimer
20 Robert Cochran	53 John Filmond
21 Hutchens Burton	54 James Jacobs
22 John Rainey	55 William Buchannon
23 Charles Ward	56 Leonard Morris
24 John R Eskrigo	57 Vinson Tapp
25 William Gill	58 John Elmore
26 Giles Rogers	59 John Moore
27 Jeremiah Stanfield	60 David Lareson
28 John W Graves	61 John Fuller
29 Solomon Walker	62 Walter Fuller
30 William Jones	63 Reuben Corner
31 Jesse Bull	64 James Waddy
32 Thomas Lawson	65 John Toler
33 Robert Mann	66 Walter Buchannon

Eleventh Company, detached from Caswell Regiment.

1 Joseph Benton, *captain*	6 Joshua Hightower
2 John Mitchell, *lieutenant*	7 Samuel Wood
3 John Lea, *second do*	8 Richard Jones
4 William B Graves, *ensign*	9 Armstead Watington
5 Allen Gunn	10 Carter Malone

11 Goodwin Evans	52 George Brooks
12 Moses Simpson	53 Jonathan B Wattington
13 Alexander Watson	54 William H Wattington
14 Oliver Brintle	55 John Williams
15 Hiram Parks	56 James Scott
16 John Nighton	57 Parabo Bozwell
17 Tilmore Stone	58 William Terrell
18 William Night	59 John H Humphries
19 William Martin	60 John Stadler
20 Lemuel Chilton	61 Haroway Swift
21 Isham Normand	62 Joseph Burrough
22 Turner Nighton	63 Stewart Farley
23 Isaac Patterson	64 George Randolph
24 Robert Ware	65 Matthew Hubbard
25 Josiah Stanfield	66 William Kersey
26 Isaac West	67 Robert Stadler
27 Westly Normand	68 Lewis Hall
28 Richard Swift	69 Younger Hardwick
29 Lewis Ballard	70 William Nipper
30 Bartholomew Ellis	71 Edward Glore
31 Thomas Fielder	72 Sandy Smith
32 Benjamin Cantrall	73 Robert Wilson
33 Henry Collier	74 William Fullington
34 John Brown	75 James Johnston
35 John Shackleford	76 William Harwell
36 Robert Bruce	77 Virgil M Raiuey
37 Spencer Jackson	78 John B Farley
38 William Johnston	79 Stephen Burton
39 James Bruce	80 William Gordon
40 James Somers	81 Noel Burton
41 John Badget	82 Benjamin Crider
42 Eli Sharp	83 James Atkins
43 Hiram Wetherford	84 Zenas Martin
44 Daniel Morgan	85
45 Baldy Ramson	86 Daniel Smith
46 Edward Jones	87 Joshua Butler
47 Walter Brayfield	88 Laban Hunt
48 Hugh Howard	89 William Singleton
49 Francis Wattington	90 Pleasant Rudd
50 Henry Booker Hailey	91 Benjamin Loafmand
51 Jepthah Parks	

SIXTH REGIMENT,

Detached from the eighth Brigade.

John Martin, Lieutenant Colonel Commandant.
George Lemmond, First Major,
James Johnston, Second Major.

First Company, detached from the second Guilford Regiment.

1 William Mears, *captain*	6 Arthur Forbes, **sen.**
2 William Dinkey, *lieutenant*	7 Elijah Lingold
3 Grovesnor Marsh, *ensign*	8 John Clark
4 Elias Prickhard	9 Frederick Sheaver
5 John Chance	10 David Story

11 Andrew Law
12 Stephen Griffin
13 Reuben Anderson
14 Maxwell Wilson
15 Aron Sprouts
16 Jacob Wilker
17 John Barnhart
18 John J Matthews
19 William Forster
20 Alanson Forster
21 Daniel Cobb
22 Ludwith Seabold
23 William Smith
24 Henry Swing
25 Henry Greason
26 David Glass
27 Henry Bowman
28 Henry Shaw
29 John Charles
30 John Shepperd
31 Lewis May
32 Christian Cline
33 Daniel Mitchel
34 William Tade
35 Shadrach White
36 Christian Isley
37 Peter Wamick
38 Bartin Garringer
39 Richard Fentress
40 John Wilson
41 Robert Elkins
42 Thomas Jackson
44 Levi Sullivan
44 Levin Sullivan
45 Obediah Leonard
46 Samon Wilson
47 Robert Parsons
48 Thomas Elkins
49 Solomon Ward
50 George Montgomery
51 William Jackson

52 Dempsey Whitney
53 James Leonard
54 Jhon Howell
55 John Strickland
56 James Williams
57 John Thomas
58 Andrew Thomas
59 John Spoon jr
60 Ebenezer Whitney
61 Thomas Lane
62 William Spoon
63 Samuel Horney
64 Isaac Leonard
65 Samuel Montgomery
66 Stewart Hardin
67 Benjamin Field
68 Daniel Kirkman
69 James Witherly
70 Thomas Lincheum
71 Johnston Alexander
72 Daniel Gladson
73 Robert Fields
74 Fisher B Taylor
75 William Hacket
76 William Meed
77 Elias Bowen
78 Francis Wrightet
50 Gradathan Harper
80 Isaac Rolan
81 William Dunning
82 William Watson
83 Thomas Ross
84 Elijah Ward
85 John Bpchannon
86 Charles Clemer
87 James Walker
88 Peter Wetherby
89 Wilkins Lucans
90 John Starks jr
91 Israel Brown

Second Company, detached from first ·Guilford Regiment.

1 Samuel Hunter, *captain*
2 Abraham Riples, *first lieutenant*
3 John Moore, *second do*
4 Thomas Bevill, *ensign*
5 Nicholas Ogborn, *cadet*
6 Levy Ross, *first sergeant*
7 Thomas L Moody, *second do*
8 Miat Carter, *third do*
9 Alexander Bevill, *fourth do*
10 Phillip Bevill, *first corporal*
11 James Cole, *second do*
12 Noel Parish, *third do*
13 Alfred Branner, *fourth do*
14 Charles B Harris, *private*

15 Henry Maga
16 Wilson Patterson
17 Kinchen Vaughan
18 Jonh Osburn
19 Nathan Barham
20 Aron Walker
21 Parrum Ray
22 Peyton Ray
23 Felix M Bince
24 Elijah Beasel
25 Sihon Turner
26 William Billingsby
27 Jonas Case
28 William Walker

29 David Fairbanks
30 John Walker
31 Walker Dowet
32 Levin Caulk
33 James Gaugh
34 Reuben Parish
35 Harbert Tatum
36 John Willy
37 George W Bell
38 John Flemming
39 nEoch Tumlinson
40 James Nelson
41 Valentine Garoll
42 Caleb Lawrence
43 Edward Wilson
44 John Doak
45 David Lanin
46 Isaac Howlet
47 William Winchester
48 William Parmer
49 Thomas Maga
50 Charles Case
51 Reubin Garlick
52 Archibald Whitworth
53 Bryant Pearcy
54 Lodwick B Wilson
55 Thomas Jackson
56 Robert H Brinkle
57 William A Stephens
58 David Archer
59 James Archer
60 Zenas Bunker

61 Peter Brown
62 Henry Reed
63 Thomas Dunning
64 John Pegg
65 David Beason
66 Jacob Lovell
67 William Shelly
68 George Middleton
69 Jesse Pegg
70 Joab Pegg
71 Martin Pegg
72 Danut North
73 Absalom Williams
74 Jacob Riggins
75 Joseph Edoll
76 Hezekiah Lock
77 Robert Bevill
78 Moton Riggins
79 William Riggins
80 Thomas Hunt
81 Danil Barnell
82 Jacob Waggoner
83 Argis Suthard
84 John Kindle
85 Nathan Underwood
86 William Dunning
87 Valentine Waggoner
88 Isaac Lee
89 Malcomb Morrison
90 Andrew Cain
91 Wiat Lane
92 Sihon Turner

Third Company, detached from Rockingham Regiment.

1 William Lenmon, *captain*
2 Reubin Lindsay, *Lieutenant*
3 Thomas Galoway, *ensign*
4 Jesse Vermilion, *first sergeant*
5 Elijah Thomas, *second do*
6 Enoch Hinston, *private*
7 William Berwick
8 Robert Walker
9 Edward Massey
10 Thomas Botts
11 William Hosford
12
13 William W Brown
14 James Hudson
15 Valentine Morgan
15 Robert Barnes
17 Pleasant Barnes
18 John Bundrant
19 Reece Watkins
20 William Griffith
21 Samuel Jelton
22 Zera Summers
23 Joseph Maye
24 Archills Wynn

25 William Henderson
26 James King
27 Matthew Covey
28 Peter Wall
29 Abram Jerald
30 James Young
31 Chesley Wooders
32 David Heron
33 Stewart Dramond
34 Joshua Jarrall
35 Reason Waters
36 James Sparks
37 Baldy Rice
38 Durham Sharp
39 Willima Sharp
40 Ambrose Joice
41 Pleasant Joice
42 Thomas Barfield
43 Peter Horn
45 William Haynes
46 James Lemon
47 William Alexander
48 Bartlet Grogan

49 Thomas Godsey	52 Robert Hall
50 William Smothers	53 David Buchannon
51 David Chadwell	54 Wilham W Burk

Fourth Company, (Grenadiers,) detached from Rockingham Regim.

1 James Campbell, *captain*	41 James Barry
2 William J Mongus, *lieutenant*	42 John Sinclar, jr
3 David Barry, *second do*	43 Robert Cantrill
4 George Adkins, *ensign*	44 Lewis Dodson
5 William Wardlow, *first sergeant*	45 John Cantrall
6 John Shivers, *second do*	46 Daniel Foster
7 George Cantrill, *third do*	47 James Walker
8 Eli Coram, *fourth do*	48 Lelin Molenby
9 John H Taylor, *first corporal*	49 Frederick Miller
10 Morgan Lillard, *second do*	50 Edward Godsey
11 James H Scales, *third do*	51 James Mackey
12	52 John Wollington
13 Martin Jones, *drummer*	53 James Taylor
14 Richard Coram, *fifer*	54 Jesse Thomas
15 John Serkin	55 Isaac Pitle
16 Jeremiah Nichols	56 Pleasant Mount
17 James W Olington	57 Allen Caldwell
18 William Grogan	58 Thomas Wammot
19 William Mobly, jr	59 John Jones
20 William Brown, jr	60 Lemiah King
21 John Molesby	61 John King
22 John Hancock	62 Edward Nunon
23 William Miller	63 Joseph Asbrige, jr
24 John Wall, jr	64 John Powell
25 Joseph Berry	65 Matthias Mount, jr
26 Elijah Cantrill	66 William King
27 Daniel Ellington, jr	67 William S Haney
28 Fedding Wright	68 James B Rice
29 Grieff Ellington	69 Robert S Stewart
30 John Barry	70 John Sims, jr
31 Skipwith Wray	71 Zacha Lewis
32 William Williams	72 Eli Young
33 Joseph Woldrige	73 Daniel Tucker
34 Daniel Carter	74 John Griffin
35 Henry Miller	75 Reuben Grady, jr
36 John Mount, jr	76 Thomas Jarold
37 William Coram, jr	77 George Stewart
38 George Coffer	78 William Lewis
39 Davis Heron	79 Robert Grady
40 James Wardlow	

Fifth Company, detached from the Second Stokes Regiment.

1 Alexander Moody, *captain*	11 William Dalton
2 Thomas Yarrell, *lieutenant*	12 Jesse Stewart
3 William G Haynes, *ensign*	13 Henry Doube
4 Henry Fry	14 Henry Briggs
4 Thomas Westmoreland	15 John Stofel
6 James Cooper	16 Jacob Teats
7 William Cox	17 Peter Moses
8 William Hubbart	18 Robert Hill
9 James Hargrove	19 Samuel Aldrige
10 John Cox	20 John Binkley

21 Henry Stipe
22 Leonard Conrad
23 Simon Croon
24 Jacob Miller, sen
25 Jacob Hixt
26 Elijah Purdon
27 Charles Anderson
28 Austin Smith
29 Charles Chitty
30 Christopher Zimmerman
31 Archibald Davis
32 William Boly Jack
33 Henry Hitner
34 John Hyor
35 Elisha Stator
36 Andrew Krowse
37 Abram Beck
38 Edward Tatom
39 Stephen Riddle
40 John Barr
41 John Rick
42 Joseph Holbrook
43 David Linvill

44 William Holbrook, jr
45 William Holbrook, sen
46 Willis Cooper
47 Daniel N Repton
48 James Ham
49 James Reid
50 George Hubbard
51 John Wright
52 John Smith
53 George Kennemon
54 Jesse Swim
55 Kelan Pittcord
56 Campbell Sutton
57 Francis Jackson
58 John S Leight
59 Asbury Arnett
60 James Crews
61 John Harald
62 William Beason
63 Daniel Huff
64 John McPherson
65 Solomon Fulp
66 Elijah Gerrell

Sixth Company, detached from the First Stokes Regiment.

1 William Goode, *captain*
2 David Dalton, *first lieutenant*
3 Samuel Martin, *ensign*
4 Robert Young
5 Berryman Knight
6 James Fountain
7 Joshua Southam
8 William Ward
9 Elijah Night
10 Richard Flynt
11 Bradford Vanter
12 James Marshal
13 William Smith
14 Michael Smith
15 William Riggs
16 Joel Smith
17 William Welch
18 Thomas Reddick
19 Benjamin Morgan
20 William Daggins
21 Richard Vernon
22 Samuel Heath
23 William Eads
24 William Sisk
25 Aurelua Wooldrige
26 Thomas Westbrook
27 William Harris
28 Benjamin Haynes
29 Hezekiah Tore
30 William Oliver
31 Lambert Dodson
32 Henry Baker
33 William Cannon

34 Samuel Neil
35 Pillis Priddy
36 Lewis Tilly
37 James Young
38 Benjamin Hutchison
39 Thomas Wilkins
40 John Priddy
41 Elisha Vernon
42 Thomas Jinkins
43 James Griffin
44 Clifford Yates
45 George Wilkins
46 James Beasley
47 Joel Kitchum
48 Elisha Nelson
49 Lewis Bower
50 William Nelson
51 Benjamin Fry
52 Henry Bulling
53 Larkin Burge
54 Pleasant Bridgmore
55 Moses Hiett
56 William Gregory
57 Daniel Scotte
58 James Bavick
59 Isaac Jackson
60 Samuel Jackson
61 Christopher Sponse
62 James Eaton
63 Raleigh Darnold
64 Thomas Franklin
65 Solomon Spainhour
66 Joseph Zimmerman

67 John Prather
68 William Stone
69 Henry Alberty
70 Jesse Brown
71 Clisby Robertson
72 John Crammer

73 Jesse Childress
74 John Cook
75 John Segimore
76 James Walker
77 Mereday Bennet
78 Nicholas Frost

SEVENTH REGIMENT.

Detached from the 7th and 11th Brigades.

Jesse A. Pearson, Lieutenant Colonel Commandant
David Kerr, First Major
John Still, Second Major

First Company, detached from the First Rowan Regiment

1 Jacob Krider, *captain*
2 Hugh McKnight, *lieutenant*
3 James Gelispee, *ensign*
4 Frederick Cauble
5 Henry Lippart
6 George Fisher
7 John Tinkle
8 Conrad Smitteds
9 Henry Casey
10 Jacob Lane
11 Daniel Brown
12 Pleasant Tapley
13 Sion Keeth
14 James Ross
15 Phillip Hoofman
16 John Kastor
17 William Snow
18 Solomon Miller
19 Charles Ryer
20 George Hodge
21 John Ross, sen
22 Mertin Miller
23 Mertin Happner
24 Andrew Holshouse, jr
25 Henry Caulans
26 Adam Cauble
27 John Lingle
28 John Lane
29 John Clutz
30 Jacob Lingle
31 Meihall Delow
32 Phillips Carter
33 Jacob Skussing
34 Peter Deal
35 Peter Albright
36 Henry Sudler
37 Leonard Craigh
38 John Hauston
39 Hiram Davidson

40 Edward Heulin
41 John Rudisil
42 John Smith
43 Morris Pinkston
44 Peter M Smith
45 William H Horoh
46 John Utzman
47 George Utzman
48 Jacob Utzman
49 Jesse James
50 William Dickson
51 Robert Wood
52 John Wood
53 Ralph Kasler
54 David Ewell
55 Eps Robertson
56 Skiles Foster
57 Daniel Cress
58 John B Lonona
59 Daniel Shuford
60 John Holshouser
61 George Withellene
62 Moses Lamb
63 John Lance
64 Phillip Lytiker
65 Samuel Felker
66 Peter Upright
67 Jacob Rary
68 Malikiah Bowers
69 Henry Singenwinder
70 Andrew Kincade
71 James Glenn
72 Samuel Rice
73 Samuel Kincade
74 Thomas Hutson
75 William Bar
76 William Cowin
77 John Patterson
78 Isaac Cowin

Second Company, detached from the second Rowan Regiment

1 Henry Katts, *captain*
2 John Beard, *lieutenant*
3 James Lowe, *ensign*
4 Julius Strange, *first sergeant*
5 Barnabas Bowers, *second do*
6 John Brinkhart, *third do*
7 Wilson Wiseman, *fourth do*
8 Jacob Stoner, *first corporal*
9 Thomas Ceicel, *second do*
10 Elijah Northern, *third do*
11 Even Thomas, *fourth do*
12 James Wiseman, *drummer*
13 Jacob Bringle, *fifer*
14 James Silvers, *private*
15 Benjamin Sincunger
16 Josiah Cunningham
17 Adam Hendrick
18 George Birkhart
19 Christian Sink
20 Alfred Owens
21 Shadrick Hill
22 Christian Lucanbill
23 George Bowers
24 George Myers
25 Henry Hepler
26 John Myers, sen
27 James Jones
28 James Moss
29 Bryant Fry
30 Abram Shular
31 Abraham Hunt
32 Oliver Hunt
33 Jonathan Davis
34 Michel Myers
35 Samuel Williams
36 John Sims
37 Edmond McCarn
38 Jesse Lane
39 Joseph Warford
40 Barnard Living
41 Thomas Workman
42 William Workman
43 Peter Livenger
44 Phillip Headrick
45 Micajah Hill
46 Smith Hill
47 Abram Johnston
48 Isaiah Hicks
49 James Lacey
50 Zachariah Coggins
51 Thomas Davis
52 Lewis Beard
53 James Ziveley
54 John Stoutenberg
55 Barzilla McBride
56 John Delow
57 John B Crump
58 James Owen
59 Walter Northern
60 Isaac Grist
61 Moses Holmes
62 John Williams
63 James Gallimore
64 James Green
65 Charles Savage
66 Henry Cline
67 Phillip Cline
68 Cornelius Smith
69 Jonathan Walk
70 David Bierly
71 Phillip Willis
72 Reuben Nunby

Third Company, detached from the third Rowan Regiment

1 John Frost, *captain*
2 William Duffy, *lieutenant*
3 Charles Anderson, *ensign*
4 James Wilson, *first sergeant*
5 John Ford, *second do*
6 James Gamble, *third do*
7 Samuel Diel, *fourth do*
8 William Wiatt, *first corporal*
9 Samuel Frost, *second do*
10 John Hodgers, *third do*
11 William Hutson, *fourth do*
12 James Warren, *drummer*
13 Samuel McGuire, *fifer*
14 William Bissent, *private*
15 Daniel Lark
16 George Claybrook
17 Thomas Horn
18 Howell Horn
19 William Chapman
20 Conel James
21 Isaac James
22 Inley Smith
23 Caleb Brock
24 Edward Williams
25 Richard Haxwood
26 Robert Clark
27 Thomas Smith
28 Oliver Griffin
29 Richard Jarvis
30 John Speak
31 Dennis Jarvis
32 Clare Maxlin
33 Thomas Gears
34 Baker Johnston

35 Elwin Howard
36 James Orton
37 Richard Luckey
38 Henry Luckey
39 Gustavous Boswell
40 Francis Kinshaw
41 Teneson Cheshen
42 George Taylor
43 Thomas Taylor
44 Thomas Leach
45 Richard Jones
46 Joseph Lewis
47 Brice W Isam
48 William Brogdon
49 Alfred Brogdon
50 Jonathan West
51 John Becketh
52 Daniel Cane
53 Virtue Sweat
54 Richbell Mott
55 Samuel Beaman
56 Jacob Newton

57 William K Aire
58 Jacob Gawood
59 Isaac Gawood
60 Edward Buckner, jr
61 Zachariah Booth
62 James Owens
63 Aron Tucker
64 Enoch Chamberlain
65 David Hampton
66
67 James Park
68 John Douthet
69 Thomas Gentle
70 Freeman Bate
71 George Smith
72 John James
73 Zachariah Tenneyhill
74 Christopher Erwin
75 John Graham
76 John Buck
77 Andrew Morrison
78 Arthur Smith

Fourth Company, detached from the Fourth Rowan Regiment

1 Thomas M Times, *captain*
2 Jones Enoch, *lieutenant*
3 George Lowry, *ensign*
4 John Wilborn, *first sergeant*
5 Micajah Eagle, *second do*
6 William Cerill, *third do*
7 Benjamin Pain, *fourth do*
8 George Snider, jr *first corporal*
9 Brummel Sap, *second do*
10 George Kelly, *third do*
11 Edmond Cawil, *fourth do*
12 John Farrington, *drummer*
13 Micajah Haworth, *fifer*
14 George Saner, *private*
15 Jacob Douthit
16 Abraham Brindle
17 Ransom Ellis
18 David Marklan
19 Abner Brown
20 William Swim
21 James Kelly
22 Phillip Smith
23 Daniel Chriswell
24 Jaret Wood
25 Jeremiah Haworth
26 William Welborn
27 John Cerill
28 Obadiah Twidwell
29 William Twonay
30 Samuel Ceril
31 Daniel Waworth
32 Meredith Pearce
33 Barnabas Idol
34 Hugh Robertson

35 Matthias Idol
36 John Donaway
37 Jacob Miller
38 Francis Barncastle
39 Henry Hill
40 Christian Fash
41 Henry James
42 Larkin Scott
43 John Oaks
44 Joseph Farabee
45 Andrew Clinard
46 Abraham Everitt
47 William Pain
48 Samuel Weer
49 Samuel Spurgin
50 William Weer
51 Jacob Williams
52 John Merick
53 Adam Fritz
54 David Darr
55 Henry Long
56 John Grub
57 Jacob Averhart
58 Jacob Sowens
59 Jacob Grub
60 James Skider
61 George Myers
62 Jacob Kesler
63 Richard Graham
64 Macoy Gallispie
65 Daniel Lynch
66 Moses Tompson
67 Jonathan Burns
68 James McLaughlen

69 Richard Foster
70 Andrew Morrison
71 Caleb Webb
72 William Dickey

73 John Hugey
74 Andrew Renshaw
75 William Summers

Fifth Company, detached from Iredell Regiment

1 John Moody, *captain*
2 William Carson, *lieutenant*
3 William Moody, *ensign*
4 Thomas Prather, *first sergeant*
5 Caleb Conbey, *second do*
6 Joseph Duporster, *third do*
7 Samuel Hayes, *fourth do*
8 Henry Marshall, *first corporal*
9 Milus Privitt, *second do*
10 David Fox, *third do*
11 Richard Privitt, *fourth do*
12 Richard Cook, *drummer*
13 Harris Swivit, *fifer*
14 William Millsaps, *private*
15 William Martin
16 William Gordon
17 James Martin
18 Samuel Mackoy
19 George W Robertson
20 Erwin Privitt
21 George Lackey
22 Richard Sparks
23 William Blackenship
24 Sake Harris
25 John Teague
26 James Lack
27 Walter Beill
28 John Cash
29 Henry Giddens
30 Thomas Green
31 James Templeton
32 Samuel Templeton
33 Hugh B King
34 Joseph Edson
35 John McConnell
36 Solomon Claywell
37 Samuel Mitchel
38 Hugh Currant

39 Greenbury Haire
40 John Hath
41 Reuben Barnard
42 Turner Welch
43 Ashiey Johnston
44 John Rector
45 Bleasant Owen
46 Benjamin Moody
47 Bresom Heziap
48 Benjamin Brantly
49 Henry Carson
50 John M Clerland
51 Nathan Baker
52 Michael Tague
53 Lovet Phelps
54 Abram Cook
55 Samuel Henderson
56 William Looper
57 Allison Gapp
58 Richard Mears
59 Hiram Flecher
60 Thomas Lovelus
61 Reason Beill
62 Elias Lazenbury
63 Thomas Galloway
64 Alexander Read
65 Andrew Well
66 Joseph Moon
67 John Young
68 Phillip Phillips
69 Randolph Roads
70 Benjamin Brown
71 Richard Booker
72 Henry Buck
73 Joseph Donalson
74 George Masters
75 Samuel Hart

Sixth Company, detached from Iredell Regiment

1 Neil McCoy, *captain*
2 Abram Nelson, *lieutenant*
3 Alexander McCoy, *ensign*
4 Thomas Davidson, *first sergeant*
5 James Jones, *second do*
6 William Freeland, *third do*
7
8 Andrew Kilpatrick, *fourth do*
9 Benjamin Sterns, *first corporal*
10 John Fenster, *second do*
Elijah Tucker, *third do*
11 Thomas Campbell, *fourth do*
12 Daniel Rector, *drummer*

13 William Arthur, *fifer*
14 George L Davidson
15 Thomas Crawford
16 Robert Allison
17 Theophilus Simonton
18 Theophilus Falls
19 John Cleton
20 John Parker
21 John Beil
22 John Murdock
23 Ephriam Ewin
24 James Parker
25 William Preil

26 James Templeton
27 Henry Conner
28 Robert Westmoreland
29 David McCrery
30 Andrew Caldwell
31 Joseph Rogers
32 Joseph Templeton
33 Ephraim Ewing
34 Edmond Taylor
35 Robert M Hughs
36 William Horsliam
37 John Scott
38 Neil Brawlie, jr
39 Robert West
40 David Mulholland
41 David Currell
42 John Bector
43 Michael White
44 Hezekiah Grey
45 Neil McCastle
46 William Wintosh
47 Thomas Morrison
48 David Moore
49 Archibald Essleman
50 Samuel McMillan
51 John Wintosh

52 Alexander Wintosh
53 Joseph Alexander
54 Mosey Stephenson
55 John Houp
56 James Hill
57 Samuel Freeland
58 James Freeland
59 Thomas Morrison
60 Andrew Watts
61 Andrew Morrison
62 Samuel Wah
63 John Morrison
64 Alexander Kilpatrick
65 George Braddy
66 And' McAdams
67 Joel Bruce
68 Hugh Copland
69 David Potts
70 Levi Moore
71 Laban Bracker
72 Ninian Steel sen
73 Thomas Archibald
74 John Gay
75 Reason Bell
76 John Hait
77 Samuel Chambers

Seventh Company, detached from the First Mecklenburg Regiment

1 Joseph Douglass, *captain*
2 William M Kary, *lieutenant*
3 William Walker, *ensign*
4 Hemden Brevard, *first sergeant*
5 David Gibony, *second do*
6 Samuel Brown, *third do*
7 William M Barrett, *fourth do*
8 Thomas Allen, *first corporal*
9 John Solon, *second do*
10 Isaac V Pitt, *third do*
11 Robert Duchworth, *fourth do*
12 Adam Harrison
13 Hugh Wiley
14 James Moore
15 John Caldwell
16 Junius Hood
17 David Alexander
18 James Parker
19 Matthew Wallace
20 Thomas McRae
21 John Phillips
22 Henry Farr
23 Hugh Todd
24 Hugh Elliott
25 Arthur Jimison
26 Nicholas Parish
27 Andrew Walker
28 Upton Roden
29 David B Wilson
30 Joseph Love

31 Isaac Beaty
32 Joseph Bingham
33 William Sharply
34 Hugh Greggs
35 Francis Erwin
36 Richard Mason
37 John B Elliott
38 John L Darnell
39 William Camerson
40 Samuel J Hutchison
41 Joshua Clark
42 James Hutchison
43 John McLure
44 John Darnell
45 Benjamin Thompson
46 Alexander Moore
47 Alexander Smith
48 William Darnel
49 David Darnel
50 Jacob I Cunningham
51 Hugh Harris
52 Eli Alexander
53 Mitchel Johnston
54 Allen Lucas
55 William Downy
56 Samuel Graham
57 Will Bushbey
58 Thomas Shepherd
59 Allen Sloan
60 John Fat

61 Andrew M Lane
62 Alexander Washam
63 Howard Weir
64 William Sullivan
65 John Ferret, sen
66 David Henderson
67 Arthur Garretson
68 Will Robertson

69 James Simmimer
70 Drury Solomon
71 Hugh Holmes
72 Thomas McIlie
73 Hugh Stephenson
74 William Munteeth
75 Will Scott
76 Palau Alexander

Eighth Company, detached from the Second Mecklenburg Regiment

1 Robert Wood, *captain*
2 Jacob Shaver, *lieutenant*
3 Peter Mape, *Second do*
4 John Wilson, *ensign*
5 William Fleningan, *first sergt.*
6 John Hooker, *second do*
7 John Barnes, *third do*
8 James Watson, *fourth do*
9 John Hammuns, *first corporal*
10 Obed Dafter, *second do*
11 Will John, *third do*
12 Charles Hart, *fourth do*
13 Allen Stewart, *drummer*
14 John Rice, *fifer*
15 James Walker, *private*
16 John Brown
17 Robert Flenigan
18 William Sharp
19 Elias Flenigan
20 Randolph Cheek
21 Samuel E Flanigan
22 Elias McCallok
23 Andrew Stewart
24 Samuel Wiley
25 Ash John
26 Cunningham Sharp
27 John Wiat
28 John Black
29 Paten Bambow
30 Joseph Bryan
31 Antheris Purvins
32 Henry Clontz
33 Charles Crowell
34 John Cathberton
35 Wm L Lemmond
36 John Flow

37 Jacob Starns
38 Robert Boid
39 Daniel McLoyd
40 Roderick McReley
41 Moses Stunford
42 Allen Broom
43 Charles Lancey
44 John None
45 Brelon Belk
46 Samuel Holden
47 Valentine Prifly
48 Michael Flenigan
49 Henry Moser
50 Eli Coughran
51 James Robertson
52 William Redford
53 Jesse Yandles
54 Will Rea
55 Thomas Henley
56 Samuel Ormand
57 John Fobes
58 Adam Ormand
59 Lewis Howard
60 John McCorkle
61 Will U Irvey
62 James Thompson
63 John Long
64 Thomas Miller
65 Samuel Givens
66 William Martin
67 Robert Shannon
68 William Barnes
69 Solomon Morris
70 William Pirant
71 William Pool

Ninth Company, detached from the Second Mecklenburg Regiment

1 John Garretson, *captain*
2 Isaac Wiley, *lieutenant*
3 Nathiel Sims, *ensign*
4 Archibald Sawyer, *first sergeant*
5 Ire B Dixon, *second do*
6 William Smith, *third do*
7 Joro Kimmons, *fourth do*
8 William Mays, *first corporal*
9 John Holbrooks, *second do*

10 Frederick Kiser, *third do*
11 Andrew M Grady, *fourth do*
12 George Kenty, *drummer*
13 John Jaccour, *fifer*
14 John Irwin, *Private*
15 Saml. H Harris
16 James Ross
17 Houston Harris
18 John Alexander

19 Isaac Harris
20 Laid Alexander
21 Cyrus Campbell
22 Robert M Cochran
23 Jno Morrison
24 Robert C Morrison
25 Hugh McCain
26 Daniel Bost
27 Jacob House
28 Henry Miller
29 Jacob Rhinehart
30 Henry Rowe
31 Matthias Bost
32 Michael Owrey
33 John Light
34 Robert Carrigan, sr
35 Robert Carrigan, jr
36 Theophilus Gayler
37 John Correll
38 Joseph Hamilton
39 David Houston
40 Andrew Neele
41 James Neele
42 George Flemming
43 Martin Icehour
44 George Dove
45 William Smith
46 George Linker
47 Daniel Smith
48 John Barnhard

49 Son Fink
50 Andrew Carriher
51 Phillip Fink
52 John S Taylous
53 John Johnston
54 Rufus Johnston
55 David H Black
56 John Black
57 Johnston N Biggers
58 William Newit
59 George Right
60 Josiah Gilmore
61 Edward Martin
62 William Kelly
63 William Wines
64 Ebeneser Keelough
65 James Hall
66 Jacob Gaugus
67 John Goodnight
68 Adam Freeze
69 John Fereland
70 John Clisk
71 Jesse Chaple
72 Reuben Sneed
73 John Goodman
74 James McGraw
75 Charles Walter
76 Martin Shank
77 Daniel Luther
78 Jacob Simmon

Tenth Company, detached from Montgomery Regiment

1 Elijah Hattam, *captain*
2 William Moor, *lieutenant*
3 Hardy Morgan, *second do*
4 Wyett Scott
5 Hamlin Freeman
6 Stephen Morton
7 William Folks
8 Sion Pearce
9 William Gillan
10 Jacob Cockran
11 Allen McKackle
12 James Hellen
13 Hector McKinsie
14 Matthew Ingram
15 Joseph Killis
16 Nimrod Bradly
17 Robert B Wood
18 Richard Urry
19 William Thompson
20 William Trusty
21 William Eights
22 Daniel Hurley
23 Robert Berton
24 James Wiot
25 James Stephens
26 Zachariah Collins

27 William Johnston
28
29 Etheldred Blake
30 Micajah Rogers
31 Abraham Cochran
32 Daugle McDuffy
33 Colin Pall
34 Joseph Blake
35 Benjamin Jonhston
36 Hennith McKinsey
37 Myerdoh Loyd
38 Abel Rolan
39 John McRae
40 Aulas McCalar
41 Patrick Thompson
42 Joseph Hattom
43 Marrel Suggs
44 James Bennett
45 David Blallock
46 William Morgan
47 Nathaniel Mekins
48 John Still
49 William Morton
50 William Holton
51 George Heair
52 Rolen Crump

G

53 Wiley Harris
54 John Crump, jr
55 West Harris, jr
56 Allen Harris
57 Ezekiel Hearn
58 Daniel Redwine
59 William Hurley
60 Banister Porter
61 Frederick Randle
62 John Smith
63 John Durgan
64 Jept a Milton
65 John Merrett
66 Abram Trusty
67 Robert G Steele
68 James Balton
69 Joseph Morgan
70 Ephraim Coker
71 Majro Russell
72 Francis Jordan
73 Brantley H Gallihan

74 Terrel Blalock
75 Drury Bennett
76
77 Reuben Hicks
78 George Martin
79 John Beaves
80 Green Harris
81 Thomas Morris, jr
82 Eli Harris son of J
83 William Hanisen
84 Darby Jones
85 John Hancock
86 Jesse Bell
87 Elijah Grisham
88 Elias Morris
89 John Cotton
90 William Harris, son of K
91 David Tillman
92 Nelson Smith
93 John Poplin

EIGHTH REGIMENT.

Detached from the 9th, 10th and 15th Brigades

Nathan Horton, Lieutenant Colonel Commandant
Merritt Burgin, First Major
Samuel Davidson, Second Major

First Company, detached from the First Surry Regiment

1 William McCraw, *captain*
2 John Shipp, *first lieutenant*
3 Bernard Franklin, *second do*
4 William Potter, *ensign*
5 Eleon G Moore, *cadet*
6 Bailey Johnston, *private*
7 Micajah Reaves
8 Watson Holifield
9 Richard Reaves
10 Ezekiel Desern
11 William Holder
12 Charles Combs
13 John Parish
14 Charles Bryant
15 David Gerwin
16 Ralph Holifield
17 Joseph Cartwright
18 Joseph Muncas
19 Seward McCraw
20 Elijah Muncas
21 Jesse Howard
22 Solomon Griffith
23 Benjamin Baker
24 Isaac Puckett
25 Martin Forkner
26 Joshua Garrett
27 Samuel Laurence

28 William Smallwood
29 John Griffith
30 Samuel McCraw
31 Calvin Robertson
32 Henry Sparger
33 Isaac Holbrook
34 Daniel Reece
35 Lewis Raper
36 Gentry Hodges
37 William Hodges
38 John Ryan
39 Thomas Ketchum
40 William Vest
41 Thomas Bray
42 Benjamin Cummin
43 Dudley Reynolds
44 Daniel Barker
45 Thomas A Ward
46 Ephraim Stone
47 Jonathan Reynols
48 John Watson
49 James Graves
50 Moses Smith
51 Peter Graves
52 Richard White
53 Robert Baber
54 Conway Stone

Second Company, detached from the Second Surry Regiment.

1 Samuel Speer, *captain*
2 Thomas D Kelly, 1st *lieutenant*
3 Bowen Whitlock, *ensign*
4 John Kelly, jr, *cadet*
5 William D. Kelly, *private*
6 Benjamin Howard
7 Edmond Swenny
8 William Frady
9 William Spelman
10 Allen Willard
11 Asa Dinkins
12 Isaac Jones
13 Francis Moreland
14 Samuel Goff
15 Thomas Oliver
16 Strangerman Johnston
17 Abraham Wooten
18 Joshua Angel
19 David Anthony
20 Jesse Folbet
21 John Parks
22 Thomas Osbourn
23 Stephen Wood
24 Solomon Johnston
25 Joseph Phinney
26 William Masters
27 James Harris
28 William Sparks
29 Joel Patterson
30 Daniel Teasly
31 George Speer
32 Robert Martin
33 Robert Lyon
34 Thomas Dyal
35 James Lakey
36 Archer Poindexter
37 Joseph Lovill
38 Edward Lovill
39 John Logan
40 Joshua Pumm
41 William Pigg
42 Jacob Shouse
43 Joseph Hickman
44 Ephraim Williams
45 Jonathan Pendry
46 John Martin
47 Jesse Chinn
48 Garrett Mahaly
49 James Pilcher
50 William Brown
51 Johnston Lindsay
52 Wilie Dickinson
53 John McDonald
54 Thomas Kell
55 Richard Cook
56 Jonathan Roses
57 William Holloman
58 John Sutliff

Third Company, detached from Wilkes Regiment

1 Walter R Lanoir, *captain*
2 Michel Swain, *First lieutenant*
3 Lewis Carlton, *ensign*
4 William Ferguson
5 James Davis
6 Thomas Lands
7 Aron Fox
8 Jesse Crouch
9 Thomas Carlton
10 William Brookshire
11 Smith Ferguson
12 Joseph Howard
13 Isaac Vanderpool
14 David Robertson
15 Clifton Keeton
16 Charles Ragen
17 Elijah Dyer
18 Alexander Brown
19 John Vannoy
20 William Gullet
21 William Goforth
22 Francis Fox
23 David Hickerson
24 Ebenezer Castle
25 John Lipe
26 David Laird
27 Adam Kilby
28 Joel Foster
29 John N Broyhill
30 William Morgan
31 John Hall
32 Charles Main
33 Joshua Morgan
34 William Broyhill
35 Joel Dyer
36 William Kilby
37 Abner Trebble
38 Lewis Cash
39 Martin Baker
40 John Eversale
41 William Bingham
42 Laban Adams
43 Aron Wiatt
44 Enoch Chapman
45 Edmond Dorson
46 Thomas Craton
47 James Brown
48 Stephen Roberts
49 Joseph Teague
50 John Carnest

51 Thomas Crumpton
52 Achillis Stipp
63 William Alloway

54 Jeremiah Hendrickson
55 Richard Hawkins

Fourth Company, detached from Wilkes Regiment

1 James Martin, *captain*
2 Moses East, *lieutenant*
3 James Benge, *ensign*
4 Benjamin Rose
5 John Martin
6 Sterling Rose
7 Henry Welborn
8 William Curby
9 William Denny
10 Thomas Ellis
11 Edmund Bryan
12 Isaac Martin
13 John Green
14 William Green
15 Joseph Johnston
16 Abel Nichilson
17 William McBride
18 James McBride
19 Joseph Longbottom
20 Ephraim Nichilson
21 John Sale
22 Hyram Ryan
23 Barney Carter
24 David Caperham
25 John Cockerham
26 Stephen Gentle
27 Richmond Gordon
28 John Shoemaker
29 John Hawkins
30 Isaac Adams
31 Thomas Keelin
32 Henry Trusty
33 John Brooks
34 Gorden Chavers
35 Joseph James
36 James Matthews
37 Eli Brown
38 William Underwood
39 George Combs
40 Benjamin Gamble
41 George Laurence
42 Henry Gamble
43 Benjamin Adams
44 John Adams
45 James Tolby
46 Thomas Roberts
47 Willis Alexander
48 John Brown
49 John Blackburn
50 Aron McDaniel
51 John Chustley
52 Jeremiah Abshire
53 John Abshire
54 William Donally
55 Colin Edwards
56 George Brown

Fifth Company, detached from Ashe Regiment

1 William Horton, *captain*
2 Squire Wilcoxen, *lieutenant*
3 Phillip Baker, *ensign*
4 William Johnston
5 John Kerby
6 William Tolliver
7 Stephen Crow
8 Moses McBride
9 David Maxfield
10 James McMillan
11 James Hatt
12 Jacob Stamper
13 Alexander Cox
14 John Price
15 Elijah Smith
16 William Ellison
17 Edward Hart
18 Thomas Collins
19 Matthias Williams
20 Archibald Blankenship
21 William Baker
22 George Cider
23 Samuel Wilcoxen
24 David Horton
25 Joseph Green
26 Lewis Trackler
27 James Fatam
28 John Bear
39 Henry Holsclaw
30 George Brown
31 Benjamin Chambers, *fifer*

Sixth Company, detached from the First Lincoln Regiment

1 Edward Boyd, *captain*
2 Edwin S Gingles, *lieutenant*
2 John Hill, *ensign*

4 Mason Harwell, *first sergeant*
5 Joshua Abernathy, *second do*
6 David Linebarge, *corporal*

7 John Club, *corporal*
8 Samuel Harwell
9 Gardner Merys
10 Levi Perkins
11 Frederick Abernasty
12 Thomas Long
13 Michel Sides
14 Henry Eddlemon
15 Moses Abernathy
17 Jacob Eddman
18 Joseph Burk
19 Peter Evans
20 George Club, jr.
21 Ezekiel Abernathy
22 James McGinnis
23 Robert Ramsey
24 Martin Gruson
25 Robert McCullock
26 Henry Holland
27 Matthew Holland, jr
28 William Robison, jr.
29 Robert Huggins, jr.
30 James Rhodes
31 David Rine, jr.
32 John Ryne
33 Joseph Senter
34 Frederick Hovis
35 Jacob Dutcherow
36 Jonathan Nardike
37 Nicholas Dillin
38 John Friday
39 Samuel Armstrong

40 Matthew Armstrong
41 John Neagle
42 Alexander Irwin
43 George Oliver
44 William Oliver
45 John Henderson
46 William Hawkins
47 John Linebarger
48 Archibald Cathy
49 Daniel Morrison
50 Alexander Moore
51 Adam Clominger, jr.
52 Jonathan West
53 George Hager
54 William Stephenson
55 Thomas Henry
56 Andrew Forguson
57 William Falls
58 Samuel Carson
59 John Hager
60 Daniel Tucker
61 Robert Beale
62 Levi Sides
63 William Hinkle
64 William Hunt
65 John Blalock
66 John Little
67 George Ferguson, *sergeant*
68 Miles Farrer
69 Sherod Little, *Corporal*
70 John Ganny   *do*

Seventh Company, detached from the First Lincoln Regiment

1 Henry Rudasil, *captain*
2 Robert Oats, *lieutenant*
3 Phillip Hain, *ensign*
4 Moses Herring, *first sergeant*
5 Peter Crites, *second do*
6 Christopher Lewis, *third do*
7 William Fullbright, *fourth do*
8 Abraham Wiatt, *corporal*
9 Linas Sanford, *second do*
10 David Cline, *third do*
11 Samuel Edgin, *fourth do*
12 John Master, *private*
13 John Tucker
14 Jepeth Sham
15 James Clark
16 Henry Barclay
17 Jesse Wheeler
18 John Ballard
19 George Sifford
20 Menucan Shelton
21 George Freet
22 William Sifford
23 Isaac Flemming
24 John Sifford
25 Gatlip Sifford

26 Adam Hoppis
27 Martin Delinger
28 Robert Williams
29 William Lowe
30 Isaiah Abernathy
31 Drury Baggett
32 Abram Bagget
33 Absalom Bungarner
34 George Moore
35 William Walker
36 Nicholas Laurence
37 Thomas Ash
38 Moses Bungarner
39 Colbert Sherrel
40 Isaac Robertson
41 Jacob Burns
42 John Caldwell
43 Frederick Summey
44 Jacob Fingo
45 Elias Plot
46 Henry Chipperd
47 Christopher Hoffman
48 Jacob Isaac
49 Jacob Dunsill
50 Solomon Cline

51 Elijah Call
52 John Wilson
53 Alfred Moore
54 Aron Moore
55 William Johnston
56 Francis Asbury
57 John Kistler
58 James Martin
59 Samuel Turner
60 John Brim

61 Thomas Hannon
62 Edward Sneed
63 William Bennett
64 Jacob Miller
65 Robert Wilson
66 John Crago
67 John Murphy
68 James Lindsay
69 Adam Speight
70 Christy Speight

Eighth Company, detached from the Second Lincoln Regiment

1 George Hoffman, *captain*
2 David Bailey, *Lieutenant*
3 Daniel Cline, *ensign*
4 John Jarratt, *first sergeant*
5 Jacob Conner, *second do*
6 Thomas Bandy, *third do*
7 Robert H Simpson, *fourth do*
8 Phillip Fry, *first corporal*
9 Thomas Sampson, *second do*
10 John Norman, *third do*
11 Christopher Acer, *fourth do*
12 Daniel Shuford, jr
13 Daniel Whitener, jr
14 Adolph Fadz
15 Michel Prolst
16 David Bost
17 John German
18 Andrew Seiter
19 Abram Kilyon
20 Jacob Kink
21 Daniel Peterson
22 Abraham Sieter
23 George Fisher
24 Payton Vaughan
25 Conrad Yoder
26 George Mosteller
27 Silas Wilson
28 Jacob Thorne
29 George McEntosh
30 Thomas Huskey
31 Reuben Copelin
32 William Harlson
33 Peter Harman
34 Ephraim Davis
35 James Patterson
36 Samuel Gladdon

37 Benjamin Waterson
38 William Scoggin
39 Solomon Harmon
40 Abner Camp
41 David Wier
42 Perry G Reynols
43 Uell Reynolds
44 John Rudaice
45 John Turner
46 Cyrus Peed
47 Isaac Williams
48 Benjamin Edwards
49 Jacob Raugh
50 Micheal Hepner
51 John Miller
52 John Taylor
53 William Caldwell
54 William Hull
55 William Bird
56 William Carrol
57 John Trout
58 Peter Howzer
59 Jacob Spengler
60 James Center
61 John Eders
62 Wiley Harris
63 John Harvener
64 Robert Watts
65 Joseph Kyson
66 Thomas Laming
67 Adam Husslatter
68 Feter Beem
69 John Vickers
70 Joseph Carpenter
71 Peter Kiser

Ninth Company, detached from the first Rutherford Regiment

1 John Goodbread, *captain*
2 Robert Baber, *lieutenant*
3 John H Crow, *ensign*
4 Michel Hudlow, *first sergeant*
5 Jesse Milton, *second do*
6 Robert Porter, *third do*
7 Edward Elms, *fourth do*

8 William McCurry, *first corporal*
9 James Griffy, *second do*
10 Littleton Parram, *third do*
11 Charles Chitwood, *fourth do*
12 Samuel Campbell, *private*
13 Joseph Harmon
14 Benjamin M Gakey

15 Leonard Painter
16 Coleby Sutton
17 William Wood
18 Jeremiah Bennik
19 Thomas Davis
20 William Early
21 Richard Fortune
22 William Fortune
23 Abner Green
24 Henry Norbet
25 Archibald Weeks
26 Queen Hicks
27 Daniel Hicks
28 Christy Mooney
29 Samuel Miltoe
30 John Jones
31 William Milton
32 James Sargent
33 James Thompson
34 John Guffy

35 John Walker
36 Julias Logan
37 William Carson
38 James Dalton
39 Joseph Hunter
40 William Watson
41 George Fluman
42 William Freeman
43 William Vickers
44 William Adain
45 Jonathan Hill
46 Edward F Fennington
47 Peter Coon
48 John Ownley
49 William Fluman
50 Thomas Williams
51 Summons Bradley
52 Terry Bradley
53 Isaiah Wadkins
54 Hiram Dunkin

Tenth Company, Detached from the Second Rutherford Regiment

1 Abram Irvine, *captain*
2 John Craw, *lieutenant*
3 John Alexander, *ensign*
4 Isom Weather, *first sergeant*
5 William Harder, *second do*
6 Abner Wessen, *third do*
7 John Williams, *fourth do*
8 James Lemons, *first Corporal*
9 Mark Harder, *second do*
10 James Lefever, *third do*
11 Archibald Moore, *fourth do*
12 Henry Johnston, *private*
13 Jacob Smith
14 John Levan
15 Hillery Scott
16 Larkin Lea
17 Richard Afria
18 David Briars
19 William Lea
20 Richard Carver
21 Charles West
22 James Lea
23 John Allison
24 Jesse Huskey
25 Robert Herren
26 Hiram Hector
27 James Thompson

28 Wekins Nilman
29 James Braley
30 Isaac Brooks
31 Samuel Scoggin
32 John Gregory
33 Joseph Smart
34 Elijah Surrasy
35 Levi Burn
36 Robert Haney
37 John Gibbs
38 James Roach
39 Aron Bridges
40 James Hamsick
41 John Lea
42 Lewis Blanton
43 Samuel Humphries
44 Byard McCraw
45 Samuel Hamsick
46 George Blanton
47 Richard Bridges
48 Charles Durham
49 James Hall, *fifer*
50 Morris Quinn, *drummer*
51 John Blanton
52 Francis Young
53 Charles Scoggin

Eleventh Company, detached from the third Rutherford Regiment.

1 Major R Alexander, *captain*
2 Christholm Daniel, *lieutenant*
3 Robert Marlan, *ensign*
4 Joseph Holbert, *sergeant*
5 John Price, *second do*
6 Ezekiel Waldrop, *third do*

7 Aasa Hill, *fourth do*
8 Squire Cockeran, *first corporal*
9 William Redman, *second do*
10 Thomas Cook, *third do*
11 Jonathan Aldridge, *fourth do*
12 James Cockeran, *private*

13 Joseph Robins
14 Thomas Robins
15 Jacob Cantrel
16 John Martin
17 George King
18 William Owens
19 Robert Suttle
20 William McKennoy
21 John Rivis
22 John Davis
23 James Wrier
24 William Walker
25 Henry Cockeran
26 John Porter
27 James M Erwin
28 Thomas Prater
29 John Furlly
30 John Anderson
31 Chisolm Daniel
32 James Early

33 James Hood
34 John Owens
35 John Spencer
36 John Grizzle
37 Luke Wilson
38 John Blackwell
39 Raleigh Owens
40 James Jackson
41 Jeremiah Martin
42 Patrick Scott
43 Lemuel Milican
44 Charles Wilson
45 Solomon Blackwell
46 David Dellbuck
47 Daniel Foster
48 George Logan
49 Mathew Garrett
50 John Forster
51 John Hannon
52 Robert Thompson

Twelfth Company, detached from the Second Rutherford Regiment

1 John C Elliott, *captain*
2
3 Samuel Bridges, *ensign*
4 William Porter, *first sergeant*
5 James Hunter, *second do*
6 James Purrucks, *third do*
7 John Dyer, *fourth do*
8 Joshua Hawkins, *corporal*
9 John Proctor, *second do*
10 William Daggett, *third do*
11 Jacob Gage, *fourth do*
12 William Wilson, *private*
13 John Waters
14 Jesse Chitwood
15 John Washburn
16 Henry Lawson
17 Samuel Gates
18 James Parks
19 Lewis Levity
20 Cazor McCurry
21 Jacob McCurry
22 Nicholas Nancy
23 Samuel Kirkland
24 Robert Rickets
25 Leroy Curruth
26 William Holeyfield

27 John McDonald
28 Joseph Nichols
29 Arthur Owenby
30 James Anthony
31 William Anthony
32 Asa Lovelace
33 Marsy D Holland
34 James G Beatty
35 Samuel Downy
36 Samuel M Bryer
37 Charles Y Daggett
38 Jonathan Harder
39 Thomas Downy
40 Jesse Hill
41 John McFarland
42 Robert Lirk
43 Samuel Garland
44 Henry Workman
45 John Jarrels
46 John Hoyle
47 Thomas McReely
48 Thomas Reader
49 William Downs
50 Joseph Willis
51 James Newton
52 Abner Wilson

Thirteenth Company, detached from the second and Part of the first Burke Regiment.

1 Cinton Harthy, *captain*
2 Benjamin Parks, *lieutenant*
3 Mathew Cox, *ensign*
4 Isaac Harris, *private*
5 John Waggoner
6 John Hilemon

7 Joseph Hilton
8 William Fincannon
9 Peter Constable
10 Jacob Rample
11 Alexander Moore
12 Thomas Foster

13 Elisha White
14 Micajah Paine
15 Leonard Keller
16 Balum Ducary
17 Abner Presnal
18 Lewis Alman
19 Reuben Henson
20 Reuben White
21 Thomas White
22 John Wakefield
23 Moses Jackson
24 James Jackson
25 Reuben Webb
26 John Gibson
27 Abner Staples
28 John Staples
29 William Farmer
30 Samuel Gibson
31 Thomas Green
32 Joseph Green
33 Thomas Simes
34 Samuel Amburn
35 William Amburn

36 John Emmett
37 Jacob Hise
38 James Hust
39 John Phillips
40 James Penland
41 Reuben Parks
42 Ellis Marquis
43 James Branch
44 John Gibson
45 Frederick Huffman
46 Daniel Watman
47 Daniel McFalls
48 Abram Huffman
49 Leonard Higdon
50 William Poteet
51 William Neill
52 George Duckworth
53 Jonathan Duckworth
54 Thomas Colby
55 Ephraim Evans
56 John Deal
57 Jacob Hips

Fourteenth Company, deached from the Third and part of the First Burke Regiment.

1 Kenneth McKinsey, *captain*
2 Jesse Brevard, *first lieutenant*
3 William Mifee, *ensign*
4 John Perkins
5 Jeremiah Boon
6 William Kinkaid
7 John Boon
8 Enoch England
9 John Kinkard
10 Athan McDowell
11 James Davies
12 Joseph Little
13 Joseph Hood
14 John McClure
15 John Gribble
16 Thomas Monteath
17 Thomas Robertson
18 Alexander Harris
19 William Standford
20 Alexander Glass
21 John McDowell
22 William Hicky
23 James Warlow
24 Benjamin Wise
25 David Stroud
26 Richard Bell

27 Thomas Cripson
28 Peter Strond, jr
29 Peter Epley
30 Freeman Tomberlin
31 Thomas Glass
32 William Sanders
33 John Oaks
34 Daniel Stillwell
35 Robert Childers
36 Tillman Stillwell
37 John Lowry
38 Barnard Oaks
39 Solomon Ellis
40 George Triplett
41 Joshua Jones
42 William Triplett
43 Solomon Wright
44 Charles Medlock
45 William Hill
46 Charles Baley
47 William Riddisk
48 William Rickets
49 James Hunhill
50 Benjamin Allison
51 Lemuel Paget
52 Benjamin McDowell

Fifteenth Company, detached from the First and Second Buncombe Regiments.

1 Thomas Rhodes, *captain*
2 Eli Merrell, *lieutenant*
3 Thomas Moore, *ensign*

4 James Kincade
5 Francis Byers
6 John Gargely

7 William Wilson
8 Benjamin Wilson
9 Samuel J Murry
10 Thomas Justice
11 Cornelius Caps
12 Nathan Fletcher
13 Edward Shipman
14 Nimrod Merrell
15 John Caneade
16 William Murry
17 William Janes
18 Henry Cary
19 Andrew Garron
20 Joshua Owens
21 Lewis Ward
22 John Drake
23 John Love
24 James Case
25 Reuben Step
26 James Abel
27 Sion Cook
28 George Story
29 Robert Byers
30 John Story
31 James Hickson
32 Jonathan Cinard
33 Mathew Patterson
34 David Johnston
35 Easly Dasson
36 Thomas Kelley
37 James Kitchen
38 John Robertson

39 Samuel Scott
40 Benjamin Rickets
41 George D Davis
42 Joel McKey
43 Daniel Davin
44 John Rutherford
45 Albert Arcory
46 William Spivey
47 Sim Cannon
48 Charles Hayes
49 John Weaver, jr
50 John Plemmons
51 John Frisby
52 Joseph Black
53 John Plemmons, jr
54 John Plemmons
55 Andrew Plemmons
56 Stephen Rogers
57 Joseph Gudger
58 Nathaniel Person
59 Elsey Reynolds
60 Mitchell Alexander
61 James Irwin
62 Jonas Burns
63 John Palmer
64 John Harriss
65 Jesse Selah
66 Jacob Dunket
67 William Brown
68 William Carpenter
69 Peter Mason
70 Pendleton Underwood

Sixteenth Company, detached from the Haywood Regiment

1 Joseph Hughey, *captain*
2 Robert Love, jr, *lieutenant*
3 John Anglin, *ensign*
4 Samuel Brittain
5 James Avery
6 David Vance, jr
7 John Killian
8 Daniel Killian
9 Azra Roberts
10 John Dowell
11 William L Dalton
12 John M Patton
13 George C Alexander
14 Lylas Ray
15 James Rine
16 James Welch
17 William Welch
18 Dell'd Love
19 Charles Toler
20 Marsh Coleman, jr
21 Henry Anderson
22 Eli N Henry
23 Uriah Burns

24 Hezekiah Burns
25 J Smith Armstrong
26 John Bryson, jr
27 Joseph Morrow
28 William Goodin
29 Martin Helpley
30 Philly Hyley
31 Garret Gordon
32 Thomas Hall
33 Benjamin West
34 Benjamin McMullen
35 Benjamin Clark
36 Josiah Crawford
37 Enos McHenry
38 John McHenry
39 Prico Adams
40 William Davied
41 David Rogers
42 George Reed
43 William Murry
44 David Elders
45 Henry Wild
46 James Carson

47 Daniel Giles
48 John J Wild
49 John Anderson, jr
50 James Greenlee, jr
51 George Stanton
52 John Griffith
53 Charles Hensley
54 Ephraim Piercy
55 John Baker
56 James Edwards
57 Robert Patterson
58 John Edwards
59 Joseph Shepherd
60 Jesse Radford

61 Niram Allen
62 James Wood
63 James Redman
64 James Runnion
65 Henry Keith
66 Coleman Murry
67 John Wild
68 John Sams
69 Philip Wilson
70 John Rice
71 Isaac Rice
72 Barney Landers
73 James Thomas

MUSTER ROLL OF THE CAVALRY

Detached from the Militia of North Carolina, in pursuance of a Requisition from the President of the United States, by virtue of an act of Congress Passed 10th April, 1812.

REGIMENT

Edmund Jones, Lieutenant Colonel Commandant
Isham Edwards, First Major
Henry Taylor, Second Major

First Company, detached from the Fifth Brigade

1 William G Jones, *captain*
2 William R Bennet, *first lieut*
3 Marma D Jeffery, *second do*
4 Frederick Jones, *cornet*
5 Archibald Yarborough
6 Robert Hill
7 Samuel Thomas
8 William Jenkins
9 Robert Gill
10 Parker Murphrey
11 John Kelley
12 Joshua Johnston
13 James Cheaves
14 Richard Hall
15 Robert Gupton
16 Benjamin Hertee
17 Charles Hayes
18 Thomas E Hill
19 Richardson Finch
20 John F Foster
21 Mathew Strulland
22 Benjamin Carpenter
23 Willie Williams
24 Robert C Hall
25 Etheldred Pippin

26 David Bowers
27 Abner Cheaves
28 Cafferld Harris
29 Laban Webb
30 Isaac House
31 William Lancaster, jr
32 William H Strother
33 Allen Minnis
34 William D Freeman
35 Jesse Pearce
36 Joseph Ballard
37 Jason Purvin
38 John Skiles
39 Arden Andrews
40 John Barnhill
41 William Cockburn
42 Henry Wyne
43 Collen Robeson
44 Darling Cherry
45 James Barner
46 Benjamin Edmonds
47 William M West
48 Iravin Jones
49 Abner Read
50 John B Massey

51 Frederick Campbell
52 Robert B Daniel
53 William Eskins
54 Pendleton B Isbell
55 Jared Weaver

56 Hardy Newell
57 Thomas Newell
58 Absalom Brown
59 Jesse Newell
60 William F Irrard

Second Company, detached from the Sixteenth Brigade

1 Thomas Cooke, *captain*
2 Leonard Cardwell, *first lieut*
3 Joseph Bowell, *second do*
4 Silas High, *cornet*
5 William Mallery, *first sergeant*
6 John Cheaves, *second do*
7 Hiram Taylor, *third do*
8 Robert Paine, *fourth do*
9 John O'Brien, *first corporal*
10 Thomas Atkins, *second do*
11 Groves Howard, *third do*
12 James Jeffers, *fourth   "*
13 Nelson Thomason, *trumpeter*
14 Isaac Hirter, *dragoon*
15 Benjamin Thomason
16 Pleasant Pearce
17 George Stroud
18 William Griffin
19 Burford Twitty
20 Jethro Lowry

21 William Williams
22 John Reaves
23 Willis Newman
24 Mathias Williams
25 Daniel S Barringer
26 Anderson Hunter
27 Green Alfred
28 Robert H Jackson
29 John Baxter
30 Thomas Matthis
31 William Brown
32 Hugh Cobb
33 Alexander Grav
34 Thomas Libscomb
35 Samuel Mitchel
36 Thomas Walton
37 Samuel Day
38 Benjamin Speed
39 John Daniel
40 Charles Parrot

Third Company, detached from the Sixth Brigade

1 John Mebane, *captain*
2 James Forest, *lieutenant*
3 Hardy Ward, *second do*
4 Younger McLastro, *first sergt.*
5 Daniel Fossee, *second do*
6 Asin Moore, *dragoon*
7 David Craig
8 Absalom Bulbee
9 Charles Jones
10 Jonathan Jones
11 William McMillion
12 Elam Hinton
13 Noah Rhodes
14 Samuel McBroom
15 Joseph B Shaw
16 Elias Forte
17 Thomas Hargis
18 Alexander Mebane
19 William Thompson

20 David Patterson
21 Samuel Nelson
22 John Rogers
23 Jacob Thomas
24 William York
25 Peter Croom
26 William Elliott
27 Tobias Moser
28 Anarser Riddle
29 John Spivey
30 Anderson Williavy
31 John W Dismaks
32 James Bell
33 William Brinkley
34 John Norwood
35 Ferrington Burnett
36 Patrick Pool
37 John Smith
38 Henry Whishenhunt

Fourth Company, detached from the Eighth Brigade

1 William Doak, *captain*
2 Sampson Smith, *first lieutenant*
3 John Stewart, *second do*
4 John Wharton, *cornet*
5 Robert Woodburn, *first sergeant*
6 Leaven Ross, *second do*

7 Francis Bell, *third do*
8 David Wiley, *fourth do*
9 Mark Gannon, *first corporal*
10 Sample Garrigan, *second do*
11 William Brown, *third do*
12 Josiah Wiley, *fourth do*

13 Peter Monet, *dragoon*
14 James Gillaspie
15 Abdi Gillaspie
16 Ralph Forbis
17 Alexander Hanner
18 Robert Gillaspie
19 Abner Hannah
29 Eli Hannah
21 John Morrow
22 Evan Wharton
23 William Akin
24 Findlay Shaw
25 Thomas Gilbreath
26 Wenright Burns
27 John Gillaspie
28 Benjamin Alexander
29 James Alexander
30 John Harden

31 Thomas W Clands
32 Levi Huston
33 John Hannah
34 James Hendrick
35 George Sullivan
36 William Gannon
37 James Gilbreath
38 Charles Harden
39 William Dyer
40 John Alcorn
41 William Gilbreath
42 Isaac Wetherly
43 Isaiah Wetherly
44 James Russand
45 Christopher Field
46 Thomas McCullock
47 Mathew Young
48 Robert Johnston

Fifth Company, detached from Seventh Brigade

1 Robert Lock, *captain*
2 John Smith, *first lieutenant*
3 Francis Penny, *second do*
4 John McCullock, *cornet*
5 John Brandon
6 Joshua Gay
7 John Pool, *saddler*
8 Thomas Smith
9 George T Smith
10 George Lock
11 John Locke
12 Francis Locke
13 John Brandonn, *fourth creek*
14 David Stewart
15 Henry Verval
16 Christian Farr
17 Harman Fisher
18 Andrew Cook
19 Henry Allimony
20 Jacob Cauble
21 Elias Caruthers
22 William Henby
23 Gassaway Gaither
24 Scarlet Glasscock
25 Jacob Kinkle
26 Joseph Howard
27 John Bailey
28 Peter Rupard

29 John Jones
30 Daniel Bore
31 John Hughs
32 Richmond Hughs
33 Jonathan Hunt
34 Phillip Craven
35 Elijah Daniel
36 Levi Reed
37 Jonathan Hoge
38 John Bodenhammer
39 Killion Phelps
40 James Flemming
41 John Davidson
42 John Falls
43 John Kin
44 Ross Nesbet
45 Anguish McKinzie
46 James Hughs
47 John Crawford
48 Howell Alby
49 Ross M Clenning
50 Edward Mills
51 Thomas Bell
52 William Erwin
53 Robert Johnston
54 Thomas Sloan
55 John Bell
56 Tarlton Shoemaker

Sixth Company, detached from Eleventh Brigade

1
2
3
4
5 Hugh H McCane
6 Joseph Robeson
7 John Robison

8 Solomon Gibbans
9 John Shillington
10 James Martin
11 Henry Coruner
12 John D O K Pettes
13 Alexander Ross
14 William Duncan

15 William Allison
16 John Knox
17 Jacob Barringer
18 George Chits
19 William Verner
20 Zeblone Ford
21 Robert Kirkpatrick
22 Jeremiah Hood
23 John Ford
24 Joseph Johnston
25 Nathan Orr
26 James Plummer
27 Isaac Price

28 B. W. Darrison
29 Thomas Duckworth
30 Samuel Portor
31 Mathew Houston
32 Griffith Graham
33 Thomas Blewet
34 John Pemberton
35 Thomas Pemberton
36 Anguish Campbell
37 William Burton
38 John Asher
39 Edmond Almond
40 Barrum Kirk

Seventh Company, detached from Tenth Brigade

1 Henry Ramsour, *captain*
2 William Green, *first lieutenant*
3 Jacob Summers, *second do*
4 John Zimmerman, *cornet*
5 John Falls, *first sergeant*
6 John Slagle, *second do.*
7 Henry Smith, *third do*
8 Moses Sides, *fourth do*
9 George Fry, *sadler*
10 Ezekiel Hazelett, *trumpeter*
11 Elias Bost, *dragoon*
12 William Bost
13 Jacob Smoyer
14 Hiram Harbeson
15 Alexander Nail
16 Henry Smith
17 Charles Reinhart
18 Edward Sanders
19 Mathew Haynes
20 Absalom Taylor
21 Allen Wetherly

22 William Price
23 John Henry
24 Moses Heron
25 John Rhine, jr
26 Edward Scarboro
27 David Ramsour
28 James Grist
29 Richard Maze
30 James Knox
31 Samuel McMin
32 John Wilkinson
33 Alexander McCorcle
34 John Cornelius
35 Hardy Abernathy
36 William Porter
37 Frederick Kimmy
38 Benjamin Suttle
39 William Hannon
40 Jeremiah Runyan
41 Timothy Hanny
42 Isaac Vanzant

Eighth Company, detached from Ninth Brigade

1 William P Waugh, *captain*
2 John Jones, *first lieutenant*
3 John W Gorden, *second do*
4 Samuel Parks, *cornet*
5 Nathaniel Gorden
6 Alexander Nesbitt
7 Hugh Jones
8 Wiley G Gorden
9 John Reynolds
10 Mechat McDowell
11 Jesse Minton
12 Andrew Shepherd
13 Payten Gwynn
14 Thomas A Gorden
15 David Waugh
16 Braxton McLiven
17 Ralph McGee
18 James Huket

19 John Finley
20 John Johnston
21 Lancaster Cunningham
22 Willim F Camble
23 Little Hickason
24 William Laws
25 Abner Tribble
26 Joel Vancy
27 Joel Chandler
28 Samuel Wellbourn
29 John Hickeson
30 John Pumphrey
31 James M Parks
32 Charles Adams
33 Henry Brown
34 William Hudson
35 Blewford McGee

Ninth Company, detached from Fifteenth Brigade

1 Ezebulon Baird, *captain*
2 John Weaver, *first lieutenant*
3 Mathew Baird, *second do*
4 William Alexander, *cornet*
5 Samuel Semple
6 Samuel Hunter
7 George Patton
8 William Gillaspie
9 David Gillaspie
10 William Greenlee
11 John Young
12 Charles Carrell
13 Nathaniel Culberson
14 William Sedford
15 Alexander Perkins
16 Charles McDowell
17 Obadiah H Erwin
18 Thomas Flemming
19 John Harbison
20 John Kinkaid
21 Roberd Cobb, *sergeant*
22 Elisha Baird
23 Joshua Conely
24 Moses Cobb
25 Elisha Dockry
26 Henry McCall
27 John Paxton

MUSTER ROLL OF THE ARTILLERY

Detached from the Militia of North Carolina, in pursuance of a Requisition of the President of the United States, by virtue of an Act passed in Congress, 10th April, 1812.

First Company, detached from Wake Regiment

1 Elhannon Nutt, *captain*
2 Benjamin Rogers, *first lieutenant*
3 Willis Whitaker, *ensign*
4 Nathaniel Whitaker, *first sergt*
5 Samuel Rogers, *second do*
6 Osborn Lockhart, *third do*
7 James Nance, jr *fourth do*
8 Robert Nutt, *first corporal*
9 Mark Moore, *second do*
10 Jesse Roads, *third do*
11 Freeman Broadwell, *fourth do*
12 John A Smith, *drummer*
13 Turner McInvail, *fifer*
14 Wilie Nichols
15 Alsey Rockett
16 Jones Fowler
17 Durham Hall
18 William Rigsby
19 Robert Hall
20 Wiley Freeman
21 Brittain Boykin
22 David Jones
23 Oram Muller
24 Jacob Williams
25 John Ames, jr
26 Alfred Acock
27 Hardy Dean, jr
28 Oram Tamon
29 Miles Allen
30 Edward Moore
31 Alsey Nichols
32 Reason Rabourn
33 Kade Alfred
34 Micajah Stricklin
35 Cader Bunn
36 Israel Privett
37 James Chamblee
38 Elijah Todd
39 Jeptha Massey
40 Micajah Jordan
41 William Griffin
42 Littleton Ivey
43 Solomon Hartsfield
44 Samuel Thompson
45 Charles Sandiford
46 Miles Scarbrough
47 James Bell
48 James Peace
49 Bailey Alfred
50 Gilbert Alfred
51 Kinchen Medlin
52 James Lewis, jr
53 Joshua Beasley
54 Daniel Beasley
55 Jacob Utley
56 Lemuel Jones
57 Robert Edwards
58 Michel Duskins, jr

59 Howard Pool
60 John Hutchins jr
61 Gillis Brown
62 John Hull
63 Taban Armstead
93 Arthur Reaves
65 Peter Amget
66 William Holand
67 Noel Norris
68 Isma Killum
69 Anthony Pilkinton
70 Miller Sexton
71 Giles J Bledsoe
72 Darling Jones
73 John Band
74 John Watson
75 Wiley Wemack
76 Tyrel Parish
77 Alvin Utley

78 Whitmill Hunter
97 Frederick Spain
80 Jesse Powell
81 Isham Holding
82 Jesse Turner
83 Robertson Ward
84 George Kith
85 Donas Yeargan
86 Aaron Shiner
87 David Geer
88 Richard Ferguson
89 Richard White
90 James Hicks
91 Elija Kimbrough
92 David Read
93 Harbut Hobby
94 Williams Ladd
95 John Holloway, jr
96 Thomas Parham

Second Company, Detached from Edgecombe Regiment

1 John Thomas, *captain*
2 Lat. Vins., *first lieutenant*
3 Thomas Amosin *second do*
4 John Bridges, *ensign*
5 Theophilus Thomas, *first sergt*
6 Benjamin Sharp, *second do*
7 William O Carter, *third do*
8 William Williams, *fourth do*
9 Henry C Knight, *first corporal*
10 James Pender, *second do*
11 Ithiel Eason, *third do*
12 William White, *fourth do*
13 James Cobb, *drummer*
14 May Moore, *fifer*
15 John Barrow
16 Jesse C Knight
17 Levi Long
18 Robert Long
19 John Stallings
20 Elijah Williams
21 Henry Walter
22 James Permerter
23 Elisha Fellon
24 Benjamin Varnel
25 John Taylor
26 Reddin Thigpen
27 William Gay
28 Thomas Moore
29 Dempsey Hicks
30 Abram Coles
31 David Wollard
32 Martin D Liles
33 Hausford Burress
34 Hardy Simpson
35 James Moore
36 Ephraim Wooten
37 John Peele

38 Lemuel Lancaster
39 William Williams, sen
40 Edward Sherod
41 Daniel Land
42 John Thomas
43 Thomas Williams
44 David Thomas
45 Jethro Weaver
46 Stephen Bullock
47 John Brantly
48 Accles Barnes
49 Dixon Summuns
50 Isaac Daniel
51 James Daniel
52 John Johnston
53 William Johnston
54 Asahel Bateman
55 Ashael Farmer
56 John Farmer
57 Reddick Barnes
58 John Barnes
59 Haman Mann
60 Enos Barnes
61 Jesse Parker
62 John B Cobb
63 Barnvill Moore
64 Bryant Schoots
65 Jesse Hedgepeth
66 Silas Mitchel
67 Thomas Whitly
68 Rickmon Cobb
69 Benjamin Sumerlin
70 Isaac Hobbs
71 Timothy Harris
72 Enoch Robertson
73 Moses Moore

Third Company, detached from Bertie Regiment

1 Joseph H Bryan, *captain*
2 Augustin Pugh, *lieutenant*
3 Lodswick Pruden, *ensign*
4 William McGruder
5 Isaac Wilson
6 Hardy Hunter
7 Anthony Wiggins
8 Benjamin Brogdon
9 Washington Turner
10 John A Cordle
11 Rheuben Wilkes
12 David Harrell
13 Fred Wimberly
14 John Wilkes
15 Henry Wilkes
16 Jesse Powell
17 John Ruffin
18 Thomas Bickell
19 Turner McGlawhon
20 Edward Turner
21 Elijah C Bryan
22 John B Everitt
23 John Minor
24 John Stewart, jr
25 Richard L Bowers
26 John Brickell
27 Linus Leonard
28 Shade Britt
29 John Brantly
30 William Brickell
31 Cader Bunch
32 Samuel Hobbs
33 Edward B Baker
34 John Allen
35 Edward Gill
36 Edmond Fleetwood, jr
37 Frederick Miller
38 Reuben Lawrence
39 Wil Wilkins
40 Asa Radett
41 Levi Todd
42 Joshua P Brantly
43 James Boswell
44 Asa Gregory
45 John Ramsey
46 Josiah Miller
47 John Rhodes
48 Haller Calway
49 Richard Bagwell
50 William H Greem
51 Nathaniel Culeper
52 Benjamin Winburn
53 James Simonds
54 Benjamin James
55 Thomas Corbett
56 William Gardner
57 David Garrett
58 Ryan Jonagon
59 Abner Aaron, jr
60 Samuel Martin
61 Elisha Pritchard
62 Cader Mitchel
63 Jacob Pruden
64 Levi Outlaw
65 David Fleetwood
66 Neal Nicholas
67 James Carley
68 Thomas Hogard
69 Lawrence Cook
70 William Roll
71 Jesse Garrett
72 George Wilson
73 Cader Hunter
74 Dred Evans
75 Silas Wilson
76 Thomas Sorrell
77 William Brogdon
78 William Hunter
79 Stephen Hymon
80 James Ryman
81 John West
82 Hardy Clements
83 Benjamin Rogers
84 William Robertson
85 Malacha Green
86 Isaac Wiggins
87 William Higgs
88 James Wilkes
89 Augt. Callum
90 West Tines
91 David Folk
92 Redden Rutland
93 George Core
94 Johnston Rutland
95 Simeon Harrell
96 Joseph Harrell
97 W M Bishop
98 David Outlaw
99 John Waltan
100 Nathl Wattoman
101 William Holloman
102 John Holly
103 Moses Freeman
104 George Ward
105 Cader White
106 Hardy White
107 Miles Rollins
108 William Evans

I

Fourth Company, detached from Carteret Regiment

1 Jacob Henry, *captain*
2 William Jasper, *first lieutenant*
3 Samuel Leffers, *second do*
4 David Wallace, *ensign*
5 Thomas Howland
6 John Rigs
7 Elijah Canaday
8 John Linch
9 Joseph Fulford, jr
10 Anthony Davis
11 George Gibble
12 Timothy Small
13 James Johnston
14 John Simmons
15 Zacheus Green
16 Archibald Greenn
17 Abram Wilder
18 John Sanders
19 Elias Meadors
20 Nevil Russell
21 Elijah Gardner
22 Thomas Willis
23 John Bell
24 Benjamin Willis
25 Loftin Quin
26 Francis Gardner
27 William Lewis
28 Joseph Salter
29 Walace Salter
30 Cason Willis
31 Jacob Smith
32 James Dixon
33 William Gaskill
34 David Ireland
35 George Golding
36 John Lewis
37 Caleb Wade
38 Eliza Wade
39 John Wharton
40 Clifton Fulford
41 Benjamin Guthrie
42 George Price
43 Beliher Hakee
44 Elijah Guthrie
45 Zachariah Willis

Fifth Company, detached from Brunswick Regiment

3 John Sullivan, *second lieutenant*
4 David Tolson
5 Richard Harris
6 Burnel Cason
7 John Cherr
8 William Pound
9 Joel Robins
10 Allegood Suggs
11 Eldred Tellers
12 William Key
13 William Hankens
14 Randal Hewet
15 John Clemons
16 Levi Swain
17 Abram Wilder
18 William Bennett
19 Josiah Little
20 Coleman Runnels
21 Benjamin Sellers
22 Samuel Harris
23 Arthur Pinner
24 Josiah Cox
25 Alexander Campbell
26 Moses King
27 James Ellis
28 Niram Skipper
29 Jonathan Rothwell
30 Joseph Walters
31 Thomas Vines
32 Jonathan Keater
33 Benjamin Purrell
34 John Spencer
35 Daniel Bennett
36 William Gilbert

MUSTER ROLL OF THE RIFLEMEN,

Detached from the Militia of North Carolina, in pursuance of a Requisition of the President of the United States, by virtue of an Act of Congress, passed 10th April, 1812.

First Company, detached from Cumberland Regiment

1 William Loyd, *captain*
2 Robert Carver, *first lieutenant*
3 George Kenedy, *second do*
4 Richard Watson, *ensign*
5 James Holmes, *first sergeant*
6 John Rhea, *second do*
7 Jesse Townsend, *third do*
8 John Dixon, jr

9 Isaac Howard
10 Menas Howard
11 Allen Brown
12 Egbird Hall
13 Isham Carver
14 William Gyton
15 Elijah Ward
16 John Campbell
17 Isaiah Toler
18 Samuel Taylor
19 Daniel Pharis
20 Josiah Culberson
21 Frederick Brewer
22 Aron Smith
23 James C Myrick
24 Jesse Ritter
25 Julius Brewer
26 John Corkman
27 Mitchel Rowland
28 John Milton
29 Gideon Moore
30 Louis Williamson
31 Louis Russell
32 Thomas D King
33 Hardy Chesnut

34 Willie Dodd
35 Jesse Oats, *fourth sergeant*
36 Richard Clinton
37 Joshua Chesnut
38 William Blackman
39 Nathan King
40 Louis F Peck
41 Daniel Cogdell
42 John Turner jr.
43 Travers Beddoe
44 Archibald McMillan
45 Stephon Hester
46 David Thomas
47 John Robertson
48 James Jackson
49 Cornelius Kellyham
50 Arthur Hardy
51 David M Kemp
52 William Lewis
53 Warren Baldwin
54 John Bright
55 William Huff
56 Jonathan Cribb
57 John Graham
58 Thomas Carteret

Second Company, detached from Fourteenth Brigade

1 Nell Buie, *captain*
2 William Leod
3 James McFarland
4 Malcom Gills
5 Neil Curry
6 Alexander McKay
7 Alexander McDonald
8 Malcom Yates
9 Malcom Curry
10 John Rainwater
11 Elisha Gibson
12 John Gillis
13 Hugh Gillis
14 Dugald McDuffy
15 Moses Parker
16 John Little
17 John McDuffy
18 John Turrege
19 Stephen Dees
20 Levy Dees

21 Daniel McEathan
22 William McNeil
23 Duncan Mathews
24 Alex McNabb
25 Daniel Calbroth
26 Dugald Stewart
27 Hugh Curry
28 Hector Bethune
29 Archibald Curry
30 Neil McNeil
31 Archibald McNeil
32 Duncan McGregar
33 Daniel Smith
34 Peter Livington
35 John Sinclair
36 John Wilkinson
37 Peter McArthur
38 Duncan McMillan
39 James Watson
40 Neil Ferguson

Third Company, Detached from the Ninth Brigade

1 Gideon Lewis, *captain*
2 Elijah Wilcoxen
3 Jonathan Taylor
4 Matthias Langly
5 Fulty Miller
6 Isaiah Miller
7 Elias Robeson
8 Theophilus Baldwin

9 David Bogan
10 Larkin Bunyard
11 Fulty Miller
12 John Ray
13 James Kethhorn
14 Richard Allen, jr *first lieutenant*
15 Jacob Pilear
16 John Foss

17 John Sparks, jr
18 Francis Kurby
19 Jacob Hoots
20 Solomon Sparks
21 Isaac Stover
22 Jeremiah Johnston
23 John N Green
24 John Chapman
25 James Robinet
26 James Franklin, *second lieut*
27 John Shipp, *ensign*

28 William Oglesby, *cadet*
29 Bartlet Hanmock
30 John Snow
31 Miley Cave
32 Thomas Cox
33 Thomas Oglesby
34 William Potter
35 Ephraim Witcher
36 Levi Snow
37 William Hammonds
38 Bernard Franklin

Fourth Company, detached from the Seventh Brigade

1 Francis Young, *captain*
2 Samuel Young
3 William McOnnel
4 Richard Harris
5 Solomon Ellis
6 William Tomlinson
7 John Young
8 John Dobson
9 John Green
10 William Murdy
11 Fans Sharp
12 Solomon Jacobs
13 Robert Callahan
14 Thomas Francis
15 John Veark
16 James Beil
17 Enos Campbell
18 Erasmus Lazenby
19 Ezekiel Pearce
20 George Summers
21 Daniel Brown, *lieutenant*
22 Daniel Starns
23 Benjamin Agender
24 Jacob Trees
25 Henry Eller
26 David Butner
27 John Rainy
28 Joseph Graham

29 David Masters
30 Henry Berger
31 Isaac Cummins
32 Peter Mourey
33 Jacob L Peterson
34 Peter Agender
35 John Hartman
36 John Bose
37 Edward Burgess
38 William Glasscock
39 Jacob Booe
40 Jacob Helfer
41 Daniel Booe
42 Joshua Brinigan
43 Phillip Baker
44 Georges Graves
45 Jacob Call
46 Zedediah Jarvis
47 Jacob Hoover
48 David Larkabee
49 George Bodenhammer
50 Thomas Newcomb
51 George Miller
52 John Michel
53 John Long, jr
54 Andrew Yoakley
55 Jacob Sink

Fifth Company; detached from the second Rutherford Regiment, Tenth Brigade.

1 John C Elliott, *captain*
2 William Porter, *first sergeant*
3 Samuel Bridges, *ensign*
4
5 James Hunter, *second sergeant*
6 James Parrish, *third do*
7 John Dyer, *fourth do*
8 Joshua Hawkins, *first corporal*
9 John Proctor, *second do*
10 William Daggett, *th'd do*
11 Jacob Gage, *fourth do*
12 William Wilson
13 John Waters

14 Jesse Chitwood
15 John Washburn
16 Henry Lanon
17 Samuel Gates
18 James Parks
19 Lewis Levity
20 Cazor W Curry
21 Jacob McCurry
22 Nicholas Nancy
23 Samuel Kirkland
24 Robert Rickets
25 Leroy Curretch
26 William Holyfield

27 John McDonald
28 Joseph Nichols
29 Arthur Owerly
30 James Anthony
31 William Anthony
32 Asa Labeless
33 Marcus D Holland
34 James G Beaty
35 Samuel Downy
36 Samuel McBroyer
37 Charles Y Dogget
38 Jonathan Harder
39 Thomas Downy

40 Jesse Hill
41 John McFarland
42 Robert Link
43 Samuel Garland
44 Henry Workman
45 John Jarrels
46 John Hoyle
47 Thomas McReely
48 Thomas Reader
49 William Downs
50 Joseph Willis
51 James Newton
52 Abner Wilson

Sixth Company detached from the Eleventh Brigade.

1 David Long
2 Robert Farr
3 Samuel McCurdy
4 Eli Newell
5 Peter J Bane
6 George Sifford
7 Jacob Cruise
8 Francis Newel
9 John W Davis
10 Jacob Stough
11 William Gray
12 Charles Juhu
13 Francis McClosky
14 Henry Fisher
15 Isaac Helms
16 Aley McCorkle
17 Robert Givens
18 Andrew Walker
19 William Campbell
20 John Campbell
21 Henry Lewis
22 John Price
23 James Todd
24 James Thompson
25 Robert Robinson

26 Milton Harris
27 Cyrus Harris
28 Solomon Ballard
29 Charles Cupples
30 Thomas Frasure
31 James Haywood
32 Will Johnston
33 James Lesbury
34 Benjamin Williams
35 John Layton
36 Laban Carter
37 Zachariah Walker
38 John Hasley
39 Henry Goodman
40 John Reddell
41 Isom Williams
42 Adam Shular
43 John Ball
44 Jesse Gallimore
45 Robert C Davis
46 David Davenport
47 John Milsaps
48 John Loftin
49 Solomon Heath
50 Jacob Myers

MUSTER ROLL
OF THE DETACHED MILITIA, ORGAN-IZED IN AUGUST, 1814

General Officers designated to command in this Detachment of Militia: MONTFORT STOKES, Major General,

JEREMIAH SLADE,
JESSE A PEARSON, } Brigadier Generals.

THE FIRST REGIMENT to be composed of the counties of Chowan, Currituck, Camden, Pasquotank, Perquimans, Gates, Hertford, Bertie, Northampton, Halifax, Warren, and Nash.

OFFICERS.—Duncan McDonald, Lieutenant Colonel commandant; Andrew Joyner, Lieutenant Colonel; Joseph F Dickerson, First Major, John C Green, Second do.

SECOND REGIMENT of Washington, Tyrrell, Hyde, Beaufort, Craven, Carteret, Jones, Lenoir, Greene, Pitt, Martin, Edgecombe, and Wayne.

OFFICERS.—Simon Bruton, Lieutenant Colonel commandant; Nathan Tisdale, Lieutenant Colonel; Thomas H Blount, First Major; James W Clark, Second do.

THIRD REGIMENT of Onslow, New Hanover, Bladen, Brunswick, Columbus, Duplin, Sampson, Robeson, Cumberland, Moore, Richmond, and Anson.

OFFICERS.—Maurice Moore, Lieutenant Colonel commandant; Richard Nixon, Lieutenant Colonel; Archibald McNeil, First Major; Edward B Dudley, Second do.

FOURTH REGIMENT of Wake, Johnston, Franklin, Granville, Person, Orange, and Chatham.

OFFICERS.—Richard Atkerson, Lieutenant Colonel commandant, Maurice Smith, Lieutenant Colonel; John C Wyatt, First Major; Benjamin Chambers, second do.

First Major; Benjamin Chambers, second do.

FIFTH REGIMENT of Caswell, Guilford, Rockingham, Stokes, Surry, Wilkes, Ashe, and Randolph.

OFFICERS.—Alexander Murphy, Lieutenant Colonel commandant; Samuel Hunter, Lieutenant Colonel; James Campbell, First Major; Joseph Winston, jr. second do.

SIXTH REGIMENT of Rowan, Montgomery, Mecklenburg, Cabarrus, and Iredell.

OFFICERS.—Richard Allison, Lieutenant Colonel commandant; John H Freeling, First Major, Amos Sharpe, Second do.

SEVENTH REGIMENT of Lincoln, Rutherford, Burke, Buncombe, and Haywood.

OFFICERS.—Andrew Irwin, Lieutenant Colonel commandant; William Cathey, First Major; Nathan A McDowell, Second do.

FIRST REGIMENT.—CHOWAN COUNTY.

1 James Iredell, *captain*
2 Joseph Manning, *first lieutenant*
3 John M Roberts, *second do*
4 Myles Wilder, *ensign*
5 John D Castillow
6 John Bond, sr.
7 Charles Simpson
8 Jones Parish
9 James Hinsley
10 Edwin Bond
11 Hardy Morgan
12 John Evans
13 Richard Paxton
14 Nathaniel Miller
15 Samson Wilder
16 Thomas Mires
17 James R Creecy
18 Martin Noxon
19 Edmond Hoskins
20 Clement H Blount
21 Samuel Charlton
22 Michael Hendrick
23 Benjamin Whidler
24 William Nickolls
25 Jackson S Hoyle
26 Obediah Roberts
27 Jonathan Parks
28 Henry Evans
29 Isaac Boice
30 **Charleston Ward**
31 Joseph. Winslow
32 William Jordan
33 Josiah Ward
34 Thomas Smith, sr
35 Michena Trulove
36 John Wilder
37 Thomas Rhea
38 Alfred M Gatlin
39 George Waff
40 William Cheshire
41 George Mewbern
42 Edmond Bunch
43 John Ashley
44 William Todd
45 John Boyce
46 John Rhody
47 Joseph Small, jr
48 Jesse Mitchel
49 Stacy Floyd
50 William Ashley
51 John Reddic
52 Jethro Woodard
53 Alexander Parish
54 Julius Deale

CURRITUCK COUNTY

1 William Bray, *captain*
2 John Baxter, *first lieutenant*
3 Phillip Dozier, *second do*
4 Thomas Summon, *ensign*
5 William Etheridge
6 Lemuel Ferebee
7 Samuel Gregory
8 Malachi Holstead
9 Charles Seears
10 Tully Dozier
11 Samuel Glasgow
12 Peter Ferebee
13 William Spence
14 Iles Collins
15 Arthur Heath
16 Wilson Nash
17 Anthony Simmons
18 Caleb Woodard
19 Martin McBride
20 Dempsey Gregory
21 Willoughby Boswood
22 Jordan Dozier
23 Jasper Dozier
24 Grandy Barnard
25 William Dozier
26 Willoughby Barnard
27 William Ferebee
28 William Guilford
29 John Baxter
30 Wallis Hutchins
31 Hillary Finters
32 Jeremiah Mercer, jr
33 Enoch Whithurst
34 Samuel Whithurst
35 Josiah Etheridge

36 Hillary Fanchier
37 John C Glasgow
38 Cornelius Mercer
39 Branson Bell
40 William Messenger
41 Peter Parr
42 Peter Gregory
43 James Parr
44 Samuel Nicholson
45 Levi Etheridge
46 Arthur Spence
47 William Hanners
48 John Gregory
49 Jacob Aydelotte
50 Frederick Northern
51 Ralph P Beeling
52 James Northern
53 Charles Sawyer
54 Jesse Robinson
55 John Morse
56 John Bunnell
57 Joseph Sawyer
58 John Floro
59 John Brickhouse
60 James Bunnell
61 Aaron Floro
62 Henry Bright
63 Willoughby Whally
64 William Etheridge
65 Charles Perkins
66 James Brabble
67 John W Hughs
68 William Brumsey
69 James White
70 Jesse McClannan
71 John Lee
72 Enoch Lee
73 Joseph Tatum
74 Tatum Brabble
75 Jesse Balance
76 John Brabble
77 Bartholomew Thompson
78 Isaac Snowden
79 Dempsey Doxey
80 Matthias Bell
81 George Cason
82 Daniel Tatum
83 Mixey Tatum
84 John Caps
85 John Brabble, jr
86 Thomas Balance
87 James Poyner
88 Dempsey Douglass
89 Isaac Roberts
90 James Fentus
91 John Baxter
92 Alexander White
93 George Perkins
94 James Snowden
95 Samuel Payner
96 Peter Barco
97 Thomas Etheridge
98 Francis Camp
99 Spencer Oneal
100 Reuben Taylor
101 John Forbes
102 Thomas Roberts
103 Mitchell Simmons
104 Joseph Baxter, jr
105 Moses Cox
106 Amos Davis
107 James Lee
108 John Wilson
109 Willis Ballentine
110 William Cilgrow
111 Henry Williamson
112 Nicholas Ellison
113 Stephen Etheridge

CAMDEN COUNTY

1 James S Garlington, *captain*
2 Archibald Sawyer, *lieutenant*
3 John H Wright, *ensign*
4 John A Brockett
5 William Mercer
6 John Jerrell
7 Thomas Berry
8 Nathan Harrison
9 John Pue
10 Malachi Collins
11 Frederick Gregory
12 James Owens
13 Edward Cerlin
14 Cader Wright
15 Dempsey Collins
16 Malachi Knight
17 Charles Wright
18 Asa Cartwright
19 Wilson Coats
20 Miles Mercer
21 Thomas Surry
22 William Garrett
23 Thomas Bray
24 Adam Baum
25 Bradly Smith
26 Reuben Gibson
27 Job Gregory
28 William Collin
29 Elijah Staples
30 Simeon Jones
31 Ferebee Sanderlin
32 Silas Forbes
33 Joseph Bell
34 Seth Wright

K

35 Isaac Burges
36 Joab Bell
37 John Jones
38 Frederick Daily
39 James Sawyer
40 Frederick Kanady
41 Samuel Godfrew
42 Jonathan Gregory
43 Abner Cooper
44 William Dowtey
45 Dempsey Squiers
46 Nathan Gregory
47 Miles Williams
48 James Beales
49 Henry H Wright
50 Samuel Needham
51 Zephaniah Sawyer
52 Freeman Sawyer
53 John Godfrey
54 Josiah Sanderlin
55 Jeremiah Jones
56 James Godfrey
57 Benjamin Douge
58 Densey Dunkin
59 Caleb Forbes

60 Peter Pugh
61 Joseph Love
62 Maxsey Sawyer
63 Jesse Douge
64 Hiram Godfrey
65 James McHarney
66 Jesse Temple
67 Dempsey Riggs
68 Silas Riggs
69 Dempsey Forbes
70 Isaac Harrison
71 Cornelius Wright
72 Berket Beales
73 Joseph Seamon
74 Levi Wright
75 William Kanady
76 Abraham Cartwright
77 Joseph Barco
78 Samuel Gregory
79 Depmsey Douge
80 Edmond Gregory
81 Lot Needham
82 Samuel Jarvis
83 Amos Pue

PASQUOTANK COUNTY.

1 Carter Bernard, *captain*
2 Abraham Simons, *lieutenant*
3 Miles Jones, *ensign*
4 William Gammon
5 Henry Keaton
6 James Sawyer
7 James Turner
8 Jesse Maddux
9 Thomas Lowry
10 John Lester
11 Thomas Marknm
12 Joshua Trueblood
13 Alfred Turner
14 John White
15 Richard Clayton
16 Miles Brothers
17 Caleb Brothers
18 Robert Cartright
19 David Davis
20 Malachi Davis
21 Thomas Palin
22 Cyprian Chopard
23 Jesse Walden
24 Keder Morgan
25 Richard Madrew
26 William Casey
27 James Cartwright
28 Thomas Pritchard
29 Harvey Hairis
30 James Jackson
31 Thomas Cartwright
32 William Morris

33 Isaac Williams
34 Kader Perry
35 Hezekiah Jackson
36 James Munden
37 Charles Roberts
38 Nathan Small
39 Daniel White
40 Caleb Bundy
41 William Mnnden
42 Daniel Spence
43 Thomas Burnham
44 Evergain Carver
45 William Cartwright
46 Joseph Haireld
47 John Hallstead
48 Harvey Stokely
49 Robert Sawyer
50 Henry Temple
51 James Williams
52 John Williams
53 Peleg Prichard
54 David Frew
55 Johnson Davis
56 William Smithson
57 Isaac Sawyer
58 Stephen Richardson
59 Adam Stafford
60 Grandey Pritchard
61 Stephen Hooker
62 Thomas Madrew, jr
63 Jesse Gray
64 William Allen

65 Thomas McKey
66 Willam Jackson (son of Thos.)
67 Jabez Bright
68 Joseph Brothers (son of Jos.)
69 Joshua Pool

70 William Albertson
71 William Bumbough
72 Daniet Bray
73 Henry Pendleton.

PERQUIMANS COUNTY

1 William R Sutton, *captain*
2 Alfred Moore, *lieutenant*
3 John Branch, *ensign*
4 Benjamin Smith
5 Charles Elliott
6 Caleb Chappel
7 Joseph Roberts
8 Joseph Elliott
9 Jesse Elliott
10 John White
11 Foster Elliott
12 Henry Smith
13 John Rogerson, jr.
14 Hugh Morgan
15 Joseph W Weeks
16 Barnabas Ward
17 Francis Godfrey
18 Harrison Turner
19 James Tweedy
20 Purry Weeks
21 Thomas Feveash
22 John Jackson jr.
23 Nathaniel Cole
24 Robert Harrison
25 John Madre
26 Charles Hall
27 John Bunch
28 Joseph Jordan
29 James Thach
30 Willis Butter
31 John Wingate
32 William Thach

33 William Tailor
34 William Thorn
35 Charles W Skinner
36 Seth Hendricks
37 Thomas Hasket
38 Mexum Newby
39 Josiah Smith
40 John Woodley
41 George Low
42 William Bagley
43 Hezekiah Savage
44 William Gregory
45 Willis Morgan
46 John Hasket
47 Nathan Bagley
48 Joseph Cooper
49 Dempsey Webb
50 John White (of John)
51 John Simpson
52 James Perry
53 Moses Boyce
54 William Walton
55 Asa Pelon
56 Samuel Barclift, sen.
57 Robert Reed
58 William Humphries
59 John Stanton
60 James Needham
61 James Tatlock
62 John Stephenson
63 James Gipson

GATES COUNTY.

1 Henry Pugh, *captain*
2 Isaac K Hunter, *lieutenant*
3 George Kittrell, *ensign*
4 John Gordon, *first sergeant*
5 William Kitrell, *second do*
6 John Barnes, *third do*
7 Robert Powell, *fourth do*
8 Jonas Franklin, *first corporal*
9 Whitmill Hill, *second do*
10 Joseph Harrell, *third do*
11 Jethro Brinkley, *fourth do*
12 William White, *private*
13 Elijah Lyons
14 Amos Hobbs
15 William Hofler
16 Jesse Hyett
17 Anson Williams

18 Joseph Derden
19 James Eure
20 Timothy Spivey
21 Solomon Eason
22 William Pearce
23 William Blanchard
24 Seth Blanchard
25 Edward Briggs
26 Samuel Green
27 Robert Simons
28 Miles Knight
29 Richard Farlass
30 Francis M Foster
31 Edward Daughtie
32 Henry Holt
33 Samuel Smith
34 Frederick Williams

35 Kindred Parker
36 Kinchen Taylor
37 Benjamin Eure
38 Elisha Ump l t
39 Thomas Collins
40 William Crofford
41 Lewis Lee
42 Elisha Pyland
43 Jesse Parker
44 James Williams
45 Miles Williams
46 John Evens
47 Jethro Reddick
48 Shedric Pyland
49 Watson Hilley
50 William Pyland
51 Dempsey Hall
52 James Lapland
53 Kader Briggs
54 Reuben Miller

55 James Jones (of John)
56 Jesse Mathias
57 Noah Speight
58 Joshua Small
59 Robert Parker
60 Harmon Hayes
61 Robert Wilson
62 Hardy Williams
63 John Polson
64 David Brown
65 John Shearod
66 Elisha Duke
67 James Parker
68 Henry Crafford
69 Jacob Ealey
70 Joshua Lang
71 William March
72 John March
73 William Spivey

HERTFORD COUNTY

1 Irvin Jinkins, *captain*
2 Benjamin Hill, *lieutenant*
3 Henry G Darden, *ensign*
4 Benjamin Brown, *drummer*
5 Silas Shewcraft, *fifer*
6 William Brown
7 James Johnston
8 Willie Willoughbee
9 Luke Hare
10 John Brown
11 Burrell Eur
12 Jacob Overton
13 Elisha Overton
14 Jeremiah Aikin
15 William Wynns
16 Wm W Whitfield
17 Jeremiah D Aikin
18 James Raiberry, jr
19 Allen Moore
20 William Downing
21 James Barns
22 Willie Cullan
23 Jesse Harrison
24 William Sessoms
25 George Hollomon, jr
26 Justin Hollomon
27 Samuel Britton
28 Jethro Sowell
29 Aaron Hare
30 Isaac Baker
31 David Welch, jr
32 William Sewell
33 Thomas Elerton
34 Benjamin Hocall
35 George H Bond
36 Isaac Taylor
37 William Purnell
38 William Yeats

39 Samuel Parker
40 William Peaster
41 Benjamin Wyuns
42 Samuel Ely
43 Eli Harrell
44 Boan Driver
45 John Dickinson
46 Thomas Early
47 John P Hare
48 Stephen Howell
49 John A Anderson
50 Benjamin Blan
51 Sterling Francis
52 Arthur Vick
53 George Whitley
54 John Seall
55 David Williams
56 James Skinner
57 Henry Brantley
58 Daniel Williams
59 James Worrell
60 Thomas Faircloth
61 Benjamin Williams
62 Lemuel Sanders
63 Gray Mabane
64 John Vinson
65 John Vaughn
66 Jonas Clifton
67 William Rodgers
68 Nelson Joyner
69 William Andrews
70 Robert Montgomery
71 William Parker
72 Mathias Cook
73 Hilary Vaughn
74 Joel Grizzard
75 Hardy M Banks

BERTIE COUNTY

1 Jonathan H Jacocks, *captain*
2 Powell Harrel, *lieutenant*
3 James Wilson, jr, *ensign*
4 Thomas Morgan, *private*
5 Miles Gilliam
6 William G Terrell
7 William M Darlett
8 Simon A Bryant
9 William B Mastin
10 Joseph Blount
11 Gaven Hogg
12 William P King
13 Lewis Wimberly
14 Levi Kenaday
15 Thomas Liversage
16 James Duglas
17 William W Johnson
18 Kenneth Clark
19 Cullen Shoolders
20 Thomas Ruffin
21 Wm R W Bozman
22 Hatter Calloway
23 Asa Gregory
24 Aquilla Harden
25 Josiah Reddit
26 William Simons
27 Jasper Ward
28 William Castellow
29 Trustum Capehart
30 Thomas L West
31 Curry Butler
32 Josiah Bird
33 Benjamin Baker
34 Benjamin Bowen
35 John Bowen
36 Levi Jennings
37 John P Butler
38 Silas Butler
39 Reuben Barns
40 Nehemiah Bunch
41 Cullen Bazimore
42 William K Miller
43 Stephen Bazimore
44 James Cherry, jr.
45 Ralph Outlaw
46 Lodowick Jenkins
47 Elisha Cook
48 James Early
49 James Williford
50 Isaac Early
51 Willie Jenkins
52 John Cobb
53 Lawrence Mizells
54 John Lassiter
55 Joshua Harrell
56 Thomas Harrell
57 Josiah Davidson
58 Isaac White
59 Peter White
60 Zachariah Ellison
61 George Mizells
62 Charles Miller
63 Meredith Harrell
64 Benjamin B Williams
65 George White
66 James Mizell
67 Whitmell White
68 Joshua Hale
69 Charnley C Dundalow
70 Noah Outlaw
71 Elisha Hoggard
72 David White
73 Lewis Miller
74 King Mitchel
75 William Griffin
76 Hatton Fleetwood
77 John Hunter
78 Timothy Mizells
79 Seth Morgan
80 Michael Mardre
81 Henry Tood
82 Luke Smithwitk
83 John Watson
84 Jeremiah Legett
85 James Baswell
86 Hardy Clements
87 Leven McTuller
88 Jonathan Zaloe
89 David Calloway
90 John Mhoon
91 John Boyd
92 Henry Lee
93 Henry Harrell
04 John Murdough
95 Dancy Harrell
96 Whitmell Ruffin
97 Moses Purvis
98 Jesse Brown
99 Jason Minton
100 John Higgs
101 Kinchen Wilks
102 Cullen Grimmer
103 James Hoggard

NORTHAMPTON COUNTY

1 John F Walker, *captain*
2 Darius Parker, *first lieutenant*
3 Solomon B Goodson, *second do*
4 Sterling Finnie, *third lieut*
5 John C Wood, *ensign*
6 Henry Adams, *private*

7 Burges Burkett
8 Lemuel Burkett
9 Robert Baum
10 Bennet Boon
11 Brittain Brittle
12 John T Benns
13 William Boon
14 Elijah Brewer
15 John Cornwall
16 James Day
17 Goodwin Daniel
18 David C Dardin
19 Britain Doles
20 Thomas Deloach
21 William Draper
22 Lewis Davis
23 Jesse Deloach
24 Pink Edwards
25 Thomas Ellis
26 Williamson Edwards
27 Ricks Elliott
28 John Edwards
29 Sterling Faison
30 William Futrell
31 Enos Futrell
32 Winborne Futrell
33 Claiborne Griffin
34 Edward Gatlin
35 Jossph Griffin
36 Armstead Grizzard
37 William Gay
38 Green Hart
39 William Harriss
40 Gideon Harriss
41 Elias Harriss
42 William Hicks
43 Henry Hailey
44 Henry Hart
45 John Holmes
46 James Hill
47 Jeremiah Horton
48 Moore Higgs
49 William Ingram
50 John Jenkins
51 John Johnson
52 John Jordan, sen.
53 Elias Johnson
54 Robert Johnson
55 Nathaniel Ingram
56 Benjamin Jenkins

57 Jesse Jones
58 George Key
59 Robert Little
60 Edward Liles
61 Henry Leek
62 Lemuel Lane
63 Benjamin Lawrence
64 Joshua Morgan
65 John Maughon
66 Jesse Morgan
67 Wilson Mongar
68 Bartlett McDonald
69 Samuel Norwood
70 William Naresworthy
71 Burwell Norwood
72 Everet Oliver
73 Samuel Patterson
74 William Pledger
75 George W Pledger
76 Barnaby Pope
77 Joel Peele
78 Jesse Philips
79 Philip Poyland
80 James Pierce
81 Robert Roe
82 Thomas Richards
83 Willis Roane
84 Boswell Smith
85 John B Stanback
86 Robert Snipes
87 William Short
88 Benjamin Strickling
89 Matthew Spivey
90 Benjamin Sweter
91 Henry Sweter
92 Britain Smith
93 James Sumner
94 John Thompson
95 Edmond Wilson
96 James Wheeler
97 Jsseph T Wornam
98 Sion Wheeler
99 Simeon Wood
100 Samuel Warren
101 Abraham Wall
102 Lemuel Winborne
103 Lemuel Warr
104 John E Wallace
105 Jan Wade, (const.)

HALIFAX COUNTY, FIRST REGIMENT

1 William Price, *first lieutenant*
2 William Brinkley *Ensign*
3 John Allen
4 Ludwell Allen
5 German Baker
6 William Curliles
7 Anderson Clardy

8 John Crawly
9 William Campbell
10 Stephen Eubank
11 John Fulgem
12 Nathaniel Gilliam
13 Alfred Harwell
14 Jesse Harlow

15 Robert Hynes
16 Orren Harris
17 Hugh Hatheway
18 Hall Hudson
19 Joseph C Justiss
20 Willis Johnsion
21 Henry Jones
22 Willis Johnston
23 Samuel King
24 William Keeter
25 Gregory Moore
26 Henry Morris
27 Willie Matthews
28 Eli Marshall
29 Eaton Morris
30 Elijah Nevill
31 William Onions
32 James Powell, jr.
33 Benjamin Partin
34 Isham Perdue
35 John Pitts
36 Irby Powell
37 Edmond Powers

38 Allen Rainey
39 Edward Robinson
40 Jacob Sykes
41 Caleb Smith
42 Lodiman Shelton
43 Isham Sykes
44 James Shaw
45 Battie Smith
46 Peter Smith
47 Daniel L Sturdivant
48 Joel Smith, jr.
49 Joseph A Sturdivant
50 Laban Vinson
51 Warren Vinson
52 Richard Vick
53 Lewis Willls
54 Samuel Weldon
55 Sharp Wright
56 James Wood
57 Joseph Williams
58 Thomas Weldon
59 Guilford Williams
60 Washington Yarborough

HALIFAX COUNTY, SECOND REGIMENT

1 Jeptha A Barns, *captain*
2 John Peebles, *first lieutenant*
3 John Bradford, *second do*
4 William Brinkley, *ensign*
5 Thomas Cochran
6 Micajah Alsobrook,
7 Benjamin Vick
8 Abud Gray
9 Samuel Murder
10 Henry Harris
11 Benjamin Jones
12 James Lipscomb
13 Turner Brewer
14 John Sills
15 Joel Carlisle
16 John Roan
17 Mills Parker
18 Jesse Curling
19 Josiah Fort
20 Wilson Brantly
21 William Brantly
22 David Brantly
23 William T Bryant
24 Thomas Drew
25 John Dawson
26 Benjamin Paull
27 Cordy Drew
28 Ira Coffield
29 Edmund Wiggins
30 Whitmell Braswell
31 General Dawson
32 Marmaduke Braswell

33 Aquilla Lock
34 Dempsey P Hillman
35 Jesse Hayes
36 Nathaniel Mullen
37 Valentine Minton
38 Edward H Davis
39 James Northcut
40 Thomas Gall
41 Thomas Jolly
42 Richard Doggett
43 Henry Doggett
44 Thomas Lowe
45 Joseph Randolph
46 James Turner
47 Peter Brunt
48 Herbert Warner
49 Thomas Merritt
50 Landin Smith
51 John Archer
52 Ralph Skinner
53 James Bachelor
54 Matthew Holtfoot
55 Daniel Glover
56 Augustin Willis
57 Elisha Euse
58 Samuel Davis
59 Joshua Manning
60 Blake Davis
61 Peyton R Tunstall
62 James Young
63 Dempsey Pittman

WARREN COUNTY

1 Amos P Sledge, *lieutenant*
2 John Munholland, *ensign*
3 James Powell, *sergeant*
4 John Alleh, *do*
5 Wilmot Egerton, *serg'nt*
6 William Powell, *do*
7 James Tolley, *corporal*
8 Owen F Myreck, *do*
9 Henry Person, *do*
10 Doctor G Robberson, *do*
11 Allen Wren
12 Bird Ellington
13 Cudberth Neal
14 Charles Stewart
15 Claton Lambert
16 Daniel A Perdue
17 Drury Thompson
18 Daniel White
19 Elish Sheerren
20 Edward Patillo
21 George Hazelwood
22 Hardaway Davis
33 Henry James
24 James Edwards
25 Joseph Whaer
26 Joshua Harper
27 James Alston
28 James Thomas
29 James C Bennet
30 James Smith
31 Joel Tolley
32 Joel Ellington
33 Jiles Carter
34 Jeptha Caps
35 Ira Allen
36 John Hawks
37 John Lancaster
38 Kinchen Williamson
39 Lemuel Mitchell
40 Lewis Sherren
41 Littleton B Roberson
42 Lewis Ellis
43 Lunceford Baker
44 Michael Bell
45 Miles Ellis
46 Obediah Ellis
47 Philemon Perdue
48 Peter Randolph
49 Richard Allen
50 Ransome Acock
51 Richard Davis
52 Ransome Worrell
53 Richard Brook
54 Samuel Dowton
55 Thomas Newsman
56 Thomas Walker
57 Thomas Harton
58 Thomas Davis
59 Thomas Tolley
60 William Oliver
61 Willis Person
62 William Sherren
63 William Breedlove

NASH COUNTY

1 Isaac Watkins, *captain*
2 Joseph Vick *lieutenant*
3 Willie Rick, *ensign*
4 Henry Hedgepeth
5 Joseph Griffen
6 James Beckworth
7 Elijah Whelas
8 William Walker
9 Solomon Thomas
10 Thomas Cobb
11 Holliday Hedgepeth
12 Nelson Bowie
13 William Langley
14 Lewis Tucker
15 Robert Crickmore
16 William Ballard
17 Asberry Lindsey
18 Briant Lewis
19 Willis Hammons
20 Allen Brantley
21 Hopni Pucket
22 John Perry
23 John Rice
24 Joseph Bissit
25 Reuben Strickland
26 William Colston
27 William Bunn
28 Whitmell Ricks
29 Samuel Vick
30 James W Daniel
31 Henry Bunn
32 Valentine Chapman
33 Thomas Valentine
34 Duncan Ricks
35 Oran D. Powell
36 Thomas Pott
37 Bennet Mason
38 James Manning
39 John Williams
40 Frederic Parish
41 Henry Blount
42 Tompkins Rose
43 Thomas Aven
44 Enoch Flood

45 Samuel Williams
46 Samuel S Lampkin
47 Valentine Perkinson
48 Edward Strickland
49 David Hunt
50 Major Potter
51 German Mann
52 Clairbourn Mann
53 Peter Prigen
54 Irwin Eatman
55 Elisha Tisdal
56 Eli Never
57 Everret Morriss
58 Griffin Lewis
59 Irvin Boykin
60 James Duck
61 Lee Horn
62 Thomas Landers
63 Thomas Williamson
64 William Landers

65 Amden Horn
66 William Braswell
67 Sion Beckworth
68 Arch G Whitfield
69 John Harris
70 Alfred Strickland
71 Edwin Harris
72 Thomas White
73 Jesse Thorp
74 James Hunter
75 Reddick Massengill
76 Joab Tucker
77 Wright Bachelor
78 Cornelus Taylor
79 Boen Wren
80 Joseph Brown
81 William Bilbes
82 Joseph Bachelor
83 Wilson Bachelor

SECOND REGIMENT

WASHINGTON COUNTY.

1
2
3 David Airs
4 Joseph H Adams
5 Joshua Alexander
6 Anthony Alexander
7 Andrew Bateman
8 Evin Bateman
9 James Blount (3d or son of Steph.)
10 Isaac Brown
11 Reuben Carnel
12 Robert McClary
13 Richard Corprew
14 Elijah Etherige
15 Robert Everitt
16 Solomon Armstrong
17 Aaron Fagan
18 James Forlaw
19 Jacob N Gordon
20 Josiah Haughton
21 Daniel Barns

22 Edward Hollis
23 George Harrison
24 John Jethro
25 Harman Legett
26 Downing Leary
27 Joshua Long
28 Charles Wiley
29 Aquilla Norman
30 Frederick Oliver
31 William Readit
32 Evin Phelps
33 Hezekiah Phelps
34 Willibough Phelps
35 Edward J Ransom
36 John M Roulhac
37 Roger Snell
38 Stephen Swain
39 William H Star
40 James Walker, sen.
41 Martin Walker
42 Joshua Young

TYRRELL COUNTY.

1 Richard Hawett, *captain*
2 Benjamin Clayton, *ensign*
3 Jeremiah Giles
4 Daniel Ensley
5 Eli Woodley
6 Henry Mariner
7 Abel Cahoon
8 Talket Davenport

9 Samuel Davenport
10 Ebenezer Peettigrew
11 Charles Phelps
12 Uzziah Spruell
13 Willis Sawyer
14 Edward Man
15 Lewis Mydgett
16 Benjamin Mydgett

F

17 Major Brickhouse
18 Gardener Alexander
19 Richard Brickhouse
20 Elikin Swain
21 John Cooper
22 Matthew Brickhouse
23 Henry Norman
24 Darius Phelps
25 Seth Sanders
26 Silas Etherige
27 Peter Wynn
28 Spence Hooker
29 Joseph Pledger
30 David Alexander
31 Joshua Swain
32 Zadock Hassel
33 William Ranton
34 Thomas Sweedy

35 Isaac Liverman
36 James McKinney
37 Joseph Swain
38 William Edwards
39 Charles Johnson
40 Josiah Jermanny
41 Carney Spinner
42 Henry Baker
43 Lilby Bilangey
44 John Cahoon (of John)
45 Benjamin Cooper
46 Thomas Clayton
47 Willis Liverman
48 Hardy Powers
49 Ebenezer Smith
50 Miles Sawyer
51 James Cahoon (of John)

HYDE COUNTY.

1 Seth B Jordan, *captain*
2 Wyriott Windley, *lieutenant*
3 Christopher Gaskins, *ensign*
4 David Paine
5 Asa Oneal
6 Benjamin Turner
7 Henry Clark
8 Mathew English
9 William Meekins
10 Sparrow Midgett
11 Josiah Knox
12 Stephen Owens
13 Samuel Selby
14 Daniel Seabrook
15 William B Spencer
16 Benjamin Brinn
17 John Swindell
18 Thomas Mason
19 Samuel Williamson
20 Edward Rose
21 Uriah Lewis
22 Elias Mooney
23 Thomas Moore
24 Wilson Sawyer
25 Clement Daniels
26 Thomas Daniels
27 Zedekiah Swindell
28 Frisby Spencer
29 Morris Daniels
30 Henry Delow
31 Alexander Cohoon
32 Israel Henry
33 Robert Hopkins
34 Samuel Gibbs, sen.
35 Selby Spencer
36 Thomas Sanderson
37 Jeremiah Hall
38 Stephen Gibbs

39 Washington Gibbs
40 William Cohoon
41 Thomas Gurganus
42 Zachariah Wilkinson
43 Zachariah Bishop
44 John Allen
45 Mark Smedick
46 Martin Davis
47 Henry Hobbs
48 William Eborn
49 Robert Barnett
50 John Shavener
51 Mouncen Peckham
52 Henry Blount
53 Enoch Robins
54 Zachariah Kipps
55 Richard Jordan
56 Thomas Moore
57 William Hooten
58 Lewis Blount
59 Nathan Harvey
60 Moses Windley
61 John James
62 William Barrow
63 William Fetterton
64 Richard Sadler
65 Robert Harris
66 Bartee Gibbs
67 David Gibbs
68 Josiah Harris
69 John Silverthorn
70 William Easter, sen
71 Solomon Easter
72 Sheldon Tooley
73 John Dixon
74 Thomas Mason
75 John Gaylard
76 William Easter, junr.

77 Franklin Dixon
78 Valentine Slade
79 Jeremiah Tooley

80 Timothy Parmarle
81 Hosea Tyson
82 James Loyd

BEAUFORT COUNTY.

1 John Cox, *captain*
2 Henry Williams, *first lieutenant*
3 Samuel Taylor, 2nd *lieutenant*
4 Wilson B Hodges, *ensign*
5 Achilles Hawkins
6 Richard Mastin
7 Jesse Godley
8 William S Holmes
9 Allen Grist
10 William McDonald
11 Charles Holland
12 Jesse Swonner
13 James Sworner
14 Christ Crandell
15 Benjamin Legget
16 Joseph Legget
17 John Brown
18 David Latham
19 Major Ball
20 Eden Beacham
21 James Gorden
22 Joel Dickenson
23 Isaac Peacock
24 Peter Demill
25 William D Barr
26 Michael Hanrahan
27 James Kelly
28 Hugh McCullough
29 William Shaw
30 Solah Mammon
31 Levin Wallace
32 Willie Bagner
33 Alfred Bagner
34 Benjamin Braddy
35 John Wollard
36 Jacob Allegood
37 James B Ellison
38 Littleton Hawkins
39 Nathan Cutler
40 Slamil Bagner
41 Thomas Hawkins
42 Isaac Chauncey
43 Irra Paul
44 John Seaward
45 John Pilley
46 Jacob Cordin
47 Israel Windley
48 J Gardner
49 Thomas Floyd
50 William Fortisque
51 John Whitley
52 Aaron Gurganus

53 Jacob Wilkinson
54 John Kelley
55 Jeremiah Garrot
56 William Sleatey
57 James Harris
58 George Harris
59 James Waters
60 Dempsey Martin
61 Elisha Harris
62 Shadric Downs
63 Noah Spear
64 John G Hill
65 Joseph Millar
66 Thomas Morris
67 William E Edwards
68 William N Edwards
69 Willie Hill
70 William Telliton
71 Richard Blacklidge
72 Israel Harching
73 Uriah Slade
74 John Evitt
75 Daniel Warren
76 Hardy Rue jun
77 Lott Evitt
78 William Dixon
79 Thomas Robason
80 Hilery Whitehurst
81 William Hudnal
82 Will Bond
83 Jesse Puiser
84 John Danals
85 Zadock Ives
86 David Camper
87 Frederick Watson
88 Luke Lenton
89 Zedekiah Mirow
90 Burage Linton
91 Jeremiah Slade
92 Nathaniel Woodard
93 James Jones
94 Thomas Cox
95 William Springle
96 Joshua Moore
97 Price Wm Lewis
98 Solomon Brag
99 Archibald Wilcox
100 William Walker
101 William Thomason
102 John Roll
103 William Hollowell
104 John Dowty

CRAVEN COUNTY.

1	Minor Huntington, *captain*	
2	John S Smith, *first lieutenant*	
3	Isaac Hellen, *second do*	
4	Uriah Sandy, *third do*	
5	John Forlaw, *ensign*	
6	Moses H Stephens, *sergeant*	
7	Abner Heartley	*do*
8	Lewis Griffien	*do*
9	Isaac Patrick	*do*
10	Hrrvey Morris, *corporal*	
11	Mason Ives,	*do*
12	William Caruthers	*do*
13	Nathaniel Clark	*do*
14	Moses Prescott	
15	Will Whitford	
16	James Daniels	
17	Jesse Collins	
18	Joseph Stephens	
19	Jesse Hampton	
20	David B Gibson	
21	Michael Fisher	
22	John Shipp	
23	Kinchen Canaday	
24	George Lane	
25	Jesse Weatherington	
26	Samuel Avery	
27	Amos Hudler	
28	William Sanders	
29	Jacob Dudley	
30	Levin Dunn	
31	George Lewis	
32	Linkfield Perkins	
33	Robert Barns	
34	Stephen Hawkins	
35	Elisha Arnold	
36	Edmund Heath	
37	Henry Shute	
38	Isaac White	
39	John Arnold	
40	Frederick Heath	
41	William West	
42	Cason Fell	
43	Elijah Wheedleton	
44	William Spikes	
45	James Edwards	
46	Moses Caton	
47	Jos S Brinson	
48	Rollin Dixon	
49	Jordan Butler	
50	John Clark	
51	Joseph Bryan	
52	Lewis Warren	
53	Stephen Chapman	
54	Will Griffin	
55	Levi Griffin	
56	Jesse Griffin	
57	Daniel Daughety	
58	Elijah Randal	
59	Louis Cox	
60	William King	
61	Zach Barrot	
62	Shad Holloway	
63	Allen Smith	
64	Ervin Taunt	
65	Ennis Cooper	
66	William Hall	
67	William Mills	
68	Reding Harrison	
69	John Kirk	
70	Levi Gallin	
71	John Taylor	
72	John Sparrow	
73	John Griffin	
74	John S Brown	
75	John Jones	
76	Nathaniel Lewis	
77	Elijah Dunn	
78	Evan Jones	
79	Andrew Morgan	
80	Thomas Hall	
81	Lazarous Ipock	
82	John Ipock	
83	John Kemp	
84	Aaron Eventon	
85	Abner Gatlin	
86	Henry Ipock	
87	Thomas Carraway	
88	Parks Ryal	
89	James Masters	
90	John Pittman	
91	Job Smith	
92	Richard Parsons	
93	John Holley	
94	Jephthy Simpson	
95	Duran Ives	
96	Isaac Reed	
97	Fredrick Folson	
98	Peter Parris	
99	William S Brinson	
100	Robert Philips	
101	Elijah Ives	
102	William Harper	
103	Thomas King	
104	Jesse Lawson	
105	James Vendrick, jr	
106	Ezekiel Simpkins	
107	John Woods	
108	William Williams	
109	Cornelius Dixon	
110	Samuel Collins	
111	Thomas Hamilton	
112	Lewis Dawson	

113 Murphy Trott
114 John Smith
115 Joshua Mitchell
116 Elijah V Pittman
117 Benjamin Marriner
118 John Herrington

119 Thomas McKelroy
120 Thomas Pittman
121 William Muse
122 Francis Beasley
123 Reuben Prentiss

CARTERET COUNTY.

1 Nathaniel Pinkham, *captain*
2 David A Wallace, 1st *lieutenant*
3 Thomas Martial, *second do*
4 James Chadwick, *third do*
5 Jacob Paquanett, *ensign*
6 John Paquanett, *first sergeant*
7 Jesse Prescott, *second do*
8 Alexander Hamilton
9 Samuel Sanders
10 Uriah Suggs
11 Thomas Meadows
12 Hardy Lane
13 Wilboga Prescott
14 Fama Gaskett
15 John Simmons
16 Allen Robinson
17 Samuel Piver
18 Daniel Dickerson
19 Barton Hendesty
20 James E Gibble
21 Joseph Hall
22 Samuel Guthree
23 Samuel Buckman
24 John Martial
25 Logan Key
26 Zemeriah Harris
27 Jesse Haskett
28 John Weaks
29 Thomas Elliott
30 Josiah Harris
31 Samuel Gardener
32 James Piver
33 David Gould

34 Joseph Morton
35 Counsel Fealds
36 Thomas Louis
37 Archibald Louis
38 John S Davis
39 Zephaniah Howland
40 Washington Willis
41 Newel Bell
42 William Morton
43 William Pigett
44 Williams Brooks
45 Joseph Willis
46 Uriah Gillikan
47 George Gillikan
48 Richard Arthur
49 George Linguish
50 Isaac Wade
51 Martin Chadwick
52 William Howland
53 David Gabriel
54 Joseph Willis
55 Thomas Nelson
56 Abisha Nelson
57 Littleton Willis
58 David Gaskitt
59 David Hamilton
60 Henry Saulter
61 William Smith
62 Joseph Tulcher
63 David Mason
64 James Styson
65 Reubin Willis

JONES COUNTY.

1 Sears Bryan, *first lieutenant*
2 Jonathan Wood, *ensign*
3 Jonathan Kay
4 James Mades
5 Aaron Eubanks
6 John Dudley
7 James Frazer
8 Theolifus Odium
9 William Foskey
10 Amos Sanderson
11 James Griffith
12 Joshua Millar
13 Joseph Wallis
14 Josiah Taylor

15 Benjamin McKinney
16 James Monford, sen
17 Frederic J Becton
18 John Wilcox
19 James Reynolds
20 Robert Reynolds
21 Thomas Mackney
22 Jonathan Lee
23 Thomas McQuillan
24 Alfred Harget
25 Ivey Anders
26 Daniel Mallard
27 Adam Anders
28 Shadrich Mallard

29 Joseph Killingsworth
30 Benjamin D Gray
31 John Overton
32 Ariel Jones
33 Daniel Smith
34 Hezekiah Alphin
35 John Shelfer
36 Lewis Kinsey
37 William Garman
38 William Wilcox
39 John Gilbert
40 Kesdon McDaniel
(son of Risdon)

41 William Harget
42 James Monford, jr
43 Alfred McDaniel
44 Daniel Stanley
45 John Barrington
46 John McDaniel
47 James Oliver
48 Jesse Alphin
49 Abner Harrison
50 Samuel Dillahunta
51 Durant Green
52 Peter Harget

LENOIR COUNTY.

1 Joshua Mosley, *captain*
2 Richard Aldridge, 3rd *lieutenant*
3 Thomas Aldridge,
4 William Benton
5 Silas Bowen
6 Lewis O'Bryan
7 Bartholamy Cauley
8 John Slismore
9 Jesse Slismore
10 William F Davis
11 Reading K Davis
12 David Evans
13 John Evans
14 Major Fields
15 Zachariah Gray
16 David Griffin
17 Samuel Hines
18 Rigdon Henry
19 William Hood
20 David Hartsfield
21 Burwell Herring
22 Kenon Hudlow
23 Josiah Horton
24 Isam Jackson
25 Isaiah Johnston
26 Isham Lassiter

27 Herod Lovit
28 Thomas Midlin
29 Kenon Meloney
30 William Moore
31 William Mosely
32 Walker Moore
33 Radner Moore
34 William Potter
35 John Philips
36 Moses Pool
37 Farniford Pool
38 William Pearson
39 Abraham Peacock
40 Bryan Pate
41 Thomas Rows
42 Edward Smith
43 William Sutton
44 Patrick Sparrow
45 John Tilman
46 Arthur Tull
47 Jeremiah Waters
48 John Westbrook
49 Garrot Williams
50 Thomas Witherington
51 William Vause
52 Briton King

GREEN COUNTY.

1 Henry Miller, *first lieutenant*
2 James Miller, *second do*
3 Joseph Harrel, *ensign*
4 John Gardner
5 John Andrews
6 Mark Taylor
7 Jonathan Parker
8 James Wasden
9 Aven Lane
10 Willis Newsom
11 John Goff
12 Henry David
13 Joel Mears
14 Gardner Jones
15 Silas Lassiter

16 Abraham Grizzard
17 William Britt
18 William Barrow
19 Joseph Williams
20 Beverly Belsher
21 John Murrah
22 Haswell Hay
23 Woody Belsher
24 James Rogers
25 Charles Tindall
26 Samuel Harrel
27 Benjamin Hardy
28 Lemuel Hardy
29 David Shirley
30 Henry Moring

31 Nicholas Smith
32 Samuel Forrest
33 John Potter
34 Allen Stanul
35 Simon Jones
36 William Harper
37 William Farmer
38 Owen Lockhart
39 Abram Joyner
40 William Turnage
41 Jesse Cunninggem
42 Stuart Summerlin

43 Augustin Moore
44 James Hill
45 Spears Denny
46 Micajah Kenaday
47 James Edmonson
48 Fountain Ward
49 Nehemiah Garras
50 Timothy Roddick
51 Stephen Tison
52 James Ranch
53 Noah Dunn

PITT COUNTY.

1 George Eason, *captain*
2 Summer Adams, *first lieutenant*
3 Samuel Albritton, *second do*
4 Gideon Brindon, *third do*
5 William Briley, *ensign*
6 John Stocks
7 Burrel Bell
8 John Moye
9 Jacob Rogers
10 Samuel Truss
11 James Johnston
12 David Hathway
13 Kedar Randolph
14 William Whitehurst
15 Turner House
16 Jacob Moore
17 William Nichols
18 Reuben Gardener
19 Isaac Gardener
20 William Quinley
21 Stephen Quinley
22 Hardy Trip
23 Jonathan Pelt
24 James Bell
25 Jesse Cherry
26 Thomas Adams
27 John Duvol
28 John Eason
29 William Mills
30 Daniel Duvol
31 James Bryant
32 Caleb Nelson
33 Bryant Grimes
34 Jordan Nelson
35 Joseph Boyd
36 Naisby Mills
37 Naboth Nelson
38 Noah Adams
39 John Arnold
40 William Boyd
41 William Barber
42 Moses Herrington
43 Arthur Magleham

44 Franklin Moye
45 Gilford Broom
46 Isaac Turner
47 Joab Smith
48 Noah Harriss
49 Worley White
50 Ervan Dudley
51 Erandal Little
52 Hugh Telfair
53 Joseph Griffin
54 Samuel Moore
55 Silvenus Harris
56 Willie Daniel
57 James Buch
58 Amos Joyner
59 Icabod Moore
60 Willis Hodges
61 Sparkman Smith
62 Abner Askew
63 Absalom Page
64 Thomas Flanigen
65 David Leget
66 Willis Flemming
67 Mansel Flake
68 Miles Spier
69 Allen Moore
70 John Harriss
71 Charles Tison
72 William Bird
73 William Norriss
74 James Grist
75 John Willoughby
76 John Wallace
77 Joseph Judkins
78 John Smith
79 Richard Gammon
80 Bryant Corbet
81 Richmon Cobb
82 William Braddy
83 John Teal, jun
84 Samuel Williams
85 Elisha Braddy
86 Frederick Barfield

87 Micajah Teal
88 Allen Mayo
89 William Thomas
90 Benjamin Bell
91 Simpson Meeks
92 Frederick Sommerlin
93 John Thomas
94 Alvin Mayo
95 Elisha Taylor
96 William Downs
97 Henry Jolley
98 Henry Moore
99 Solomon Harriss
100 Richard Carson
101 Amos Pelet

102 John Cox
103 James Wilson
104 Henry Cannon
105 William Emery
106 Edmond Evans
107 James Whitehead
108 William Brooks
109 Hugh Pritchett
110 John Barnhill
111 Willie Gurganus
112 Henry Barnhill
113 Edward Acrey
114 Jonathan Briley
115 John Bullock

MARTIN COUNTY.

1
2
3 Lemuel Ballard
4 Obediah Bullock
5 James Belflower
6 Barnaby Brown
7 Redding Brown
8 Zachariah Browney
9 Hardie Cobb
10 Littleberry Carlisle
11 Harrod Craft
12 Jesse Cow, jr
13 Jonathan Callaway
14 John Douglas
15 Wright Evans
16 Michael Ellis
17 Jesse Griffin
18 Edward Griffin
19 Joshua Griffin
20 John Haislip
21 Branson Haislip
22 William Hassel
23 Joshua Hodge
24 Edward Hardison
25 Jesse Harrel
26 Benjamin F Hallsey

27 Theophilus Jenkins
28 Lemmuel James
29 Lovett Lanier
30 Josephus Moore
31 Ith Medford
32 Marcum Manning
33 Mathew Pickolson
34 Simon Perry
35 John Petty
36 William Pennywell
37 Hardy B Price
38 John Quin
39 William Roebuck
40 Reddick Rawls
41 Abraham Rawls
42 Joshua Robinson jr
43 Josiah Rogerson
44 Bond Stawls
45 Joel Smithwick
46 Reuben Salenger
47 William Swain
48 James Swain
49 Samuel Spruel
50 David Wynns
51 Henry Wynns
52 George Wynns

EDGECOMBE COUNTY—FIRST REGIMENT.

1
2
3 Abraham Taylor
4 Amos Walston
5 Allin Balton
6 Brient Evens
7 Benjamin Larder
8 Benjamin Granthon
9 Bryant Little
10 Bryant Stallons
11 Burwell Page

12 Culin Andrews
13 Dempsey Owens
14 Dempsey Gardner
15 Edwin Sherwood
16 Edward Amison
17 Eanos Askin
18 Elisha Jones
19 Ephraim Wooton
20 George Moore
21 George H Killibrew
22 Henry Waller

23 Henry Wooten
24 Isaac Scarborough
25 James Harman
26 Hilliard Thomas
27 Jonathan Thomas
28 Jordan Bruce
29 Jacob Barnes
30 Jonas Williford
31 Joshua Taylor, jun
32 Joseph Farmer
33 Jacob Sims
34 John Evins
35 John Sharpe
36 Joseph Pittman
37 James Tart
38 Jeremiah Horne
39 Joseph Ruffin
40 John Holomon
41 John Thespin
42 Joshua Killibrue
43 Joseph Page, jun
44 James Ambrose
45 John Dowdin

46 Joseph Ansley
47 James Norvil
48 Jessy Morris
49 Lawrence Page
50 Lewis Peele
51 Marshal White
52 Martin B Horne
53 Mills Harvil
54 Moses Moore
55 Perry White
56 Hobbert Coleman
57 Robert Long
58 Richard Singleton
59 Samuel R Jenkins
60 Thomas Dixon
61 Thomas Morris
62 Thomas Barrow
63 Uriah Stallings
64 William Dixon
65 Whitmel C Bullock
66 William Webb
67 William Singleton

EDGECOMBE COUNTY—SECOND REGIMENT.

1
2
3 William P Coleburn
4 William Savage
5 Maurice Redmond
6 John Parker
7 Stephen West
8 Robert Broadstreet
9 James Griffis
10 Berry Brown
11 Lott Killibrew
12 Laden Abrahams
13 Luke Nowells
14 Daniel Conner
15 James Cobb
16 John Anderson
17 John Moon
18 John Knight
19 Drury Mayo
20 Charles Knight, jun
21 Hardy Harrill
22 Geraldus Batts
23 Littlebury Edwards
24 David Pender
25 Thomas Hayner
26 James Everitt
27 William Bayton
28 James Taylor
29 James Rainer
30 Reading Crisp
31 Moulden Loops
32 Jesse Turner
33 Michael Horn
34 J Jolly Horn

35 James Williams
36 Vincen Vaughn
37 Elijah Jackson
38 Robert Barnes
39 John Hines
40 Joseph Stallions
41 John Penney
42 David Lain
43 James Foreman
44 John Garrock
45 Jason Matthews
46 William Armstrong
47 John Sarsnot
48 James Mayo
49 Kenneth Coopper
50 Lewis Purvis, jun
51 Stancel Hoard
52 Thomas Wiggins, jun
53 William Exum
54 James Petman
55 Thomas Jones
56 Book Dickson
57 Levi Denton
58 John Lain
59 Joseph Sessums
60 Spier Bradley
61 Stephen White
62 Archibald Pope
63 Reuben Taylor
64 John Spyva
65 Thomas Strickland
66 William Kea
67 Joseph Loyd

WAYNE COUNTY.

1 John Flowers, *captain*
2 Hilliary Hooks, 1st *lieutenant*
3 Major Blont, 2nd *do*
4 David Thompson, 3d *do*
5 Willis Hall, *ensign*
6 Henry Roberts
7 Burwell Martin
8 Jeremiah Smith
9 John Wasdon
10 Thomas Beard
11 Pearce Brogden
12 Kenrard Holland
13 Matthew Gennet
14 Bryan Bradberry
15 Joseph Smith
16 Jesse Taylor
17 Caleb Howell
18 Edward York
19 Anson Gurly
20 Raiford Wiggs
21 Lewis Forehand
22 John Hardy
23 Jethro Barns
24 Simon Barns
25 Hermant Hooks
26 Joseph Ware
27 Miles Lamb
28 William Bass
29 Cornelius Durden
30 Levi Winflet
31 Ransom Comanch
32 Samuel Barns
33 Elisha Devoun
34 Bryan Bass
35 John Mitchell
36 Lewis Powell
37 Joel Ellis
38 Noah Bass
39 Johnston Corbet
40 Michael Watson
41 John Skipper
42 Ephraim Grant
43 Kelly Creamer
44 Joseph Smith
45 Samuel Pope
46 Richard Langston
47 Miles Rodford
48 Thomas Grant
49 Richard Ivy
50 James McCullin
51 Jesse Warturs
52 Bryan Rhodes
53 Bryan Pipkin
54 Arthur Pearce
55 James Britt
56 Henry Cannon
57 William Atwill
58 Rolen Coley
59 Williams Bundy
60 Joshua Fletcher
61 William Ham
62 Taylor Smith
63 Henry Britt
64 Henry Ham
65 Wm Landcaster
66 William Lasser
67 Isaac Hill
68 Henry Boget
69 Everit Thompson
70 Bryan Thompson
71 Richard Worrel
72 Wiley Peacock
73 Handy Alfred
74 Jesey Worrel
75 Matthew Bradford
76 John Thompson
77 James Futcret
78 Jeremiah Bunton
79 James Bartlet
80 John Elventon
81 Richard Wodel
82 Noah Peacock
83 Henry Hare
84 Elisha Cook
85 Nathan Bremon
86 William Deal
87 Simon Peacock
88 Thomas Outland
89 Arthur Bogan
90 John Heath
91 James Bridger
92 Matthew Grace
93 Joseph Herring
94 James Tindal
95 John Harrass
96 William Kelly
97 Richard Carey
98 John Cox
99 Richard Kelly
100 Jesse Peacock
101 Rheuben Mitch
102 John Bizzel
103 Sion Granthon
104 William Dunn
105 Jacob Sims

ONSLOW COUNTY—THIRD REGIMENT.

1 William Mitchell, *captain*
2 Titus Howard, 1st *lieutenant*
3 Hardy Pitts, 2nd *do*
4 Lewis Oliver, 3d *do*
5 Hilory Henderson, *ensign*
6 Lott Huffman
7 George Williams
8 James Mills
9 William Calvet
10 Henry Foster
11 Henry Hyde
12 James Strange
13 Charles Cox
14 James Harvey
15 Jesse Wilder
16 Thomas Hawkins
17 Absalom Barber
18 Stephen Calvet
19 John Brown
20 Hillkiah Horn
21 Nathan Futral
22 Rigdon Whaley
23 Peter Ambrose
24 Edmund Littleton
25 William Parker
26 John Ellis
27 Isaac Simpson
28 Reuben Melton
29 James Barrow
30 Josiah Hawkins
31 Everitt Simmons
32 Edward Kellam
33 Charles Thompson
34 Benjamin Littleton
35 John Murrel
36 John Edmondson
37 Dexter Farnel
38 Hawkins Marshall
39 Kilby Henderson
40 John Enbanks
41 Otway Hawkins
42 Purnal Haskins
43 Robert Caston
44 John Marshall
45 John Morton
46 Enock Haskins
47 John Gibson, jun
48 Ezekiel Enbanks
49 Brice Fields
50 Henry Wells
51 Elijah Enbanks, jun
52 Bryan Barber
53 John Gilbert
54 Jos Collins, jun
55 William Gibson, jun
56 William Carraway
57 John Garrett
58 Richard Simmons
59 Alexander Gray
60 Edmund Milson
61 Solomon Davis
62 Josiah Ward
63 Elijah Taylor
64 William Bell
65 Charles Scott
66 James Hurst
67 Jesse Hardison
68 John Edens
69 Samuel Nicholas
70 Peter Venters
71 Leckariah Evins
72 Laben Justice
73 Simon Hobbs
74 Whitlift Casten
75 Frederick Mills
76 John Shepard
77 James Lloyd
78 Lewis Thompson
79 Thomas King
80 Jesse Fryer
81 John Higgs
82 George Hinkley
83 William Sammons
84 John Goints
85 David Horn
86 Henry Milton
87 Edward W Shiver
88 Hosiah Clark
89 Josiah Fayles
90 Moses Jinkins
91 James Baker
92 Ohed Eason
93 William A Pearce
94 James Oman
95 Daniel Mashborn
96 Henry Howard
97 William Orme
98 Thomas Fryer
99 John Bell
100 Samuel Howard
101 John Jones
102 David Riggs
103 James Caston
104 Jackariah Jackson
105 Amos Goints

NEW HANOVER COUNTY.

1 Montesquien W Campbell, *captain*
2 James Nixon, *lieut*
3 Joel E Larkins, *lieut*
4 William Lewis, *ensign*
5 William McCurdy
6 Stephen Notton
7 Richard Saunders
8 James Larkins
9 Robert Rankin
10 Reuben Loving
11 John Walker
12 Joseph Jones
13 William S Nickols
14 Donald R McLeod
15 Jesse Scarborough
16 Jonathan J Long
17 Moses Sholders
18 William Taylor
19 Aaron Alexander
20 Woodman S Ledbury
21 Joshua McClammy
22 David Eddons
23 Buckner Stokely
24 Jacob Pickett
25 Jeremiah Nickols
26 Thomas Coston
27 William Nixon
28 Robert Nickols
29 Henry King
30 John James
31 Edmond Hansley
32 John Riley
33 James Ratcliff
34 William Revenbark
35 John Wood
36 William George
37 Daniel George
38 Richard Millar
39 Joseph Mumford
40 Robert Larkins
41 John Parker
42 John Beesley
43 Solomon Beesley
44 John Moore
45 John Highsmith
46 Anthony Williamson
47 Hugh Lamb
48 Nickolas Boon
49 Berd Boon
50 Samuel Gerganious
51 William Gerganious
52 James Malfrass
53 John Register
54 Jame Bonbam
55 David Bonbam
56 James Busby
57 Obed Smith
58 Dempsey Powell
59 Francis Devane
60 William Corbet
61 George Corbet
62 James Lee
63 Duncan Sellars
64 Timothy Johnson
65 John Airs
66 Ross Cogdell
67 James Roe
68 Frederic Simpson
69 Luton Orr
70 John Black
71 Benjamin Moore
72 William Malpass
73 George Moore
74 John B Bourdeaux
75 Benjamin Due
76 John Bainhill
77 Timothy Rooks
78 Joseph Rooks
79 Benjamin Mott
80 Morris Bishop
81 William Adkins
82 Daniel Adkinson
83 Fredric Gerganious
84 Thomas Bishop, jun
85 William Robeson
86 Ensign Hinklin
87 Joseph Farrow
88 William Goodman
89 Benjamin Rockell
90 Jacob Castill
91 Alfred Wadkins
92 Lawrence Mason
93 Henry Dickson
94 James Evans
95 Daniel Bucher
96 Gilbert New
97 Hardy Bowen
98 Samuel Straughan
89 Duncan Henderson
100 Daniel Henderson
101 John Taylor
102 Matthew Johnston
103 David Paget
104 Isaac Taylor

BLADEN COUNTY.

1 John Sellars, *captain*
2 John Andres, 1st *lieut*
3 John Andres
4 Matthew Sikes
5 James Sikes
6 Nathaniel Sutton

7 David Sikes
8 Aaron Larkins
9 Peter Cromartee
10 Beatty Sikes
11 Ever McMillan
12 Nehemiah Done
13 Charles Oliver
14 Elisha Baker
15 James Benson
16 Matthew Benson
17 Elijah Smith
18 James Counsel
19 Alfred Sikes
20 William Jones
21 Cornelius' Ray
22 Samuel Smith
23 William Anderson
24 Philemon S Hodges
25 Philip Cheshire
26 James Singletary
27 Morgan Allan
28 John Beard
29 Aaron Plummer
30 Samuel Cain
31 Neil McArthur
32 Colin Monroe
33 Joseph Allan
34 Neil Clark, jun
35 David Perry
36 John Robeson
37 Simon Smith
38 Duncan Clark, jun
39 Angus Clark
40 Willis Hudson
41 David Russ
42 John Mulford
43 Ever McMillan
43 Sion Callum
45 William White
46 Benjamin Singletary
47 William Wood
48 George Russ
49 Willis Singletary
50 Zadock Hillbourne

51 Samuel Pool
52 Henry Hillbourn
53 Abraham Blackwell
54 Jesse Jones
55 William Jones
56 William Robeson
57 Absalom Mairs
58 William McEwen
59 William Mooney
60 Archibald Robeson
61 John Bluie
62 John Lisley
63 Randolph McMillan
64 James Rising
65 William Lewis
66 Daniel McEwen
67 Samuel Singletary
68 John Hair
69 Jonathan Lock
70 Edward Plummer
71 Brayton Singletary
72 John Martin
73 Alexander Watson
74 Richard Taylor
75 Jacob Long
76 Thomas Bedsold
77 Henry Bullard
78 Thomas Davis
79 Lewis Suggs
80 John McDonald
81 Shadrack Wethersby
82 William Smith
83 John New
84 Travis Bedsold
85 Daniel Sellars
86 William Simmons
87 Duke Edge
88 John Smith
89 Arthur Smith
90 John Edwards
91 John Davis
92 Daniel Melvin
93

BRUNSWICK COUNTY.

1 John Bryan, *lieutenant*
2 Thos Flowers, *do*
3 Moses Bruton
4 John Liles
5 William Sellers
6 George Oliphant
7 James Keath
8 George Keath
9 Bennet Flowers
10 William Taylor
11 Samuel Tharp

12 Samuel Hill
13 Meady Osby
14 Henry Rainy
15 Peter Stanaland
16 James Highsmith
17 John Barns
18 Henry Stanaland
19 William Gause
20 Bryan Gause
21 Elisha Sellers
22 John Ward

COLUMBUS COUNTY.

1 Caleb Stephens, *captain*
2 Josiah Powell, *ensign*
3 William Bryan, *private*
4 Armilain Bryan
5 Meskick Wilson
6 Duthan Hammons
7 Dempsey Worrell
8 William Register
9 Jonathan Dial
10 Robert Ward
11 James Campbell
12 Andrew Coleman
13 Henry Coleman
14 John Campbell
15 William Faulk
16 Asa Coleman
17 Elisha Nickols
18 John Gore
19 Levi Stephens
20 Malachiah Hews
21 Hinnant Faulk
22 Joseph Gore
23 Needham Fairfax
24 Jonathan Beech
25 William Flinn
26 Nathaniel Ward
27 William Stubbs
28 Henry Johnston
29 George Stubbs
30 James Lasser
31 John Barefoot
32 John Lasser
33 Arthur Mooney
34 Isaac Dage
35 John Wilson, jun
36 Thomas Faulk
37 John Billberry
38 Shadrick Wilson [*enlisted*]
39 Amos King
40 William Hook
41 Goldsberry Boswell
42 Reuben Stephens
43 Gilbert McKeithan
44 Eli Nobles
45 William Mooney
46 John Addison
47 James Jones
48 William Little
49 Curtis Fields
50 Henry Billbinny
51 Lewis Price
52 John Wilson [*enlisted in U S A*]
53 Austin Innman
54 John Faulks

DUPLIN COUNTY.

1 John E Hussey, *captain*
2 Amos J Walker, 1st *lieut*
3 Abraham Glisson, 2nd *do*
4 John Swinson, 3d *do*
5 John T Grady, *ensign*
6 Charles Bowan
7 William Streets
8 David Teachey
9 Jonathan Allen
10 Caldwell Thalley
11 George Mallard
12 Isaac Allen
13 James Norriss
14 John F Bowey
15 Lemuel Thigper
16 Tobias Fountain
17 William Fountain
18 James Scarborough
19 James Borcy
20 Felic Hancock
21 Nathan Murray
22 Henry Hollingsworth
23 Noah Lanier
24 John Bishop
25 Caleb Ostien
26 Owen Bishop
27 Joseph Brooks
28 John Farrier
29 William Sandler
30 Daniel Kenady
31 David Farrier
32 William Nuthercut, jun
33 Benjamin Pearce
34 William Farrier
35 Joseph Brooks, sen
36 Jonas Jones
37 Nathan Kennady
38 Reding Smith
39 Thomas Davis
40 Jesse Grimes
41 Theophilus Williams
42 James Stuart
43 Richard Matthews
44 Michael Matthews
45 Enock Quin
46 William Macner
47 Felix Sullivan
48 Stephen H Glisson
49 William Hardison
50 Henry Deal
51 Benjamin Herring
52 Theophilus Blount

53 John Beardan
54 William Connerly
55 Henry Moore
56 Lemuel Guy
57 Isaac Gore
58 John Pollock
59 Archibald McCaleb
60 Benjamin Rivenbark
61 John Bennet
62 Solomon Kenady
63 Joel Burnham
64 Daniel Parker
65 John Barfield
66 Bennet Millard
67 Lewis Rouse
68 Daniel Jones
69 Dickson Sullivan
70 Henry Sommerlin
71 Thomas Jones
72 Daniel Swinson
73 Thomas Brock
74 John Swinson
75 Reading Bowden
76 Joseph Sollace
77 Jesse Brock
78 Henry Boyt
79 James Wade

80 Moses Bourdeaux
81 Elam Lea
82 Allen Jones
83 John Hines
84 David Floan
85 Alexander Heath
86 David Brock
87 James Morris
88 John Miller, jun
89 Jacob Mallard
90 Samuel Chambers
91 George Cummings
92 Patrick Ezell
93 Nicholas Rogers
94 Isaac Taylor
95 Samuel Grier
96 Nathan Jones
97 William White
98 Isaac Wilson
99 Byrd Williams
100 John Oneal
101 Stephen Noles
102 Joseph Waller
103 Jacob Taylor
104 Elijah Jones
105 Daniel Cannon

SAMPSON COUNTY.

1 Payton R Parker, *captain*
2 Thomas Sutton, 1st *lieut*
3 Ira Tucker, 2nd *do*
4 Burrel Register, *ensign*
5 James Pennington
6 John Brewer
7 Zackariah Parker
8 Thomas James
9 Cornelius McKay
10 John Cook, jun
11 Levi S Mars
12 Joshua S Mars
13 Zepheniah Parker
14 Felix Merritt
15 Levi Register
16 Manassah Williams
17 Lewis Williams
18 Michael Shurly
19 Aaron Marlin
20 Lowamy Flowers
21 Whitfield Sutton
22 Wiley Merrit
23 Philip Flowers
24 Wm Hope
25 Gabriel Peterson
26 Wm Stephens
27 William Robinson, jun
28 George Robinson, jun

29 William Edge
30 Allen Jones
31 Needham Watkins
32 James Chesnut
33 Joseph Chesnut
34 Joseph Kelly
35 John Boon
36 Abraham Joiner
37 Robert Wilkins
38 James Hall
39 Cornelius Autrey
40 Ezekiel Owens
41 Sherrod Simmons
42 John Faircloth
43 Isom Faircloth
44 Raphial Faircloth
45 Curtis Nillens
46 Juni Pope
47 Thomas Owens
48 John McLewinnen
49 Jesse Carr
50 Thomas Britt
51 Stephen Pope
52 Jonathan Carrold
53 John W Turner
54 Martin Hare
55 Thomas Howard
56 Nathan Williams

57 Nathan Strickland	81 John Tart
58 William Stewart	82 David Rainer
59 Tobias McGee	83 James Wilson
60 James Faircloth	84 Felix Bass
61 Martin Strickland	85 William Williford
62 Matthew Porter	86 James Anderson
63 Elbert Strickland	87 Hardy Warrick
64 Henry Hall	88 Duncan Peterson
65 Drew Daughtery	89 Joseph Lorraman
66 William Goodwln	90 Clemm Sales
67 Hardy Danghtrey	91 Robert Wilson
68 David Strickland	92 Malcom McCorquadale
69 Jonas Quimby	93 David Dudley
70 Michael Hobbs	94 Hugh McQueen
71 Henry Woods	95 Neil Stewart
72 John Royals Owmson	96 Lurrel Mobley
73 Robert Dardin	97 James Rench
74 Nias Waters	98 John Hare
75 Uriah Westbrook	99 James Rainer
76 Green Hill	100 Ervin Jackson
77 Jordan Coats	101 Willlam Chesnut
78 Barney Blackman	102 John Royal [Isom's son]
79 Young Wood	103 Bailey Chesnut
80 John Tallow	104 Owen Page

ROBESON COUNTY—FIRST REGIMENT.

1 John McPhattair, *captain*	34 Willis Jones
2 Duncan Murphy, 1st *lieutenant*	35 Richard Watson
3 James McRee, 2nd *do*	36 Richard Small
4 Jacob Little, 3d *do*	37 John Townsend
5 John McPhaul, *ensign*	38 Burwell Britt
6 Archibald McIntyre	39 Stephen Land
7 Stephen Cumboe	40 John Philips
8 Neil McMillan	41 James Wilcox
9 Jesse Manuel	42 Benjamin Lovet
10 Jesse Pittman	43 William Histers
11 Dempsey Powell	44 Zachariah Pate
12 Aaron Braswell	45 Reuben Musslewhite
13 William Shipwash	46 Charles Pate
14 Elias Bullard	47 Michael Baxley
15 Richard Bullard	48 Joel Stephens
16 Anderson Taylor	49 John Hammons
17 Horny Trawick	50 Cade Barfield
18 James Brassie	51 Albertain Barnes
19 Charles Williams	52 Erick Legget
20 John McNeil	53 Asa Daniel
21 John McDonald	54 James Taylor
22 John Walker	55 Burwell Lee
23 James Watson	56 Giles Herring
24 Peter Nickolson	57 Elijah Pittman
25 Peter Munroe	58 Needham Barfield
26 Malcom McEachern	59 John Parnell
27 Duncan McEachern	60 John Powers
28 Lanchlin McLanchlin	61 Moab Willis
29 Stephen Powell	62 Paul Allen
30 Henry Bullock	63 Thomas Wilson
31 Sterling Powell	64 James Bourne
32 Stephen Ammons	65 Hardy Cox
33 Lalathel Pippin	

ROBESON COUNTY—SECOND REGIMENT.

1
2
3 Willis Baslay
4 Neill Thompson
5 Malcom McRainey
6 Edward Malloy
7 Robert McAlpin
8 James McMillan
9 John McMillan
10 Neel McKennon
11 John Davis
12 Daniel Stewart
13 Daniel McAlpin
14 Hugh Carmickdet
15 Hugh Mathews
16 John Shaw, jun
17 Daniel Ruthoen
18 Elijah Wilks
19 Duncan Smith
20 Hugh McKenzie
21 John McKay
22 Neill Wilkinson
23 Alex McNeill
24 Alex Johnson
25 Archibald McNeel
26 Angus McAlpin
27 Gadi Strickland
28 James Furguson, jun
29 Malcom McAlpin
30 Neil McNeill
31 Daniel Buie
32 Marsh Barlow
33 Hugh McKay
34 Daniel McNeill
35 Hugh McPherson
36 John Smith
37 John Powell
38 John Currie
39 John Farrell
40 Malcom Smith
41 Malcolm McLoud
42 Peter McEacheron

CUMBERLAND COUNTY—SECOND REGIMENT.

1 John Burt, *captain*
2 John Armstrong, 1st *lieut*
3 Murdoch Ochiltree, 2nd *do*
4 Neil McArthur
5 James Cameron
6 Wm Kennaday
7 Archibald Patterson
8 Malcom Clark
9 Duncan McLean
10 Archibald McGregor
11 Murdock McLeod
12 John Morrison
13 Hugh McLean
14 James Huckaby
15 James Ferguson
16 Ica Parker
17 Lewis Walker
18 John Dollihit
19 Young Blanchet
20 Jones Stephen
21 John Knight
22 James Stewart
23 Asey Pearson
24 Asa Matthews
25 Durham Aven
26 Elijah Spencer
27 Henry Urquhart
28 John Eley
29 James Christian
30 Tapley Johnston
31 William Watson
32 Duncan McDongald
33 Hardy Parker
34 Duncan Dorman
35 Wm Smith
36 James Campbell
37 Neil McAllister
38 James Dean
39 Alex McAllister
40 John Evans
41 James Kellin
42 Allen Godwin
43 David Balentine
44 Daniel McLeod
45 George Learcey
46 John Avery
47 John Johnston
48 Jonathan Smith
49 Levie Ennes
50 Leml Searcy
51 Norman Urquhart
52 Norman Urquhart
53 Saml Card

MOORE COUNTY.

1 Wm Dowd, *captain*
2 John Oats, 1st *lieut*
3 Alex McNeill, 2nd *do*
4 John Stuart, *ensign*
5 Archibald Graham
6 John Blackman

N

7 Kenneth Black
8 Ezra Russel
9 Martin Eagle
10 Wm Barrot
11 John Moore [*drummer*]
12 Merriman Ball [*fifer*]
13 James Spicer
14 Daniel Kelley
15 John MacBeth
16 Benjamin Siler
17 Abner Hawser
18 Alex Curry
19 James Curry
20 Peter Kelly
21 Burwell Maples
22 James Ringstaff
23 John Hancock
24 Henry Philips
25 Hugh Kelly
26 Thomas Muse
27 Joseph Johnston
28 Henry Stuts
29 Malcom McCrommon
30 Duncan McLanchlin
31 Kindrick Brickhead
32 William Jinkins
33 John Mac Donald
34 George Ritter
35 Neil Black
36 George Fry
57 John Rouse
38 John McLane
39 Duncan McInnish
40 Angus McNeill
41 Peter Blue
42 Neil McMillan
43 Malcom Buchan
44 John Black
45 Neil Sulivant

46 Joseph Robeson
47 John Morris
48 Martin Thomas
49 John MacIver, jun
50 James Walker
51 Duncan Baker
52 Edward Walker
53 Robert McIver
54 Malcolm MacFarland
55 Martin Dye
56 Bartholomew Dunn
57 Wm Smith, jun
38 John Gibson
59 Thomas Dunn
60 John Smith
61 William Britt
72 Angus McKennon
63 Wm Jones
64 Daniel Buchan
65 Thomas Keyson
66 Alexander MacLane
67 John Nickolson
68 Dahald Campbell
69 Allen McLeod
70 Wm Milton
71 Daniel Buie
72 Duncan Thompson
73 Duncan McDuffee
74 Wm Brown
75 Gardener Rowling
76 Joseph Owens
77 Wm Smith
78 John Dunlop
79 William Brewer, jun
80 Kindrick Williamson
81 Jacob Ormand
82 Moses Myrick
83 Isaac Teaque
84 Robert Brady

RICHMOND COUNTY.

1 Pleasen M Mask, *captain*
2 Henry Thomas, 1st *lieut*
3 John MacKinnon, 2nd *do*
4 John Carmichael, 3d *do*
5 Shelsby Cobman, *ensign*
6 Thomas H Lewis
7 David D Tedder
8 John Steele
9 John Buck
10 John Kelly
11 Absalom Wall
12 James Gorden
13 William Robeson
14 Joseph Dark
15 Daniel Smith
16 Thomas Cope

17 William Long
18 Isham Shepard
19 Thomas Shepard
20 Culiver Britt
21 Daniel Laslie
22 Israel Luced
23 Moses Overstreet
24 Daniel McLeod
25 Lewis Thomas
26 William Scott
27 Burrel Graham
28 Stephen Herring
29 Benjamin Scott
30 Nehemiah Hadder
31 John Pate
32 Archibald Macgee

33 Silas Norton
34 Benjamin Watkins
35 Richard Welsh
36 John Webb, jun
37 Jacob Lampley
38 Alexander Oliver
39 Moses Watkins
40 Thomas Serjiner
41 Daniel Munroe
42 Malcolm Morrison
43 John Quick
44 Neill Laslie
45 Alexander McCall
46 Alexander Martin
47 Archibald McCattum, jun
48 John MacDonald
49 Dugal MacDuffie
50 Archibald Graham, jun
51 John Leech
52 Dugal Leech
53 John Morrison
54 Jonn McQuain

55 Miles K Well
56 Norman Campbell
57 Alex Cunningham
58 Noah Sanderford
59 Vincent Rainwater
60 Roland Hammons
61 John Powell
62 Eli MacDonald
63 John MacInnis
64 Gooden Capell
65 Huncan MacRae
66 Alfred Balding
67 George Dawkins
68 Duncan Cunningham
69 Alexander Gordon
70 Landerford Loving
71 Briant Loving
72 Archibald McCabler
73 Alex Cunningham
74 John Stewart
75 Isham Scott

ANSON COUNTY—FIRST REGIMENT.

1 Benjamin A Laniere, *captain*
2 Thomas Godfrey, 1st *lieut*
3 Gideon Threadgill, 2nd *do*
4 John Lockhart, 3rd *do*
5   , *ensign*
6 Nathaniel Hales
7 John Legoe
8 Micajah Dawkins
9 James Runnols
10 Joshua Legoe
11 Hugh Monroe
12 John Martin
13 John F Russell
14 Theophilus Hopgood
15 Joseph Parish
16 Ezekiel Wynn
17 Abner Beverly
18 Emanuel Courtney
19 Henry Gullidge
20 Leroy Pounds
21 Isaac Boggaw
22 Thomas Ward
23 William Davis
24 William Taylor
25 Philip Gathings
26 William Howell
27 John Howell
28 John Patterson
29 Daniel McKay
30 Willis Struter
31 William Dilport
32 James Short

33 John Hopkins
34 John Hinson, jun
35 John Harrington
36 Daniel May
37 Daniel MacRae
38 John Plunkett
39 John Launcan
40 Daniel Murphy
41 Elias Best
42 Charles Gathings
43 William Johnson
44 Axum Turner
45 Burwell Messer
46 Freeman Winkfield
47 Jeremiah Messer
48 Jacob Pope
49 Peyton Lunsford
50 Richard McBride
51 Shadrick Brazil
52 Wright Lee
53 John Lockhart
54 John Gewin
55 John Ingram
56 Thomas Smith
57 Wm Vandiford
58 Angus Murchison
59 Joel Hamn
60 John Morel
61 William Wallace
62 Jonathan Boggan
63 Jesse McLindon
64 Jesse Little

65 Wm Bailey, jun
66 Colin Evans
67 John Cockran
68 Ashur Myres
69 William Rivers
70 William McDonald

71 Needham Eddins
72 Enock Little
73 Levi Medor
74 John H German
75 Isaac Morce

ANSON COUNTY—SECOND REGIMENT.

1 Obadiah Curbee, *captain*
2 Solomon Trull, 1st *lieut*
3 James White, 2nd *do*
4 Stephen Rushing, 3d *do*
5 Hardy Harton, *ensign*
6 Abraham Griffin
7 Saunders Taylor
8 John Parker
9 William Trull
10 William Gurly
11 Solomon Tragall
12 Thomas Trull
13 Joel Williams
14 Charlton Joiner
15 Enock Griffin
16 Moses Pearce
17 Horantio Rosser
18 Reuben White
19 Thomas Jones
20 John Meggs
21 John Jones
22 Asa Pearce
23 John Lassiter
24 John Davis
25 Jesse Green
26 John Wm Thomas
27 Philip Hagler
28 David Tomerlin
29 Nathaniel Bibby
30 William Shelby
31 David Medcalf
32 Joseph Price
33 Jordan Drake

34 Joshua Hudson
35 Wyatt Nance
36 William Hatcher
37 James Bawcom
38 Jephthah Beverly
39 James Dunn
40 Hansel Horn
41 George Hobbs
42 Isaac Williams
43 John Hyatt
44 James Hill
45 George Nash
46 Willis Williams
47 David Allen
48 John Wilkerson
49 William Morgan
50 Elijah Cook
51 John Holifield
52 Joel Meador
53 George Duran
54 Thomas Moss
55 Isham Harrell
56 David Prince
57 Robert Leonard
58 George Williams
59 Elijah Carthedge
60 Wm McMillan
61 Jeremiah Anderson
62 John Jones
63 Charles Trull
64 Stephen Williams
65 David Brumblow

FOURTH REGIMENT.

WAKE COUNTY—FIRST REGIMENT.

1 John Bell, *captain*
2 William Battle, *lieut*
3 Zenas O'Kelly, *ensign*
4 Joel H Lane
5 Wm W Mason
6 William Wiggins
7 Dennis Wilson
8 William M White
9 Charles Gilliam
10 Thomas Hill
11 Thos R Cooke

12 John Vandigriff
13 John Terry
14 Hardy Dodd
15 Charles Stewart
16 Newton Wood
17 Benjamin Brantly
18 Charles Johnson
19 Williams Damsell
20 James Reddish
21 John Luced
22 John Smith

23 John Andrews
24 John Cooke
25 Isham McGee
26 Wm Buffalo
27 Thomas Neal
28 Lewis Bunn
29 Harris Liles
30 Robert Hicks
31 Bennet Brown
32 Reuben Mitchell
33 Thomas Williams
34 Micajah Wall
35 Charles Horton
36 William Learcey
37 Berry Ambrous
38 John Butter
39 Hardy Peane
40 William Boyakin
41 Budd Bagwell
42 Dickson Jordan
43 Burwell Fowler
44 William Hopkins
45 Mark Cole
46 Reddick Massey
47 Jedemiah Pulley
48 John Jones
49 Isaac Massey
50 Benjamin Marriott
51 William Reddish
52 Jerrod Chamblee
53 Budd Bunn
54 Wm Philips
55 John Perry
56 Henry Culpepper
57 Robert B Williams
58 Seth Jones
59 Hinton Pugh
60 John Leopard
61 Elie Alford
62 Samuel Landiford
63 Bennet Perry

64 William Clark
65 William Reaves
66 Thomas Garrott
67 Shadrack Bolar
68 Josiah Battle
69 Brittain Acock
70 Thos Alston
71 David Williams
72 Simon Williams
73 Peter Porter
74 James Williams
75 Samuel Sugg
76 Acril Myatt
77 Ephraim Messer
78 Wm Rand
79 Wm Roads
80 Hardy McGuffe
81 Willie Pollard
82 Wm Canwadd
83 Samuel Slaughter
84 Jacob Baltin
85 Henry Smith
86 Osbourn Jordan
87 Bryan Ferrill
88 Hardy Lewis
89 Ansel Price
90 Brittain Deloach
91 Bennet Bawcom
92 David Hutchins
93 William Todd
94 Jesse Fason
95 John Traywick
96 Simon Stephens
97 Joseph Shaw
98 Johnson Britt
99 Samuel Jones
100 David Slawson
101 Allen Parker
102 William King
103 Thomas Spiar

WAKE COUNTY—SECOND REGIMENT.

1 John Green, *captain*
2 Willis Whitaker, 1st *lieut*
3 Joseph Barbee, 2nd *do*
4 Jephthah Tyrrell, 3d *do*
5 John W Lee, *ensign*
6 Alexander Smith
7 Allen Jones
8 Aaron Matthis
9 Alsey Yates
10 Anda Burges
11 Asa Blake
12 Abner Green
13 Anthony Bledsoe
14 Alfred Wilkins

15 Absalom Hayes
16 Aquilla Hubbard
17 Bradford Jones
18 Burwell Brown
19 Britain Smith
20 Benjamin Ashworth
21 Britain Mills
22 Benjamin Davis
23 Christopher Woodard
24 Christopher Spier
25 Daniel Jackson
26 Daniel Matthis
27 Dawson Adkinson
28 Eldah Brown

29 Edward Bledsoe
30 Ewell Watts
31 Francis Jones
32 Gideon Vaughn
33 Green Hill
34 Hillsman King
35 Henry Haley
36 Hillsman Parish
37 Hinton Courtis
38 Henry Moore
39 Harwell Sims
40 James King
41 John Tedrick
42 Jacob Vandigriff
43 Isham Olive
44 Joseph H Hill
45 Joseph Woodard
46 John W Lee
47 John Crocker
48 John Peddy
49 John Betts
50 John Fadgett
51 John Surls
52 Jacob Sorrel
53 John Luallen
54 James Walker
55 Johnston Loyd
56 John Carpenter
57 John Moore
58 John Jarral
59 James Thompson
60 Jonathan Hall
61 James Estes
62 John Geer
63 John Holloway
64 John Ward
65 Isham Goodwin
66 John Marshall
67 James Rigsby

68 John Edwards
69 Kinchen Griffin
70 Laban Jones
71 Martin Mann
72 Mordecai Joplin
73 Mathews Goodwin
74 Major Bradley
75 Nash Standley
76 Neal Womble
77 Peyton Norris
78 Robert Ray
79 Robert Glenn
80 Stephen King
81 Samuel Narris
82 Sion Uutly
83 Stephen Seagroves
84 Seth Sexton
85 Stephen Pearson
86 Samuel Reaves
87 Timothy W Jones
88 Thomas Dennis
89 Thomas Edwards
90 Thomas Laffoon
91 Wm Evans, jun
92 William Silvey
93 Westley Jones
94 William Woodard
95 William Braker
96 William Eves
97 William Yates
98 Ridley Jones
99 William King
100 Walter Marshal
101 William Harris
102 Willie Harrison
103 Woodson Allen
104 William Marshall
105 Young Allen, jun

JOHNSTON COUNTY.

1 Harry Bryan, *captain*
2 Thomas J Walton, 1st *lieut*
3 David Bryan, 2nd   *do*
4 Hardy Pool, *ensign*
5 Hartwell Ivey, 1st *sergt*
6 Young Allen, 2nd   *do*
7 David Bridgers, 3d *do*
8 Godfrey Stansill, 4th *do*
9 Rice Price, *fifer*
10 Futrill Cockrett, *drummer*
11 Ambrose Ingram
12 William Johnson
13 Averytt Holston
14 Nelson Andrews
15 Burwell Blackburn
16 Thomas Price

17 Allen Watson
18 Martin Price
19 James Smith
20 Bridgers Porch
21 John Brown
22 William Pullen
23 Larkin Smith
24 Joel H Atkinson
25 Dixon Philips
26 William Willons
27 John Patterson, jun
28 John Evans
29 Henry Capps
30 William Braddy, jun
31 William Edwards
32 Noel West

33 John Hobby
34 Hartwell Ivey
35 William Jones
36 James Ivey
37 Elisha Stanley
38 Benjamin Stephens
39 James Dozier
40 John Woodall
41 Moses Johnson
42 Alexander Woodall
43 Sion Hill
44 Samuel Wilder, jun
45 John Nawl
46 Eunuch Whitley
47 James Hinton
48 Theophilus Biddingfield
49 John Cooper
50 John Pullen
51 Wm Cockrill
52 Isaac Keen
53 Stephen Williamson
54 William Watson
55 Edmond Balance
56 Arthur Pearce
57 Stephen Lasser
58 John Lamb
59 Silas Horn
60 Nathan Morris
61 Samuel Mitchiner
62 Wm Thompson
63 Wm Farrow
64 Asa Learcey
65 Osborn Howell
66 John Powell
67 Samuel Learcey
68 Nathaniel Hood
69 Lewis Tiner
70 Irvin Price, jun
71 George Bayett

72 Micajah Oneal
73 Jacob Peacock
74 Willie Price
75 John Eatman
76 Stephen Oneal
77 Stephen Price
78 Willie Hall
79 John Stansill, jun
80 Jonathan Austin
81 Nathaniel Jones
82 Alexander Franklin
83 Jacob Vincent
84 Zadock Gower
85 Willis Hayes
86 Benjamin Stephenson
87 William Stephenson
88 Wm Snipes
89 Thomas Frail
90 Jonathan Baker
91 Willie Junigan
92 Nathan Almond
93 John Jordan
94 Joseph Bryan
95 Edward Stevens
96 James Brown
97 Lewis Smith
98 William Noals
99 John Warwick
100 John Kelly, jun
101 John Turner, jun
102 Abner Smith
103 Jesse Ellington
104 Theophilus Pool
105 Reddin Johnson
106 Isaac Pinney
107 Alsey Busby
108 Elisha Redding
109 James Pool
110 Willie Jones

FRANKLIN COUNTY.

1 Jones Cook, *captain*
2 Sherrod Sanders, *lieut*
3 Benjamin Carpenter, *ensign*
4 Hicks Wynne
5 Nathan Patterson
6 Jeremiah Solomon
7 John B Debnam
8 Richard Caisar
9 Micajah T Cotten
10 Samuel Johnson
11 William Asque
12 James Langon
13 Peter Denton
14 William Denton
15 Solomon Perry
16 MacKollach Stone

17 Thomas Gay
18 Charles Hines
19 Willis Peale
20 Arthur Fassel
21 Charles Coppage
22 John Nelms
23 Jones Walker
24 Jesse Winston
25 Robert Robertson
26 Nathaniel Nickolson
27 William Duke
28 Ransom Brogdon
29 William Browning
30 Reuben Neale
31 David Cook
32 Benjamin Priddie

33 John Arnolds
34 Benjamin Thomas
35 Joseph Bledsoe
36 George Bledsoe
37 William Murphree
38 Patrick Bledsoe
39 Miles King
40 Thomas Driver
41 James Upchurch
42 William Owens
43 John Bell
44 Isaac Griffin
45 Banister Peppin
46 Berkely Upchurch
47 Richard Spivey
48 William T Hollingsworth
49 Elisha Sandeford
50 William Phelps
51 James Medlin
52 William Sanders
53 James Cooley
54 John Harriss
55 Jos Young
56 Jacob Alford
57 Henry Harriss
58 Nathaniel Williams
59 John Deuglas
60 Isaac House
61 John B Bobbit
62 John Dickson
63 James H Murry

64 James Graham
65 Sugar McLemore
66 James Moore
67 Wm Loyd
68 John Merrit
69 Wm Pulliam
70 Thomas Wise
71 James Wiggins
72 Joseph Pleasants
73 Joseph Heltan
74 John Fuller
75 John Hornsby
76 Malachi Simmons
77 Jeremiah Cook
78 James C Jones
79 Caswell Finch
80 Josiah Jackson
81 Dickson Cour
82 Oram Jackson
83 Peyton Tunstall
84 John Gill
85 Turner Gupton
86 James Nelms
87 Jacob Gupton
88 John Cook
89 Joel Parish
90 Benjamin Hamm
91 Willie Alford
92 John Farmer
93 Robert Cary

GRANVILLE COUNTY—FIRST REGIMENT.

1 Willis Johnson, *captain*
2 Wm Nailing, *lieut*
3 William Mann, *ensign*
4 Absalom Parish
5 Lemuel Kittrell
6 Micajah Harris
7 John Inscore
8 Anthony Moore
9 Malachiah Frazer
10 Edward Sutton
11 Richard Harris
12 Harrel Wiggins
13 John Wiggins
14 James Conway
15 Beriman Ham
16 Wm W Reavis
17 Alfred Hicks
18 Joshua Archer
19 Edward Bryant
20 James Bryant
21 David McGlanklin
22 William Warrels
23 Reuben Harris
24 Egrippy Nance

25 Gideon H Macon
26 Thomas White
27 James Tate
28 John Floyd
29 Green B Walker
30 Dick H Dalby
31 Zachariah Lyon
32 James Bowers
33 Taswell Spain
34 Littleton Spain
35 Alexander Walters
36 Nathaniel M Taylor
37 James Suite
38 Joseph Hister
39 Wm Brogdon
40 Leonard Bullock
41 John Haley
42 James Arnold
43 Ezekiel Wheeler
44 Gideon Davis
45 Edward Chappel
46 Joseph Lysle
47 Burges Walls
48 John Stephenson

49 Samuel Forsythe
50 Archibald Mitchell
51 Wm McFarland
52 Micajah Dally
53 Thomas Forsythe
54 Jeremiah King
55 John Adams
56 William Adams
57 John Fuller
58 Abner Fletcher
59 Hezekiah Jones
60 James Allison
61 Gilliam McGehe

62 James Cook
63 Gilford Ball
64 Washington Womouth
65 Dempsey Brown
66 Willie Jones
67 Winkfield Morgan
68 Gideon Gill
69 Isham Huskey
70 Barnett Jeter
71 John W Finch
72 William Hiflin
73 James B Eustis

GRANVILLE COUNTY—SECOND REGIMENT.

1
2
3
4 George Parker
5 John P Beasly
6 Matthew Chandler
7 Robert Blackwell
8 Anderson Satterwhite
9 William Amos
10 John Whitamore
11 Francis Oliver
12 Robert Hester
13 James Smith
14 George Lumpkin
15 Joseph Ames
16 Graves Hart
17 Robert Knott
18 James Falconer
19 John Finch
20 Bird Lofter
21 Robert Lewis
22 Samuel Lewis
23 Bussee Lewis
24 Charles Yancey
25 Samuel Daniel
26 John Royster
27 John J Inge
28 Wm Martin
29 James Lewis, jun
30 Richard Brown
31 Willis Hanks
32 Thomas Grissom
33 Thomas Terry
34 Nathaniel Roberson
35 John Hanks
36 John Dorch
37 Laban Grissom

38 John Cretcher
39 Archibald Gordon, jun
40 Allen Jones
41 Wm Longmire, jun
42 William Frazier
43 Larkin Curren
44 Thomas Morris
45 John Sander
46 Alfred Hester
47 Richard Lemay
48 Samuel Ussery
49 Thomas Rice
50 Evan Raglin
51 Richard Ball
52 Abner Hicks
53 James K Clark
54 Pumphrett Gooch
55 Abraham Eastwood
56 Simon Clements
57 John Hopkins
58 Riley Meadows
59 Elkanah Lyon
60 John Dodson
61 Young Montague
62 Bennet Foster
63 Ephraim Frazier
64 Thomas Hunt
65 John Cobs
66 Anthony Wood
67 John Duncan
68 Woodson Washington
69 Daniel Tucker
70 John Bowls
71 Jordan Bowls
72 Thomas Hayes
73 Benjamin Hester

PERSON COUNTY.

1 John Bradshaw, *captain*
2 William Bagley, 1st *lieut*

3 Bradshaw Fuller, 2nd *lieut*
4 Jeremiah Dixon, *ensign*

5 John Scoggin
6 Morgan Fitts
7 Elijah O'Briant
8 Robert Carter
9 Samuel Wheeler
10 John Russel
11 Downey Wade
12 John Riggs
13 Samuel Burke
14 Richard Broach
15 Robert Jones
16 Churchwell Jones
17 Anderson Jones
18 James Jones
19 Mark Glenn
20 Daniel Meadows
21 Richard Farrar
22 Samuel Mangrum
23 Riley Suit
24 Caswell Vaughan
25 Jeremiah Roberts
26 Wm Cates
27 Seth Coleman
28 James Cozort
29 Daniel Hicks
30 Ambrose Day
31 Ambrose Dary
32 Archibald Day
33 Grant Allen
34 James Hay
35 John Parrot
36 Wyatt Painter
37 Wm Bumpass
38 Thomas Gill
39 Wm Elliot
40 Josiah Oliver
41 Gilliam Mitchell
42 Peter Warren
43 Pleasant Hall
44 John Harralson

45 Archibald Harralson
46 Wm Martin
47 George Berry
48 Edward Johnston
49 James Johnston
50 Richard Jones
51 David Bell
52 James Bradshaw
53 Henry Worsham
54 Henry Lipscomb
55 James Dollerhide
56 Vincent Bradshaw
47 Vincent Lea
58 McFarland Oakley
59 Samuel Winstead
60 Wm Royster
61 Reuben Lea
62 Wm Southward
63 Richard Harris, sen
64 Drury A Pulliam
65 Thomas Marit
66 Joseph M Stanfield
67 Ransom Austin
68 John Brooks
69 Samuel Bull
70 Drury Pulliam
71 Daniel Rease
72 John Jas Brooks
73 Allen Green
74 Henry Bailey
75 John Buckanan
76 Daniel Walker
77 Thos Townsen
78 Wm Buckanan
79 Wyatt Ford
80 John Wilkerson
81 Hastin Blalock
82 Wm Mann
83 Wm Hill
84 Benjamin Sampson

ORANGE COUNTY—FIRST REGIMENT.

1 John Young, *captain*
2 Arthur Bobbit, *lieut*
3 Isaiah Davis, *ensign*
4 James Linsey
5 Elijah Hunt
6 Alfred McDaniel
7 John Cummins
8 Thos Ward
9 Wm Ringstaff
10 James Guttis
11 John Crabtree
12 Wm Wllson
13 Lemuel Carrol
14 Green Williams
15 Joseph Proctor

16 Levy Cole
17 Timothy Cate
18 Isaac Wood
19 Archibald Carrington
20 Thomas Cate
21 Wm Carrington
22 Zilmon Allison
23 Jos McCullock
24 John L Woods
25 Jesse Clark
26 John Jordan
27 David Ray
28 Green Richards
29 James Lindsey
30 Wm Herndon

31 Edmond Linch
32 John Browning
33 John Carden
34 Bartlet Hinchey
35 May Desern
36 John Scarlett
37 John Hutchins
38 James Raney
39 Daniel Boothe
40 George Nickolas
41 Wm Woods
42 Hugh Riggs
43 John Woods
44 Bradley Collins
45 Robert Turrentine
46 Jesse McGee
47 Carter Garrard
48 Wilie Sweaney
49 Mark Oakley
50 Harrison Parker
51 George Moore
52 John Taylor
53 Willis Roberts
54 Amos Nickolas
55 John Garrard
56 Arthur Stephens
57 Charles Roberts
58 Ephraim Carrington
59 Thornton McFarland
60 James Stagg
61 John Roberts
62 James Parish
63 Levi Owens
64 John Tilly
65 Robert Clinton
66 Wiley Glenn
67 Canady Horton

68 Joshua Horton
69 Westly Rhodes
70 Lewis Hutchins
71 Moses Dorsett
72 Delamy Chizenhall
73 Daniel Holden
74 James Browning
75 Laney Chizenhall
76 Samuel Strayhorn
77 Anderson Whithead
78 Benjamin Haswell
79 Newcomb Thompson
80 Pleasant Herndon
81 James Whithead
82 Edward McDade
83 Thomas Ruffin
84 James Thompson
85 Morris Henderson
86 Thomas Walker
87 David Strain
88 Thomas Gattis
89 Joseph Dawson
90 Bennet Pattin
91 Patterson Yeargin
92 Wm Kirkland
93 Lewis Pattin
94 Andrew McCauley
95 James Woods
96 Willis Marcomb
97 Drury Leigh
98 John Browning
99 Asa Brown
100 Thos Luter
101 James Shepard
102 Daniel Holden
103 Willie Marcomb

ORANGE COUNTY—SECOND REGIMENT.

1 David Tate, *captain*
2 Joseph Allison, *lieut*
3 Egbert Shepherd, *ensign*
4 Wm Mabane
5 George Mebane
6 Henry Mulhollan
7 Allan Mebane
8 Thomas Tinnon
9 Burk Walker
10 Robert Smith
11 Robert Shanklin
12 Samuel Gilston
13 Alex Criswell
14 Thomas Finnen
15 Thomas Woods
16 Hunter McCulloch
17 Will Campbell
18 Joseph Smith

19 Larkin Sanders
20 Thos McClushy
21 John Bain
22 Walter Murray
23 John Wilson
24 Wesley Carson
25 Walker Pickett
26 James Davis
27 Robt Dickee
28 Barnabas Perry
29 William Wilson
30 William Price
31 George Jordan
32 Frederick Bason
33 Sterling Price
34 Alex Lasly
35 John Woody
36 James Grimes

37 Wm Clendinen
38 Wm Stewart
39 Elisha Pickhart
40 John Thompson [miller]
41 James Pindar
42 James Thompson, jun
43 Thomas Rhadshaw, sen
44 Simon Buckum
45 Matthew Tutral
46 David Ray
47 Jesse Ray
48 Samuel Kirkpatrick
49 Berry Duke
50 Stephen Glass
51 Alex Patten
52 James Webb
53 Erasmus Compton
54 Leroy Acros
55 Alfred Compton
56 Jeremiah Compton
57 Robert Faucett
58 Eli Faucett
59 Anderson Faucett
60 Thos Millington
61 Andrew Murray
62 Peter Belvin
63 Joshua Ward
64 Thomas Ward
65 Richard Hayes

66 Jesse Pickhart
67 Thos Durham
68 Benj Cruchfield
69 Richard Cate
70 Richard Workman
71 Green O Daniel
72 James Minnis
73 Wm Workman
74 Alex NayBo
75 Alex NayUts
76 Reuben Owens
77 Thos Moore
78 Thos Durham
79 Thos Williams
80 James Weaver
81 Wm Beaver
82 George Haywood
83 James Crabtree
84 Wm Caven
85 Wm Ivey
86 James Miles
87 Wm Brewer
88 Thos Cate
89 Anderson Blackwood
90 Benj Bridges
91 Jasper Glawson
92 John Fowler, *drummer*
93 John Webb, *fifer*

ORANGE COUNTY—THIRD REGIMENT.

1 James Grahams, *captain*
2 Wm Holt, *lieut*
3 Absalom Harvey, *ensign*
4 Henry Holt
5 Thos Powell
6 David Parks
7 Isaac Rainey
8 Jacob Whitsell
9 Richard Wilkins
10 Jeremiah Grant [son of John]
11 James Faddis
12 Jacob Albright
13 Charles Webster
14 Alex McDaniel
15 Joseph Albright
16 John McDaniel
17 George Ephland
18 Wm Hashford
19 Wm Caps
20 Joseph Smith
21 Nickolas Troxler
22 John Troxler
23 John Coe
24 James Wilson
25 Barney Troxler
26 Oliver Powell

27 Anderson Thompson
28 Simpson Harris
29 Avery Coe
30 Daniel Theek
31 George Spoon
32 Frederick Moser
33 John Wells
34 John Kimbro
35 Stephen Wells
36 Wm Thompson
37 John Ray
38 Philip Rose
39 Ezekiah Hendley
40 George Martinn
41 Robert Fausett
42 Wm Cooke
43 Thos Rumbley
44 Wm Jones
45 Joseph West
46 Nathaniel Jones
47 Robert Lackey
48 Joseph Hughes
49 George McCulley
50 Andrew McCulley
51 Edmund Branock
52 Alfred Moore

53 Wm Dickey
54 James Jackson
55 James Busick
56 James Burnet
57 Levi Kilton
58 James McPherson
59 Jos Marshall
60 Wm Carter
61 Richard Cambel
62 Timothy Weaver
63 George Stafford

64 Caleb Busick
65 Boston Tiley
66 James Melvan
67 Daniel Johnston
68 Jacob Huffins
69 Stephen Willis
70 Zackeriah Philips
1 John Cocke
72 Matthew Cotner
73 Jacob Cockcleress

CHATHAM COUNTY.

1 Aaron Evans, *captain*
2 Richard C Cotten, *lieut*
3 Isaac Headen, *ensign*
4 Mial Ramsey, 1st *serg't*
5 John Taylor, 2nd *do*
6 Wm Underwood, 3rd *do*
7 Wm Duty, 4th *do*
8 Thomas Craver, 1st *corp'l*
9 Stephen Cruchfield, 2nd *do*
10 Asa Stone, 3rd *do*
11 Rufus McMasters, 4th *do*
12 Alex Boyd, *drummer*
13 Henry Harris
14 George Harman
15 Ira Rosson
16 Thos Beal
17 Thos Clark
18 David Blalock
9
20 Jephthy Fooshee
21 Reuben May
22 Allen Goodwin
23 Bennona Rosson
24 Jonathan Lindley
25 John Lewis
26 Jos Blaylock
27 Peter Quakenbush
28 George Rodgers
29 Wm Lea
30 Saml Jackson
31 John Powell
32 Edward Caudle
33 Nathaniel Roberson
34 Richard Cates
35 James Crow
36 Hasten Poe
37 Jos Wilkerson
38 John Glass
39 John Fields
40 Jos Glass
41 Jonathan Green
42 Jonathan Miles
43 Tabner Beal
44 Wm Tilman

45 James Jones
46 Joel Edwards
47 Jesse Bray
48 Samuel Elkins
49 James Limbory
50 John Moorcy
51 Eli Bone
52 John Purvis
53 John Mann
54 John Brown
55 John Brigat
56 Asa Gunter
57 Alex Lassiter
58 Wm Thomas
59 Jourdan Davis
60 Archibald Little
61 John MacIver
62 Thomas Bland
63 Burwell Williams
64 John Clegg
65 Whitmil Little
66 James Ward
67 Charles Johnston
68 Abner Minter
69 Wm Lassater
70 George Drake
71 Alfred Buckannan
72 Robert Wicker
73 Wm Hinton
74 Benj Teddar
75 Stephen Loot
76 Wm Smith
77 Harman Cox
78 Jos Pearson
79 Benj Philips
80 Jesse Hicks
81 Claiborn Deaton
82 Gambol Powers
83 Daniel Brown
84 Tyson Womble
85 Jesse Highland
86 Aaron McMasters
87 Wm Perry
88 Isaac Phillips

89 Isaac Harrington
90 Jos May
91 Ephraim Oldham
92 Henry Fields
93 John Gilman
74 Peter Smith
95 James Burns, jun
96 Wm Smith
97 Joseph Holliday
98 Reuben Reeves
99 Jos Whitehead
100 Elisha Harris
101 Frederick Philips
102 Henry Smith
103 Daniel Smith
104 Rufus MacMasters
105 Nickolas Fox, sen
106 David Vestal, sen
107 Jesse Nelson
108 Nathaniel Whitehead
109 Amos Ward
110 Joseph Allen
111 James Smith
112 John Norwood
113 Hiram Burns [112]
114 John Wesly Bynum, *lieut*
115 John Cocke, *ensign*
116 John Smith, 1st *sergt*
117 Avent Cotten
118 James Thomas
119 Rora Womack
120 John Bowers
121 Thos Williams
122 Joseph Mims

123 Richard Holt
124 Ransom Byrum
125 John Bishop
126 Henry Williams
127 James Boling
128 Thomas Garner
129 Allen Riddle
130 Guilford Garner
131 Green Straughan
132 Samuel Brewer
133 Elbert Williams
134 Watson Mitchell
135 Henry Wilson
136 Wm Pennington
137 Thos M Sturdivant
138 Samuel Wilson
139 Elijah Willis
140 Wilson Willis
141 John Parker
142 Britain Hatley
143 Elijah Bell
144 Jacob Womble
145 Allen Parker
146 John Clark
147 Ruffin Upchurch
148 Allen Rhodes
149 Nickolas Long
150 Robert Council
151 Britain Harwood
152 John A Mason
153 Thomas Oliver
154 Presley Moore
155 James C Barbee

FIFTH REGIMENT.

CASWELL COUNTY.

1 James Holder, *captain*
2 John Johnston, *lieut*
3 John Roan, *ensign*
4 Francis H Burton
5 Wm Eddins
6 James Darby
7 Drucis Briggs
8 Wm P Jackson
9 Thos Dameron
10 Adam Stafford
11 John Tirrell
12 Spencer Ball
13 Wm Nelms
14 Harbert Samuel
15 Archibald Samuel
16 Edward Kersey
17 James Gordon
18 Samuel Johnston
19 Timothy Warren

20 John Hodge
21 Wm Johnston
22 James Johnston [son of Jas]
23 Alex Jackson
24 Charles Connally
25 Giddal Gillaspie
26 Thos Evans
27 James White
28 John Gunn
29 James Ingram
30 Thos Pittard
31 Birditt Escridge
32 Dempsey Sargent
33 Abraham Price
34 James Florence
35 Wm Murry
36 Absalom Burton
37 Christopher Matthews
38 John Love

39 Wm Tolloch
40 Eli Stafford
41 James McCain
42 Noel Burton
43 John Farley
44 Newman Durham
45 David Ball
46 Bird Wisdom
47 Virgil M Rainey
48 James Swann
49 Laban Farland
50 Wm Tirrell
51 Williamson Moore
52 Lewis Tirrel
53 Paul Tirrel
54 Henry Wilson
55 Major Stanfield
56 Henry Mahoon
57 Robert Malone
58 John N Fuller
59 Peter P Stublefield
60 Levi Simpson
61 Thos Brinsfield
62 Philip Eubank
63 Richard Gates
64 James Baldridge
65 Benj B Nelson
66 Luke Sanders
67 John Norris
68 Thos Hobbs
69 Matthew Walker
70 Wiley Mason
71 James Nighton
72 Jos Swann
73 James H Pass
74 Wm W Price
75 John Thompson
76 Robt Ware
77 Thos Penix
78 Joseph Burroughs
79 Thomas Swann
80 David Farley
81 Nathaniel Lea

82 Christopher Dameron
83 John Wray
84 James Thompson
85 Lewis Samuel
86 Abraham Montgomery
87 John Montgomery
88 Rowzee Samuel
89 Wm Randolph
90 George Finlay
91 Thos Turner
92 Isaac Patterson
93 Edley Campbell
94 Wm Fullington
95 Christopher Spencer
96 Jos Swann, jun
97 Robt Yealock
98 John Covington
99 John Mansfield
100 Gabriel B Lee
101 John Woods
102 Nickolas Thompson
103 Anderson Smith
104 Stephen Stuart
105 John Stuart
106 Sandy Smith
107 Wm Culberson
108 John Fitch
109 James Johnston
110 Jesse Corbith
111 David Culberson
112 David Mitchell
113 Oney Randolph
114 Robt Randolph
115 James Underwood
116 Wm Jones
117 Edw Moore
118 Jonson Brooks
119 Edward Wattington
120 James Rozwell
121 Henry Willis
122 Edward Jones
123 James Holdesnes
124 George Brooks, jun

GUILFORD COUNTY—FIRST REGIMENT.

1 Robt McEuiston, *captain*
2 Moses Owens, 1st *lieut*
3 Wm McBride, 2nd *do*
4 Jesser McCurston, *ensign*
5 John Grogan
6 Levi Fosbers
7 Samuel Hillmon
8 James Donnel
9 John McCurston
10 John McCain
11 Wm Adams
12 John Hoskins

13 Amos Page
14 Nathan Lester
15 Caleb Hillmon
16 Wm McCuiston
17 Samuel Kellum
18 Jos Hoskins
19 James Lap
20 Thos Hister
21 Elijah Owen
22 Wm Hutchinson
23 Elisha Coffin
24 Joshua Hillmon

25 Daniel Caulk
26 Aaron Binny
27 Tilmon Clark
28 Robert Burney
29 John Nickolson
30 Wm Claton
31 Lemmuel Oaks
32 James Hutchison
33 James Bevill
34 Taylor Holloway
35 Moses Elliott
36 Henry Bevill
37 James McCuiston
38 Hartwell Knight
39 Turner Irby
40 Jos Simmons
41 Alexander Hutchinson
42 James Loar
43 Ellis Hoskins
44 Isaac White
45 Wm Wilson
46 Wm Dennis
47 Agbert Landingham
48 Wm Knight
49 Robert Spivert
50 Mark Caps
51 Tandy Bell
52 John Starnt
53 Benj Allen
54 Shadrach Allen
55 James Brown
56 Electris Johis
57 Robert Flemming
58 John Perdue
59 Henry Anthony

60 Nickolas Edwards
61 James Tobin
62 Marmon Strawn
63 David Burney
64 Robert Middleton
65 Abraham Burt
66 George Kinnodle
67 Beniah Fleming
68 Hugh McCain
69 Amous Wilson
70 David Madaris
71 Thos Daugherty
72 James Clark
73 Harvey King
74 John Pegram
75 Henry Wilson
76 Garrison Justice
77 Jesse Knott
78 Hooper Caffer
79 James Ross
80 Jasper Gent
81 William Shelby
82 Thomas Parker
83 David Loyd
84 Adam Boyd
85 David Edwards
86 Elias Morgan
87 Robert Russel
88 Samuel Barney
89 George Donner
90 David Allin
91 Henry Clark
92 Wm York
93 Harbert Brown
94 Sutton Taylor

GUILFORD COUNTY—SECOND REGIMENT.

1 Wm Clapp, *captain*
2 Henry Humphreys, *lieut*
3 Robert Ervin, *ensign*
4 Aaron Williams
5 Andrew Garenger
6 Adam Trollenger
7 Andrew Gamble
8 Daniel Geringer
9 David Edwards
10 Ephraim Burrow
11 Enos Frazer
12 Francis Simpson
13 George Sullivan
14 George Stephens
15 Henry Weatherly
16 Henry Camplain
17 Isaac Wolfingtan
18 Isaac Lamb
19 Isaac McDill
20 Jesse Forbes

21 Jacob Hager
22 John Rarden
23 John Amick
24 Jos Shaw
25 Jacob Coble
26 Jacob Greason
27 John Kinman
28 John Fogleman
29 James Foster
30 Zedekiah Smith
31 Jesse Shaw
32 James Grissom
33 John Dickson
34 Jesse Holton
35 Joel Lowden
36 John Boyd
37 John Tucker
38 Joseph Quaits
39 John Ingle
40 Jonathan Short

41 John Murphy
42 James Suduth
43 John Hemphill
44 Leonard Phillippic
45 Major Underwood
46 Martin Fifer
47 Moses Job
48 Michael Swain
49 Moses Gibson
50 Nehemiah Whittington
51 Obed Gardner
32 Richard Williams
53 Robert Morgan
54 Reuben Dick
55 Robert Wood
56 Robert Wilson
57 Robert Field

58 Robert Patterson
59 Solomon Burrow
60 Samuel Dick
61 Samuel Irwin
62 Wm Thomas
63 Wm Fryer
64 Wm Simmons
65 Wm Swain
66 Wm Richardson
67 Whittenton Sullivan
68 Wm Fifer
69 Winwright Barns
70 Wm Humphries
71 Wm Watson
72 Wm Suits
73 John Humphreys

ROCKINGHAM COUNTY.

1 Geo W Barker, *captain*
2 Howel Harris, 1st *lieut*
3 David Smith, 2nd *do*
4 James Fewel, *ensign*
5 Joel Cardwell
6 John Guy
7 John Smith
8 George Jackson
9 Pleasant Dearing
10 Pleasant Tod
11 Reuben Lindsay
12 Dillard Allen
13 Josiah Settle
14 Leonard Carney
15 Alfred Bethell
16 Absalom Wall
17 Philip Gates
18 Wm Wall
19 John Scales
20 Geo W Jennings
21 Samuel Dalton
22 Alfred Scales
23 Green Vernon
54 Wm H Rice
25 Jos G Porter
26 John J Wright
27 Zack Strong
28 Elisha Hancock
29 Zack Fewee
30 Zack Wall
31 Thomas Smith
32 James Wall
33 James Webster
34 John C Overton
35 John Webster
36 Thos Barker
37 John Gilliland
38 Silas Padge

39 Joel Fagg
40 John Barker
41 Martin Roberts
42 Robert Hall
43 James Vaughan
44 Wm Whitworth
45 Jonathan Aldridge
46 Pleasant Black
47 Pleasant Webster
48 Samuel Vernon
49 Robert Joyce
50 Philip Ision
51 Jacob Crawford
52 Jeremiah Barns
53 Wm Reynolds
54 John D Vernon
55 Josiah Vernon
56 Bartlet Edwards
57 John Sharp
58 Willie Dearing
59 John Parish
60 Shelton Foster
61 Thos Robertson
62 And Robertson
63 John Vaughan
64 Hardiman Strong
65 Samuel Page
66 Samuel Moxley
67 John Cody
68 James Walker
69 Milton Grant
70 Powhattan May
71 Wm Duncan
72 Francis Hains
73 John Wilson
74 John Carter
75 John Geesling
76 Fountain Purrell

P

77 Thos Carter
78 James Andrews
79 Wm Gedsey
80 Robert Hudson
81 Wm S Tucker
82 Freeman Greer
83 John Tucker
84 Isaiah Hancock
85 Alam Boak
86 Pleasant Gorman
87 Peter Lyon
88 Isaac Philips
89 David Kellam
90 Lee Bondusant
91 Stephen Gibson
92 Wm Mangham
93 Stephen Pratt
94 Robert Gibson
95 Robt H Coats
96 Anthy N Millar

97 Cooper Jordan
98 Signor Ahorn
99 George Wright
100 James Underwood
101 John Robertson
102 John Kelly
103 Benjamin Ladyman
104 Thos Underwood
105 Wm Small
106 Edward King
107 John B Curry
108 Noah Cardwell
109 James Norman
110 John Smith
111 John Joyce, jun
112 Pleasant Gibson
113 John Claridge
114 Eli Hancock
115 Jos Bishop
116 John Dilliard

STOKES COUNTY—FIRST REGIMENT.

1 Sam Martin, *captain*
2 Thomas Smith, *lieut*
3 Newton Ladd, *ensign*
4 Elijah Nelson
5 Jacob Nelson
6 Jeremiah Cloud
7 James Lawson
8 Larkin Burge
9 Joel Ketchum
10 Edward Yates
11 Ezekiel Collins
12 Wm Blanchet
13 Benj Fry
14 Jas G Lyon
15 Wm Johnson
16 Thomas Doss
17 Bartlet Shipp
18 Joseph Martin
20 John Cox
19 Wm Shipp
21 Reuben Tilley
22 Lambert Dodson
23 Wm Stanly
24 James Hutchens
25 Benj Thomas
26 James Perkins
27 Matthew Moore
28 Wm Young
39 George Breedlove
30 Hansford Pollard
31 John Pollard
32 Floyd Webb
33 John Jones
34 Wm Cannon
35 Jeremiah Cisk

36 George Neele
37 Samuel Angel
38 Wm Ladd
39 James Powers
40 Benj D' Angle
41 Wm Carr
42 Wm Gibson
43 Robert Neele
44 David D Bostick
45 Thos Martin
46 Wm Poindexter
47 John Tilley
48 Wm Slaughter
49 George Booth
50 Richard Flynt
51 James Davis
52 Wm Welch
53 Thomas Evans
54 John Harvey
55 John Hoover
56 Thos Reddick
57 Henry Spainhower
58 James Ridley
59 Jacob Wolf
60 Jacob Helsepeck
61 John Brabin
62 Jesse Brown
63 John Edwards
64 Jacob Fiscus
65 John Prater
66 David Spainhower
67 Frederic Fulk
68 Wm Childress
69 Shedrack Reddick
70 James Merrit

71 John Kances
72 Isaac George
73 John Hooker
74 Jacob Denton
75 James Bowleyjack
76 Samuel Riggs
77 John Neal

78 Samuel Neale
79 Jesse Dunlap
80 Kelly Shirley
81 Jesse Banks
82 John Brown
83 Arthur Muskram

STOKES COUNTY—SECOND REGIMENT.

1 John L Hausar, *captain*
2 Benj Briggs, *lieut*
3 Solomon Fulps, *ensign*
4 Duncan C McCocklin
5 Alex McKay
6 Wm G Parish
7 Peter Shamell
8 David Jean
9 Jacob Neel
10 John Myers
11 Thos Snow
12 John Snow
13 Matthew Marshall
14 Martin W Marshall
15 James Allen
16 John Boswell
17 Thos Marshall
18 John Bibee
19 Christian Waggerman
20 Stephen McFerson
21 Wm Frazier
22 Matthias Maston
23 Thos Walker
24 Owen Walker
25 Israel Robinson
36 John Oens
27 Elijah Harrell
28 Fredrick Millar
29 Fracis Rose
30 Jacob Huphines
31 Charles Vest
32 Wm Blackburn
33 Thos Jinkens
34 Robert Cornelious
35 Henry Fidler
36 John Oens
37 John Karney
38 John Strape
39 John Haning
40 Jacob Shamel
41 Daniel Hauser
42 Abram Lash

43 Henry Ripple
44 John Fidler
45 John Rell
46 Thos Rell
47 Charles Chube
48 John Todd
49 Philip Huffman
50 Abram Johnson
51 Elisha Johnson
52 Jonathan Sell
53 John Styers
54 John Johnson
55 Richard Clampit, jun
56 Joseph Idol
57 John Whitehead
58 Hampton Bynum
59 Julius Patterson
60 John Blume
61 Christian Ebert
62 David Patterson
63 John D Salmons
64 Wm Golding
65 Andrew Bowman
66 Thos Westmoreland
67 Elijah Fowler
68 Seth Hamm
69 George Lenville
70 Moses Lenville
71 John Forrester
72 John Campbell
73 Wm Branson
74 Lawrence Angel
75 John Sprinkle
76 Wm Branson
77 Godfrey Millar
78 Isaac Church
79 Robert Hill
80 John Cornelius
81 Harman Millar
82 Mickael Sailer
83 Henry Doub

SURRY COUNTY—FIRST REGIMENT.

1 David Freeman
2 Joseph Bunham

3 Michael Teag
4 Enoch Stone

5 Henry Fulks
6 Joel Bray
7 Joseph Chandler
8 Ezekiel Kenny
9 Jesse Lam
10 Jesse Peal
11 James Martin
12 Edmund Fleming
13 Mordecai Fleming
14 John M Fleming
15 James Bays
16 Wm B McCraw
17 James Roberts, jun
18 Wm Williams
19 Coleby Cruid, jun
20 Abraham Cruid
21 Hail Snow
22 Thos Snow
23 Elijah Aubury
24 Jesse Prichet
25 Wm Golden
26 Matthew Davis
27 Robert Ship
28 James Cockram
29 James Smyth
30 Charles Tucker
31 James Smith, jun
32 Solomon Center
33 Isaac Bartlett
34 Elijah Thompson
35 John Thompson
36 Stephen Potter
37 Henderson Thompson
38 Barnard Franklin
39 Joel Canada
40 Andrew Willie
41 Wm Mash
42 Thos Franklin
43 John Mash

44 Wm Paul
45 Jesse Burch
46 Lemuel B Jones
47 John Collins
48 John Whitlock
49 Jacob Jones
50 Aaron Andres
51 Isaac Winfrey
52 James Kyle
53 Jacob Dobbins
54 Jesse Jones
55 John Thomason
56 Wm Car
57 Jesse Whitaker
58 Achilus Key
59 Littleton Isbell
60 James Fitzgerald
61 Lawrence Morris
62 James Harrison
63 Asa Earley
64 John Aulberty
65 Wm Whitaker
66 Isaac Whitaker
67 Charles Hunn
68 James McDonald
69 Richard Studard
70 Daniel Griffith
71 Zachariah Clandler
72 Barajah Reynolds
73 David Love
74 James Rorden
75 Lewis Forkner
76 Isaac Norman
77 Eli Tansey
78 Jeremiah Rorden
79 Robert Blackville
80 Wm Holifyeld
81
82

SURRY COUNTY—SECOND REGIMENT.

1 Capt Abner Carmichall
2 John Welch, *lieut*
3 George Hudspith, *private*
4 Richard Walker
5 Wm Petty
6 George Debode
7 Willie Harp
8 Daniel Brandle
9 Henry Millar
10 Aaron Nooton
11 Samuel Speak
12 John Parks
13 Benj Brewer
14 George Tipps
15 John Brown, jun
16 Wm Sparks

17 Joel Sparks
18 Stephen Denny
19 Joshua Fenny
20 Joseph Horton
21 Nathan Ratcliff
22 Jonathan Ratliff
23 Wm Hunt
24 Abraham Swain
25 Davis Bagley
26 Hawkins Cook
27 Nickolas Cook
28 Hempley Hart
29 Jssse Collins
30 John Southan
31 Levy Johnson
32 Thomas Hampton

33 John Castephens
34 Neal Bohannon
35 Joshua Carter
36 Isaac Vestal
37 Joseph Carter
38 Berry Patterson
39 Charles Davis
40 George Hobson
41 Jonathan Hinshaw
42 Lewis Wyles
43 Henry Hoots
44 John Frady
45 Charles Stedman, jun
46 Fredric May
47 John Rutledge
48 Matthew Johnson
49 Edmond Lovelepe
50 Wm Eaperson
51 Henry Peace
52 Benj Pitell

53 Wm Lane
54 Benj Glenn
55 Bennet Philips
56 Henry Shore
57 Wm Robertson
58 Edmund Philips
59 Isaac Jarrat
60 Francis A Poindexter
61 James Ball
62 Benj Kelly
63 John Spillman
64 Henry Skidmore
65 George Ball
66 John Pilcher
67 Francis Moreland
68 Thos Thornton
69 Giles Coe
70 John McGuire
71 Peter Vest
72 Peter Sprinkle

WILKES COUNTY.

1 Ambrose Carleton, *captain*
2 Andrew Vannoy, 1st *lieut*
3 Saml Johnston, 2nd   *do*
4 Elijah Coffey 3rd   *do*
5 Lewis Walters, *ensign*
6 David Allison
7 Hiram Pipes
8 Martin Livingston
9 Moses Stansberry
10 Samuel Brown
11 Samuel Neathery
12 Thos Barlow
13 Wm Hagler
14 Thomas Steed
15 Hughs Napper
16 Thos Potts
17 John Allen
18 John Ferguson
19 Joel Watters
20 Edward Watkins
21 Benj Foster
22 Christopher Gullet
23 Daniel Gullet
24 Eli Hamby
25 Jacob Lipps
26 John Craine
27 Joel Vannay
28 Thos Summers
29 Wm Church
30 James Bradley
31 Hezekiah Paisley
32 Cewen Humphry
33 Isaac Hogler
34 Joshua Hendrickson
35 Peter Elerod

36 John Coffey
37 Archibald Brown
38 Wm Murphy
39 Joshua Brown
40 Elijah Barns
41 Solomon Saunders
42 John Barns
43 Joon Pearson
44 Larkin Kerly
45 Samuel Newsom
46 Simon Shaw
47 Charles Vickers
48 George Gilbreath
49 Helen H Gilbreath
50 Frederic Tyser
51 Javan Ball
52 Marshall McDaniel
53 Allen Robinett
54 Hiram Gilbreath
55 John Rains
56 Gideon Gilbreath
57 Hiram Smoot
58 Wm Smith
59 John Norris
60 Joel Johnson
61 Reuben Hamby
62 James Morgan
63 Daniel Holderfield
64 Sylvester Adams
65 Benj Treble
66 George Barns
67 Wm Morgan
68 Larkin Sheppard
69 Gibson Adams
70 Whitfield Brown

71 Eli Brown
72 Isaac Adam
73 David Trusty
74 John Bruce
75 Daniel Hayes
76 John Robards
77 John Brown
78 Wm Walsh
79 Peter Brown
80 Wm Amburgy
81 Malachai Lawrence
82 John Sparks
83 Beorge Crouse
84 John Dunkin
85 Thos Rigsby
86 George Sparks
87 Jeremiah Caudill
88 Wm V Lyon
89 John Gilliam
90 James Tucker
91 Thos Wood
92 John Bensel
93 Wm Toliver
94 Joshua Parks
95 Elisha Brown
96 George Sparks
97 Joseph Gregory

98 Robert Layle
99 Wm Gray
100 Joseph Brown
101 Elisha Felts
102 Robert Perdue
103 Ramsome Shore
104 Jonathan Sparks
105 Daniel McDaniel
106 Presly Bussill
107 Daniel Norman
108 Levi Wilsen
109 Charles Bewsey
110 James Lewis
111 James Morgan
112 George Norman
113 Luke Rash
114 Wm Combs
115 Wm Darnall
116 Ezekiel Brown
117 Hezekiah Sebastian
118 Jonathan Walsh
119 Jesse Adams
120 Hopkins Pratt
121 Edward Turner
122 Samuel Spier
123

ASHE COUNTY.

1 Gideon Lewis, *captain*
2 Isaac Weaver, *lieut*
3 Wm Toliver, *ensign*
4 Henry Graybeal
5 Eli Ragon
6 Henry Millar
7 James Duncan
8 David Graybeal
9 David Carpenter
10 Samuel Griffith
11 Isaac Taylor
12 Frederick Staley
13 Isaac Lewis
14 Wm Morefield
15 Abraham Miller
16 John Millar
17 Mark Weaver
18 Peter Hart
19 Absalom Bower
20 John Faw
21 Jacob Mikel
22 David Hartzog
23 Aaron Owens
24 Peter Feese
25 Andrew Shearer
26 Wm Cox
27 Isaac Smith

28 Wm Mink
29 Edmond Tilley
30 Joshua Pennington
31 David Horton
52 Phineas Horton
33 Reuben Hartley
34 Lewis Fairchilds
35 Jacob Ingerham
36 Levi Blackburn
37 John Shearer
38 Joel Dugger
39 David Dugger
40 Thomas Swift
41 Henry Hately
42 John Vanderpool
43 Wm Brewer
44 Jacob Brinegar
45 John Hoppass
46 John Brower
47 Wm S Edwards
48 Young Edwards
49 Alex T Conley
50 Enock Passmoer
51 Joel Rose
52 Richard Perry
53 Wm Vanover
54 Joseph Colwell

55 Enock Baldwin	59 William Taylor
56 John Rutherford	60
57 John Quinley	61
58 John Williams	62

RANDOLPH COUNTY—FIRST REGIMENT.

1 Zebidee Rush, *captain*	38 Andrew Fouts
2 Wm Welborn, *lieut*	39 Whitlock Crage
3 , *ensign*	40 Jacob Lamm
4 Isaac Elliott	41 Reuben Alexander
5 Laza Merril	42 Benj Wright
6 John McGee	43 Enock Spinks *sergt*
7 Seth Dickson	44 Branson Lawrann, *do*
8 Isaac Hannah	45 Enock Tucker
9 Matthew Davis	46 Wm Pearce
10 Mark Stud	47 Michael Cole
11 Solomon Hannah	48 Daniel Cast
12 Wm Crawford, jun	49 John Bowdown
13 Wm Morris	50 John Haskitt
14 John Hannah	51 Wm Swafford
15 Wm Coggin	52 Joseph Hinson
16 Solomon Farmer	53 John Wormington
17 Jeremiah Bailey	54 Micajah Brewer
18 Benj Fuller	55 Jonathan Moffet
19 James Skeen	56 Wm Macon
20 Stephen Hulgan	57 Doran Yeorgan
21 John Gibson	58 Thos Yeorgan
22 Richard Gallimore	59 Thos Pain
23 Jos Nicolson	60 Samuel Milliken
24 James Harvey	61 Thos Clark
25 John Mills	62 Daniel Robins
26 Jesse Blair	63 John Miller
27 Robert Gray	64 John Jordan
28 Andrew Johnston	65 Nathan Goddin
29 Benj Sanders	66 George Williams
30 Nathan Hoedridge	67 Wm Presnall
31 Lewis Walton	68 Barnabas Hobbs
32 Isaac Coltrane	69 Johnson King
33 Thos White	70 Benj Page
34 Reuben Rush, *sergt*	71 Isham Hancock
35 Thos Pearce	72 Jos Luther
36 Wm Varner	73 Wm Laitham
37 Benj Cooper	

RANDOLPH COUNTY—SECOND REGIMENT.

1 John Ramsour, *captain*	12 Samuel Royer
2 Minos, Ward, *lieut*	13 Aaron Kivet
3 Richard Richardson, *ensign*	14 Jabaz York
4 Elias Hayes, *serjeant*	15 Goshen Gennings
5 Ivy Richardson, *do*	16 Timothy Cude
6 Aaron Moffet, *do*	17 Reuben Aldred
7 Nathan Swafford, *fifer*	18 Adam York
8 Enock Swafford, *drummer*	19 Wm Lochlan
9 Samuel Aldridge	20 James Lowe
10 Christian Brower, jun	21 John Wren
11 David Ameck	22 Isaac McCollum

23 David Campbell
24 Wm Norman
25 Samuel Russell
26 Moses Johnston
27 Wm Underwood
28 Daniel Smith
29 Charles Jones
30 Vestal Beeson
31 Thos Underwood
32 Iri Richardson
33 Joseph Lamb
34 Gabriel Lamb
35 Michael Swean
36 John Robbins
37 Marmaduke Vickery
38 Wm Robbins [of Danl]

39 John Ruston
40 Benjamin Johnston
41 James Philips
42 Henry Williams
43 Richard Caveness
44 James Warren
45 Joshua Brown
46 James Cruthes
47 Ezekiel Matthews
48 Henry Moffet
49 John Cravan
50 Eli Lambert
51 John Deaton
52 Wm Vestal
53 Gabriel Lamb

SIXTH REGIMENT

ROWAN COUNTY—FIRST REGIMENT.

1 Thos Matthews, *capt*
2 Truth Wood, *lieut*
3 Johnsten Neblock, *do*
4 Richman Hughes, *do*
5 David Cowan, *ensign*
6 Thos Allison
7 Michael Bruner
8 John Albright
9 Henry Allemony
10 Jos Daniels
11 Zekial Dekison
12 Jacob Delow
13 John Weaver
14 Jos Chamblers, sen
15 Thos Reaves
16 Joseph Agnor
17 George Dunn
18 Wm Gardnor
19 Samuel Bunch
20 Littleton Rainey
21 Philip Rumple
22 Wm Rogers
23 Daniel Murphy
24 Caleb Curfise
25 Christ Blackwelder
26 Jacob Corisher
27 Judson Brown
28 John Minster
29 Michael Biley
30 Wm Williamson
31 Elijah Marlin
32 Wm Thompson
33 Wm Rice
34 Peter Traxler
35 Levi Mays
36 Wm Henlin
37 Jos Marlin

38 James Sammons
39 John Yost
40 Adam Eddleman
41 Andrew Boston
42 John Shulleberger
43 Wm Rose
44 Abraham Zickler
45 Henry Arenhart
46 Henry Snider
47 Nathan Morgan
48 Jonathan Miller
49 John Paim
50 Noah Parks, jun
51 Jacob Shover
52 Michael Pittman
53 James Hutson
54 George Knox
55 Joseph Clotfelter
56 John Mills
57 Samuel Graham
58 Samuel Reaves
59 Zekiah Cowan
60 John Cowan
61 Reuben Yearborough
62 Kisman Linn
63 John H Brandon
64 Henry Hill, jun
65 Wm Anderson
66 Henry Stillar
67 Enock Philips
68 Fred Menos
69 Wm Barber
70 Jos Cowan
71 Wolter Rigdon
72 Burrage Davenport
73 John McConnibery
74 John Craig

75 Thomas Willis
76 Jacob Weant
77 Jacob Cross
78 Thomas Craig
79 William Long
80 Samuel Anderson
81 Solomon Hall
82 William Anderson
83 William Price
84 Matthias Phifer
85 John Weab
86 Thomas Renshaw
87 Wilson Niblock
88 Daniel Bogar
89 Martin Clutz
90 Anthony Pealor
91 Peter Cruse
92 John Lippert
93 John Wasnor
94 Jacob Poole
95 John Thomas
96 Volentine Rimer
97 George Waller
98 Thomas Cunningham
99 Hermon Walton

100 Peter Brown
101 Jerry Arey
102 George Smithall
103 John Crotzer
104 John Hartman
105 George Eller
106 Peter Agnor
107 John Gardener
108 Daniel Swink
109 Jacob Thomas
110 Henry Castor
111 Philip Edlinian
112 George Agle
113 Christian Rinchart
114 Fred Holshausen
115 Jacob Fulwider
116 Joseph Cowan, Sen
117 Joseph Cowan, Jun
118 Timothy McNealey
119 David Cooper B S
120 Samuel McLaughlin
121 James Short
122 James McLaughlin, Sen
123 James Brigs
124 James Locke

ROWAN COUNTY—SECOND REGIMENT.

1 George Smith, *Captain*
2 George Miller, 1st *Lieut*
3 John Wilson, *ensign*
4 David Billiny
5 Samuel Spafford
6 Elisha Word
7 Peter Frank
8 Henry Workman
9 Isaac Kinney
10 George Gregson
11 Peter Whitaker
12 John Gregor
13 William McCarn
14 William Jarrat
15 John Garvay
16 Lennard Smith
17 William Peacock
18 James Jackson
19 Jesse Pealer
20 John Houser
21 Walter Northern
22 Mashack Green
23 John Goss
24 John Briggs
25 Jonathan Barclay
26 Joseph Goss, jun
27 Isaac Cobble
28 Isaac Margan
29 Alex Yarborough
30 Joseph Clark

31 William Stout
32 Jessee Harris, jun
33 Edward Davis
34 Peter Riley
35 William Hughs
36 Joseph Shoulse
37 David Garner
38 James Hughes
39 Jonathan Coggins
40 Isaick Russell
41 Cornelius Loftin, jun
42 Edmond Smith
43 Henry Shemeel
44 Isaac Thompson
45 James Johnston
46 John Shipton
47 John Davis, jun
48 Robert Lacey
49 James Morgan
50 William Sorrat, jun
51 James Davis
52 Abraham Owen
53 James Wiseman
54 David Smith
55 James Elliot
56 Ebenezer Moore
57 Noah Huut
58 Ezekiah Owen
59 David Grub
60 John Shoaf

61 Martin Owen
62 James Womack
63 Warren Roberts
64 Hugh Cunningham
65 George Grub
66 Michael Sink
67 Thismothy Wiseman
68 John Macray
69 Thomas Sullivan
70 Joseph Black
71 David Bower
72 Adam Black
73 Ruedolph Yonce
74 John Wortman
75 Philip Myre
76 William Goodman
77 John Moss

78 Daniel Myre
79 Michael Myre
80 Matthew Byrns
81 Christopher Hepler
82 Nathan Lambeth
83 Philip Hapler
84 John Beck
85 Jacob Hasby
86 Thomas Owen
87 Lewis Robling
88 Peter Winklar
89 William Ball
90 John Hill
91 James Pickler
92 James Dedman
93 James Coaths

ROWAN COUNTY—THIRD REGIMENT.

1
2
3
4 Thomas Mumford
5 Ishmael Cordle
6 Jacob Lain
7 Daniel Click
8 William Call
9 James O'neal
10 Jesse Hendricks
11 Drury Jones
12 Abraham Allen
13 Enoch Ellis
14 John Peck
15 David Harris
16 William Guy
17 Thomas Skinner
18 William Dulin
19 Stephen Williams
20 William Edwards
21 Samuel Poyner
22 Joshua Hindrix
23 Isaac Twoney
24 Jesse Swan
25 John Hare
26 William Madden
27 Samuel Gray
28 Joseph Forcum
29 John Taylor
30 John Brandon
31 Joseph Beal
32 William Dockins
33 Saul Price
34 Thomas Smoot
35 Laurence Hudson
36 John Gabard
37 Alfred McCullock
38 George Wilson
39 Charles Detheridge

40 John Smart
41 Thomas Hendrix
42 Christopher Killer
43 Frost Nelson
44 John Ijams
45 Daniel Earnest
46 Johnsey Gaither
47 Daniel Helfer
48 William Nelson
49 Jacob March
50 Wilson Austin
51 John Bryan
52 John Douge
53 Peter Mock
54 John Etchison, jun
55 Henry Brickhouse
56 Jesse Bowden
57 William Chapman
58 Elijah Adams
59 John West
60 Isaac Creef
61 Samuel Ward
62 Smith Cox
63 Thomas Chaffin
64 John Renair
65 Hamilton Gatton
66 William Foster
67 Thomas Foster
68 Thomas Foster
69 Ignatius McDonnell
70 John Philips
71 William Hainline
72 Abraham March
73 Thomas Owens
74 William Batey
75 Elisha Leach
76 Henry Hendrix
77 Jonathan Cronfell
78 Jonathan Jones

79 John Pierce
80 John Johnson
81 William Humphries
82 William Holomon
83 Abijah Irwin
84 Conrad Mires
85 George Gullet
86 Anthony Silvey
87 John Sparks
88 David Sheets
89 John Thornton
90 George Howard
91 Samuel Brannock
92 Henry Call
93 William Johnson
94 John D Ballard

ROWAN COUNTY—FOURTH REGIMENT.

1 Moses Welborn, *captain*
2 Moses Welborn, jun, *lieut*
3 Adam Huffman
4 Christian Zimmerson
5 Cage Ferril
6 David Bodenhamer
7 David Clinard
8 Daniel Motsinger
9 David Weer
10 David Michael
11 Emsley Burton
12 George Zink
13 George Grimes
14 George Jush
15 Henry Little
16 Henry Sawers
17 Henry Wood
18 Henry Mires
19 Hugh Robertson
20 Henry Barrier
21 James Pope
22 James Evans
23 James Jeague
24 John Pain
25 Jesse Farabe
26 Joseph Stone
27 John Weer
28 John Jush
29 John Charles
30 Jacob Nailor
31 Jacob Hague
32 Jacob Bominger
33 John White
34 Jacob Snider
35 John Hague
36 John Frits
37 Jacob Myers
38 Jacob Lopp
39 John Miller
40 John Markland
41 John Clemmons
42 John Lockinbill
43 James Garrett
44 Moses Stokes
45 Moses Teague, sen
46 Michael Easter
47 Moses Teague
48 Michael Worlaw
49 Philip Cecil
50 Philip Leonard
51 Philip Mock
52 Stephen Dowthard
53 William Hayworth
54 William Cook
55 William Bodenhamer
56 William Robertson
57 William Brookshire
58 William Danaway
59 Wilson Rodes
60 Thomas Phelps
61 Samuel Bird
62 Zachariah Stout
63 Basdel Burton
64 Ice Long
65 Thomas Hartte
66 Daniel Wood, jun
67 Robert Green
68 William Sweeney
69 Jacob Bodenhamer
70 John Gobbel
71 John Farabee
72 Thomas Cecil

MONTGOMERY COUNTY—FIRST REGIMENT.

1 Willis Haris, *captain*
2   1st *lieut*
3 William Lilly, 2d *lieut*
4   *ensign*
5 John Hunt
6 Basel Denton
7 James Parson
8 Edward Mund
9 Daniel Garriot
10 Thomas Deaton
11 Malcom Gillis
12 John Yarborough
13 William Russell, sen
14 Jespry Reavis
15 Joseph Russel
16 Hugh Steward
17 Levi Coggins
18 Joseph Steward

19 John Steward
20 James Taylor
21 John Partin
22 Jarrett Russell
23 Abraham Beaman
24 William Green
25 George Allen
26 John Townsend
27 Noah Randle
28 Reuben Smith
29 David Taylor
30 George Calicoat
31 Talton Johnson
32 William Spencer
33 William James
34 John Arnet
35 Nicholas Rynalds
36 David Beamon
37 John Holton
38 Jonathan Harris
39 Samuel Webb
40 Elisha B. Smith
41 Jeptha Harris
42 Levi Reddin
43 Anguish Chisholm
44 Isaiah Hogan
45 Daniel Manus
46 Moses Yarborough
47 Welcome Ussery
48 Wilson Andress
49 John Chisolm
50 Thomas Parsons
51 Joel Harris
52 John Alley
53 John Wilson
54 John Hill
55 Aaron Russell
56 James Ussery

57 James Cook
58 James Mills
59 Levi Russel
60 Martin Russel
61 Thomas Bledsoe
62 Willie Scarborough
63 William Seagraves
64 Willam Christoon
65 Wiley Johnston
66 Andrew Dennis
67 Malcom McCullum
68 Bannet Brown
69 Cobelas Hunley
70 Elisha Smart
71 George Coggins
72 Harbert Suggs
73 John Calicoat
74 James G Mask
75 Moses Steed
76 Peter Edward
77 William A Scott
78 William Russel
79 Eli Townsend
80 Thomas Kirk
81 Samuel Scarborough
82 Benjamin Merrit
83 John Rolins
84 Thomas Davis
85 Charles Reynolds
86 John Townsend
87 Lovin Bennet
88 David Sedberry
89 Jacob Luken
90 John Mills
91 Jesse Haygood
92 Kenneth McClenon
93 Thomas Williams
94 Moses Batton

MONTGOMERY COUNTY—SECOND REGIMENT.

1 David Green, 1st *lieut*
2 Charles Culpepper, 3d *lieut*
3 George Little, *ensign*
4 Burwell Braswell
5 William Buress
6 Andrew Bird
7 Stephen Crump
8 Abraham Cooper
9 Washington Coaley
10 Leonard Cagle
11 Thomas Cox
12 George W. Davidson
13 James Floyd
14 Daniel Ford
15 Richard Greene
16 Isham Honeycut
17 Samuel Honeycut

18 George Hearn
19 Philip Hegler
20 Reuben Honeycut
21 Jacob Hartsoll
22 Leonard Hartsell
23 Willie Harris
24 John S Kindall
25 Henry Kimry
26 Henry Kipley
27 Stephen Kirk
28 William Lyerly
29 Joseph Milton
30 Frederick Mossman
31 William Moss
32 Jonathan McDonald
33 Mathew Parham
34 George Poplin

35 Jarrot Pritchard
36 Jesse Poplin
37 Michael Ritchie
38 George Read
39 Joel Rowland
40 Jordan Russel
41 George D Smith
42 John Smith
43 Richard Stoker
44 George Sydes

45 James Townsell
46 William Tomlinson
47 Jonathan Wilkerson
48 Hewet Weaks
49 John Walker
50 George Whitley
51 George Palmer
52 Farley Hopkins
53 Bennet Solomon

MECKLENBURG COUNTY—FIRST REGIMENT.

1 James Wilson, *captain*
2 Thomas Boyd, Esq., 1st *lieut*
3 Joseph Blackwood, 2nd *do*
4 Isaac Price,   3rd *do*
5 Charles Hutchinson, *ensign*
6 William Carson
7 John Wynens
8 Barzilla Garner
9 James McCombs
10 John Barnett
11 William McKelvia
12 John Hawkins
13 Amos Barnett
14 Ezekiel Alexander
15 William Shelvey
16 John C Garrison
17 James Means
18 Thomas Hope
19 Robert Coldwell
20 John Price
21 John Parkes, sen
22 Samuel Johnston, jun
23 William Wolles, jun
24 Mathew Wallis, jun
25 Samuel Parks
26 Robert Coldwell, jun
27 Ann Wynns
28 John Sadler
29 John Barnhill
30 Jacob Julin
31 James Henderson
32 Elisha McCracken
33 Christopher Love
34 Robert Dunn, jun
35 Andrew M Parish
36 William Dunn
37 Andrew Lewing, jun
38 Francis Perry
39 John Farra
40 John Lewing
41 James Carothers
42 James Dinkins
43 Robert Bigham, jun
44 John Johnston
45 William Johnston

46 Samuel Neeley
47 David Reed
48 Joseph Whiteside
49 Augustus Miles
50 Mathew West
51 Thomas Connel
52 William Benhill
53 Robert McKnight
54 Michael Baker
55 Abel Baker
56 Hugh McDowel
57 William Kerr
58 John Towd
59 Aaron Baker
60 Andrew Walker
61 James Porter
62 John Beaty
63 Samuel Bigham
64 Simon V Pelt
65 John Beaty
66 Peavon Jackson
67 John Blackburn
68 John Wilson, jun
69 John Brown
70 William S Norman
71 Daniel Baxter
72 Benjamin Wilson
73 Thomas Elliott
74 James Conner
75 Daniel Davis
76 William Elliott
77 Richard Hartley
78 George Duckworth
79 James Meek
80 James Alexander
81 Joel Jones
82 James Sloan
83 Isaac Morrison, jun
84 John Parker
85 James Mentith
86 Joseph Williams
87 Andrew Prim
88 Robert A Orsburn
89 John White
90 Michael Channels

91 Gabriel Ferrel
92 Giles Irwin
93 John Ferrel
94 Joseph Wallis
95 Henry Hunter, jun
96 William Ferrel
67 James Steele
98 Nelson Gray

99 John Steel
100 Robert Montgomery
101 Richard Peoples
102 James A Braddy
103 Joseph McKellerand
104 George Goforth
105 John D Alexander

MECKLENBURG COUNTY—SECOND REGIMENT.

1 David Moore, *captain*
2 John Wilson, 1st *lieut*
3 Solomon Reed, 2d *do*
4 William John, 3d *do*
5 Albertes Alexander, *ensign*
6 Richard Barflet
7 Mathew McCall
8 James McCall
9 Henry Thompson
10 Alexander Stewart
11 William Cheery
12 James Robertson
13 Samuel Yaudles
14 James Harbeson
15 William Shelby
16 Gideon Freeman
17 John Morrison
18 John Allen
19 John Forsythe
20 Games Barnes
21 Moses Purser
22 Micajah Barns
23 Osburn Wilkinson
24 Robert Allen
25 Groves Vinson
26 William Helmes
27 Charles Helmes
28 Frederic Starns
29 Nathaniel Starns
30 Morris Shehorn
31 William Yerby
32 James Rone
33 John Belk
34 Dan'l Rich
35 John Junderbusk
36 Henry Flowers
37 David B Yaudles
38 Salamachus Alexander
39 Abdon Alexander
40 Osburn Smart
41 Elisha Smart
42 John McCullock
43 Robert Cook
44 Stephen Hanson
45 Moses Craig
46 Wm. McCoy
47 Robert Howood
48 William Woodall

49 Jacob Gray
50 Aaron Howie
51 Andrew King
52 Joshua Finsher
53 Samuel Rape
54 Samuel Rener
55 James Hambleton
56 Moses Vick
57 John Philips
58 James Train
69 George Berns
60 William Fisher
61 Daniel Button
62 Hugh McAlroy
63 Jess Ivey
64 John Hauley
65 Benjamin Spravey
66 Joseph Reed
67 Adam Karr
68 John Mathews
69 George Parke
70 William Reed
71 Wm. Downs
72 Wilson Taylor
73 John Maglauchlin
74 Joseph Hall
75 William Maygeehee
76 Henry Hargett
77 William Hargett
78 Joel Helmer
79 John Crowel
80 Peter Chainey
81 David Harkey
82 George Tuter
83 Elias Stilwell
84 James Morrison
85 Moses Tomberlin
86 Edward Reak
87 Neel Morrison
88 James Costley
89 Thomas S Cochran
90 Wm Housten, jun
91 Robert Cochran
92 Hugh Wilson
93 Reuben Hood
94 Charles Dennis
95 Samuel Neele
96 John Harkey

97 James Rogers
98 Robt. Harrison
99 John Hodge
100 Richard Lambert
101 David W Story

102 John Fuller
103 James Shaw
104 Lewis Webb
105 James Story, sen

CABARRUS COUNTY

1 Even S Willey, *captain*
2 George Fogleman, *lieut*
3 Christopher Milken, *ensign*
4 Alexander W Harris, 1st *sergt*
5 Ozni Rogers, 2nd *do*
6 John Long, 3rd *do*
7 Andrew Kemmons, 4th *do*
8 Peter Alles, 1st *Corporal*
9 John Drye, 2nd *do*
10 Daniel Drye, 3rd *do*
11 Andrew Trulman, 4th *do*
12 Daniel Mooss
13 Daniel Ritengous
14 Henry Hover
15 Andrew Blackwater
16 John Nusman
17 John Goger
18 Jacob Overcast
19 Jonathan Stanford
20 Alexander Bain
21 Methias Passenger
22 Jacob Stirwatt
23 William Bell
24 John Hall
25 William Pelt
26 Samuel Neel
27 James Ross
28 George Long
29 James Gray
30 George Kegle
31 David White
32 John Mathews
33 James Love
34 James McMahew
35 John Haskey
36 Adam Richey
37 George Trutman
38 James Buchanon
39 John Snider
40 George Miller
41 Moses Conel
42 Andrew Yaw
43 Jacob Bager
44 John Bager
45 David Nisler
46 William Scott
47 Jacob Croner
48 Christopher Hattaman
49 John Mitchell
50 Peter Walter

51 Paul Walter
52 Charles Hartman
53 George Lefort
54 Jacob File
55 Cirus Alexander
56 Silas McCinlay
57 Richard D Plunkett
58 James Welch
59 John Eliot
60 Andrew Walker
61 John Clay
62 John Davis
63 John Morris
64 Robert Dixon
65 Isaac McClerland
66 Hugh Dixon
67 Hezekiah Davis
68 Jacob Goodman
69 John McCinley
70 John Bradshaw
71 Isaac Howell
72 John Johnston
73 William Houston
74 John Mullen
75 John Green
76 William Simons
77 John Mclain
78 Joel S Houston
79 Henry Petery
80 Jacob Cline
81 Tobias Mesthinghams
82 James Hadley
83 James Nicholson
84 John Davis
85 William G. Harris
86 David Winecof
87 Samuel Holebrooks
88 Cirus Wedenton
89 George Goodnight
90 David McRee
91 William Houston
92 Tobias Goodman
93 Joseph G Spires
94 John Garman
95 Beverly Gray
96 John Sossiman
97 Christopher Osburn
98 Durum Cuzine
99 Caleb Blackwater
100 Moses Archabb

101 Samuel H Cochran
102 John Cuzine
103 David Linker
104 Adam Cariker
105 David Miskingham
106 Jacob Tucker
107 Jacob Hegles

108 Jacob Funn
109 Daniel Funn
110 David Fink
111 Matthias Miskingham
112 Henry Himpman
113 George Barnhart

IREDELL COUNTY.

1 John McKee, *captain*
2 William Kerr, *lieutenant*
3 Thomas Forterner, *ensign*
4 Andrew McKenzie
5 William Hicks
6 Charles Summers
7 Alexis Alexander
8 James Crawford
9 William Jacobs
10 John Bone
11 Alexander Watts
12 John Freeland
13 Alexander Hall
14 Andrew W Davidson
15 John Woodard
16 Daniel Brawley
17 Aaron Downs
18 James McKnight
19 John Sloan
20 John Huggins
21 John Atwell
22 James Maulholland
23 Robert Brawley
24 Ruel Walles
25 Hiram Lawson
26 James McRee
27 John McDate
28 Robert Elliott
29 David McRee
30 Jeremiah Whiley
31 James B Thomas
32 Angus McRoy
33 Robert McFarland
34 Samuel McFarland
35 Ralph Stewart
36 Henry Morrison
37 James Alexander
38 Jacob Bostion
39 John Carter
40 John Wilkinson
41 Tobias Miller
42 Martin Cryder
43 Thomas Elliott
44 Hamelton McClatchy
45 Abner Feamster
46 George Erwin
47 James Gilley
48 William Morrison

49 Jaran Fortune
50 Joseph Wright
51 Andrew Davis
52 Rhoda Westmoreland
53 Abner York
54 Samuel Honeycutt
55 Alfred Kerr
56 Robert Timpleton
57 Richard F Houston
58 James Alley
59 Peterson Westmoreland
60 William Mayhew
61 Joseph Rogers, jun
62 James Randels
63 John Lippard
64 Joseph Parks
65 Mathew Calaher
66 Windle Holshouser
67 Abraham Ritchey
68 David Clodfelter
69 Neal McKay, jun
70 John Wilson
71 Neal McKay, sen
72 Andrew Neil
73 John Fleming
74 James Morten
75 John Erwin, sen
76 John Steel
77 William Lipperd
78 William King
79 John Harchie
80 William Allison
81 William Gay
82 Samuel Archibald
83 Ninia Steel
84 Robert McGuire
85 Thomas Allison
86 Maxwell Chambers
87 George Mair
88 Samuel Timpleton
89 Daniel Lewis
90 Kinchen Walls
91 Robert Lazenby
92 Lebishes Gaither
93 Greenberry H Johnston
94 John Fitzgerril
95 David Holleman
96 Leonard Wishon

97 William Mason
98 Solomon Sumners
99 John McLelland
100 John Claggett
101 William Summers
102 Humphrey Tomlinson
103 Thomas Kerney
104 James Thompson, *captain*
105 Isaac Smith, *lieutenant*
106 Perry Tomlinson, *ensign*
107 Ezekiel Morgan
108 Jacob Privit
109 William Mitchell
110 James Williams
111 John Mears
112 Robert Coleman
113 Mark Marlow
114 Gideon Deboard
115 Anderson Johnson
116 Ezekiel Mires
117 William Bogle
118 Charles Hatten, jun
119 Elisha Farmer
120 Isaac Kena
121 James Bogle
122 James Reynold
123 James King
124 James Harbin
125 Lemuel Beckhan
126 Samuel Meadows
127 William Jolley
128 David Roberts
129 James Barnard
130 Henry E Williams
131 Enock Gaither

132 John Dilliard
133 Adam Campbell
134 William Marlow
135 Archibald Cast
136 Plesabo Hueston
137 Isaac Wailes
138 David Marmon
139 Thomas Marmon
140 John Maiden
141 Joseph Milsaps
142 Alexander Lackey
143 Dearling Allen
144 Elihugh King
145 John Guider
146 Nathan Guiltney
147 William Guiltney
148 Robert Guiltney
149 Wallis Privit
150 John S Patterson
151 John Griffith
152 Ruton Jordan
153 Ezekiel Edis
154 George Flowers
155 James Dishman
156 Richard Cook
157 James Bentley
158 John Arrington
159 Alexander McHague
160 Armold Holland
161 John Maxwell
162 Joseph Shelby
163 Alexander Long
164 James King
165 James Gregory
166 John King

LINCOLN COUNTY—FIRST REGIMENT.

1 James Finley, *captain*
2 William J Wilson, 1st *lieut*
3 Richard Cowan, 2nd *do*
4 Andrew Barry,   3d *do*
5 John Beard, *ensign*
6 Ambroze Gaultney
7 Andrew Slinkard
8 John Hogan
9 Henry Sadler
10 George Berry
11 Jacob Troutman
12 William Short
13 James Graham
14 Isaac Murrell
15 John Hunt
16 Benedict Jetton
17 Benjamin Proctor
18 John Litz
19 William Little

20 Richard Proctor
21 William Nance, jun
22 James White
23 William Nance
24 William Tucker
25 Ambrose Cobb
26 Jacob Cloninger
27 Samuel Pew
28 Thomas Sadler
29 Needam Wingate
30 David Smith, jun
31 Robinson Moore
32 William Meginess
33 John Rhodes
34 John Meginess
35 William Sutton
36 John Mahew
37 Bedford Childers
38 Thomas Tucker

R

39 Samuel Abernathy
40 Red Errowood
41 Robt Lucky
42 Charles Edwards
43 Anthony Long
44 Freeman Shelton
45 Reuben Grice
46 John Bynum
47 William Hill
48 Willis Ballard
49 William Killian
50 Robinson Harris
51 Anthony Hinkle
52 Ashman Gwin
53 James Hicks
54 Daniel Killian
55 Frederic Killian
56 Edward Carroll
57 John Jinkens
58 Thomas Dickson
59 John Venable
60 Austin Ford
61 Peter Titman
62 James McCarver
63 William Rockford
64 Robert Alexander
65 William McCarver
66 Wiertt Jenkins
67 Reuben Jenkins
68 Jacob Rhine
69 Adam Rhine
70 Solomon Rhine
71 John Rhodes
72 John Bynum

73 David Costner
74 Jacob Smith
75 George House
76 Amos Robeson
77 Alexr McCullock
78 Keece Price
79 Moses Grissom
80 Thomas Groves
81 Hiram Harris
82 James Shannon
83 Jacob Fite
84 Ezekiel McClure
85 John Merner
86 Samuel Williams
87 James McClure
88 William Lettimore
89 John Damon
90 Anderson Wells
91 William Hamilton
92 John Leeper
93 John Glover
94 Alexander Rankin
95 William Reed
96 Steward Jinkens
97 William Bluford
98 John Hanks
99 Ebner Rumfelt
100 John Carthy
101 Jacob Kenedy
102 John Oats
103 John Parmer
104 William Adams
105 John Blackwood

LINCOLN COUNTY—SECOND REGIMENT.

1 Daniel Hoke, *captain*
2 John B Harris, 1st *lieut*
3 Gilbert Milliken, 2nd *do*
4 Isaac Mauney, 3rd *do*
5 Peter Hoke, *ensign*
6 John Carpenter
7 Henry Huffsteddler
8 Moses Barr
9 Jacob Plunk
10 William Carpenter
11 Joseph Black
12 William Ferguson
13 Cudias Smith
14 Jonas Rudisil
15 Peter Mauney
16 David Kezer
17 Peter Eaker
18 George Seller
19 Peter Costner
20 John Huffsteddler
21 William Guntlesey
22 Daniel Glotfelder
23 Elias Glotfelder

24 John Teague
25 George Glotfelder
26 Rudolph Glotfelder
27 Lewis Huet
28 Philip Skerd
29 Thomas Smith
30 John Bumgarner
31 Willie Hops
32 Archibald Cobb
33 Elisha Saunders
34 Joshua Hunter
35 Conrade Heldebrand
36 Peter Reymer
37 Bostian Best
38 John Houser
39 Solomon Shoup
40 Samuel Bigham
41 William Willis
42 Charles Williams
43 James Chapman
44 Nathaniel Pew
45 Jacob Houser
46 John Watterson

47 Joseph Wear
48 James Patterson
49 Preston Goforth
50 Hugh Sprulin
51 Isaac Mullinax
52 James Elliott
53 Thomas Earwood
54 George Goforth
55 Jacob Harman
56 Robert Barber
57 Young Marden
58 Thomas Black
59 David Dickson
60 Hardy Long
61 Solomon Childers
62 Christopher Carpenter
63 James Endsley
64 Anthony Clerk
65 David Bookout
66 Archibald Endsley
67 John Wright
68 Thomas Crags
69 Philip Haynes
70 John Whitworth
71 Joshua Howell
72 Samuel Collins
73 John Monser
74 Casper Bolick
75 George Bowman
76 Henry Lickman
77 Mathew Boovey
78 Charles Ward
79 William Harman
80 David Huntley
81 Martin Lickman
82 George Turner
83 Abraham Tray
84 Henry Lickman, jun
85 Samuel Sullivan
86 Christian Bollinger
87 Christopher Hope
88 Michael Ingle
89 William Cline
90 John Shafer
91 Henry Houser
92 Ransom Husky
93 Matthias Barringer
94 Michael Dillenger
95 Daniel Blackburn
96 Jacob Harner
97 Aaron Moore
98 David Dick
99 Joseph Heldebrand
100 Joseph Lenhart
101 James Lemons

102 Daniel Fullbright
103 Francis Summitt
104 Daniel Summitt
105 Nicholas Carpenter
106 Peter Lorance
107 Joseph Ashe
108 John Earncy
109 Alfred Sherril
110 Elias Shine
111 Conrade Ward
112 Avery Guant
113 Andrew Yant
114 Phillips Hedrick
115 Benedict Levant
116 John Cowan
117 George Shook
118 Jacob Fullbright
119 Leonard Kagle
120 Ephraim Christoph
121 William Echard
122 John Hadrick
123 Aaron Downson
124 Peter Keller
125 Gabriel Isaac
126 Samuel Peterson
127 Frederick Knup
128 Francis King
129 Peter Raby
130 Michael Sattonfield
131 Jonathan Robinson
132 Miles Abernathy
133 David Hawn
134 Valentine Taylor
135 John Stamy
136 Peter Frey
137 James Gilleband
138 John Snyder
139 James Bridges
140 James Jones
141 Benjamin Newman
142 Sterling Singleton
143 John Ward
144 John Glotfelder
145 James Fisher
146 Samuel Setton
147 William Black
148 David Warlic
149 Elisha Winson
150 Nimrod Winson
151 Henry Killian
152 Solomon Killian
153 Daniel Coulter
154 Henry Coulter
155 John Shufford

RUTHERFORD COUNTY—FIRST REGIMENT.

1 John Oliver, *captain*
2 John Moore, 1st *lieut*
3 Joseph Taylor, 3rd *do*
4 Lindsey Fortune, *ensign*
5 Adam Hampton
6 Vincent Wood
7 John McHan
8 James Hill
9 Jonathan Mullens
10 William Hicks
11 Jonathan Hampton
12 Harbert Horton
13 Ransom Edgarton
14 David Wamock
15 Hamilton Freeman
16 Carter Johnston
17 Beuben Melton
18 Robert Webb
19 Leonard Deck
20 John Melton
21 Richard E Allen
22 Thomas Wamock
23 Jeremiah Webb
24 Asaph Hill
25 Moses White
26 Samuel Bickerstaff
27 Robert Johnston
28 John Crow
29 Thomas Stockton
30 John Bradey
31 Josiah Jones
32 Isaac Rhom
33 Benjamin Grayson
34 William Grayson
35 William Melton
36 Elijah Pool
37 William Hunt
38 Elijah Sparks
39 Thomas Brackett
40 Simon Steet
41 William Hutchins
42 William Street
43 James Taylor
44 Hugh Watson
45 Daniel Watson
46 William Reed
47 John Guffy
48 Archy Reed Guffey
49 James S Guffey
50 Jesse W Grove
51 Benjamin Andrews
52 James Thompson
53 James Moore
54 George Ross
55 James Irvine
56 William Sprat
57 Richard Neweam
58 David Hodge
59 Rial Hill
60 Henry Camp
61 Noah Sergant
62 Benjamin Ketor
63 Wade Bates
64 Eli Hanes
65 James Ketor
66 William Marshall
67 Micajah Bankenship
68 James Naney
69 Ephraim Cook
70 William Wallace
71 Jacob Venzant
72 John Cook
73 Howard Williams
74 Henry Morris
75 Zedekiah Harris
76 William Whitesides
77 Sterling Lewin
78 John Hunter
79 Mark Moore
80 William Harris
81 Andrew H Eliott
82 James Ward
83 Miner Winn
84 Jesse Morgan

RUTHERFORD COUNTY—SECOND REGIMENT.

1 Abram Irvine, *captain*
2 John Fonetren, *lieut*
3 Joseph Willis, *ensign*
4 Micajah Davis
5 John Blanton
6 Byard McCraw
7 James Wilkins
8 Jesse Blanton
9 John Rippy
10 Elijah Hamrick
11 Richard Bridges
12 Samuel Fonetren
13 Absalom Ellis
14 Nehemiah Padgett
15 Benjamin Burns
16 Valentine Martin
17 Richard Lea
18 George Bridges
19 Jesse Rippy
20 Samuel McIntire
21 Robert Smith
22 Joseph Luguire

23 Henry Ledbetter
24 Daniel King
25 James McEntire
26 Henry Weston
27 Thomas Downey
28 James Wilson
29 Alfred Moore
30 James Crane
31 Samuel Wilson
32 Jesse Braddy
33 Solomon Harrelson
34 David Lissum
35 John Bailey
36 Henry White
37 Alfred Moore
38 Constant Brooks
39 James Wilson
40 James Dickus
41 Jenky Jenkins
42 Lewis Johnson
43 Elisha Stacy
44 William Holland
45 Zeckariah McDaniel
46 John Green
47 Darlin Webb
48 Gilbert Harrel
49 Richard Bostick
50 Henry Grigs
51 Jacob Willis
52 Jacob McKinney
53 John White
54 Henry Workman
55 William Newton
56 John Rooker
57 Hugh McRannolds
58 William York

59 Blueford Randal
60 James Arrowood
61 Jesse Grigg
62 Bannester Grigg
63 Richard Gibbs
64 William Wilkey
65 Mosse Black
66 Samuel Julin
67 Jabes Murry
68 John Smith
69 John Barker
70 James Chitwood
71 Jesse Ledford
72 Thomas Hill
73 Abel Beaty
74 William Dedman
75 Allen Mathis
76 John Handcastle
77 Martin Beam
78 Samuel Mode
79 Thomas Garner
80 William McEntire
81 Isham Julin
82 John Alexander
83 Elijah Holifield
84 Robert Scruggs
85 Joel Williams
86 Abraham Pagett
87 William Lea
88 Elias Scruggs
89 John Robeson
90 David Beheler
91 John Amos
92 David Pope
93 Arther Clarke

RUTHERFORD COUNTY—THIRD REGIMENT.

1 Ephraim Carruth
2 James Braden
3 William Newman
4 Andrew Thompson
5 Leander P Carruth
6 James Ruth
7 Joseph Wood
8 Robert Baicly
9 William Colier
10 James Crawford
11 Noah Hampton
12 Austen Musuck
13 Thomas Prator
14 Gabriel Wilmath
15 John Ownsby
16 Sims Ownsby
17 John Lowther
18 Isaac Goforth
19 Cornelius Clemmons
20 Greenbury Griffen

21 John Dolton
22 David Turlly
23 John Going
24 William Wooten
25 Charles Edwards
26 Pleasant Whirly
27 Elijah Dolten
28 Thornton Randal
29 Dennis Duff
30 Edward McGuin
31 Ephraim Jackson
32 Luke Woldson
33 John Hiflin
34 Samuel Thompson
35 John Skipper
36 Burges Smith
37 Jonathan Ellison
38 George McKinney
39 Jeremiah Smith
40 William Thompson

41 Robert Cockrum
42 Joseph Studman
43 James Menice
44 John Sutton, jun
45 Thomas Dills, sen
46 James Henderson
47 William Giles
48 William Sutton, jun
49 John Logan
50 James Miller Erwin
51 William Wilson
52 William Clinton
53 Edley Hambleton
54 George Musick
55 Archibald Sohlar
56 An'd Young

57 Claton Brown
58 William Ownby
59 John Dillbark, jun
60 Burrel Utly
61 Thomas Blackurl
62 George Fry
63 Caleb Williams
64 Joshua Wells
65 Thomas Steedman
66 Solomon Blackurl
67 Richard Sisemore
68 Joseph Willson
69 John Smith
70
71
72

BURKE COUNTY—FIRST REGIMENT.

1 Frederick Sluillei, *captain*
2 Elrod Pobete, 1st *lieut*
3 John F O'Neill, 2nd *lieut*
4 John Riel, *ensign*
5 William Brittain, 1st *sergant*
6 Jacob Keller, 2nd *do*
7 John Walker, 3rd *do*
8 Henry M Oneal, 4th *do*
9 Swipton Lowdon, *drummer*
10 Stephen Ballow, *fifer*
11 Ezekal England
12 Peter Wisenghunt
13 John Williams
14 Peter Mull
15 Frederick Bottles
16 Garrat Garratson
17 James Largant
18 Thomas Moody
19 Philip Pitts
20 William Sorrals
21 Joseph Thompson
22 James McFalls
23 Reuben Walker
24 Samuel Lockrage
25 William Oglesby
26 Archibald Oglesby
27 Thomas Michaels
28 Robert Good
29 William Reed
30 Andrew England
31 Joseph Baker
32 John Bottles
33 Elijah Walker
34 John Good
35 William Hartley
36 Joseph Murphy
37 John H Singling
38 Philip Shufler
39 Joseph England, M

40 William England, jun
41 Solomon Good, jun
42 John Powell
43 Michael Wisinghunt
44 Demmon Dossey, jun
45 John Derryburry
46 Alexander Deal
47 Henry Deal
48 John Jones
49 John Poteete
50 Peter A Bry
51 Michael Wehunt
52 John Martin
53 William Deal
54 John Black
55 John Kennedy
56 John Hartley
57 Abraham Deal
58 William Brackett
59 John Airwood
50 George Reider
61 William Wenters
62 John Eavins
63 Elijah Powell
64 Lewis Powell
66 Henry Wilds
66 John Bial
67 Jacob A Bey
68 Andrew Kincaid
69 James McDowell
70 John Hayse
71 Elijah Hayse
72 Isaac Tunmire
73 Henry Winkler
74 John Killian
75 John Purson
76 Thomas Bryant
77 Perian Daniel
78 Jesse Smith

79 John Smalley
80 Henry Kyles
81 William Pyott

82 Archibald Gibbs
83 James Hill
84 Micajah Lisk

BURKE COUNTY—SECOND REGIMENT.

1
3
2
4 Larkin Kerby
5 Andrew Reid
6 Joel Williams
7 William Turner
8 William Roberts
9 James Collins
10 John Fincannon
11 Thomas Bean
12 Jesse Berry
13 Abraham Melone
14 Samuel Smith
15 John Bovey, jun
16 John King
17 Leps Helton
18 Joshua Harshaw
19 Henry Cook
20 Alexander Campbell
21 John Ernest
22 Solomon Crisp
23 James Fletcher
24 William Coffey
25 Colbert Hays
26 John Harriss
27 Reuben Coffey

28 James Gilbert
29 John Sumpter
30 Joseph Owens
31 John Prock
32 Alexander West
33 Samuel Howell
34 Thomas Blair
35 Justice Beech
36 Frederick Tucker
37 John Brown
38 Christian Hass
39 John Litten (in dispute)
40 Robert Riner
41 Philip Rough
42 Joseph Kerby
43 Jonathan Penly
44 Lemuel Holt
45 John Fritt
46 William Reed
47 Matthew Winkler
48 Daniel Whittenburg
49 Thomas King
50 Enock Presnill
51 Thomas Dorsett
52 Eli Justice
53 Thomas Forrester

BURKE COUNTY—THIRD REGIMENT.

1 Jason Carson, *captain*
2 James Burgen, *lieut*
3 Pleasant Cashin
4 Burret Rickets
5 James Smith
6 Jonathan Allison
7 John Ross
8 Dennis Ross
9 Ben. Curtis
10 Lavender Fortune
11 George Darnald
12 Alexander Porter
13 George Edmison
14 Johnson Allison
15 Samuel Cockhorn
16 William Barley
17 Swinefield Hell
18 Henry Crown
19 William Guy
20 Jesse Henil
21 William Hughs
22 Andrew McKimy

23 Abner Devenporte
24 William Waldriss
25 Elis Waldriss
26 Thomas Devenporte
27 Manual Lamb
28 William Dickson
29 William Voun
30 Austin Pack
31 William Bright
32 Joab Goodbread
33 Joseph Lanner
34 Thomas James
35 Thomas Gribble
36 Mitchel Parham
37 William Henderson
38 Joseph Civins
39 John Queen
40 John Morris
41 William Duncan
42 John W Carson
43 Stogdol Wilson
44 David Curtis

45 Man Shote
46 Thomas Hancy
47 Daniel Morrow
48 John Biddicks

49 James Reves
50 Jacob Martin
51 William Jones
52 William Lackey

BUNCOMBE COUNTY—FIRST REGIMENT.

1 Clayton Neel, *captain*
2 Andrew Wilson, *lieut*
3 John Sutton, *private*
4 Samuel McCarson
5 Charles McLain
6 Lewis Herrin
7 William Wilson
8 James Brevard
9 Robert Wilson
10 Thomas Jones
11 Charles Adams
12 James Erwin
13 Cajer Smith
14 Abraham McGuffee
15 George Justin
16 James Jones
17 Nathan Fletcher
18 John Justice
19 Jesse Case
20 Andrew Lockhart
21 James Maxwell
22 William Justice
23 William Case
24 Andrew Lockart
25 James Maxwell
26 Archibald Edmiston
27 James S Smith
28 Jesse Causby
29 William Carn
30 Davis Rhodes
31 Ninnion Edmeston
32 William Cincard
33 Ezekiel Sandelin
34 John Osborn

35 Jeremiah Osborn
36 Daniel Allen
37 Henry Studer
38 Matthias Little
39 Samuel Corn
40 James Tweed
41 Hugh Johnston
42 David Evins
43 Enock Williams
44 Robert Orr
45 James Nickolson
46 Peter Sheperd
47 William W Lain
48 Richard Sceutill
49 Daniel Hefner
50 Eli Merrill
51 Ballard Lake
52 John Clayton
53 George D. Davis
54 David Fains
55 Burges Lake
56 George Erwin
57 Samuel King
58 Walter Burwell
59 James Clark
60 Mathew Wilson
61 James Kitchins
62 David Johnson
63 Alexander Jordan
64 Jonathan Lincard
65 Grady Johnson
66 Solomon Farker
67 John Galloway
68 Lewis Ransom

BUNCOMBE COUNTY—SECOND REGIMENT.

1
2
3 John Smith
4 John Hawkins
5 Aaron Javette
6 Elsy Rundles
7 Joseph Gudger
8 John Gooch
9 Joseph Wright
10 Nimrod Merril
11 Amos Lanning
12 Eli Rimon
13 Aaron Banks
14 Andrew Gorran
15 Thomas Snelson

16 Thomas Rogers
17 George Lindsey
18 John Frisby
19 William Spivey
20 David Rogers
21 David Vance
22 James Wever
23 William Button
24 David K Baty
25 George Corn
26 Richard Daff
27 James Dilliard
28 Robert Britton
29 James Rogers
30 Jacob Carber

31 Joseph Carver
32 Joseph Millsaps
33 William Mason
34 David Millar
35 Malley Reeves
36 Thomas Jones
37 Irea Javiette
38 Joseph Hays
39 George Brock
40 Elisha Spivey
41 Jacob Fortunberry
42 Abraham Penland
43 Aswell Phillips
44 James Rice
45 William Crage
46 Samuel Mafee
47 William Murray
48 John M Patton
49 William Wafer
50 John Henry
51 John Palmer
52 Andrew Garron
53 John Gearron
54 William H Murrey
55 M Haustin Patton
56 Jacob Jaron
57 William Gudger
58 Thomas Murry
59 Thomas Taylor
60 Samuel Jinkins
61 Adam Garron
62 John Patton
63 Cilas Rhea
64 Azra Jinkens
65 Samuel J Mavey

BUNCOMBE COUNTY—THIRD REGIMENT.

1 Levi Bailey, *captain*
2 Joseph Shepard, 1st *lieut*
3 David Hughey, *ensign*
4 William Keith
5 Henry Keith
6 James Wood
7 Mark Roberts
8 Thomas Roberts
9 Edward Robertson
10 Reuben Keith
11 John Cody
12 Tavner Moore
13 Joseph Ponder
14 Thomas Gaines Roberts
15 Nimrod Buckner
16 Robert Roberts
17 Jesse Giles
18 John Green
19 William Carson
20 John Greenwood
21 James Hurstle
22 Samuel Hughey
23 Shadrack Guthry
24 Garrat Deweese
25 William Williams
26 Augustine Prestwood
27 John Lams
28 James Lams
29 Britain Williams
30 John Arrowood
31 Benjamin Webb
32 Richard Holland
33 Joseph Callihorn
34 Absalom Medcalf
35 Sperlin Bowman
36 John Cornwell
37 John Garrett
38 John Stanton
39 John Slanlon
40 George Stanton
41 John Randolph
42 George Robertson
43 William Byrd
44 John Edwards
45 Samuel Byrd
46 William Dayton
47 James Edwards
48 William Taylor
49 Jacob Silver
50 James Angel
51 Jacob Killian
52 James McMahan
53 Maxamilian Harriss
54 Uriah Honeycutt
55 Angel Cook
56 John Anglin
57 John Poteet
58 James Poteet
59 William Calliway
60 Abner State
61 Jesse Radford
62 Edmond Edwards
63 Thomas Wilson
64 Thomas Lawson
65 Joseph Ray

S

HAYWOOD COUNTY.

1 John McClure, *captain*
2 Elijah Dever, *lieut*
3 John Dever, *ensign*
4 John Welsh
5 Joseph Cathey
6 Jethro Cathey
7 Christian Howel
8 Benjamin Hatfield
9 Jonathan Hains
10 James Campble
11 Andrew McClor
12 William McClure
13 Benjamin McMullen
14 Charles Evenes
15 Richard Clark
16 Abraham Eaton
17 William Goodwin
18 Lazarus Eaton
19 James Chambers
20 William Chambers
21 James McFarland
22 Bailey Fleming
23 Champ Langsford
24 David Elder
25 John Dillord
26 John Oliver
27 Benjamin Enloe
28 Edward Coiter
29 Jesse Enloe
30 James A Ellis
31 George Penland
32 William Rogers
33 James Williams
34 John Telley
35 Robert Penland
36 Hirom Gray
37 William Murray
38 William Crawford
39 Josiah Crawford
40 Joseph Chambers
41 John Lord
42 Andrew McLon
43 Joseph Dunn
44 John Bell
45 Andrew Bryson
46 John Middleton
47 Jonas Denton
48 Andrew Hopper
49 Jonathan Denton
50 James Peterson
51 Malachai Boland
52 John Middleton
53 William Watson
54 John Nelson
55 Henry Anderson
59 Martin Hefley
57 Nicholas Massey
58 William Montgory
59 George Hiffley
60 John Anderson
61 Isom Gurly
62 James Welsh
63 Hugh Donalson
64 Mark Colmer
65 Elisha Foller
66 John Mann
67 John Tollor
68 Samuel Corter
69 Samuel Robeson
70 Thomas Watson
71 John Watson
72 James Love
73 Loyd Heyson

MEMORANDA.

The following Counties of the Detached Militia of 1814, were called into service at Norfolk, in Virginia, by orders issued in September, A. D. 1814, to wit: Granville, Wake, Johnston, Franklin, Warren, Halifax, Northampton, Nash, Edgecombe, Martin, Bertie, Hertford, Gates, Chatham Orange, Person.

N. B. The detached Militia from the Counties of Chatham, Orange and Person were ordered to return to their respective homes before they arrived at Gates Court House, the place of rendezvous.

The Detached Militia from the following Counties were called into service at Wilmington, North Carolina, by orders issued September 29th, A. D. 1814, to wit: New Hanover, Brunswick, Bladen, Columbus, Robeson, Cumberland, Duplin, Sampson.

The following Counties of the Detached Militia were called into service at Newbern, North Carolina, by orders issued September 17th, A. D. 1814, to wit: Pitt, Wayne, Greene, Jones, Lenoir, Craven, Beaufort.

The detached Militia from the following Counties were called to Hillsborough, the place of rendezvous, on the 28th of November, A. D. 1814, where they were organized and from thence they were marched to Norfolk, in the service of the United States, agreeable to a requisition made by the President to the Governor of this State: The Counties to wit: Orange, Chatham, Person, Caswell, Rockingham, Guilford, Randolph, Stokes, Surry, Wilkes.

The officers of this regiment were,

RICHARD ATKERSON, of Person, as Lieutenant Colonel Commandant.
SAMUEL HUNTER, of Guilford, as Lieutenant Colonel.

JAMES CAMPBELL, of Rockingham, 1st }
JOSEPH WINSTON, junr. of Stokes, 2nd } Majors.

A requisition was made by Major General Thomas Pinckney, for one Regiment to march to the defense of the Southern Frontier of the Sixth Military District of the United States. In consequence of which, orders were issued from this office, calling forth the Detached Militia from the following Counties, to wit: Anson, Richmond, Moore, Cabarrus, to rendezvous at Wadesborough, in Anson County, on the 24th February, A. D. 1815. Also, to Ashe, Wilkes, Burke, Rutherford, Buncombe, Haywood, to rendezvous at Wadesborough, in Anson County, on Wednesday the 1st day of March, A. D. 1815.

Of this Regiment the following officers were designated to the command, to wit:

ANDREW IRWIN, as Lieutenant Colonel Commandant.
JOHN McGIMPSEY, of Burke, as Lieutenant Colonel.

JESSE ALLEN, of Wilkes, 1st }
THOMAS LENOIR, of Haywood, 2nd } Majors.

N. B. The orders from this office were dated on January 25th, A. D. 1815.

I do hereby certify, to the best of my knowledge and belief, that the foregoing is a true copy of the names of the Officers and Soldiers of the Detached Militia of North Carolina, in pursuance of a Requisition of the President of the United States, in virtue of an act of Congress, passed 10th April, 1812.

ROBERT W. HAYWOOD.
Adjutant General of the
Militia of N. Carolina.

NOTE BY THE PUBLISHER

The names of the Soldiers are spelled just as we find them on the Muster Roll, which will account for the *seeming* inaccuracies in the list, according to the present orthography of proper names.

INDEX

- A -

Aaron, Abner, Jr. 65
Abbot, Samuel 12
Abel, James 58
Abernasty, Frederick 53
Abernathy, Ezekiel 53
    Hardy 62
    Isaiah 53
    Joshua 53
    Miles 131
    Moses 53
    Samuel 130
Abington, James 18
Abrahams, Laden 89
Abshire, Jeremiah 52
Acborn, Will 33
Acer, Christopher 54
Acock, Alfred 63
    Brittain 101
    Jesse 33
    Ransom 23,80
Acrey, Edward 88
Acros, Leroy 108
Adain, William 55
Adam, William 13
Adams, Andrew 16
    Benjamin 52
    Bryan, Jr. 14
    Charles 62,136
    Elijah 122
    Gibson 117
    Hardy 14
    Harmon 29
    Henry 77
    Isaac 52,118
    Jacob 15
    Jesse 118
    John 52,105
    Joseph H. 81
    Laban 51
    Martin 35
    Noah 87
    Price 58
    Summer 87
    Sylvester 117
    Thomas 87
    William 13,105,111,
        130
Adcock, George 40
    Henry 26
    Jesse 37
    William 36
Adkins, William 92
Adkinson, Daniel 92
    Dawson 101
    William 26
Adkison, Wilie

Afria, Richard 55
Agender, Benjamin 68
    Peter 68
Agle, George 121
Agnor, Joseph 120
    Peter 121
Ahorn, Signor 114
Aikin, Jeremiah 76
    Jeremiah D. 76
Aims, Benjamin 22
Airbury, Elijah 116
Aire, William K. 45
Airs, David 81
    John 8,92
    Richard 21
Airwood, John 134
Akin, William 61
Albertson, William 75
Albird, William 10
Albright, Jacob 108
    Joel 33
    John 32,120
    Joseph 108
    Peter 43
Albritton, John H. 13
    Samuel 87
    Simon 13
Alby, Howell 61
Alcorn, John 61
Aldred, Reuben 119
Aldridge, Jonathan 55,113
    Richard 86
    Samuel 118,41
    Thomas 86
Aldrige, Samuel 41
Alexander, Aaron 92
    Abdon 126
    Albertes 126
    Alexis 128
    Anthony 81
    Benjamin 61
    Cirus 127
    David 47,82
    Eli 47
    Ezekiel 125
    Gardner 82
    George C. 58
    Harmon 9
    James 61,125,128
    John 48,55,133
    John D. 125
    Johnston 39
    Joseph 47
    Joshua 81
    Laid 49
    Major R. (capt.) 55
    Mitchell 58
    Palau 48
    Robert 130

    Salamachus 126
    Thomas 34
    William 9,40,63
    Willis 52
Alford, Elie 101
    Jacob 104
    Julius 24
    William 24
    Willie 104
Alfred, Bailey 63
    Gilbert 63
    Green 60
    Hardy 90
    Kate 63
    Macomb 24
Allan see Allen
Allegood, Jacob 83
Alleh, John 80
Allemony, Henry 61,120
Allen, Abraham 122
    Amos 28
    Benjamin 112
    Charles 22
    Daniel 136
    David 15,100,112
    Dearling 129
    Dillard 113
    Eaton F. 19
    George 124
    Grant 106
    Ira 80
    Isaac 94
    Ivy 22
    James 36
    Jesse 139
    John 14,23,65,78,80,
        82,117,126
    Jonathan 94
    Joseph 93,110
    Ludwell 78
    Miles 63
    Morgan 93
    Niram 59
    Paul 96
    Richard 67,80
    Richard E. 132
    Robert 32,126
    Shadrach 112
    Thomas 4,5,6,47
    Vine 11
    Walter 12
    William 9,32,74
    Woodson 102
    Young, Jr. 102
    Young, 2d 102
    Zachariah 19
Alles, Peter 127
Alley, James 128
    John 124

Allimony see Allemony
Allin see Allen
Allison, Benjamin 57
    David 117
    Egbert 107
    James 105
    John 55
    Johnson 135
    Jonathan 135
    Thomas 120,128
    William 62,128
    Zilmon 106
Alloway, William 52
Alman, Lewis 57
Almond, Edmond 62
    Nathan 103
Alphin, Frederick 7
    Hezekiah 86
    Jesse 86
    John 7
    Thomas 17
Alsobrook, James 20
    Micajah 79
Alston, James 23,80
    John 19
    Joseph 34
    Thomas 101
Ambrose, James 89
    Jehu 8
    Levi 8
    Peter 91
Ambrous, Berry 101
Amburgy, William 118
Amburn, Samuel 57
    William 57
Ameck, David 119
    John 112
Ames, John, Jr. 21
    Joseph 105
Amget, Peter 64
Amick see Ameck
Amis, John 21
Amison, Edward 88
Ammonds, John 12,57
Ammons, Stephen 96
Amos, John 133
    Joseph 105
Amosin, Thomas 64
Amyett, Darius 11
Ananias, William W. 36
Anders, Abner 17
    Adam 85
    Ivey 85
Anderson, Andrew 27
    Charles 42,44
    Francis 19
    George 27
    Henry 58,138
    James 96
    Jeremiah 36,100
    John 56,89,138
    John, Jr. 59
    John A. 76
    Reuben 39
    Samuel 121
    Scarlet 36
    William 25,28,120,121
Andres(s) Aaron 116
    John 92
    Wilson 124
Andrews, Arden 59
    Benjamin 132
    Culin 88
    Hezekiah 33
    James 114
    John 12,86,101
    Nelson 35,102
    Vinston 12

    Warren 11
    William 8,76
Angel, James 137
    Joshua 51
    Lawrence 115
    Peter 35
    Samuel 114
Angle, Benjamin D. 114
Anglin, John 58,137
Ansley, Joseph 89
Anson, Jesse 25
Anthony, David 51
    Henry 112
    James 56,69
    William 56,59
Antry, Frederick 27
Appleshite, Thomas 18
Applin, William 21
Archabb, Moses 127
Archer, David 40
    Elijah 8
    James 40
    John 79
    Joshua 104
    Mathuel 8
    Moses 34
Archibald, Samuel 128
    Thomas 47
    William 10
Archland, Thomas 3
Archlin, Bryan 10
Arcory, Albert 58
Arendel, Thomas B. 23
Arenhart, Henry 120
Arey, Jerry 121
Argoe, Joseph 33
Armond, James 13
Armstead, Taban 64
Armstrong, Andrew 8
    J. Smith 58
    John 97
    Matthew 53
    Samuel 53
    Selby 9
    Solomon 81
    William 89
Arnet(t), Asbury 42
    John 124
Arnold, Edward 11
    Elisha 84
    James 104
    John 7,84,87,104
Arrenton, Edward 6
    Joseph 6
    Thomas 6
Arrington, John 124
    Levi C. 22
Arrowood, James 133
    John 137
    Red 130
Artis, Cullen 20
    Kinchen 20
Asburge, Joseph, Jr. 41
Asbury, Francis 54
Ash, Halvin 19
    James 19
    Thomas 53
Ashe, Joseph 31
Asher, John 61
Ashley, James 32
    John 72
    William 72
Ashworth, Benjamin 101
Asken, George 8
Askin, Eanos 88
Askins, Ezekiel 17
    Josiah I. 8
Askew, Abner 87

Asque, William 108
Atherly, James 12
Atherton, Richard 71,139
Atkins, Jacob 22
    James 38
    Jonas 8
    Thomas 60
Atkinson, Dawson 35
    Joel H. 102
    Richard 31
Atwater, Moses 31
Atwell, John 128
Atwill, William 90
Aulberty, John 116
Austin, Jonathan 103
    Ransom 106
    Wilson 122
Auston, Cornelius 4
    Moses 4
Autrey, Ezekiel 95
Avem, Durham 97
    Thomas 80
Avera, Jacob 14
Averhart, Jacob 45
Averit, Thomas 24
Avery, Henry 36
    Isaac 4
    James 58
    John 97
    Samuel 84
Aycock, James 14
Aydelotte, Jacob 73

- B -

Baber, Robert 50,54
Bachelor, Daniel 22
    James 79
    John 81
    Wilson 81
    Wright 81
Badget, John 38
Bager, Jacob 127
    John 127
Bagget, Abram 53
Baggett, Drury 53
Baggott, Asa 28
Baglas, Hugh 32
Baglen, Joseph 4
Bagley, Davis 116
    Joseph 6
    Nathan 6,75
    William 75,105
Bagly, Etheldred 14
Bagner, Alfred 83
    Slamil 83
    Willie 83
Bags, Hall 16
Bagwell, Budd 101
    Richard 26
Baicly, Robert 133
Bailey, David 15,54
    Henry 106
    Jeremiah 119
    John 61,133
    John T. 12
    Jonathan 20
    Levi 137
    Robert 133
    William 100
Baily, John T. 12
Bain, Alexander 127
    John 107
Bainhill, John 92
Baird, Elisha 63
    Mathew 63

Zebulon 63
Bake, Samuel 35
Baker, Aaron 125
  Abel 125
  Benjamin 50,77
  Blake 18
  Duncan 30,98
  Edward B. 65
  Elisha 93
  German 78
  Henry 42,82
  Isaac 76
  James 91
  John 3,8,23,28,59,91
  Jonathan 103
  Joseph 134
  Lunceford 80
  Martin 51
  Michael 125
  Nathan 8,46
  Philip 52,68
  Samuel 35
  William 23,52
Balance see Ballance
Balding, Alfred 99
Baldridge, James 111
Baldwin, David 28
  Enoch 119
  James, Jr. 28
  Theophilus 67
  Warren 67
Balentine see Ballentine
Baley, Charles 57
  Drury 15
Ball, David 111
  George 117
  Gilford 105
  James 117
  Javan 117
  John 69
  Major 83
  Merriman 98
  Mills 29
  Richard 105
  Spencer 110
  William 122
Ballance, Edmond 103
  Jesse 73
  Merrit 3
  Thomas 73
  William H. 19
Ballard, Drewry 32
  Edwin 7
  Gardner 31
  John 53
  John D. 123
  Joseph 59
  Lemuel 88
  Lewis 38
  Solomon 69
  William 80
  Willis 130
Ballenger, Allen S. 14
Ballentine, David 97
  Willis 73
Ballester, William 8
Ballie, Mills 29
Ballow, Stephen 134
Baltin, Jacob 101
Balton, James 50
Bambow, Paten 48
Band, John 64
Bane, Peter J. 69
Bankenship, Micajah 132
Banks, Aaron 136
  Hardy 8
  Hardy M. 76
  James 3

Jesse 115
John 9
William 10
Banley, Stephen 30
  William 54
Bar see Barr
Barbee, James C. 101
  Joseph 101
Barber, Absolam 91
  Brittain 14
  Bryan 91
  David 32
  John 14,29
  Johnson 34
  William 87,120
Barclay, Henry 53
  Jonathan 121
Barclift, Samuel, Sr. 75
Barclipt, Samuel 6
Barco, Baley 4
  Joseph 74
  Peter 73
Barefoot, John 94
  Noah 14
Barfield, Allen 28
  Benjamin 21
  Bryan 13
  Cade 96
  Frederick 87
  Henry 14
  John 94
  Littleberry 20
  Needam 96
  Thomas 40
Barflet, Richard 126
Barham, Nathan 39
Barker, Daniel 50
  George W. 113
  James 33
  Jeremiah 33
  John 113,133
  Robert 34,131
  Thomas 113
  William 6
Barley, William 135
Barlow, Marsh 97
  Thomas 117
Barnacastle, Francis 45
Barnard, Grandy 72
  James 129
  Reuben 46
  Willoughby 72
Barnell, Daniel 40
Barnett, Amos 125
  Jesse 28
  John 4,10,36,125
  John, Jr. 36
  Luke 29
  Robert 82
Barnes, Aceles 64
  Albertain 96
  Daniel 81
  David 20
  Elijah 117
  Enos 64
  George 117
  James 59,76,126
  Jeptha A. 79
  Jeremiah 113
  Jethro 90
  John 48,64,75,93,117
  Jordan 89
  Micajah 126
  Pleasant 40
  Reddick 64
  Reuben 77
  Robert 40,84,89
  Samuel 90

Simon 90
William 36,48
Winwright 113
Barney, Samuel 112
  Simon 11
Barnhard, John 49
Barnhart, George 128
  John 34,49
Barnhill, Henry 88
  John 59,88,125
  Robert 31
Barns see Barnes
Barr, John 42
  Moses 130
  William 43
  William D. 83
Barrat, Asa 9
Barrett, William M. 47
Barrier, Henry 123
Barringer, Matthias 131
Barrington, Daniel S. 60
  Jacob 62
  Jesse 12
  John 86
  Lemuel 5
Barrot, William 98
  Zach 84
Barrow, Benjamin 17
  James 23,91
  John 10,64
  Jordan 22
  Thomas 89
  William 82,86
Barry, Andrew 129
  David 41
  James 41
  John 41
Bartholemew, Jacob 18
Bartlett, Isaac 116
  James 90
Baslay, Willis 97
Basom, Frederick 107
Bass, Bryan 90
  Cader 22
  Felix 96
  Guilford 24
  Jesse 13
  John 36
  Lioratta 36
  Moses 31
  Noah 90
  William 13,90
Baston, David 22
Baswell, Edward 32
  James 77
  Matthew 32
Bate, Freeman 45
Bateman, Andrew 81
  Asahel 64
  Benjamin 6
  Cornelius 11
  Evin 81
  Hardy 6
  James 81
  Jeremiah 11
  Lemuel 6
Bates, Wade 132
Batey, David K. 136
  William 122
Baton, Thomas 20
Batten, Amos 14
  Hardy 14
  William 14
Battle, Josiah 8,101
  William 100
Batton, Moses 124
Batts, Geraldine 89
  Lott 15

Baum, Adam 73
  Robert 78
Bavick, James 42
Bawcom, Bennet 101
  James 101
Baxley, Michael 96
Baxter, Daniel 125
  John 60,72,73
  Joseph, Jr. 73
  Joshua 44
Bayett, George 103
Bays, James 116
Bayton, William 89
Bazimore, Cullen 77
  Stephen 77
Beach, John 22
  Richard 23
  William 21
Beacham, Eden 83
Beal, Joseph 122
  Tabner 109
  Thomas 109
Beale, Robert 53
Beales, Berket 74
  James 74
Beals, Josiah 4
Beam, Martin 133
Beaman, Abraham 124
  David 124
  Samuel 45
Bean, Thomas 135
Beane, Nathaniel 31
Bear, John 52
Beard, John 44,93,139
  Lewis 44
  Thomas 90
Beardan, John 95
Beasley, Daniel 63
  Francis 85
  James 42
  Joshua 63
  Samuel 3
  William 3
Beasly, John P. 105
Beason, David 40
  William 42
Beatty, James G. 56
Beaty, Abel 133
  Isaac 47
  James G. 56,69
  John 120
Beaver, William 108
Beaves, John 50
Beck, Abram 42
  John 122
Becketh, John 45
Beckham, Lemuel 129
Beckwith, Amos 22
  James 80
  Thomas 22
Becton, Frederic J. 85
Bector, John 47
Beddoe, Travers 67
Bedsold, Thomas 93
  Travis 93
Beech, Jonathan 94
  Justice 135
Beeling, Ralph P. 93
Beem, Peter 54
Beesley, John 92
  Solomon 92
Beeson, Vestal 120
Beheler, David 133
Beil, James 68
  John 46
Beill, Reason 46
  Walter 46
Belcher, George 14

Belflower, James 88
Belinger, Julian D. 5
Belk, Brelon 48
  John 126
Bell, Benjamin 88
  Branson 73
  Burrel 87
  David 106
  Elijah 110
  Francis 60
  George W. 40
  Hillary 4
  James 60,63
  Jeremiah 35
  Jesse 50
  Joab 74
  John 61,66,100,104,
    138
  Joseph 73
  Joshua 9,26
  Matthias 73
  Michael 80
  Newel 85
  Reason 47
  Tandy 112
  Thomas 61
  William 35,91,127
  William W. 35
Belsher, Beverly 86
  Woody 86
Belvin, Peter 108
Bendon, Charles 13
Benge, James 52
Benhill, William 125
Bennet see Bennett
Bennett, Benjamin C. 28
  Charles 23
  Daniel 13,66
  Drury 50
  James 49
  James C. 23,80
  John 95
  Lovin 124
  Luke 21
  Mereday 43
  Thomas 15
  William 54,66
  William R. 59
Bennick, Jeremiah 55
Benns, John T. 78
Bensel, John 118
Benson, James 93
  Matthew 93
Bentholl, John 8
Bentley, James 129
Bently, Benjamin 11
Benton, Abbey 7
  David 7
  Francis 12
  Henry H. 7
  Jacob 7
  Jethro 7
  John 20
  Joseph 37
  Joshua 5
Berbank, Paul 12
Bereman, Kader 7
Berger, Henry 68
Bernard, Carter 74
Berns, George 126
Berring, William 17
Berry, David 16
  George 106,129
  Isaac 4
  Jesse 135
  Joseph 41
  Miles 4
  Thomas 73

Timothy 4
  William 4,10
Berryman, Stephen 27
Berton, Robert 49
Berwick, William 40
Beson, Samuel 33
Best, Bostian 130
  Elias 99
  Henry 21
  Theophilus 16
  William 15
Bertha, Jesse 24
Bethell, Alfred 113
Bethune, Hector 67
Betts, John
Beverly, Abner 99
  Jephthah 100
Bevers, Thomas 33
Bevill, Alexander 39
  Henry 112
  James 112
  Phillip 39
  Thomas 39
Bewsey, Charles 118
Bey, Jacob A. 134
Bial, John 134
Bibby, Nathaniel 100
Bibee, John 115
Bickerstaff, Samuel 132
Biddicks, John 136
Biddingfield, Theophilus
    103
Bierly, David 44
Biggener, Frederick 15
Biggers, Johnston N. 49
Biggs, Davis 8
Bigham, Robert, Jr. 125
  Samuel 125,130
Bilberry, James 21
Bilbes, William 81
Biley, Michael 120
Billberry, John 94
Billbinny, Henry 94
Billings, David 121
Billingsby, Hezekiah 29
  William 39
Billing, David 121
Bince, Felix M. 39
Bingham, Joseph 47
  William 51
Binkley, John 41
Binny, Aaron 112
Bird, Andrew 124
  Bright 14
  James 31
  John 26,27
  Joseph 31
  Joshua 12
  Josiah 77
  Nathan 12
  Raphael 13
  Samuel 123
  William 23,54,87
Bird see also Byrd
Birkhart, George 44
Bishop, John 94,100
  Jos. 114
  Morris 92
  Owen 94
  Thomas, Jr. 92
  W. M. 65
  William 32
  Zachariah 82
Bissent, William 44
Bissit, Joseph 80
Bizzel, John 90
Bizzett, John 8
Black, Adam 122

Andrew 17
David H. 49
George 34
John 30,48,49,92,98,
134
Joseph 58,122,130
Kenneth 98
Mosse 133
Neil 98
Pleasant 113
Thomas 131
William 131
Blackburn, Asa 19
Burwell 102
Daniel 131
Jesse 19
John 21,52,125
Levi 118
William 115
Blackenship see Blaken-
ship
Blackledge, Richard 83
Blacklock, David 34
Blackman, Barney 96
Jeremiah 14
John 97
William 67
Blackurl, Solomon 134
Thomas 134
Blackville, Robert 116
Blackwater, Andrew 127
Caleb 127
Blackwelder, Christ. 120
Blackwell, Abraham 93
John 27,56
Robert 105
Solomon 56
Blackwood, Anderson 108
John 130
Joseph 125
Blair, Jesse 119
Thomas 135
Blake, Asa 101
Ethelred 49
Joseph 49
Blallock, David 49
Blalock, David 109
Hastin 106
John 53
Terrel 50
Blan, Benjamin 76
Blanchard, Dempsey 7
John 7,15
Reuben 15
Seth 75
William 75
Blanchet, William 114
Young 97
Bland, George 11
Thomas 109
Blankenship, Archibald 52
William 46
Blanks, William 36
Blanton, George 55
Jesse 132
John 55,132
Lewis 55
Blaylock, Jos. 109
Bledsoe, Anthony 101
Edward 102
George 104
Giles B. 35
Giles J. 64
John 28
Joseph 104
Patrick 104
Thomas 124
Blewet, Thomas 62

Blont, Major 90
Blount, Benjamin 30
Clement H. 72
Ezekiel 9
Henry 80,82
James 81
John 27
Joseph 31,77
Lewis 82
Reading 31
Stephen 81
Theophilus 94
Thomas H. 71
Warren 15
Blue, Archibald 28
Collin 17
Duncan 27
John 27,29,93
Peter 98
Bluford, William 130
Bluie, John 93
Blume, John 115
Boak, Alam 114
Bobbit, Arthur 106
John B. 104
Bochannon, John 39
Bock, William 36
Bodenhammer, David 123
George 68
Jacob 123
John 61
William 123
Bodiford, William 30
Bogan, Arthur 90
David 67
Bogar, Daniel 121
Boget, Henry 90
Boggan, Jonathan 99
Boggaw, Isaac 99
Boggle, James 129
William 129
Bogleman, Archibald 28
Bogue, Jonathan 6
Josiah 7
Bohannon, Neal 117
Boice, Isaac 72
Boid, Major 11
Robert 48
Boland, Malachi 138
Bolar, Shadrack 101
Bolick, Casper 131
Boling, James 110
Bollinger, Christian 131
Bominger, Jacob 123
Bonbaum, David 92
James 92
Boncy, James 94
Bond, Edwin 72
George H. 76
John 6
John, Sr. 72
Will 83
Bondusant, Lee 114
Bone, David 25
Eli 109
John 128
Richard 25
Bonner, Gideon 3
Richard 10
Booe, Daniel 68
Jacob 68
Booker, Richard 46
Bookout, David 31
Boon, Abram 8
Bennet 78
Berd 92
David 19
Elisha 19

Jep 20
Jeremiah 57
John 34,57,95
Joiner 20
Kinchen 23
Lewis 8,20
Nickolas 92
Owen 24
Samuel 8
West 8
William 20,78
Bonner, John 10
Booth, Alexander 8
Arthur 8
Daniel 107
George 114
Zachariah 45
Boothe, Daniel 107
Boovey, Mathew 131
Bore, Daniel 61
Bose, John 68
Boss, Henry 33
Bost, Daniel 49
David 54
Elias 62
Matthias 49
William 62
Bostick, David D. 114
Richard 133
Bostion, Jacob 128
Boston, Andrew 120
Bostwick, John 30
Boswell, Goldsberry 94
Gustavous 45
James 65
John 3,115
Parubo 38
Boswood, Willoughby 72
Bottles, Frederick 134
John 134
Botts, Thomas 40
Bourdeaux, John B. 92
Moses 95
Bourne, James 96
Boushel, Robert 4
Bovey, John, Jr. 135
Bowan, Charles 94
Bowden, Jesse 122
Reading 95
Thomas
Bowdown, John 119
Bowell, Joseph 60
Bowen, Benjamin 77
Charles 94
Hardy 92
John 15,77
Lewis 15,42
Silas 86
Thomas 25
Bowers, Absalom 118
Barnabas 44
Bartholomew 21
David 59,122
Elias 39
George 44
James 104
John 110
Lewis 42
Malikiah 43
Richard L. 65
Bowey, John D. 94
Bowie, Neil 25
Nelson 80
Bowing, Obadiah 19
Bowls, John 105
Jordan 105
Bowman, Andrew 115
George 131

Henry 39
Sperlin 137
Boyakin, William 101
Boyce, John 72
Moses 75
Boyd, Adam 112
Alex 109
Edward 52
Henry 11,87
John 77,112
Thomas 125
William 87
Boyet, Arthur 7
Nathaniel 26
Boykin, Brittain 63
Irvin 81
John 26
Solomon 26
Thomas 26
Boylan, Abraham H. 35
Boyt, Henry 95
Bozeman, Josiah 30
Bozman, William R. W. 77
Bozwell, Parubo 38
Brabble, James 73
John 73
John, Jr. 73
Tatum 73
Brabim, John 112
Bracker, Laban 47
Brackett, Thomas 132
William 134
Bradberry, Bryah 90
Braddy, Benjamin 83
Elisha 87
George 47
James A. 126
Jesse 133
William 87
William J. 102
Braddy see also Brady
Braden, James 133
Bradford, Henry 18
John 18,79
Joseph 31
Matthew 90
Thomas 18,31
Bradley, James 117
Major 102
Richard 15
Spier 20,89
Summons 55
Terry 55
Bradly, Nimrod 49
Bradshaw, James 106
John 105,127
Thomas, Sr. 108
Vincent 106
William 32
Brady, John 132
Robert 98
Brag, Solomon 83
Brake, David 21
Jacob 21
Braker, William 102
Braley, James 55
Branch, James 37,57
John 75
John W. 18
William 17
Brand, John 13
Brandle, Daniel 116
Brandon, John 61,122
John H. 120
Brandonn, John 61
Branner, Alfred 39
Brannock, Samuel 123
Branock, Edmund 108

Branson, William 115
Brantley, Henry 76
William 35
Brantly, Alben 80
Benjamin 46,100
David 99
Edward 8
Edwin 22
Henry 8,76
James 18
John 4,65
Joshua P. 65
Robert 8
William 35,79
Wilson 18,79
Brassie, James 96
Braswell, Aaron 96
Burwell 124
Marmaduke 79
Sion 81
Whitmell 79
Braughton, James 7
Brawley, Daniel 128
Robert 128
Brawlie, Neil, Jr. 47
Bray, Daniel 75
George 15
Jesse 5,109
Joel 116
John 34
Joseph 5
Thomas 33,50,73
William 72
William, Jr. 3
Brayfield, Walton 38
Brazil, Shadrick 99
Breadlove, William 22
Breedlove, William 80
Bremon, Nathan 90
Brevard, Hemden 47
James 136
Jesse 57
Brewer, Benjamin 116
Elijah 78
Frederick 67
John 95
Julius 67
Micajah 119
Perry 21
Samuel 110
Turner 79
William 108,118
William, Jr. 98
Briars, David 55
Brickell, John 65
Samuel 18
William 18,65
Brickhead, Kindrick 98
Brickhouse, Benjamin 9
Jabez 75
John 73
Major 82
Matthew 82
Richard 82
Uzzell 9
William 9,135
Brickle, Samuel 18
William 18
Bridger, James 90
Bridgers, David 102
Bridges, Aron 55
Barnes 20
Benjamin 15,31,108
Brawell 14
George 132
Henry 22
James 23,131
John 64

Newit 14
Newsome 23
Richard 55,132
Samuel 56,68
Warren 20
Bridgmore, Pleasant 42
Brigat, John 109
Briggs, Benjamin 114
Edward 75
Henry 41
James 121
Jethro 7
John 121
Kader 76
Bright, Francis 17
Henry 73
John 67
Brigs, James 121
Briles, Jacob 33
Briley, James 29
Jonathan 88
William 87
Brim, John 54
Brindle, Abraham 45
Brindon, Gideon 86
Bringle, Jacob 44
Bringman, William 30
Brinigan, Joshua 68
Brinigar, Jacob 116
Joshua 68
Brinkhart, John 44
Brinkle, Robert H. 40
Brinkley, Henry 7
Jethro 75
Robert 19
William 60,78,79
Brinkly, Griffin 6
Brinn, Benjamin 82
Brinsfield, Thos. 111
Brinson, Jos. S. 84
William S. 84
Brintle, Oliver 38
Britt, Burwell 96
Culiver 98
David 30
Drucis 110
Drury 20
Gideon 14
Henry 90
James 96
John 13
Johnson 101
Shade 65
Thomas 95
William 30,86,98
Brittain, Benjamin 16
William 134
Brittle, Brittain 78
Britton, Benjamin 12
Robert 136
Samuel 76
Thomas 8
Broach, Richard 106
Broadway, Jesse 11
Broadwell, Freeman 63
Brock, Caleb 44
David 95
George 137
Jesse 95
Moses 5
Thomas 95
Brocket, Hiram 18
Brockett, John A. 73
Brogden, John 13
Pearce 90
Timothy 21
Brogdion, Alfred 45
Benjamin 65

Ransom 103
William 45,65,104
Brook, Richard 80
Brooks, Constant 133
David 15
Frederick 10
George 38
George, Jr. 111
Isaac 55
James 29
Jesse A. 18
Joab 34
John 52,106
John James 106
Johnson 111
Joseph 94
Joseph, Sr. 94
William 85,88
Brookshire, William 51,
124
Broom, Allen 48
Gilford 87
Brothers, Benjamin 5
Caleb 74
Joseph, Jr. 75
Joseph, Sr. 75
Miles 74
Brower, Christian, Jr.
119
John 118
Brown, Aben 27
Abner 45
Absalom 60
Alexander 29,51
Allen 67
Anthony 8
Archibald 117
Asa 107
Bannet 124
Barnabas 24
Barnaby 88
Benjamin 46,76
Bennet 101,124
Berry 89
Burwell 101
Claton 134
Daniel 43,68,109
David 76
Dempsey 105
Eldah 101
Eli 52,118
Elisha 25,118
Ezekiel 118
Fountain 16
Francis 12
Frederick 33
George 52
Gillis 64
Harbert 112
Henry 62
Isaac 81
Israel 39
James 10,16,30,51,
102,112
Jesse 43,77,114
John 24,34,38,48,52,
76,83,91,102,109,
115,118,125,135
John, Jr. 116
John S. 84
Joseph 81,118
Josiah 13
Judson 120
Peter 40,118,121
Redding 88
Richard 105
Samuel 47,117
Stephen 14

Sylvester 12
Thomas 3,7,12,22,24
Whitfield 117
Wiley 8
William 8,19,30,33,
35,51,58,60,76,98
William, Jr. 41
William G. 35
William W. 40
Zachariah 8
Browney, Zachariah 88
Browning, Edward 11
James 31,107
John 107
William 10,103
Broy, Edward 26
Broyhill, John N. 51
William 51
Bruce, James 38
Joel 47
John 118
Jordan 89
Robert 36
Brumblow, David 100
Brumsey, William 73
Bruner, Michael 120
Brunt, John 14
Peter 79
Bruton, Moses 93
Simon 9,71
Bry, Peter A. 134
Bryan, Armelain 94
Aron, Sr. 34
Bartholomew 20
David 102
Edmund 52
Elias 22
Elijah C. 65
Harry 102
John 19,25,34,93,122
Joseph 84,48,103
Joseph H. 65
Nathan 14
Samuel 19
Sears 85
Thomas 21
William 94
Bryant, Charles 50
Edward 104
James 87,104
John 18
Simon A. 77
Thomas 22,134
William T. 79
Bryer, Samuel M. 56
Bryon, Cornelius 5
Bryson, Andrew 138
John J. 58
Buch, James 87
Buchan, Daniel 98
Malcom 98
Buchanan, Alfred 109
David 41
James 127
John 106
Walter 37
William 37,106
Bucher, Daniel 92
Buck, Henry 46
John 45,98
Buckman, Samuel 85
Buckner, Edward 34
Edward, Jr. 45
Nimrod 137
Buckum, Simon 108
Bue, Archibald 28
Buie, Allen 30
Daniel 97,98

Duncan
Nell 67
Bukerdete, Ezra 33
Bulbee, Absalon
Jonathan 35
Bull, Samuel 106
Bullard, Elias 96
Henry 93
Richard 96
William 31
Bulling, Henry 42
Bullock, Henry 96
John 88
Leonard 104
Obadiah 88
Stephen 64
Whitmel C. 89
Bultry, William 21
Bumbough, William 75
Bumgarner, John 130
Bumgarner see also Bun-
garner
Bumpass, William 106
Bunch, Cader 65
Edmund 72
John 75
Julius 6
Nathaniel 7
Nehemiah 77
Salter 6
Samuel 120
Bundrant, John 40
Bundy, Caleb 5,74
Jesse 5
Nathan 5
William 90
Bungarner, Absolam 53
Moses 53
Bunham, Joseph 115
Bunker, Zenas 40
Bunn, Alfred 22
Barnabas 26
Benjamin 10
Budd 101
Cader 63
Henry 80
Lewis 101
William 10,80
Bunnell, James 73
John 73
William 3
Bunton, Jeremiah 90
Bunyard, Larkin 67
Burbage, George C. 10
Burch, Jesse 116
Burdeaux, Israel C. 18
Buress, William 124
Burfield, Zachariah F. 18
Burge, Larkin 42
Burgen, James 135
Burges, Anda 101
John 35
Burgess, Dempsey J. 5
Edward 68
Isaac 74
John 26,34
Burk, Joseph 53
Milliner 34
Burke, Hugh 26
Samuel 106
Burkett, Burges 78
Lemuel 78
Burkin, Larkin 114
Burkly, Donald C. 16
Burn, Levi 55
Burnet, James 109
Burnett, Abram 17
Ferrington 60

Iredell 11
  Robert 20
Burney, Abel 24
  David 112
  Lewis 11
  Robert 112
Burnham, Joel 95
  Thomas 74
  William 6
Burns, Benjamin 132
  Hezekiah 58
  Hiram 110
  Jacob 53
  James, Jr. 34,110
  Jonas 58
  Jonathan 45
  Levi 55
  Reddick 34
  Wenright 61
Burod, John 14
Burrage, James 33
Burress, Hausford 64
Burroughs, Joseph 38,111
Burrow, Ephraim 112
  Solomon 113
Burrus, Zachariah 4
Burt, Abraham 112
  John 97
Burton, Absalom 110
  Bartlett 3
  Emsley 123
  Francis H. 110
  Henry 33
  Hutchens 37
  Noel 111
  Samuel 124
  Stephen 38
  Thomas Halley 37
  Zachariah 124
Burwell, Walter 136
Busby, Alsey 103
  James 92
Bushbey, Will 47
Bushnell, Mathew 29
Bushup, Benjamin 28
  John 28
Busick, Caleb 109
  James 109
Bussill, Presly 118
Butler, Arthur 24
  Charles 27
  Curry 77
  John P. 77
  Jordan 84
  Joshua 38
  Samuel 25
  Silas 77
  William 11
  Zachariah 25
Butner, David 68
Butter, John 101
  Willis 75
Button, Daniel 126
  William 136
Butts, James 14
Byam, John 7
Byers, David 36
  Francis 57
  George 36
  Robert 58
Bynum, Hampton 115
  John 130
  Kinchen 36
Byrd, John 12
  Samuel 137
  William 137
Byrns, Matthew 122
Byrum, Ransom 110

- C -

Cable, John 33
  Joseph 32
Cade, Richard 25
  Waddell 25
Caffee, James 10
Caffer, Hooper 12
Cagle, Leonard 124
Cahoon, Abel 81
  James 82
  John, Jr. 82
  John, Sr. 82
Cain, Andrew 40
  Samuel 93
Caisar, Richard 103
Calaher, Mathew 128
Calbroth, Daniel 67
Caldwell, Allen 41
  Andrew 47
  John 47,53
  Robert 125
  Robert, Jr. 125
  William 54
Calicoat, George 124
  John 124
Call, Elijah 54
  Henry 123
  Jacob 68
  William 122
Callahan, Robert 68
Callaway, Jonathan 88
Callihorn, Joseph 137
Calliway, William 137
Calloway, David 77
  Hatter 77
  Jonathan 21,88
Callum, Augt. 65
  Sion 93
Calum, Robert 35
Calvet, Stephen 91
  William 94
Calway, Haller
Cam, James M. 15
Cambell, Lemuel 5
Camble, William F. 62
Cameron, Hugh 28
  James 97
  John A. 24
Camerson, William F. 47
Camp, Abner 54
  Francis 73
Campbell, Adam 129
  Alexander 66,135
  Allen 25
  Anguish 62
  Charles 30
  Cyrus 49
  Dahold 98
  David 120
  Edley 111
  Enos 68
  Frederick 60
  James 24,41,94,97,
    138,139
  John 24,67,69,94,115
  Montesquien W. 92
  Murdock 25
  Neel 27
  Roderick 30
  Samuel 10,54
  Shadrick 12
  Thomas 46
  Will 107
  William 12,69,78
Campble, James 138,139
Camper, David 83

Camplain, Henry 112
Canada, Joel 116
Canaday, Elijah 66
  Kinchen 84
Canady, Right 13
Candy, Felix 15
Cane, Daniel 45
Caneade, John 58
Canley, Charles 31
Cannon, Dennis 11,95
  Henry 11,88,90
  John 11
  Palmer 11
  Sim 58
  William 42,114
Cantrall, Benjamin 38
Cantrel, Jacob 56
Cantrell, John 41
Cantrill, Elijah 41
  George 41
  Robert 41
Canwadd, William 101
Capehart, Trustum 79
Capel, James 29
Capell, Gooden 99
Caperman, David 52
Capps, Henry 102
  Jasper 23
Caps, Cornelius 58
  Jeptha 80
  John 73
  Mark 112
  William 108
Capts, Dennis 3
Car, William 116
Caraway, James 21
  William 11
Carber, Jacob 136
Card, Samuel 97
Carden, John 107
Cardwell, Joel 113
  Leonard 60
  Noah 114
  Thomas F. 32
Carey, Richard 90
Cariker, Adam 128
Carley, James 65
Carlisle, Joel 79
  Littleberry 88
  Richard 22
  Robert 28
Carlton, Ambrose 117
  George 27
Carman, Joshua 25
Carmichael, Abner 116
  Daniel 30
  John 98
  Norman 99
Carmickdet, Hugh 97
Carmon, Stephen 16
Carn, William 136
Carnel, Reuben 81
Carnest, John 51
Carney, James, Sr. 11
  John 35
  Leonard 113
  Robert 12
Carothers, James 125
Carpenter, Benjamin 59,
    103
  Christopher 131
  David 118
  John 130, 102
  Joseph 54
  Nicholas 131
  William 58,130
  Wylie 35
Carr, Balis 28

David 15
Jesse 95
William 114,116
Carraway, James 21
Thomas 84
William 11,91
Carrel, Charles 63
Carrigan, Robert, Jr. 49
Robert, Sr. 49
Carriker, Andrew 49
Carrington, Archibald 106
Ephraim 107
Murwin 25
William 106
Carrol, Lemuel 106
William 54
Carrold, Jonathan 95
Carroll, Edward 130
Carrow, Henry 11
Jordan 10
Carruth, Ephrain 133
Leander P. 133
Carson, Alexander 23
Henry 46
Jason 135
James 58
John W. 135
Richard 88
Samuel 53
Wesley 107
William 125,137
Carter, Barney 52
Benjamin 5
Daniel 41
Isaac 27
James 15
Jesse 7
Jiles 23,80
John 27,113,128
Joseph 117
Joshua 117
Laban 69
Lewis 8
Miat 39
Phillips 43
Robert 106
Samuel 19,138
Thomas 114
William 5,12,109
William O. 64
Wilson W. 18
Zachariah 15
Carteret, John 28
Thomas 67
Carthedge, Elijah 100
Carthy, John 130
Carton, John 34,37
Cartwright, Abraham 74
Asa 73
Christopher 5
James 74
John 5
Joseph 50
Joshua 5
Robert 74
Thomas 5,74
William 5,74
Caruthers, Elias 61
William 84
Carver, Evergrain 74
Isham 67
John 25
Joseph 137
Richard 55
Robert 66
Cary, Henry 58
Miles 24
Richard 90

Robert 104
Thomas 22
Casa, John 5
Case, Charles 40
James 58
Jesse 136
Jonas 39
William 136
Casey, Henry 43
John 13
William 74
Cash, Boggan 29
John 46
Lewis 51
Cashin, Pleasant 135
Cason, Burnel 66
George 73
Casons, William 10
Cassons, Witham 11
Cast, Archibald 129
Daniel 119
Castellow, William 79
Casten, Whitlift 91
Castephens, John 117
Castill, Jacob 92
Castillon, John D. 72
Castle, Ebenezer 51
Caston, Jacob 17
James 91
Lewis 51
Olivier 17
Robert 91
Thomas 51
Castor, Henry 121
Cate, Richard 108,109
Thomas 32,106,108
Timothy 106
Cates, Richard 109
William 106
Cathberton, John 48
Cathey, Jethro 138
Joseph 138
William 72
Cathy, Archibald 53
Caton, Moses 84
Cauble, Adam 43
Frederick 43
Jacob 61
Caudell, Jeremiah 118
Caudle, Edward 109
Cauley, Bartholamy 86
Caulk, Daniel 112
Henry 43
Levin 40
Causby, Jesse 136
Cave, Miley 68
Caven, William 108
Caveness, Richard 120
Cazart, Wyat 36,37
Cecil, Philip 123
Thomas 123
Ceicel, Thomas 44
Center, James 54
Solomon 116
Cerlin, Edward 73
Chace, Levi 17
Chadwell, David 41
Chadwick, James 85
Martin 85
Chaffin, Thomas 122
Chainey, Peter 126
Chamberlain, Enoch 45
Chambers, Benjamin 52,71
James 31,138
Jos., Sr. 120
Joseph 138
Maxwell 128
Samuel 47,95

William 138
William W. 37
Chamblee, James 63
Jerrod 101
Chamblers, Jos., Sr. 120
Chambles, Henry 36,37
Chance, Allen 11
John 38
William 11
Chandler, Joel 62
Joseph 116
Martin 33
Matthew 105
Chaner, Cannon 11
Chaney, Stephen 5
Channels, Michael 125
Chaplain, John 33
Chaple, Jesse 49
Chapman, Enoch 51
James 130
John 68
Stephen 84
Valentine 80
William 44,122
Chappel, Caleb 75
Edward 104
Chapter, Jonathan 4
Charles, Harry 9
John 39,123
Charlton, Samuel 72
Chase, John 30
Chauncey, Isaac 83
Chavers, Gorden 52
Chaves, Banston 34
Chavis, John 36
Cheaves, Abner 59
James 59
John 60
Cheek, Joab 27
Randolph 48
Cheery, William 126
Cherr, John 66
Cherry, Benjamin 10
Darling 21,59
Humphrey 10
James, Jr. 77
Jesse 87
Samuel 15
Chesenhall, William 31
Cheshen, Teneson 45
Chesire, Philip 93
Turpin 24
William 72
Chesnut, Bailey 96
Hardy 67
James 95
Joseph 95
Joshua 67
Philip 26
William 96
Chester, Stephen 14
Cheves, James 9
Chewning, John 29
Childers, Bedford 129
Robert 57
Solomon 131
Childress, Jesse 43
William 114
Chilton, Lemuel 51
Chinn, Jesse 51
Chipperd, Henry 53
Chisholm, Alexander 30
Anguish 124
Daniel 30
John 124
Chistoon, William 124
Chits, George 62
Chitty, Charles 42

Chitwood, Charles 54
  James 133
  Jesse 56,68
Chizenhall, Delamy 107
  Laney 107
  William 31
Chopard, Cyprian 74
Chrisenberg, Aron 37
Christian, James 97
  Michael 36,37
Christie, Jesse 19
Christon, Michel 36
Christoph, Ephraim 131
Chube, Charles 115
Church, Isaac 115
  William 117
Chustley, John 52
Cider, George 52
Cilgrow, William 73
Cinard, Jonathan 58
Cincard, William 136
Cisk, Jeremiah 114
Civins, Joseph 125
Claggett, John 129
Clampit, Richard, Jr. 115
Clandler, Zachariah 116
Clands, Thomas W. 6
Clapp, William 112
Clardy, Anderson 78
  Thomas 24
Claridge, John 114
Clark, Andrew 21
  Angus 93
  Anthony 131
  Arthur 133
  Benjamin 58
  David C. 10
  Duncan, Jr. 93
  Francis 36
  Henry 82,112
  Hosiah 91
  James 53,112,136
  James K. 105
  James W. 71
  Jesse 106
  John 18,38,84,110
  Joshua 47
  Kenneth 77
  Malcom 97
  Nathaniel 84
  Neil, Jr. 93
  Reuben 8,11
  Richard 5,138
  Robert 44
  Thomas 8,109,119
  Tilmon 112
  William 101
Clarke, Arthur 133
Claton, William 112
Clay, Charles 6
  John 127
Clayton, Benjamin 9,81
  John 136,46
  Richard 5,74
  Thomas 9,82
  William 112
Claywell, Solomon 46
Clegg, John 109
Clement, Samuel 36,37
Clements, Hardy 65,77
  Simon 105
Clemer, Charles 39
Clemmons, Cornelius 133
  John 123
Clemons, John 66
  Samuel 36
  William 32
Clendenning, Fisher 32

Clendinen, William 108
Clenning, Ross M. 61
Clerk, Anthony 131
Clerland, John M. 46
Cleton, John 46
Click, Daniel 122
Clifford, Joseph 17
Clifton, Jonas 76
  Reuben 8
Clinard, Andrew 45
  David 123
Cline, Christian 39
  Daniel 54
  David 53
  Henry 44
  Jacob 127
Clinton, Richard 67
  Robert 107
  William 134
Clisk, John 49
Clodfelter, David 128
Clominger, Adam, Jr.
Cloninger, Jacob 129
Clontz, Henry 48
Clotfelter, Joseph 120
Cloud, Jeremiah 114
Club, George, Jr. 53
  John 53
Clutz, John 43
  Martin 121
Coaley, Washington 124
Coaths, James 122
Coats, Jordan 96
  Robert H. 114
  Wilson 73
Cobb, Ambrose 129
  Archibald 130
  Charles 21
  Daniel 39
  Hardie 88
  Hugh 60
  James 21,64,89
  John 77
  John B. 64
  Moses 63
  Richmon 64,87
  Roberd 63
  Thomas 80
Cobble, Isaac 121
Coble, Jacob 112
Cobman, Shelsby 98
Cobs, John 105
Coburn, Newton 21
Cochran, Abraham 49
  Robert 37,126
  Robert M. 49
  Samuel H. 128
  Thomas 79
  Thomas S. 126
Cockburn, William 59
Cockcleres, Jacob 109
Cocke, John 109,110
Cockeran, Henry 56
  James 55
  Squire 55
Cockerham, John 52
Cockhorn, Samuel 135
Cockram, James 116
Cockran, James 5
  John 100
Cockrett, Futrill 102
Cookrill, William 103
Cockrum, Robert 134
Cody, John 113,137
Coe, Avery 108
  Giles 117
  John 108
Coffer, George 41

Coffey, Elijah 117
  John 117
  Reuben 135
  William 135
Coffield, Ira 79
Coffin, Elisha 111
Cofield, Cornelius 25
Cogdell, Daniel 67
  Ross 92
Coggin, William 119
Coggins, George 124
  Jonathan 121
  Levi 123
  Zachariah 44
Cohoon, Alexander 82
  Ebenezer 9
  William 10,82
Coiter, Edward 138
Coker, Ephrain 50
Colby, Thomas 57
Coldwell, Robert 125
  Robert, Jr. 125
Coldwell see Caldwell
Cole, Abram 64
  Burnel 14
  Isaac 34
  James 39
  John 28
  Levy 106
  Mark 101
  Michael 119
  Nathaniel 75
  Thomas 25,36
  William 33
Coleburn, William P. 89
Coleman, Andrew 44
  Asa 94
  Blount 12
  Henry 94
  Hobbert 89
  Marsh, Jr. 58
  Robert 129
  Seth 106
Coles, Abram 64
Coley, John 34
  Rolen 90
Colier, William 133
Colleson, William 6
Collier, Henry 38
  William 20,133
Collin, William 73
Collins, Bradley 32,107
  David 16,23
  Dempsey 73
  Ezekiel 114
  George 13
  Iles 72
  James 135
  Jesse 8,23,84,116
  John 116
  Jos., Jr. 91
  Lewis 29
  Malachi 73
  Matthias 52
  Samuel 84,131
  Thomas 76
  William 36
  Zachariah 49
Colmer, Mark 138
Coltane, Isaac 119
Colwell, Joseph 118
Comarich, Ransom 90
Combs, Charles 50
  George 52
  Samuel 35
  William 118
Compton, Alfred 108
  Erasmus 108

Jeremiah 108
Conaway, Stephen 10
Conbey, Caleb 46
Cone, Gillum 22
Conel, Moses 127
Conely, Joshua 63
Congleton, George 10
Conley, Alex T. 118
Connally, Charles 110
Connegay, Abram 15
Connel, Thomas 125
Connell, Timothy 18
Conner, Daniel 89
  Henry 47
  Jacob 54
  James 125
  William 33
Connerly, William 95
Conrad, Leonard 42
Constable, Peter 56
Conway, James 104
Cook, Abram 46
  Andrew 61
  Angel 137
  David 103
  Elijah 100
  Elisha 77,90
  Ephraim 132
  Hawkins 116
  Henry 135
  James 105,124
  Jeremiah 104
  John 33,43,104,132
  John, Jr. 95
  Jones 103
  Lawrence 65
  Martin 35
  Mathias 76
  Nickolas 116
  Richard 46,51,129
  Robert 126
  Sion 58
  Thomas 55
  William 123
  Willis 23
  Winson 23
Cooke, John 101
  Stephen 13
  Thomas 60
  Thomas R. 100
  William 108
Cooley, James 104
  John 19
Coon, Peter 55
Cooper, Abner 4,12,14,74
  Abraham 124
  Benjamin 82,119
  Core 26
  Daniel 26
  David 22,121
  Ennis 84
  Hardy 30
  Harmon 30
  James 41
  John 30,37,82,103
  Joseph 75
  Rayford 27
  Willis 42
Coopper, Kenneth 89
Coor, Thomas, Jr. 13
Cope, Thomas 98
Copeland, James 29
  Kiah 15
Copelin, Reuben 54
Copland, Hugh 47
Coppage, Charles 103
Coram, Richard 41
  William, Jr. 41

Corbet, Bryant 87
  George 92
  Johnston 90
  William 92
Corbett, Amos 29
  George 18
  Grove 11
  Samuel 11
  Thomas 65
Corbith, Jesse 111
Cordin, Jacob 83
Cordle, Ishmael 122
  John A. 65
Core, Aurthur 25
  George 65
Corisher, Jacob 120
Corkman, John 67
Corn, George 136
  Samuel 136
Corner, Reuben 37
Cornelius, John 62,115
  Robert 115
Cornwall, John 78
Cornwell, John 137
Corpew, Richard 81
Correl, William 21
Correll, John 49
Corter, Samuel 138
Costley, James 126
Costner, David 130
  Peter 130
Coston, Thomas 92
Cotner, Matthew 109
Cotten, Alexander 20
  Avent 110
  Barna 13
  Felston 7
  John 50
  Micajah T. 103
  Richard C. 109
Cotter, John M. 3
Cotton, Carney 34
  Wilie 21
Cottram, James 21
Couch, Asa 32
Coughran, Eli 48
Coulter, Daniel 131
  Henry 131
Council, Robert 110
  William 30
Counsel, James 93
Cour, Dickson 104
Courtis, Hinton 102
Courtney, Emanuel 99
Coverton, Isaac 16
Covey, Matthew 40
Covington, Henry 30
  John 111
Cow, Jesse, Jr. 88
Cowan, David 120
  John 120,131
  Jos. 120
  Joseph, Jr. 121
  Joseph, Sr. 121
  Richard 129
  Zekiah 120
Coward, Jesse 14
  Michel 13
Cowen, John B. 24
Cowin, Isaac 43
  William 43
Cowper, James 10
Cox, Abram 10
  Absolam 11
  Alexander 52
  Charles 91
  Darius 25
  Hardy 96

Harman 109
Henry 5
Jesse 29
John 41,83,88,90,114
Josiah 66
Louis 84
Matthew 56
Moses 17,73
Smith 122
Thomas 68,83,122
William 41,118
Zachariah 11
Zadock 16
Cozort, James 106
Crabtree, James 108
  John 32,106
  Uriah 32
Crafford, Henry 76
Craft, Harrod 88
  John 14
Crage, Whitlock 119
  William 137
Crago, John 54
Crags, Thomas 131
Craig, David 60
  John 120
  Moses 126
  Thomas 120
Craigh, Leonard 43
Craine, John 117
Crammer, John 43
Crandell, Christ. 83
Crane, James 133
  John 17
Craten, John 34
Craton, Thomas 51
Cravan, John
Craven, Joshua 33
  Phillip 61
Craver, Thomas 109
Craw, John 55
Crawford, Charles 28
  Henry 76
  Jacob 113
  James 128,133
  John 61
  Josiah 58,138
  Thomas 46
  William 138
  William, Jr. 119
Crawley, John 78
Creamer, Kelly 90
Crecy, Levi 8
Credworth, John 4
Creecy, James R. 72
Creed, Solomon 9
Creef, Isaac 122
Crery, James 7
Cress, Daniel 43
Cretcher, John 105
Crews, James 42
Cribb, Anthony 28
  Jonathan 67
  Thomas 28
Crickmore, Robert 80
Crider, Benjamin 38
Cripson, Thomas 57
Criscow, Daniel 33
Crisp, Reading 89
  Solomon 135
Criswell, Alex 107
Crites, Peter 53
Crocker, Francis 31
  John 102
  Josiah 31
Crofford, Henry 76
  William 76
Cromartie, Peter 93

Croner, Jacob 127
Cronfell, Jonathan 122
Croom, Peter 60
Croon, Simon 42
Cross, Benjamin 7
    Jacob 121
    Miles 18
    Whitfield 20
Crotzer, John 121
Crouch, Jesse 51
Crouse, Beorge
Crow, James 109
    John 132
    John H. 54
    Stephen 52
Crowel, John 126
Crowell, Charles 48
    Edward 22
    James B. 22
    William 18
Crown, Henry 135
Crowson, Elisha 29
Cruchfield, Benjamin 108
    Stephen 109
Cruid, Abraham 116
    Coleby, Jr. 116
Cruise, Jacob 69
Crump, Edward 8
    John, Jr. 50
    John B. 44
    Rolen 49
    Stephen 124
Crumpler, Owen 27
Crumpton, Thomas 52
Cruse, Peter 121
Cruthers, James 120
Cryder, Martin 128
Cude, James 33
    Timothy 119
Culberson, David 111
    John 34
    Josiah 67
    Nathaniel 63
    William 111
Culeper, Nathaniel 65
Cullan, Willie 76
Cullerson, John 34
Cullipher, Benjamin 8
    Isaac 8
Culpepper, Charles 124
    Henry 101
Cumboe, Stephen 96
Cummin, James C. 24
    John 106
Cummings, Aaron 27
    Benjamin 50
    George 95
    Isaac 68
Cunninggem, Jesse 87
Cunningham, Alex 99
    Alexander 33
    Duncan 99
    Hugh 122
    Jacob I. 47
    Josiah 44
    Lansater 62
    Thomas 121
Cupples, Charles 69
Curbee, Obadiah 100
Curby, William 52
Curfuse, Caleb 120
Curl, Benjamin 34
    Isham 20
    John 8
    Richard 7
Curliles, William 78
Curlin, Edward 4
Curling, Jesse 79

John 19
Curls, Thomas 4
Currell, David 47
Curren, Larkin 105
Curretch, Leroy 68
Currie, John 97
Curruth, Leroy 56
Curry, Alex 98
    Archibald 67
    Cazor W. 68
    Hugh 67
    James 98
    John B. 114
    Malcom 67
    Neil 67
Curthington, John 32
Curtis, Ben 135
    David 135
    Henry 34
    Larkin 34
Cushing, Isaac T. 26
    Noah 20
Cutler, Nathan 83
Cuzine, Durum 127
    John 128

- D -

Dabbs, William 29
Dade, Horatio 11
Daff, Richard 136
Daffin, James 16
Dafter, Obed. 48
Dage, Isaac 94
Daggett, Charles Y. 56
    William 56,68
Daggins, William 42
Daily, Frederick 74
Dain, Hardy 14
Dalby, Dick H. 104
Dale, Wiley 13
Dally, Micajah 105
Dalrymple, William 28
Dalton, David 42
    James 55
    Samuel 113
    William 41
    William L. 58
Dameron, Christopher 111
Dameron, Gideon 19
    Thomas 110
Damon, John 130
Danals, John 83
Danaway, William 123
Dancy, David 21
Danfoot, Sion 26
Danghtrey, Hardy 96
Daniel, Avra 4
    Baley 4
    Chisolm 56
    Christholm 55
    David 4,22
    Elijah 61
    Goodwin 78
    Green O. 108
    Isaac 64
    James 64
    James W. 80
    John 4,60
    Joshua 14
    Mathew 13
    Perian 134
    Robert 22
    Robert B. 60
    Samuel 105
    Thomas 4,36

William 25,36
William R. 19
Willie 87
Daniels, Clement 10,82
    James 9,84
    John 36
    Jos. 120
    Morris 82
    Shadrick 10
    Thomas 10,82
Darby, James 110
Darden, Henry G. 76
Dardin, David C. 78
    Robert 96
Dark, Joseph 98
Darlett, William M. 77
Darnald, George 135
Darnall, William 118
Darnell, David 47
    John 47
    John L. 47
    William 47
Darnold, Raleigh 42
Darr, David 45
Darrison, B. W. 62
Dary, Ambrose 106
Dasson, Easly 58
Daugherty, Drew 96
    Hardy 96
    Thos 112
Daughety, Daniel 84
Daughtie, Edward 75
Daughtrey, Hardy 96
Davenport, Abner 135
    Burrage 120
    Chancey 21
    Enoch 9
    James 9
    Samuel 81
    Talket 81
    Thomas 135
Davey, Gabriel 37
David, Henry 86
    William 58
Davidson, Andrew W. 128
    Ephraim 31
    George L. 46
    George W. 124
    Hiram 43
    John 61
    Josiah 77
    Samuel 50
    Thomas 46
Davied, William 58
Davies, James 57
Davin, Daniel 58
Davis, Amos 73
    Andrew 128
    Anthony 66
    Archibald 42
    Benjamin 23,101
    Blake 79
    Charles 117
    Daniel 125
    David 74
    Davis 24,32
    Durham 21
    Edward 121
    Edward H. 79
    Elisha 14
    Ephraim 54
    Frederick 5
    George D. 58,136
    Gideon 104
    Hardoway 23,80
    Hardy 8
    Hezekiah 127
    Isaiah 106

James 5,12,51,107,
  114,121
James W. 20
Jesse 34
John 34,36,56,93,97,
  100,127
John, Jr. 121
John S. 85
John W. 69
Johnson 74
Jonathan 44
Jones 14
Joshua 16,23
Josiah 35
Jourdan 109
Lewis 78
Martin 82
Matthew 116,119
Matthias 4
Maxy 9
Micajah 132
Michael 74
Moses 7
Nathaniel 29
Noah 21
Reading K. 86
Richard 23,80
Robert C. 69
Sampson 26
Samuel 17,22,79
Solomon 91
Stephen 23
Thomas 3,22,23,44,55,
  80,93,94,124
Westley 16
William 30,35,99
William, Jr. 24
William, Sr. 24
William F. 86
Willie O. 23
Winfield 9
Davison, Silas 33
Dawkins, George 99
  Micajah 99
Dawson, General 79
  James 30
  John 79
  Joseph 107
  Lewis 84
Day, Ambrose 106
  Archibald 106
  James 78
  Phillip 37
  Samuel 60
Dayton, William 137
Deal, Abraham 134
  Adam 5
  Alexander 134
  Henry 94,134
  John 57
  Pater 43
  William 90,134
Deale, Julius 72
Dean, Curtis 13
  Hardy, Jr. 63
  James 97
  John 13
Dearing, Pleasant 113
  Willia 113
Dease, Smith 30
Deaton, Claiborn 109
  John 120
  Thomas 123
Debnam, John B. 103
  William 24
Deboard, Gideon 129
Debode, George 116
Deck, Leonard 132

Decker, Richard 3
Dedman, James 122
  William 133
Dekison, Zekiah 120
Delamar, James 11
  Seldon 11
Delinger, Martin 53
Dellbuck, David 56
Deloach, Brittain 101
  Jesse 78
  Thomas 78
Delow, Henry 82
  Jacob 120
  John 44
  Michael 43
Demdtund, John 4
Demill, Peter 83
Denby, Thomas 5
Denmark, John 115
Dennis, Andrew 124
  Charles 126
  Joshua 116
Denny, Spears 87
  Stephen 116
  Theophilus 25
  William 52
Dent, William T. 23
Denton, Basel 123
  Drury 24
  Jacob 115
  James 25
  John 8
  Jonas 138
  Jonathan 138
  Levi 89
  Peter 103
  William 103
Derden, Joseph 75
Derryburry, John 134
Desern, Ezekiel 50
  Mary 107
Detheridge, Charles 122
Devame, Francis 92
Devenporte, Abner 135
  Thomas 135
Dever, Elijah 138
  John 138
Devoun, Elisha 90
Devout, William 4
Deweese, Jarrat 137
Dial, Jonathan 94
Dick, David 131
  Reuben 113
  Samuel 113
Dickee, Robert 107
Dickenson, Joel 83
Dickerson, Daniel 85
  Joseph F. 71
Dickey, William
Dickinson, John 76
  Wilie 51
Dickson, Book 89
  Booky 29
  David 131
  Ephraim 10
  Gibbin 10
  Henry 92
  John 112
  Joseph 16
  Patrick 13
  Seth 119
  Thomas 130
  William 43,135
Dickus, James 133
Dill, Samuel 44
Dillard, James 136
  John 114,139,138
Dillbark, John, Jr. 134

Dillenger, Michael 131
Dillin, Nicholas 53
Dillord, John 138
Dills, Thomas, Sr. 134
Dilport, William 99
Dinkey, William 38
Dinkins, Asa 51
  James 125
Dishman, James 129
Dismaks, John W. 60
Dixon, Cornelius 84
  Franklin 83
  Hugh 127
  Ire B. 48
  James 34
  Jedediah 12
  Jeremiah 105
  John 82
  Nehemiah 11
  Robert 127
  Rollin 84
  Thomas 89
  William 83,89
Dixson, Edmond 37
Doak, John 40
  William 60
Dobbins, Jacob 116
Dobson, John 68
Docherty, Scearly 32
Dockery, Alexander 33
Dockins, William 122
Dodd, Hardy 100
  John 34
  Willie 67
Dodson, John 105
  Lambert 42,114
  Lewis 41
Dogget, Charles Y. 69
Doggett, Henry 79
  Richard 79
Dolby, William 35
Doles, Britain 78
Dollar, Isaac D. 32
  James 32
Dollerhide, James 106
Dollihit, John 97
Dolten, Elijah 133
Donally, William 52
Donalson, Hugh 138
  Joseph 46
Donaway, John 45
Done, Nehemiah 93
Donell, Oliver 13
Donnel, James 111
Door, Frederick 28
Dorch, John 105
Dorman, Duncan 97
Dorset, Duty 34
Dorsett, Moses 107
  Thomas 135
Dorson, Edmon 51
Doss, Thomas 114
Dossey, Demmon, Jr. 134
Doub, Henry 115
Doube, Henry 41
Douge, Benjamin 74
  Jesse 74
  John 122
Doughty, William 13
Douglas, John 88,104
Douglass, Adam 32
  David 18
  Dempsey 73
  Joseph 47
Douthet, Jacob 45
  John 45
Dove, George 49
Dowd, William 97

Dowdin, John 89
Dowdy, Benjamin, Sr. 34
  Isaac 14
  Jesse 4
  John 11,83
  William 4,74
Dowell, John 58
Dowers, Noah 9
Dowet, Walker 40
Down, Jesse 7
  Kinyan 10
Downer, Francis 29
Downey, John 36
  Samuel 56
  Thomas 56,133
  William 47
Downing, William 76
Downs, Aaron 128
  Shadric 83
  William 56,69,88,126
Downson, Aaron 131
Downy, Samuel 69
  Thomas 69
Dowtey, William 74
Dowthard, Stephen 123
Dowtin, Samuel 22
Dowton, Samuel 180
Dowty, John 83
Doxey, Dempsey 73
  Henry 3
Dozier, James 103
  Jasper 72
  Jordan 72
  Phillip 72
  Samuel 5
  Tully 72
  William 72
Drake, Francis 22
  George 109
  John 30,58
  Jordan 100
Drammond, Stewart 40
Draper, William 78
Drew, Cordy 79
  Thomas 79
Drinkwater, John 31
Driver, Boam 76
  Thomas 104
Drye, Daniel 127
  John 127
Ducary, Balum 57
Duck, James 81
  Thaddeus 14
Duckworth, George 47,125
  Jonathan 47
  Robert 47
  Thomas 62
Dudley, Allen 26
  David 96
  Edward B. 71
  Ervan 87
  Jacob 84
  John 85
  Levan 3
  Malachi 3
  Pelasky 20
Due, Benjamin 92
  Duff, Dennis 133
  Duffey, William 44
Dugger, David 118
  Joel 118
Duglas, James 77
Duke, Berry 108
  Dabney M. 23
  Elisha 76
  William 103
Dulin, William
Dunbar, Archibald 33

Duncan, Charles 36
  Hardy 28
  James 77,118
  John 105
  Moses 28
  Stephen 16
  William 61,113,115
  Wilson 5
Dundalow, Charnley C. 77
Dunken, David 4
  Zebulin 5
Dunket, Jacob 58
Dunkin, Densey 74
  Hiram 55
  John 118
Dunlap, Jesse 115
Dunlop, John 98
Dunn, Bartholomew 98
  Elijah 84
  George 120
  James 100
  Joseph 138
  Levin 84
  Newman 11
  Noah 87
  Robert, Jr. 125
  Thomas 98
  William 90,125
Dunning, Thomas 40
  William 39
Duporster, Joseph 46
Dupree, Sterling
Duran, George 100
Durden, Cornelius 90
Durgan, John 50
Durham, Charles 55
  Mathew 32
  Newman 11
  Thomas 108
Durning, Lewis 31
Duskins, Michel, Jr. 63
Dutcherow, Jacob 53
Duty, William 109
Duval, Prosper forma 28
Duvol, Daniel 87
  John 87
Dyal, Thomas 51
Dye, Martin 98
Dyer, Elijah 51
  Joel 51
  John 56,68
  William 61

- E -

Eads, William 42
Eagle, Martin 98
  Micajah 45
Eaker, Peter 130
Eaperson, William 117
Earley, Asa 116
  Jacob 76
Early, Isaac 78
  James 8,56,77
  Thomas 76
  William 55
Earnest, Daniel 122
Earwood, Thomas 131
Easley, Allen 19
  Rhoderick 19
Eason, Abner 21
  George 87
  Ithiel 64
  John 87
  Ohed. 91
  Solomon 75

East, Moses 52
Eastbridge, John 34
Easter, Michael 123
  Solomon 82
  William, Jr. 82
  William, Sr. 82
Eastis, James 34
Eastwood, Abraham 105
Eatman, Irwin 81
  John 103
Eaton, Abraham 138
  James 42
  Lazarus 138
Eavins, John 134
Ebert, Christian 115
Eborn, James 10
  William 82
Echard, William 131
Eddins, Needham 100
  William 110
Eddleman, Adam 120
  Henry 53
  Philip 121
Eddman, Jacob 53
Eddons, David 92
Edens, John 91
Eders, John 54
Edgar, William 12
Edgarton, Ransom 132
Edge, Duke 93
  Jonathan 26
  William 95
  Willis 19
Edgin, Samuel 53
Edis, Ezekiel 129
Edlinian, Philip 121
Edmeston, Ninnion
Edmison, George 135
Edmiston, Archibald 136
Edmonds, Benjamin 59
Edmondson, James 87
  John 91
  Thomas 20
Edoll, Joseph 40
Edson, Joseph 46
Edward, Peter 124
  William 30
Edwards, Bartkett 113
  Benjamin 20,54
  Charles 130,133
  Colin 52
  David 112
  Edmond 137
  Edom 34
  James 34,59,80,84,137
  Joel 109
  John 59,78,93,102,
      114,137
  Joshua 26
  Littlebury 89
  Newit 22
  Nicholas 112
  Pink 78
  Robert 63
  Thomas 13,102
  William 82,102,122
  William E. 83
  William N. 83
  William S. 118
  Williamson 78
  Young 118
Efland, Jacob 32
Egerton, Wilmot 80
  Wilmot E. 22
Eights, William 49
Elder, David 138
Elerod, Peter 117
Elerton, Thomas 76

Eley, John 97
Eliot, John 127
Eliott, Andrew H. 132
  Elisha 6
Elixor, Alexander 37
Elkins, David 58
  Robert 39
  Samuel 109
  Thomas 39
Eller, George 121
  Henry 68
Ellington, Bird 80
  Daniel, Jr. 41
  Grieff 41
  Jesse 103
  Joel 23,80
  Pleasant 23
Elliott, Abram 33
  Benjamin 31
  Charles 75
  Foster 75
  Hugh 47
  Isaac 119
  James 121,131
  Jesse 75
  John B. 47
  John C. 56,68
  Joseph 34,75
  Miles 7
  Moses 112
  Peter 16
  Ricks 78
  Robert 128
  Saphem 6
  Thomas 85,125,128
  William 60,106,125
Ellis, Absolom 132
  Bartholomew 38
  Daniel 14
  Elkshel 36
  Enoch 122
  James 66
  James A. 138
  Joel 90
  John 91
  Josiah 7
  Levin 32
  Lewis 80
  Michael 88
  Miles 23,80
  Obadiah 23,80
  Ransom 45
  Simes 23
  Solomon 57,68
  Thomas 52,78
Ellison, James B. 83
  Jonathan 133
  William 52
  Zachariah 78
Elliston, Robert 37
Elmore, James 14
  John 37
Elms, Edward 54
Elventon, John 90
Ely, Samuel 76
Elydon, Nicholas 3
Emery, William 88
Emmerson, Benjamin 34
Emmett, John 57
Enbanks, Elijah, Jr. 91
  Ezekiel 91
  John 91
Endsley, Archibald 131
  Daniel 81
  James 131
England, Andrew 134
  Enoch 57
  Ezekiel 134

Joseph, M 134
  William, Jr. 134
English, Mathew 82
Engram, Samuel 14
Enloe, Benjamin 138
  Jesse 138
Ennes, Levie 97
Ennett, Thomas 17
  Whitehurst 17
  William 17
Enoch, Jones 45
Ensley, Daniel 81
Epes, Kinchen P. 14
Ephland, George 108
Epley, Peter 57
Eppes, Peter 13
Equals, Talbing 10
Ernell, Allen 11
  Radford 11
Ernest, John 135
Errowood, Red 130
Erwin, Christopher 45
  Francis 47
  George 128,136
  James 136
  James M. 56
  James Miller 134
  Obadiah H. 63
  Robert 112
  William 19,61
Escridge, Birditt 110
Eskins, William 60
Eskrigo, John R. 37
Essleman, Archibald 47
Estes, James 102
Etchison, John, Jr. 122
Etheridge, Caleb 3
  Elijah 81
  Josiah 72
  Levi 73
  Silas 82
  Stephen 73
  Thomas 3,73
  William 72,73
Eubank, Philip 111
Eubanks, Aaron 85
  Elijah, Jr. 91
  Ezekiel 91
  John 91
  Stephens 78
Eur, Burrell 76
Eure, Benjamin 76
  Cypron 7
  Henry 8
  James 75
  Stephen 7
Euse, Elisha 79
Eustis, James B. 105
Evans, Aaron 109
  Arthur 18
  Charles 34,138
  Colin 100
  David 25,86,136
  Dred 65
  Edmond 88
  Ephraim 57
  George 22
  Goodrum 38
  Henry 20,72
  James 15,92,123
  John 22,25,34,72,76,
    86,97,102,134
  Jonathan 25
  Leckarah 91
  Nathan 22
  Noah 8
  Peter 53
  Richard 34

Thomas 25,36,110,114
  William 36,65
  Wright 88
Evenes, Charles 138
Evens, John 76
Eventon, Aaron 84
Everington, John 11
Everitt, Abraham 45
  Daniel 26
  James 89
  John 8,26
  John B. 65
  Richard 26
  Robert 81
  William 21
Eversdale, John 51
Eves, William 102
Evett, Jesse 10
  Moses 10
Evins, David 136
  John 89
  Leckariah 91
Evitt, John 83
  Lott 83
Ewell, David 43
Ewin, Ephraim 43
Ewing, Ephraim 47
Exum, William 89
Ezell, Benjamin 8
  Jesse 26
  Patrick 95

  - F -

Faddis, James 108
Fadgett, John 102
Fadz, Adolps 54
Fagan, Aaron 81
Fagg, Joel 113
Fains, David 136
Fairbanks, David 40
Fairchilds, Lewis 118
Faircloth, Isom 95
  Jacob 26
  James 96
  John 95
  Kinchen 14
  Noah 26
  Raiford 26
  Raphael 95
  Thomas 76
Fairfax, Needham 94
Faison, Sterling 78
Falconer, James 105
Falkin, Richard 13
Falkner, Lewis 12
Falls, John 61,62
  Theophilus 46
  William 53
Fanchier, Hillary 73
Fannet, Gideon 10
Fanney, John 7
Farker, Solomon 136
Farland, Laban 111
Farlass, Richard 75
Farles, Elisha 6
Farley, David 111
  John 111
  John B. 38
  Stewart 38
Farmer, Ashael 64
  Elisha 129
  John 64,104
  Joseph 14,89
  Kedar 14
  Solomon 119

William 57
Farnel, Dexter 91
Farr, Christian 61
  Henry 47
  Robert 69
Farra, John 125
Farrand, Henry 17
Farrar, Richard 105
Farrel, John 97
Farrer, Miles 53
Farrier, David 94
  John 94
  William 94
Farrington, John 45
Farrow, Joseph 92
  William 103
Fasene, Asa 16
Fash, Christmas 45
Fassel, Arthur 103
Fat, John 47
Fatam, James 52
Faucett, Anderson 108
  Eli 108
  Robert 108
Faulk, Hinnant 94
  Sherwood 16
  Thomas 94
  William 94
Faulkner, Rowland 125
Faulks, John 94
Fausett, Robert 108
Faw, John 118
Fayles, Josiah 91
Fealds, Counsel 85
Feamster, Abner 128
Feere, Peter 118
Felker, Samuel 43
Fell, Cason 84
Fellon, Elisha 64
Fellows, Bennet 18
Felton, John 7
Felts, Elisha 118
Fennell, James 18
Fennington, Edward F. 55
Fenny, Joshua 116
Fenster, John 46
Fentress, Frederick 33
  Lot 5
  Richard 39
Fentus, James 3,73
Ferebee, Lemuel 72
  Peter 72
  William 72
Fereland, John 49
Ferguson, Andrew 53
  George 53
  James 97
  James, Jr. 97
  John 33,117
  Neil 67
  Richard 64
  Smith 51
  William 30,51
Ferrand, Bogle 25
  Henry 17
Ferrel, Gabriel 126
  John 126
  William 126
Ferrell, Burton 22
  Hutchins 22
  James 22
  Loody 22
  Zachariah 10
Ferret, John, Sr. 48
Ferril, Cage 123
Ferrill, Bryan 101
Fetterton, William 82
Feveash, Thomas 75

Fewee, Zach 113
Fewel, James 113
Fidler, Henry 115
  John 115
Field, Benjamin 39
  Christopher 61
  Council 85
  Isaac 34
  Robert 113
Fielder, Robert 39
  Thomas 38
Fielding, William 29
Fields, Brice 91
  Curtis 94
  Henry 110
  John 109
  Major 86
Fifer, Martin 113
  William 113
Figg, Willis 7
File, Jacob 127
Filgo, David 14
  John 14
Filmar, Alexander 33
Filmond, John 37
Filyaw, John 17
Fincannon, John 135
  William 56
Finch, Caswell 104
  John 105
  John W. 105
Fingo, Jacob 53
Fink, David 128
  Phillip 49
  Son 49
Finlay, George 111
Finley, James 129
  John 62
Finn, Gabriel 32
Finner, Thomas 107
Finnie, Sterling 117
Finsher, Joshua 126
Finters, Hillary 72
Fircus, Jacob 114
Fisher, George 3,43,54
  Harmon 61
  Henry 69
  James 131
  Michael 84
  Sanders 27
  William 126
Fitch, John 111
Fite, John 130
Fitt, Samuel 6
Fitts, Morgan 106
Fitzgerald, James 116
  John 128
Flake, Manuel 87
Flanigan, Samuel E. 48
Flanigen, Thomas 87
Flannigan, James 16
Flecher, Hiram 46
Fleetwood, David 65
  Edmond, Jr. 65
  Hatton 77
Fleming, Bailey 138
  Beniah 112
  Edmund 116
  John 128
  John M. 116
  Mordecai 116
Flemming, George 49
  Isaac 53
  James 61
  John 40
  Joseph B. 24
  Robert 112
  Thomas 63

Willis 87
Flenigan, Elias 48
  Michael 48
  Robert 48
Fleningan, William 48
Fletcher, Abner 105
  Hiram 46
  James 135
  Joshua 90
  Nathan 50,136
Flinn, Enoch, Jr. 9
  William 94
Floan, David 95
Floid, Aron 28
  Jesse 13
  Westley 21
Flood, Allen 19
Florence, James 110
Floro, Aaron 73
  John 73
Flow, John 48
Flowers, Bennet 93
  Bryant 26
  Gideon 129
  Henry 126
  John 90
  Josiah 3
  Lowamy 95
  Philip 95
  Samuel 13
  Thomas 93
Floyd, James 124
  John 104
  Stacy 72
  Thomas 83
Floyd see also Floid
Fleeman, George 55
  William 55
Fleery, William 6
Fly, Aaron 20
Flynt, Richard 42,114
Fobes, John 48
Foddree, Hugh 10
Fogleman, George 127
  John 112
Folbet, Jesse 51
Folk, David 65
  Richard 28
Folks, John 28
  William 49
Foller, Elisha 138
Folsom, Frederick 84
Folsome, Ebenezer 25
  Malcom 28
  Thomas 14
Fonstren, John 132
  Samuel 132
Fonville, Edward 17
Fooshee, Jephthy 107
Forbes, Arthur, Sr. 38
  Caleb 74
  Dempsey 74
  James 4
  Jesse 112
  John 73
  Silas 73
Forbis, Ralph 61
Ford, Austin 130
  Daniel 124
  John 44
  Wyatt 106
  Zeblone 62
Foreman, James 89
Forest, James 60
Forguson, Andrew 53
Forkner, Lewis 116
  Martin 50
Forlan, William 8

Forlaw, James 81
   John 84
Forns, John 10
Forrest, Samuel 87
Forrester, John 115
   Thomas 135
Forster, Alanson 39
   John 56
   William 39
Forsythe, John 126
   Samuel 105
   Thomas 105
Fort, Austin 29
   Josiah 79
Forte, Elias 60
Fortener, Thomas 128
Fortiscue, John 10
   John Russell 10
Fortisque, William 83
Fortunberry, Jacob 137
Fortune, Lavender 135
   Lindsey 132
   Richard 55
   William 55
Forum, Joseph 122
Fosbers, Levi 111
Foskey, William 85
Foss, John 67
Fossee, Daniel 60
Foster, Benjamin 117
   Bennet 105
   Daniel 41,56
   Francis M. 75
   Henry 91
   Isaac 8
   James 112
   Joel 51
   John F. 59
   Richard 46
   Shelton 113
   Shepperd 4
   Thomas 56,122
   William 122
Fountain, James 42
   Tobias 94
   William 94
Foust, John 32
Fouts, Andrew 119
Fowler, Burwell 101
   Daniel 28
   Elijah 115
   John 108
   Jones 63
   Richard 28
   Thomas 13
Fox, Aron 16,51
   Barnell 34
   David 46
   David, Jr. 34
   Francis 51
   Nickolas, Sr. 110
Frady, John 117
   William 51
Frail, Thomas 103
Francis, Sterling 76
   Thomas 68
Franklin, Alexander 103
   Bernard 50,68,106
   James 68
   Jonas 75
   Thomas 42,116
Frazer, Enox 112
   James 85
   Malachiah 104
Frazier, Ephraim 105
   James 16,27
   Thomas 27
   William 105,115

Frederick, William 15
Freeland, James 47
   John 128
   Samuel 47
   William 46
Freeling, John H. 72
   Luke 7
Freeman, David 115
   Eaton 24
   Gideon 126
   Hamilton 132
   Hamlin 49
   Joshua 9
   Mathew 26
   Mertin 36
   Miston 37
   Moses 65
   Palmer 33
   Thomas 7
   Wiley 63
   William 55
   William D. 59
Freet, George 53
Freeze, Adam 49
Freling, Luke 7
Frew, David 74
Frey, Peter 131
Friear, William 20
Frisby, John 58,136
Frits, John 123
Fritt, John 135
Fritz, Adam 45
Frost, John 44
   Nicholas 43
   Samuel 14,44
Fry, Benjamin 42,114
   Bryant 44
   George 62,98,134
   Henry 41
Fryer, Jesse 91
   Thomas 91
   William 20,113
Fulbright, Daniel 131
Fulford, Charles 3
   Clifton 66
   Joseph 3
   Joseph, Jr. 66
Fulgem, John 78
Fulghum, Joseph 13
Fulk, Frederic 114
Fulks, Henry 116
Fullbright, Daniel 131
   Jacob 131
   William 53
Fuller, Arthur 36
   Benjamin 119
   Bradshaw 105
   Edward 10
   Hosea 37
   John 37,104,105,127
   John N. 111
   Walter 37
Fullerton, Welch 6
Fullington, William 38,
     111
Fulp, Solomon 42
Fulps, Solomon 115
Fulshire, Joseph 12
Fulsum, Malcom 28
Fulwider, Jacob 121
Funn, Daniel 128
   David 128
Furguson, James, Jr. 97
Furlly, John 56
Futcret, James 90
Futral, Nathan 91
Futrell, Benjamin 21
   Daniel 20

   Enos 78
   Micajah 20
   William 78
   Winborne 78
Futtrell, Calson 20

- G -

Gabard, John 122
Gabriel, David 85
Gage, Jacob 56,68
Gaither, Enoch 129
   Gassaway 61
   Johnsey 122
   Lebishes 128
Gaker, Benjamin 54
Galden, Jacob 16
Gall, Thomas 78
Gallihan, Brantley H. 50
Gallimore, James 44
   Jesse 69
   Richard 119
Gallin, Levi 84
Gallispie, Macoy 45
Gallop, Isaac 5
Galloway, John 136
   Thomas 40,46
   William 52
Gallup, John 4
   Joshua 5
Galoway, Thomas 40
Gamble, Andrew 112
   Benjamin 52
   Henry 52
   James 44
Gammon, Richard 87
   William 74
Ganday, Griffin 22
Gandy, Alston 22
   John 22
Gannon, Mark 60
   William 61
Ganny, John 53
Ganot, Caleb 6
Gantlin, Edward 30
Gapp, Allison 46
Gardener, Isaac 87
   John 121
   Reuben 87
   Samuel 85
Gardner, Dempsey 88
   Elijah 66
   Francis 66
   Guilford 34
   John 86
   Obed. 113
   William 65
Gardnor, William 120
Garenger, Andrew 112
Gargamy, Nichodemus 17
Gargely, John 57
Gargle, Jacob 27
Garland, Samuel 56,69
   Winston 14
Garling, James S. 4
Garlington, James S. 73
   Jabez 4
Garmon, John 127
   William 86
Garner, Barzelle 125
   Brally 27
   David 121
   Guilford 110
   James 27
   John 27
   Lewis 33

Thomas 110,133
Garato, Thomas 17
Garoll, Valenitne 40
Garrard, John 107
Garras, Nehemiah 87
Garratson, Garret 134
Garret(t), David 65
  Everard 7
  Henry 6,8
  James 4,123
  Jesse 65
  John 20,91,137
  Jonathan 5
  Joshua 50
  Mathew 56
  William 3,73
Garretson, Arthur 48
  John 48
Garrigan, Sample 60
Garringer, Bartin 39
Garriot, Daniel 123
Garris, George 20
Garrison, John C. 125
Garrock, John 89
Garron, Adam 137
  Andrew 58,137
Garrot(t), James 21
  Jeremiah 83
  Thomas 101
Garvay, John 121
Garwood, Isaac 45
  Jacob 45
Gary, Rhodes 20
Gaskett, David 85
  Fama 85
Gaskill, William 66
Gaskins, Christopher 82
  James 18
Gates, Philip 13
  Richard 111
  Samuel 56,68
Gathings, Charles 99
  Philip 99
Gatlin, Abner 84
  Alfred M. 72
  Edward 78
Gattis, Thomas 107
Gatton, Hamilton 122
Gaugh, James 40
Gaugus, Jacob 49
Gaultney, Ambroze 129
Gause, Benjamin 16
  Bryan 93
  William 93
Gavin, Samuel 26
Gawood, Isaac 45
  Jacob 45
Gay, Abel 20
  Elias 35
  John 47
  Joshua 61
  Thomas 103
  William 34,64,78,128
Gaylard, John 82
Gaylord, James 15
  Theophilus 49
Gear, John 34
Gearron, John 137
Gears, Thomas 44
Gedsey, William 114
Gee, John M. 34
Geer, David 64
  John 102
Geesling, John 113
Gelispie, James 43
Gennet, Matthew 90
Gennings, Goshen 119
Gentle, Stephen 52

Thomas 45
George, Daniel 35,92
  Frederick 17
  Isaac 115
  John 35
  William 92
Gerald, Abram 40
  Thomas 15
Gerganious, Frederic 92
  Samuel 92
  William 92
Geringer, Daniel 112
German, John 29,54
  John H. 100
  Josiah 82
  William 29
Gerrell, Elijah 42
Gerwin, David 50
Gettig, John 11
Gewin, John 99
Gibbans, Solomon 61
Gibble, George 66
  James E. 85
Gibbs, Archibald 135
  Bartee 82
  Charles 15
  David 82
  Jesse 35
  John 55
  Samuel, Sr. 82
  Stephen 82
  Washington 82
Gibony, David 47
Gibson, David B. 84
  Elisha 67
  James 75
  Jasper 4
  John 57,98,119
  John, Jr. 91
  Moses 113
  Pleasant 114
  Reuben 73
  Robert 114
  Samuel 57
  Stephen 114
  William 114
Giddens, Henry 46
  John 13
Giddins, Jonathan 10
Gilbert, Benjamin 5
  Isaac 17
  James 135
  John 86,91
  Thomas 9
  William 66
  William, Jr. 91
Gilbreath, James 61
  George
  Gideon 117
  Helen H. 117
  Hiram 117
  James 61
  Thomas 61
  William 61
Giles, Jeremiah 81
  Jesse 137
Gilham, Henry 20
Gill, Daniel 59
  Edward 65
  Gideon 105
  James 36
  John 104
  Robert 59
  Thomas 25,106
Gillan, William 49
Gillaspie, Abdi 61
  David 63
  Giddal 110

James 61
John 61
Robert 61
William 63
Gilleband, James 131
Gillespie, David 24
Gilley, James 128
Gilliam, John 118
  Lestly 36
  Miles 77
  Nathaniel 78
  William 36
Gillikan, George 85
  Uriah 85
Gilliland, John 113
Gillis, Hugh 67
  John 67
  Malcolm 123
Gillmore, Jacob 15
  William 27
Gills, Malcolm 67
Gilman, John 110
Gilmore, Josiah 49
Gilston, Samuel 107
Gipson, James 75
Girkin, Harmon 21
Givens, Robert 69
  Samuel 48
Gladdon, Samuel 54
Gladson, Daniel 39
Glasgow, John C. 73
  Samuel 72
Glass, Alexander 57
  David 39
  John 109
  Jos. 109
  Stephen 108
  Thomas 57
Glasscock, Scarlet 61
  William 68
Glenn, Benjamin 117
  Elisha 31
  James 43
  John 37
  Mark 106
  Robert 102
  Sampson 37
  Wiley 107
  William 31
Glinn, William 31
Glissen, Bryan 15
Glisson, John 15,94
  Stephen H. 94
Glore, Edward 38
Glotfelder, Daniel 130
  Elias 130
  George 130
  John 130
  Rudolph 130
Glover, Daniel 79
  John 18,130
  Jones 20
Gloveyer, Benjamin 22
Gobbel, John 123
Godfrey, Francis 75
  Hiram 74
  James 4,74
  John 74
  Thomas 99
  William 4
Godfrew, Samuel 74
Godley, Jesse 83
Godsey, Edward 41
  Thomas 41
Godwin, Allen 97
  Lewis 14
Goff, James 17
  John 86

Samuel 51
Goforth, George 126,131
   Isaac 133
   Preston 131
   William 51
Goger, John 127
Going, John 133
Goings, Edward 27
   William 27
Goints, Amos 91
   John 91
Golden, Jacob 116
   William 116
Golding, George 66
   William 115
Goldsberry, Ignatius 23
Gooch, John 136
   Pumphrett 105
Good, John 134
   Robert 134
   Solomon, Jr. 134
Goodbread, Joab 135
   John 54
Goode, William 42
Gooden, Daniel 24
Goodin, William 58
Gooding, Barge 16
Goodman, Henry 69
   Jacob 127
   John 12,49
   Lemuel 7
   Tobias 127
   William 92,122
Goodnight, George 127
   John 49
Goodson, Solomon B. 77
Goodwin, Abner 7
   Allen 109
   Cornelius H. 8
   Edmond 26
   George 18
   Granbury 26
   Isham 102
   John 29
   Mathews 102
   Silas 15
   Tobias 15
   William 96,138
Gordan see Gordon
Gorden see Gordon
Gordon, Alexander 99
   Archibald, Jr. 105
   Arthur 5
   Garret 58
   Jacob N. 81
   James 83,98,110
   Jeremiah 4
   John 25,75
   John W. 62
   Nathaniel 62
   Richmond 52
   Robert 37
   Thomas 37
   Thomas A. 62
   Wiley G. 62
   William 37,38,46
Gore, Isaac 95
   John 28,94
   Joseph 94
Gorman, Pleasant 114
Goss, John 121
   Joseph, Jr. 121
Gould, David 85
Goulde, Malach 29
Gower, Zadock 103
Grace, Matthew 90
Grady, Andrew M. 48
   John T. 94

Reuben, Jr. 41
Robert 41
Graham, Archibald 97
   Archibald, Jr. 99
   Burrell 98
   Griffith 62
   James 104,108,129
   John 27,45,67
   Joseph 68
   Richard 45
   Samuel 47,120
Grant, Bazzel 17
   Ephraim 90
   Jeremiah 108
   John 17,108
   Milton 113
   Shadrack 20
   Thomas 90
   William 17
Granthon, Benjamin 88
   Sion 90
Grantum, Needham 13
Graves, Boston 33
   Georges 68
   James 50
   John 5
   John W. 37
   Peter 50
   William B. 37
Gray, Abred 79
   Alexander 60,91
   Andrew 32
   Benjamin D. 86
   Beverly 127
   Ethelred 20
   Hiram 138
   Jacob 126
   James 127
   John 3,12
   Jordan 5
   Nelson 126
   Peter 22
   Peter M. 4
   Robert 119
   Samuel 122
   William 4,12,69,118
   Zachariah 86
Graybeal, David 118
   Henry 118
Grayson, Benjamin 132
   William 132
Greason, Henry 39
   Jacob 112
Green, Aaron 6
   Abner 7,55,101
   Abraham 6
   Allen 106
   Archibald 66
   Asa 36
   Benjamin 19
   David 124
   Durant 86
   Jacob 32
   James 44
   Jesse 100
   John 52,68,101,127,
      133,137
   John C. 71
   John N. 68
   Jonathan 109
   Joseph 22,52,57
   Malachi 65
   Mashack 121
   Nicholas 36
   Reddin 15
   Robert 123
   Samuel 75
   Thomas 11,19,27,46,57

Thomas H. 19
William 7,15,52,62,
   124
   William H. 65
   Zacheus 66
Greene, Richard 124
Greenlee, James, Jr. 59
   William 63
Greenwood, John 137
Greer, Freeman 114
   John 15
Gregg, Hugh 47
Gregor, John 121
Gregory, Asa 65,77
   Dempsey 72
   Edmond 74
   Edmond, Jr. 5
   Edmond, Sr. 4
   Frederick 4,73
   Henry 4
   Herrin 26
   James 3,129
   Jess 16,74
   Job 73
   John 3,55,73
   Jonathan 4,74
   Joseph 118
   Lemuel 5
   Mitchel 3
   Nathan 4,74
   Peter 73
   Samuel 4,72,74
   Thomas 4,5
   William 42,75
Gregson, George 121
Greves, Edward 5
   William 4
Grey, Hezekiah 47
Gribble, John 57
   Thomas 135
Grice, Reuben 130
Grier, Samuel 95
Griffen see Griffin
Griffin, Abraham 100
   Allen 35
   Benjamin 20
   Claiborne 78
   David 5,86
   Edward 88
   Elisha 28
   Enoch 100
   Gilbert 20
   Greenbury 132
   Horatio 25
   Isaac 104
   James 20,42
   Jesse 84,88
   John 4,41,84
   Joseph 78,80,87
   Joshua 88
   Kinchen 102
   Levi 84
   Lewis 84
   Oliver 44
   Reuben 22
   Stephen 39
   Will 84
   William 22,36,60,63,
      77
   William H. 10
Griffis, James 89
Griffith, D. W. 17
   Daniel 116
   James 85
   John 50,59,129
   Samuel 118
   Solomon 50
   William 40

Griffy, James 54
Grigg, Bannester 133
   Jesse 133
Grigs, Henry 133
Grimes, Bryant 87
   George 123
   James 15,33,107
   Jesse 94
   John 15
   Mercer 24
   Stephen 15
Grimmer, Cullen 18,77
   Moses 18
Grimstead, Thomas Y. 19
Grisham, Elijah 50
Grissel, Bannister 15
Grissom, Benjamin 36
   James 112
   Laban 105
   Moses 130
   Thomas 105
   Willie 37
Grisson, Neal 17
Grist, Allen 83
   Isaac 44
   James 62,87
   John 10
   Rayford 27
   Sutton 27
   Will 10
Grizzard, Abraham 86
   Armstead 78
   Joel 76
Grizzle, John 56
Grogan, Bartlett 40
   John 111
   William 41
Grove, Jesse W. 132
Groves, Thomas 130
Grower, Reuben 15
Grub, David 121
   George 122
   Jacob 45
   John 45
Gruson, Martin 53
Guant, Avery 131
Gudger, Joseph 58,136
   William 137
Guffey, Archy Reed 132
   James S. 132
Guffy, John 55,132
Guider, John 129
Guilford, William 72
Guiltney, Nathan 129
   Robert 129
   William 129
Gullet, Christopher 117
   Daniel 117
   George 123
   William 51
Gullidge, Henry 99
   Jeremiah 29
Gunn, John 110
Gunter, Asa 109
Gupton, Jacob 104
   Robert 59
   Turner 104
Gurgamus, Surnion 18
Gurganus, Aaron 83
   Thomas 82
   Willie 88
Gurley, Needham 28
   William 28
Gurly, Anson 90
   John 138
   William 100
Guthree, Samuel 85
Guthrie, Benjamin 66

Guthry, Shadrack 137
Guttis, James 106
Guy, Henry 14
   John 113
   John C. 14
   Lemuel 95
   William 122,134
Gwin, Ashman 130
Gwynn, Payten 62
Gyton, William 67

- H -

Hacket, William 39
Hackney, James 22
Hadder, Nehemiah 98
Hadley, James 127
Hadnok, Seth 17
Hadock, Michael 9
Hadrick, John 131
Haffler, William 7
Hafner, Martin 43
Hager, George 53
   Jacob 112
   John 53
Hagler, John 28
   Philip 100
   William 117
Hague, Jacob 123
   John 123
Haider, Mark 55
Hailey, Henry 78
   Henry Booker 38
Hain, Phillip 53
Haines, Overton 36
Hainline, William 122
Hains, Francis 113
   Jonathan 138
Hair, John 93
Haire, Greenbury 46
Haireld, Joseph 74
Hairis, Harvey 74
Haislip, Branson 88
   John 88
Hait, John 47
Haker, Beliker 66
Hale, Joshua 77
   Owen 15
Hales, Kader 20
   Nathaniel 99
Haley, Henry 102
   John 104
Hall, Abram 18
   Alexander 128
   Charles 75
   Daniel 26
   Durham 63
   Henry 27,95
   James 49,55,95
   Jeremiah 10
   John 51,127
   Jonathan 102
   Joseph 85,126
   Lewis 18
   Martin 15
   Mathew 27
   Pleasant 106
   Richard
   Robert 14,41,63,113
   Robert C. 59
   Solomon 121
   Thomas 58,84
   William 84
   Willie 103
   Willis 90
Hallsey, Benjamin F. 88

Hallstead, John 74
Hallswell, Reddick 6
Halsey, Miles 7
Halstead, Ivy 3
   William 3
Ham, Beriman 104
   Giles 13
   Henry 90
   James 42
   William 90
Ham see also Hamm
Hambleton, Edley 134
   James 126
Hamblett, Jesse 19
Hamby, Eli 117
   Reuben 117
Hamilton, Alexander 85
   David 85
   Joseph 49
   Thomas 84
   William 130
Hamm, Benjamin 104
   Haywood 14
   Joel 99
   Seth 115
   William 14,90
Hamm see also Ham
Hammon, Washington 16
Hammonds, Absolam 25
   William 68
   Willis 80
Hammons, Duthan 94
   Elijah 31
   John 96
   Roland 99
   Wilson 22
Hammuns, John 48
Hampton, Adam 132
   David 45
   Jesse 84
   Jonathan 132
   Noah 133
   Thomas 116
Hamrick, Elijah 132
Hamsick, James 132
Hancock, Eli 114
   Elisha 113
   Felic 94
   Isaiah 114
   Isham 119
   John 41,50,98
   Thomas 29
Hancy, Thomas 136
Hand, William 17
Handcastle, John 133
Handcock, Thomas 29
Hanes, Eli 132
Haney, Robert 55
   William S. 41
Haning, John 115
Hanison, William 50
Hankens, William 66
Hankin, John 15
Hanks, John 105,130
   Willis 105
Hanley, Benjamin 29
Hanmock, Bartlett 68
Hannah, Abner 61
   Eli 61
   Isaac 119
   John 61,119
   Solomon 119
Hanner, Alexander 61
Hanners, William 73
Hannon, John 56
   Thomas 54
   William 62
Hanny, Timothy 62

Hanrahan, Michael 83
Hansley, Edmond 92
  Owen 18
Hanson, Abijah 18
  Stephen 126
Hapler, Phillip 122
Happman, Mertin 43
Harald, John 42
Harbeson, Hiram 62
  James 126
Harbin, James 129
  Milly 19
Harbison, John 63
Harchie, John 128
Harching, Israel 83
Hardee, John 11
Harden, Aquilla 77
  Charles 61
  James 26
  John 61
Harden see Hardin
Harder, Jonathan 56,69
  William 55
Hardeson, Edward 88
  Elijah 17
  James 21
  Jesse 21,91
  Joshua 21
Hardin, Stewart 37
Hardin see also Harden
Harding, Henry 10
Hardison, William 94
Hardle, John 6
Hardwick, Younger 38
Hardy, Arthur 67
  Benjamin 86
  John 90
  Lemuel 86
  Whitmell 20
Hare, Aaron 76
  Arthur 26
  Henry 90
  Jacob 8
  John 7,96,122
  John P. 76
  Jonathan 26
  Luke 76
  Martin 95
Harget, Alfred 85
  Peter 86
  William 86
Hargett, Henry 126
  William 126
Hargis, Thomas 60
Hargrove, William 36
Haris see Harris
Harker, Belcher 66
Harkey, David 126
  John 126
Harlow, Jesse 19,78
Harlson, William 54
Harman, George 109
  Jacob 131
  James 89
  Peter 54
Harmon, Joseph 54
  Solomon 54
Harner, Jacob 131
Harp, Willie 116
Harper, Absolam 33
  Cornelius 12
  Gradathan 39
  Jesse 13
  John 13
  Joshua 23,80
  Stephen 21
  William 84,87
Harralson, Archibald 106

John 6
Harrass see Harris
Harreld, Elisha 6
Harrel(1), Aaron 7
  Bray 17
  Dancy 77
  David 65
  Eli 76
  Elias 13
  Elijah 115
  Francis 14
  Gilbert 133
  Henry 77
  Isham 100
  Jacob 15
  Jesse 88
  Joel 13
  John 13
  Joseph 5,13,65,75,86
  Joshua 77
  Meredith 77
  Powel 77
  Samuel 86
  Simeon 65
  Thomas 77
Harrelson, Solomon 133
Harress see Harriss
Harrill, Hardy 89
Harrington, Isaac 110
  John 99
Harris, Alexander 57
  Alexander W. 127
  Allen 50
  Cafferld 59
  Charles B. 39
  Cyrus 69
  Daniel 7
  David 122
  Dempsey 76
  Edwin 81
  Egbird 66
  Eli 50
  Elisha 83,110
  George 83
  Green 50
  Henry 34,79,109
  Hiram 130
  Houston 48
  Howel 113
  Hugh 47
  Isaac 48,56
  Isham 33
  James 33,51,83
  Jeptha 124
  Jeremiah 82
  Jesse, Jr. 121
  Joel 124
  John 5,81
  John B. 130
  Jonathan 124
  Joseph C. 23
  Josiah 82,85
  K. 50
  Mark 4
  Micajah 104
  Milton 69
  Orren 79
  Ransom 37
  Reuben 104
  Richard 66,68,104
  Richard, Sr. 106
  Robert 82
  Robinson 130
  Sake 46
  Samuel 34,60,102
  Samuel H. 48
  Silvenus 87
  Simpson 106

Timothy 64
West, Jr. 50
Wiley 50,54
William 30,32,42,50,
  102,132
William J. 127
Willie 124
Willis 123
Zedekiah 132
Zemeriah 85
Harris see also Harriss
Harrison, Abner 86
  Adam 47
  George 21,81
  Henry W. 5
  Isaac 74
  James 23,116
  James C. 19
  Jesse 76
  John W. 4
  Nathan 73
  Owen W. 5
  Redding 84
  Richard 20
  Robert 35,75,127
  William 35
  Willie 102
Harriss, Bynum 19
  Caleb 4
  David 19
  Elias 78
  Gideon 78
  Henry 104
  John 58,87,90,104,135
  Maxamillian 137
  Noah 87
  Rinchen 18
  Solomon 88
  William 78
Hart, Alfred 13
  Charles 48
  Edward 52
  Elijah 32
  Graves 105
  Green 78
  Hardy 20
  Hampley 116
  Henry 27,78
  John 32
  Joseph 34
  Peter 118
  Samuel 46
Hartfield, Solomon 63
Harth, Clinton 56
Hartle, Thomas 123
Hartley, John 134
  Reuben 118
  William 134
Hartman, Charles 127
  John 68,120
Harton, Hardy 100
  Thomas 50
Hartsell, Leonard 124
Hartsfield, David 86
  John B. 102
Hartsoll, Jacob 124
Hartzog, David 118
Harvener, John 54
Harvey, Abraham 33
  Absalom 108
  Duncan 23
  James 91,119
  John 114
  Nathan 82
Harwell, Alfred 78
  Robert 25
  William 38
Harwood, Britain 110

Richard 44
William 35
Hasby, Jacob 122
Hashford, William 108
Hasket, John
  Thomas 75
Haskett, Jesse 85
  John 119
Haskey, John 127
Haskin, Isham 33
Haskins, Enoch 91
  Purnal 91
Hasley, John 69
Hass, Christian 135
Hassel, William 88
  Zadock 82
Hassell, Benjamin 9
  Zadock 9,82
Hastey, Williby 20
Haswell, Benjamin 107
  Mason 52
  Reddick 23
  Samuel 53
  Thomas 23
Hatch, Anthony 16
  Samuel 16
Hatcher, William 100
Hatchock, Hansel 19
Hately, Henry 118
Hatfield, Benjamin 138
  William 6
Hath, John 46
Hatheway, Hugh 79
Hathway, David 87
Hatley, Britain 110
Hatt, James 52
Hattam, Elijah 49
Hattaman, Christopher 127
Hattom, Josiah 49
Haughton, Josiah 81
  Thomas 21
Hauley, John 126
Hauser, Daniel 115
  John L. 115
Hauston, John 43
Hawes, John 19
Hawett, Richard 81
Hawkins, Achilles 82
  Gabriel 19
  John 17,21,52,125,136
  Joshua 56,68
  Josiah 91
  Littleton 83
  Micajah T. 22
  Otway 91
  Richard 52
  Stephen 17,84
  Thomas 83,91
  William 53
Hawks, John 22,23,80
Hawley, Charles 30
  John 126
Hawn, David 131
Hawser, Abner 98
Hawsley, William 18
Haworth, Daniel 45
  Jeremiah 45
  Micajah 45
Hawthorn, Nathaniel 30
Haxwood, Richard 44
Hay, George 16
  Harwell 86
  James 106
  Joseph 16
  Samuel 14
  Thomas 16
Hayes, Absalom 101
  Charles 58,59

Daniel 118
Elias 119
Harmon 7,76
Hugh 24
James 8
Jesse 79
Mathew 25
Nathaniel 23
Peyton 36
Richard 108
Samuel 46
Solomon 36
Thomas 105
Willis 103
Haygood, Jesse 124
Hayley, Lewis 15
Hayner, Thomas 89
Haynes, Armstead 34
  Benjamin 42
  Matthew 62
  Philip 131
  William 40
  William G. 41
Hays, Colbert 135
  Harmon 7
  Joseph 137
Hayse, Elijah 134
  John 134
Haysell, James 9
Haywell, Cullen 14
Haywood, George 108
  James 69
  Shadrack 35
Hayworth, William 123
Hazelett, Ezekiel 62
Hazlewood, George 23,80
Head, James 35
Headen, Isaac 109
Headrick, Phillip 44
Headrick see Hedrick
Heair, George 49
Hearing, Benjamin 12
  Nathaniel 12
Hearn, Ezekiel 50
  George 124
Heartley, Abner 84
Heath, Alexander 95
  Andrew 3
  Arthur 72
  Edmund 84
  Frederick 84
  John 90
  Samuel 42
  Solomon 69
Heathcock, Ned 33
Hector, Hiram 55
Hedgepeth, Henry 80
  Holliday 80
  Jesse 64
Hedgepith, Thompson 37
Hedrick, John 131
  Phillips 131
Hedrick see Headrick
Hefley, Martin 138
Hefner, Daniel 136
Hegler, Philip 124
Hegles, Jacob 128
Heldebrand, Conrade 130
  Joseph 131
Helfer, Daniel 122
  Jacob 68
Hellen, Isaac 84
  James 49
  Walter 17
Helmer, Joel 126
Helmes, Charles 126
  William 126
Helms, Isaac 69

Helper, Christopher 122
Helpley, Martin 58
Helsepeck, Jacob 114
Heltan, Joseph 104
Helton, Lepr. 135
Hemphill, John 113
Henby, William 61
Henderson, Daniel 92
  David 48
  Duncan 92
  Henry 17
Henderson, Hillory 17,91
  Isaac 17
  James 125,134
  John 53
  Kilby 91
  Morris 107
  Samuel 46
  Selden 10
  William 40,135
Hendesty, Barton 85
Hendley, Ezekiel 108
  Henry 36
Hendrick, Adam 44
  David 29
  James 61
  Michael 72
Hendricks, Jesse 122
  Seth 75
  Thomas 6
Hendrickson, Jeremiah 52
  Joshua 117
Hendrix, Henry 122
  Thomas 122
Henley, Thomas 48
Henlin, William 120
Henry, Eli N. 58
  Green 22
  Israel 82
  James 66
  John 62
  Rigdon 86
  Thomas 53
Hensley, Charles 59
Henson, Joseph 12
  Reuben 57
Hepler, Henry 44
Hepner, Michael 54
Herndon, Pleasant 32,107
  William 32,106
Heron, Davis 41
  Moses 62
Herren, Robert 55
Herrin, Joseph 26
  Lewis 136
  Stephen 26
Herring, Ashael 12
  Benjamin 94
  Burwell 86
  Giles 96
  Jehabud 13
  Joseph 90
  Joshua 27
  Moses 53
  Stephen 15,98
Herrington, John 85
  Moses 87
Hertee, Benjamin 59
Hervey, Stephen 33
Hester, Alfred 105
  Benjamin 105
  Jasper 24
  Joseph 24
  Ransom 36
  Robert 105
  Stephen 67
Heulin, Edward 43
Hewes, Thomas 10

Hewet, Randal 66
Hews, Malachi 94
    Reddick 14
Heziap, Bresom 46
Hickason, Little 62
Hickerson, David 51
Hickeson, John 62
Hickman, Joseph 51
Hicks, Abner 105
    Aldridge 17
    Alfred 104
    Daniel 55,106
    Dempsey 64
    Isaiah 44
    James 64,130
    Jesse 109
    Queen 55
    Reuben 50
    Robert 101
    Stephen 14
    West 33
    William 78,128,132
Hickson, James 58
Hicky, William 57
Hiett, Moses 42
Hiffley, George 138
Hiflin, John 133
    William 105
Higdon, Leonard 57
Higgs, Bernett 37
    John 77,91
    Kinchen 36
    Moore 78
    William 65
High, Julian 24
    Michel 28
    Silas 60
Highland, Jesse 109
Highsmith, James 93
    John 92
Hight, Willie 23
Hightower, Joshua 37
Hilemon, John 56
Hill, Aasa 55
    Alfred 32
    Aquila R. 17
    Asaph 132
    Benjamin 7,76
    Green 96,102
    Henry, Jr. 102
    Isaac 90
    James 47,78,87,100,
      132,135
    James J. 18
    Jesse 56,69
    John 23,52,122,124
    John J. 83
    Jonathan 55
    Joseph H. 102
    Julius 23
    Martin 12
    Micajah 44
    Rial 132
    Richard 12
    Robert 41,59,115
    Samuel 93
    Shadrack 44
    Smith 44
    Sion 103
    Thomas 100,133
    Thomas E. 59
    Whitmill 75
    William 57,106,130
    Willie 83
Hillbourn, Henry 93
Hillbourne, Zadock 93
Hilley, Watson 76
Hillman, Dempsey P. 79

Hillmon, Caleb 111
    Joshua 111
    Samuel 111
Hilton, Joseph 56
Himpman, Henry 128
Hinchey, Bartlett 107
Hindrix, Joshua 122
Hines, Alexander 13
    Charles 103
    John 21,89,95
    Samuel 86
    William 21
Hinkle, Anthony 130
    William 53
Hinkley, George 91
Hinklin, Ensign 92
Hinnant, Hardy 15
    Jonathan 15
    Josiah 14
Hinshaw, Jonathan 117
Hinsley, James 72
Hinson, John, Jr. 99
    Joseph 119
    Robert 14
Hinston, Enoch 40
Hinton, Elam 60
    James 103
    Mathew 14
    William 109
    Willis 14
Hiott, Isaac 7
Hips, Jacob 57
Hirter, Isaac 60
Hise, Jacob 57
Hister, Joseph 104
    Thomas 111
Histers, William 96
Hite, William 5
Hitner, Henry 42
Hixt, Jacob 42
Hoard, Stancel 89
    Willie 21
Hobbs, Amos 75
    Barnabas 119
    George 110
    Henry 6,82
    Isaac 64
    James 26
    Michael 96
    Miles 8
    Noah 4
    Reuben 6,12
    Samuel 65
    Simon 91
    Thomas 28,111
Hobby, Francis 25
    Harbut 64
    John 103
Hobson, George 117
Hocall, Benjamin 76
Hodge, David 132
    George 43
    John 110,127
    Joseph 31
    Joshua 88
    Phillip 33
Hodgers, John 44
Hodges, Gentry 50
    John 24
    Philemon S. 93
    William 24,50
    Willis 87
    Wilson B. 83
Hoedridge, Nathan 119
Hoffman, Christopher 53
    George 54
Hofler, William 75
Hogan, Isaiah

    John 129
    Matthew 34
Hogard, Thomas 65
Hoge, Jonathan 61
Hogg, Gaven 77
Hoggard, Elisha 77
    James 77
Hogler, Isaac 117
Hogwood, Josiah 88
Hoke, Daniel 130
    Peter 130
Holand, William 64
Holbert, Joseph 55
Holbrook, Isaac 50
    Joseph 42
    William, Jr. 42
    William, Sr. 42
Holbrooks, John 48
Holden, Daniel 107
    Samuel 48
Holder, James 110
    William 50
Holderfield, Daniel 117
    Willis 35
Holdesnes, James 111
Holding, Isham 64
Holebrooks, Samuel 127
Holefield, William 56
Holifield, Elijah 133
    John 100
    Ralph 50
    Watson 50
Holifyeld, William 116
Holland, Arnold 129
    Charles 83
    Enos 13
    Henry 53
    Kenrard 90
    Marcus D. 69
    Marsy D. 56
    Matthew, Jr. 53
    Richard 137
    Thomas 8
    William 35,133
Holleman, David 128
Holley, John 84
Holliday, Joseph 110
Hollin, Daniel 27
Hollingsworth, Henry 94
    William T. 104
Hollis, Edward 81
Holloman, Elisha 10
    George, Jr. 76
    Justin 76
    Lemuel 8
    William 51,65
Holloway, Abram 6
    John 102
    John, Jr. 64
    Luke 6
    Shad 84
    Taylor 112
Hollowday, Rinchen 13
Hollowell, Joseph 14
    Thomas 15
    William 83
Holly, John 65
Holmes, Edward 13
    George 25
    Hugh 48
    James 66
    John 17,18
    Moses 44
    Robert 9
    Solomon 19
    William S. 82
Holomon, John 89
    William 123

Holsclaw, Henry 52
Holshause, Andrew, Jr. 43
Holshauser, Fred 120
    John 43
    Windle 128
Holstead, Malachi 72
Holston, Averytt 102
Holswell, Edwin 14
Holt, Henry 75,108
    Lemuel 135
    Richard 110
    William 15,33,108
Holtford, Matthew 79
Holton, Jesse 112
    John 124
    William 49
Holtowell, Thomas 15
Holyfield, William 68
Honecutt, Brittain 15
Honeycutt, Isham 124
    Reuben 124
    Samuel 124,128
    Uriah 137
Hood, Bold Robin 14
    James 56
    Jeremiah 61
    Joseph 57
    Junius 47
    Nathaniel 103
    Reuben 126
    William 86
Hoofman, Philip 43
Hook, William 94
Hooker, Hiram 9
    Hymeriah 13
    James 13
    John 48,115
    Spencer 82
    Stephen 74
    Thomas 13
    William 13
Hooks, Hermant 90
    Hillary 90
    Phillip 13
    William 13,28
Hooper,
Hooten, William 82
Hoots, Henry 117
    Jacob 68
Hoover, Henry 127
    Jacob 68
    John 114
Hop, William 16
Hope, Christopher 131
    Thomas 125
    William 95
Hopgood, Theophilus 99
Hopkins, Farley 125
    John 99,105
    Miles 8
    Robert 10,82
    William 101
Hoppase, John 118
Hopper, Andrew 138
Hoppis, Adam 53
Hops, Willie 130
Horn, Amden 81
    David 91
    Hansel 100,118
    Harrell 22
    Henry 21
    Hillkiah 90
    Howell 44
    Isaac 21
    J. Jolly 89
    John 32
    Lee 81
    Michael 89

Peter 40
    Silas 103
    Thomas 44
    William 25
Horn see also Horne
Hornaday, John 33
    Ziah 32
Horne, Hansel 18,100
    Henry 21
    Isaac 21
    Jeremiah 89
    Martin B. 89
    Sion 25
Horner, John 32
Horney, Samuel 39
Horniday, Ziah 32
Hornsby, John 104
Horoh, William H. 43
Horslam, William 47
Horton, Canady 107
    Charles 101
    David 52,118
    Elisha 8
    Harbert 132
    Jeremiah 78
    Joseph 116
    Joshua 107
    Josiah 86
    Nathan 50
    Phillip 25
    Phineas 118
    William 52
Hoskins, Edmond 72
    Ellis 112
    John 111
    Jos. 111
Houp, John 47
House, George 130
    Green D. 23
    Isaac 59,104
    Jacob 49
    John 26
    Joseph J. 13
    Thomas 37
    Turner 87
Houser, Henry 131
    Jacob 130
    John 121,130
Housten, William, Jr.
Houston, David 49
    Joel S. 127
    Littleton 35
    Matthew 61
    Richard F. 128
    William 127
    William, Jr. 126
    William Hubbard 16
Hover, Henry 127
Hovis, Frederick 53
Howard, Alvin 45
    Benjamin 51
    Bewdie 37
    Calvin 17
    Edmund 16
    Elwin 45
    George 123
    Grovew 60
    Henry 91
    Hugh 38
    Isaac 66
    James 10
    Jesse 50
    Joseph 51,61
    Lewis 48
    Menas 66
    Richard 31
    Samuel 91
    Thomas 36,95

Titus 90
    William 17
Howe, William 34
Howel, Christian 135
Howell, Caleb 90
    Isaac 127
    James 21
    John 13,17,39,99
    Joshua 131
    Osborn 103
    Richard 9
    Samuel 135
    Stephen 76
    William 99
    Woodard 13
Howie, Aaron 126
Howington, Edward 32
Howland, Thomas 66
    William 85
    Zephaniah 85
Howlet, Isaac 40
Howood, Robert 126
Howzer, Peter 54
Hoyle, Jackson S. 72
    John 56,59
Hubbard, Aquilla 101
    George 42
    Matthew 29,38
Hubbart, William 41
Huckaby, Benjamin 28
    James 97
Hudgins, Asa 37
Hudler, Amos 84
Hudlow, Kenon 86
    Michel 54
Hudnal, William 83
Hudson, Azariah 9
    Hall 18,79
    James 40,120
    Joshua 100
    Lawrence 122
    Robert 114
    Thomas 6,43
    William 44,62
    Willis 93
Hudspith, George 116
Hueston, Plesabo 129
Huet, Lewis 130
Huff, Daniel 42
    William 67
Huffins, Jacob 109
Huffman, Abram 57
    Adam 123
    Benjamin 36
    Frederick 57
    Jacob 16
    Lott 91
    Phillip 115
Huffsteddler, Henry 130
    John 130
Hufman, Jacob 16
Hugey, John 46
Huggins, Isaac 17
    John 128
    Robert, Jr. 53
Hughes, Joseph 108
    Nathaniel 5
    Richman 120
Hughes see also Hughs
Hughey, David 137
    Joseph 58
    Samuel 137
Hughs, James 61,121
    John 61
    John W. 73
    Richmond 61
    Robert M. 47
    William 121

Hughs see also Hughes
Huit, James 5
Huket, James 62
Hulet, John 17
Hulgan, Stephen 119
Hull, John 64
    William 54
Humphis, Thomas 5
Humphrey, Burney 17
    Daniel 11
    Lewis 11
    Malachi 15
    William 17
Humphreys, Henry 112
    John 113
Humphries, John H. 38
    Samuel 55
    William 75,113,123
Hunhill, James 57
Hunley, Cobelas 124
Hunn, Charles 116
Hunnings, Elijah 4
Hunt, Abraham 44
    Charles 5
    David 81
    Elijah 106
    Henry 22
    Ishum 4
    James 24
    Jonathan 61
    John 32,123,129
    Leban 38
    Nathaniel 23
    Noah 121
    Oliver 33
    Thomas 36,40,105
    William 53,116,132
Hunter, Anderson 60
    Cader 65
    Hardy 65
    Henry, Jr. 126
    Isaac 75
    James 56,68,81
    John 77,132
    Joseph 55
    Joshua 130
    Samuel 39,63,71,139
    Whitmill 35,64
    William 65
Huntington, Minor 84
Huntley, David 131
Huphines, Jacob 115
Hurdle, Elisha 6
    Henry 33
    Kader 7
Hurley, Daniel 49
    William 50
Hurst, James 91
Hurstle, James 137
Huskey, Isham 105
    Jesse 55
    Thomas 54
Husky, Ransom 131
Hussey, John E. 94
Husslatter, Adam 54
Hust, James 57
Huston, Levi 61
    Littleton 35
Hutchens, James 114
Hutchins, David 101
    James 101
    John 107
    Lewis 107
    Wallis 72
    William 132
Hutchinson, Alexander 112
    Charles 124
    William 111

Hutchison, Benjamin 42
    James 47,112
    Samuel J. 47
Hutson, Azariah 9
    James 120
    Thomas 43
    William 44
Huut, Noah 121
Hyatt, Alsey 28
    John 100
Hyde, Henry 91
Hyett, Jesse 75
Hyley, Philly 58
Hyman, Lawrance 21
Hymon, Stephen 65
Hynes, James 22
Hyer, John 42

- I -

Icehour, Martin 49
Idol, Barnabas 45
    Joseph 115
    Matthias 45
Idol see also Edoll
Ijames, Brice W. 45
Ijams, John 122
Inge, John J. 105
Ingerham, Jacob 118
Ingle, Michael 131
Ingram, Ambrose 102
    Hezekiah 29
    Isham 29
    James 110
    John 29,37,99
    Lemuel 29
    Matthew 49
    Moody 30
    Nathaniel 78
    William 78
Inscore, John 104
Ipock, Henry 34
    John 84
    Lawarous 84
Irby, Turner 112
Iredell, James 72
Ireland, David 66
    John 32
Irvey, Will U. 48
Irvine, Abram 55,132
    James 132
Irwin, Abijah 123
    Alexander 53
    Andrew 72,139
    Giles 126
    James 58
    John 48
    Samuel 113
Isaac, Gabriel 131
    Jacob 53
Isam, Brice W. 45
Isbell, Littleton 116
    Pendleton B. 60
Ision, Philip 113
Isley, Christian 39
Ives, Duran 84
    Elijah 84
    Mason 84
    William H. 11
    Zadock 83
Ivey, Charles, Sr. 31
    Hartwell 102,103
    Isham 30
    James 30,103
    Jesse 126
    John 32

    Littleton 63
    William 108
Ivy, Richard 90
Izzard, Elijah 23

- J -

Jaccour, John 48
Jack, William Boly 42
Jackson, Abner 32
    Beverly 19
    Daniel 33,101
    Edmond 19
    Eleazer 10
    Elijah 89
    Elisha 34
    Ervin 96
    Francis 42
    George 113
    Hezekiah 74
    Isaac 42
    Isam 86
    Jacob 12,32
    Jackariah 91
    James 5,56,57,67,74,
        109,121
    John 6,13,25
    John, Jr. 75
    Joseph 7
    Joshua 5
    Josiah 104
    Law 13
    Michael 33
    Moses 57
    Oram 104
    Peavon 125
    Robert H. 60
    Samuel 42,109
    Spencer 38
    Thomas 39,40,75
    Warren 26
    William 27,33,39,75
    William P. 110
Jacobs, James 37
    Solomon 68
    Thomas 26
    William 32,128
Jacocks, Jonathan H. 77
James, Benjamin 65
    Conel 44
    Cornell 44
    David 28
    Henry 23,28,45,80
    Hosea 28
    Isaac 44
    Jacob 4
    James F. 9
    Jesse 43
    John 20,29,45,82,92
    Joseph 52
    Lemmuel 88
    Martin 30
    Osborn 33
    Thomas 95
    William 21,28,124
Janes, William 58
Jarold, Thomas 41
Jaron, Jacob 137
Jarral, John 102
Jarrall, Joshua 40
Jarrat, Isaac 117
    William 121
Jarratt, John 54
Jarrels, John 56,69
Jarvis, Caleb 4
    Dennis 44

Merese 3
  Richard 44
  Samuel 74
  Thomas B. 4
  Zedekiah 68
Jasey, Willis 19
Jasper, William 29,66
Javette, Aaron 136
Javiette, Irea 137
Jeague, James 123
Jean, David 115
Jeffers, James 60
Jeffery, Marma D. 59
Jeffreys, Marmaduke N. 23
Jeffries, Robert 32
Jelks, Jarrat M. 14
Jelton, Samuel 40
Jenkins, Benjamin 78
  Charles 8
  Henry D. 8
  Irwin 7
  Jenky 133
  John 78
  Lodowick 77
  Reuben 130
  Robert 36
  Samuel R. 89
  Simon 24
  Solomon 23
  Theophilus 88
  Wiertt 130
  William 59
  Willie 77
Jenkins see Jinkins
Jennett, Robert 10
Jennigan, David 13
Jennings, Frederick B. 9
  George W. 113
Jerald, Abram 40
Jermanny, Josiah 82
Jernigan, Buk 15
  Daniel 15
Jerrell, John 73
Jesop, Joshua 25
Jeter, Barnett 105
Jethro, John 81
Jetton, Benedict 129
Jewter, Jiles 20
Jimison, Arthur 45
Jinkins, Azra 138
  John 130
  Moses 91
  Samuel 137
  Steward 130
  Thomas 42,115
  William 98
Jinks, Matt 34
Johis, Electris 112
John, Ash 48
  Will 48
  William 126
Johnsion, Willis 79
Johnson, Abram 115
  Anderson 129
  Charles 82,100
  David 136
  Elias 78
  Elisha 115
  Grady 136
  Joel 117
  John 78,115,123
  Levy 116
  Matthew 116
  Moses 103
  Reddin 103
  Robert 78
  Samuel 103
  Shadrack 25

Talton 124
William 99,114,123
William W. 77
Willis 104
Johnston, Abram 44
  Alex 110
  Andrew 119
  Angus 27
  Ashley 46
  Bailey 50
  Baker 44
  Benjamin 14,120
  Brittain 15,59
  Carter 132
  Charles 109
  Daniel 109
  David 58
  Edward 106
  Henry 33,55,94
  Hugh 136
  Isaiah 86
  James 13,15,38,66,76,
    87,106,111,121
  James, Jr. 110
  James, Sr. 110
  Jeremiah 68
  John 25,26,28,34,49,
    62,64,97,110,125,
    127
  Joseph 52,98
  Joshua 59
  Lewis 26,133
  Mitchel 47
  Moses 120
  Nathaniel 14
  Richard 106
  Robert 61,132
  Rufus 49
  Samuel 110,117,125
  Solomon 51
  Stephen 14
  Strangerman 51
  Tapley 97
  Weat 36
  Wiley 124
  Will 69
  William 13,37,38,49,
    52,54,64,102,103,
    110,125
  Willis 35,79
Joice, Ambrose 40
  Pleasant 40
Joice see also Joyce
Joiner, Abraham 95
  Charlton 100
Joiner see also Joyner
Jolley, Gideon 21
  Henry 88
  William 128
Jolly, Thomas 79
Jonagon, Ryan 65
Jones, Alfred 35
  Allen 95,101,105
  Anderson 106
  Bartlett 9
  Benjamin 79
  Bennett 22
  Bradford 101
  Charles 60,120
  Churchwell 106
  Cornelius 3
  Daniel 95
  Darby 50
  Darling 35,64
  David 16,27,37,63
  Drury 122
  Edmund 16,57
  Edward 38,111

Elijah 95
Elisha 88
Felix 16
Francis 102
Fred 11
Frederick 59
Gardner 86
George 26
Hardy L. 11
Henry 36,37,39
Hezekiah 105
Hugh 62
Iravin 59
Isaac 51
Isaac James 16
Jacob 116
Jacob P. 7
James 26,44,46,76,83,
  94,106,109,131,
  136
James B. 8
James C. 104
Jeremiah 4,74
Jesse 78,93,116
Joel 125
John 16,19,24,29,32,
  41,55,61,62,76,
  84,91,100,101,
  114,134
John, Sr. 10
Jonas 94
Jonathan 15,60,122
Joseph 92
Joshua 57
Josiah 132
Laban 102
Lemuel 63
Lemuel B. 116
Martin 40
Maurice 9
Miles 31,74
Nathan 95
Nathaniel 103,108
Readin 13
Reddick 26
Richard 12,37,45
Ridley 102
Robert 13,19,106
Samuel 5,8,17,101
Seth 101
Simeon 73
Simon 4,87
Smith 11
Stephen 30
Thomas 6,29,89,95,
  100,136,137
Timothy W. 102
Vinson H. 7
Westley 102
William 13,18,37,93,
  98,108,111,136
William D. 23
William G. 59
Willie 103,105
Willis 96
Joplin, Mordecai 102
Jordan, Alexander 136
  Cooper 114
  Dickson 101
  Francis 50
  George 107
  Hana 7
  James 7,14
  Jesse 15
  John 19,103,106,119
  John, Sr. 78
  Joseph 75
  Leonard 34

Matthew 6
Micajah 63
Osbourn 101
Richard 82
Ruton 129
Seth B. 82
William 34,72
Joy, Andrew 18
Myrick 14
Reeves 14
Joyce, John, Jr. 114
Robert 113
Joyce see also Joice
Joyner, Abram 87
Amos 87
Andrew 71
Nelson 76
Joyner see also Joiner
Judkins, Joseph 87
Juhu, Charles 69
Julding, John 29
Julin, Isham 133
Jacob 125
Samuel 133
Julke, William 29
Junderbush, John 126
Junigan, Willie 103
Jush, George 123
John 123
Justice, Eli 135
John 136
Joseph C. 79
Laben 91
Thomas 58
William 136
Justin, George 136
Justuss, Joseph C. 79

- K -

Kallum, Shadrack 3
Kanady, William 74
Kances, John 115
Kart, John R. 35
Kasler, Ralph 43
Kastor, John 43
Katts, Henry 44
Kay, Jonathan 85
Kea, William 89
Kean, John 14
Keath, George 93
James 93
Keaton, Henry 74
Keel, John 5
Keelin, Thomas 52
Keen, Gardner 26
Isaac 103
Keeth, Sion 43
Keeton, Clifton 51
Keetor, William 79
Kegle, George 127
Keith, Henry 59,137
Reuben 137
William 137
Kell, Thomas 51
Kellam, David 114
Edward 91
Kellehan, Dennis 24
John 24
Pierce 24
Keller, Jacob 134
Leonard 57
Peter 131
Kelley, James 24
John 59,83
Thomas 58

Kellum, Isma 35,64
Samuel 111
Kelly, George 45
Hugh 98
James 45,83
John 114
John, Jr. 51,103
Joseph 95
Peter 98
Richard 90
Solomon 57
Thomas 51
William 49,90
William D. 51
Kellyham, Cornelius 67
Kemmons, Andrew 127
Kemp, David M. 67
John 84
Kenaday, Levi 77
Kenady, Daniel 94
Kence, Isaac 129
Kendrick, James, Jr. 84
Kenedy, George 66
Kennedy, John 134
Robert 27
Kenneman, George 42
Kenny, Ezekiel 116
Kenty, George 48
Kerby, John 52
Joseph 135
Larkin 135
Kerby see also Kurby
Kerney, Thomas 129
Kerr, Alfred 128
David 43
William 125,128
Kerr see also Kurr
Kersey, Edward 110
William 38
Kesler, Jacob 45
Ketchum, David 16
Joel 114
Thomas 50
Kethorn, James 67
Kethly, Daniel 16
Ketor, Benjamin 132
James 132
Key, Achilus 116
George 78
Logan 85
William 66
Keyson, Thomas 98
Kilby, Adam 51
William 51
Killegrew, William 12
Killian, Daniel 58,130
Frederick 130
Henry 131
John 58,134
Solomon 131
William 130
Killibrew, George H. 88
Lott 89
Killibrue, Joshua 89
Killingsworth, Joseph 86
Killis, Joseph 49
Killum, Irma 64
Kilpatrick, Alexander 47
Bryant 13
Francis 12
Kilton, Levi 109
Kilyon, Abram 54
Kimbrough, Elija 64
Kimmons, Joro 48
Kimmy, Frederick 62
Kimry, Henry 124
Kin, John 61
Kincade, Andrew 43

James 57
Samuel 43
Kincaid, Andrew 43,134
Kindle, John 40
Kindrick, Austin 20
King, Amos 94
Andrew 126
Briton 86
Daniel 133
David 16
Edward 18,114
Elihugh 129
Eliphlet 10
Ephraim 8,17
Frances 131
George 56
Hartsell 112
Harvey 112
Henry 7,92
Hillsman 102
Hiram 18
Hugh B. 46
James 28,40,102,129
Jeremiah 105
John 19,41,97,129,
135
Johnson 119
Lemiah 41
Leonard 23
Micajah 17
Miles 104
Moses 66
Nathan 67
Samuel 79
Stephen 102
Thomas 84,91,135
William 14,41,84,
102,112,128
William P. 77
Kinkaid, John 63
Kinkle, Jacob 61
Kinman, John 112
Kinney, Isaac 121
Kinnodle, George 112
Kinsey, Lewis 86
Kinshaw, Francis 45
Kipley, Henry 124
Kipps, Zachariah 82
Kirk, Barrum 62
John 84
Robert 56
Stephen 124
Thomas 124
Kirkland, Samuel 56,68
William 32,107
Kirkman, Daniel 38
Kirkpatrick, James 25
Kirland, William 32
Kiser, Frederick 48
Peter 54
Kistler, John 54
Kitchen, John 58
Kitchens, James 136
Kitchum, Joel 42
Kith, George 64
Kithrell, Merkle Tom 36
Kitrell, William 75
Kittral, William 12
Kittrell, George 75
Kade 36
Lemuel 104
Kivet, Aaron 119
Peter 33
Kivett, Henry 34
Kluttz see Clutz
Knight, Berryman 42
Charles, Jr. 89
Henry C. 64

James 20
Jesse C. 64
John 18
Miles 75
Samuel 11
Knott, David A. 35
Jesse 112
Robert 105
Knox, George 120
James 62
John 62
Josiah 82
Knup, Frederick 131
Koonce, George 16
Kornegay, Harget 16
Koy, William 28
Krouse, Andrew 42
Kurby, Elisha 34
Francis 68
Josiah 34
Kurby see also Kerby
Kurr, Angus 18
Kyles, Henry 135
Kysom, Joseph 54

- L -

Labeless, Asa 69
Lacey, James 44
Robert 121
Lack, James 46
Lackey, Alexander 129
George 46
Robert 108
William 136
Ladd, Newton 114
William 64,114
Laden, Tully 6
Ladyman, Benjamin 114
Laffoom, Thomas 102
Lain, David 89
Jacob 122
John 89
Lemuel 6
William W. 136
Laird, David 51
Laitham, William 119
Lake, Burges 136
Lakey, James 51
Lam, Jesse 116
Lamb, Gabriel 120
Hugh 92
Isaac 112
Joel M. 26
John 103
Manual 135
Michael 120
Miles 90
Moses 43
Silus 14
Lambert, Claton 23,80
Eli 120
Needham 14
Richard 127
Lamberton, Willis 28
Lambeth, Nathan 122
Lamer, Alexander 24
Laming, Thomas 54
Lamm, Dum 33
Henry 33
Jacob 119
Lampkin, Meredith 36
Samuel S. 81
Lampley, Jacob 99
Lams, James 137
John 137

Lancaster, John 80
John J. 24
Lemuel 64
William 90
William J. 59
Lance, John 43
Lancey, Charles 48
Land, Daniel 64
Stephen 96
Thomas 51
Landcaster, William 90
Landers, Barney 59
Thomas 81
William 81
Landiford, Samuel 101
Landingham, Agbert 112
Lands, Thomas 51
Lane, Andrew M. 48
Aven 86
George 84
Hardy 85
Jacob 43
Jesse 44
Joel 14,100
John 43
Lemuel 78
Thomas 39
Wiat 40
William 117
Lang, Joshua 76
Langdon, John 25
Langley, John 10
William 80
Langly, Matthias 67
Langoon, James 103
Langsford, Champ 138
Langston, Richard 90
Lanier, Benjamin 23
Hosea 21
John 15
Levett 88
Noah 94
Owen 15
Laniere, Benjamin A. 99
Lanin, David 40
Lanir, Alfred 10
Lanner, Joseph 135
Lanning, Amos 136
Lanoir, Walter R. 51
Lanon, Henry 68
Lap, James 111
Laplanch, James 76
Larder, Benjamin 88
Lareson, David 37
Largent, James 134
Lark, Daniel 44
Larkabee, David 68
Larkins, Aaron 93
James 92
Joel E. 92
Robert 92
William 17
William Jones 18
Lash, Abram 115
Laslie, Daniel 98
Neill 99
Lasly, Alex 107
Lassater, William 109
Lasser, James 94
John 94
Stephen 103
William 90
Lassiter, Alex 109
Brittain 20
George 26
Isham 86
Jacob 33
James 18

John 77,100
Robert 26
Silas 86
Thomas 21
Latham, Alfred 10
Arnet 10
David 83
William 119
Latta, James 31
Laughlon, John 27
Launan, John 99
Laurann, Branson 119
Laurence, George 52
Nicholas 53
Samuel 50
Law, Andrew 39
John 26
William 62
Lawler, John 34
Lawrence, Abram 36
Benjamin 78
Caleb 40
Malachi 118
Reuben 65
Laws, William 62
Laws see also Law
Lawson, Henry 56
Hiram 128
James 114
Jesse 84
Thomas 37,137
Layle, Robert 118
Layton, John 69
Lazenbury, Elias 46
Lazenby, Erasmus 68
Robert 128
Lcay, Jasse 28
Lea, Elam 95
James 55
John 37,55
Larkin 55
Nathaniel 110
Reuben 106
Richard 132
Vincent 106
William 55,109,133
Leach, Elisha 122
Thomas 45
Leach see also Leech
Lean, Aaron 13
Bird 31
George 34
Learcey, Asa 103
Samuel 103
William 101
Leary, Downing 81
Leath, Archibald 6
Thomas 11
Ledbetter, Henry 133
Ledbury, Woodman S. 92
Ledford, Jesse 133
Lee, Anthony B. 8
Burwell 96
Edward, Sr. 14
Enoch 73
Gabriel B. 111
Henry 14,26,77
Isaac 40
James 73,92
Jesse 16
John 15,73
John, Jr. 19
John W. 101,102
Jonathan 85
Josias 26
Lewis 76
Pharo 26

Richard H. 7
Thomas 15
William 26
Wright 99
Leech, Dugal 99
    John 99
Leech see also Leach
Leek, Henry 78
Leeper, John 130
Lefever, James 55
Leford, George 127
Leget(t) Benjamin 82
    David 87
    Erick 96
    Harman 81
    Jeremiah 77
    Joseph 82
Legget see Legett
Legoe, John 99
    Joshua 99
Leigh, Drury 107
Leight, John S. 42
Leimpoon, William 4
Lemay, Richard 105
Lemmond, George 38
    William L. 48
Lemon, Archibald 22
    James 40,55,131
Lemons see Lemon
Lenhart, Joseph 131
Lenmon, William 40
Lenoir, Thomas 139
    Walter R. 51
Lenton see Linton
Lenville see Linville
Leod, William 67
Leonard, Isaac 39
    James 5,39
    John 25
    Linus 65
    Obediah 39
    Philip 123
    Robert 100
Leopard, John 101
Lepford, William 22
Lesbury, James 69
Lester, John 74
    Nathan 111
Lettimore, William 130
Levan, John 55
Levant, Benedict 131
Levity, Lewis 68,56
Levy, Jacob 17
Lewin, Sterling 132
Lewing, Andrew, Jr. 125
    John 125
Lewis, Briant 8
    Bussee 105
    Christopher 53
    Daniel 128
    David 12
    George 84
    Gideon 67,118
    Griffin 81
    Guilford 81
    Hardy 101
    Henry 69
    Isaac 118
    James 11,118
    James, Jr. 63,105
    John 4,25,33,66,106
    Joseph 45
    Lewis 18
    Martin 30
    Nathaniel 84
    Price William 83
    Robert 105
    Samuel 105

Simon 26
Thomas 36
Thomas H. 98
Ully 13
Uriah 82
Wiben 13
William 16,29,41,66,
    67,92
Zacha 41
Lickman, Henry 131
    Henry, Jr. 131
    Martin 131
Lienter, George 36
Liggett, Martin 32
Light, John 49
Lile, Thomas 36
Liles, Edward 78
    Harris 101
    John 93
    Martin D. 64
Lillard, Morgan 41
Lillington, John A. 9
Lilly, William 123
Limbory, James 109
Lincard, Jonathan 136
Linch see Lynch
Lincheum, Thomas 39
Lindley, Jonathan 109
Lindsay, James 32,54,106
    Johnston 51
    Reuben 40,113
Lindsey, Asberry 80
    George 136
    James 32,54,106
Linebarge, David 52
Linebarger, John 53
Lingle, Jacob 43
    John 43
Lingle see also Tingle
Lingo, William 32
Lingold, Elijah 38
Linguish, George 85
Link, Robert 69
Linker, David 128
    George 49
Linn, Kisman 120
Linn see also Lynn
Linsey, James 106
Linton, Augustus 3
    Burage 83
    Luke 83
Linvill, David 42
Linville, George 114
    Moses 114
Lipe, John 51
Lippart, Henry 43
    John 128
Lippert, John 120
    William 128
Lipps, Jacob 117
Lipscomb, Henry 106
    James 79
    Thomas 60
Lirk, Robert 56
Lisk, Micajah 135
Lissum, David 133
Litchworth, Frederick 10
Litten, John 135
Little, Archibald 109
    Bryant 88
    Enock 100
    Erandal 87
    George 124
    Henry 123
    Isaac 29
    Jacob 96
    Jesse 99
    John 53,67

Joseph 56
Matthias 136
Robert 78
Sherod 53
Whitmel 109
William 94,129
Littleton, Benjamin 91
    Edmund 91
Litz, John 129
Livenger, Peter 44
Liverman, Daniel 7
    Isaac 9,82
    Willis 82
Liversage, Thomas 77
Living, Barnard 44
Livingston, Martin 117
    Pater 117
Lloyd, David 112
    James 83,91
    John 36
    Johnston 102
    Joseph 89
    Myerdoh 49
    Thomas 22
    William 66,104
Loafmand, Benjamin 38
Loar, James 112
Lochlan, William 119
Lock, Aquilla 79
    George 61
    Hezekiah 40
    Jonathan 93
    Robert 61
Locke, Francis 61
    James 121
    John 61
Lockhart, Andrew 136
    John 99
    Osborn 63
    Owen 87
Lockinbill, John 123
Locklear, Hugh 30
    Samuel 19
    Solomon 19
    Thomas 30
Locklier see Locklear
Lockrage, Samuel 134
Lofter, Bird 105
Loftin, Cornelius, Jr.
    121
    John 69
    William J. 11
Logan, George 56
    John 51,134
    Julias 55
Lolly, Jesse 21
Long, Adam 33
    Alexander 129
    Anthony 130
    David 69
    George 127
    Hardy 131
    Henry 45
    Ice 123
    Jacob 93
    John 33,48,68,127
    Jonathan J. 92
    Joshua 81
    Levi 64
    Nickolas 110
    Robert 64
    Thomas 53
    William 98,121
Longbottom, Joseph 52
Longmere, Robert 37
Longmire, William, Jr.
    105
Lonona, John B. 43

Looper, William 46
Loops, Moulden 89
Loot, Stephen 109
Lopp, Jacob 123
Lorance, Pater 131
Lord, John 138
    Nicholas 22
Lorrick, George P. 12
Losset, John A. 19
Louis, Archibald 85
    Thomas 85
Love, Charles 19
    Christopher 125
    Daniel 27
    David 116
    Dell'd 58
    Harrison 14
    James 20,127,138
    John 58,110
    Joseph 47,74
    Robert, Jr. 58
Loveing see Loving
Lovelace, Asa 56
    Thomas 46
Loveland, William 10
Lovelepe, Edmond 117
Lovell, Edward 51
    Jacob 40
    Joseph 51
Lovelus, Thomas 46
Lovet, Benjamin 96
    Herod 86
Lovick, James 12
Lovill see Lovell
Loving, Briant 99
    Landerford 99
    Reuben 92
    William 14
Lovit see Lovet
Lovrick, George P. 12
Low, Exum 19
    George 75
    John 5
    Nixon 5
Lowden, Joel 112
Lowe, James 44,119
    Thomas 79
    William 53
Lowry, Benjamin 5
    George 45
    Jethro 60
    John 5,57,74
Lowther, John 133
Loy, Henry 32
Loyd see Lloyd
Luallen, John 102
Lucanbill, Christian 44
Lucans, Wilkins 39
Lucas, Allen 47
Luced, Israel 98
    John 100
Luckey, Henry 45
    Richard 45
    Robert 130
Luguire, Joseph 132
Luken, Jacob 124
Lumpkin, George 105
Lunding, William 7
Lunsford, Peyton 99
Luter, Thomas 107
Luther, Daniel 49
    Joseph 119
    Solomon 33
Lyerly, William 124
Lymons, Asa 6
Lynch, Daniel 45
    Edmond 107
    Elkanah 105

    John 66
    Nicholas 14
Lynn, John 35
    Thomas 32
    William 32
Lynn see also Linn
Lyon, James G. 114
    Peter 114
    Robert 51
    William V. 118
    Zachariah 104
Lyons, Elijah 75
Lysle, Joseph 104
Lytiker, Phillip 43

- Mc -

McAdams, Andrew 47
    Archibald, Jr. 99
    Isaac 33
McAlister, Alexander 17
McAlpin, Angus 97
    Daniel 97
    Malcom 97
    Robert 97
McAlroy, Hugh 126
McAlsten, James 9
McAlston, John 29
McArthur, Neil 97
    Peter 67
McAttum, Archibald, Jr. 99
McAuley, Angus 27
    Daniel 29
McAuthur, Hector 25
McBau see Macbau
McBean, Daniel 11
McBeth, John 98
McBride, James 52
    Martin 72
    Moses 52
    Neil 29
    Richard 99
    William 11,52
McBroom, Samuel 60
McBroyer, Samuel 69
McCabler, Archibald 99
McCain, Hugh 49,112
    James 111
    John 111
McCalar, Aulas 49
McCaleb, Archibald 95
McCall, Alexander 99
    Henry 63
    James 126
    Matthew 126
McCallock, Elias 48
McCarn, Edmond 44
    William 121
McCarson, Samuel 130
McCarver, James 130
    William 130
McCastle, Neil 47
McCauley, Andrew
McCinley, John 127
    Silas 127
McClammy, Joshua 92
McClannan, Jesse 73
McClatchy, Hamilton 128
McClenon, Kenneth 124
McClerland, Isaac 127
McClosky, Francis 69
McClure, Andrew 138
    Ezekiel 130
    James 130
    John 57,130
    William 138

McClusky, Thomas 107
McCocklin, Duncan C. 115
McColl, Gilbert 25
McCollum, Isaac 119
McCombs, James 125
McConnell, John 46
McConnihery, John 120
McCorcle, Alexander 62
McCorkle, Aley 69
    John 48
McCormick, Peter 30
McCorquadale, Malcom 96
McCoy, Alexander 46
    Joseph 4
    Joshua 6
    Neil 46
    Sarrel 6
    William 126
McCracken, Elisha 125
McCrain, Archibald 24
McCraw, Byard 55,132
    James 117
    Samuel 50
    Seward 50
    William 50
    William B. 116
McCrery, David 47
McCrommon, Malcom 98
McCuiston, James 112
    William 111
McCullard, Angus, Sr. 31
McCullen, Amer 13
McCuller, William 35
McCulley, Andrew 108
    George 108
McCullin, Amer 13
    Council 25
    James 90
    Pitkin 25
McCulloch, Hunter 107
McCullock, Alexander 13,
    130
    James 17
    John 61,126
    Jos. 106
    Robert 53
    Thomas 61
McCullok, James 17
McCullough, Hugh 83
McCullum, Angus 31
    Malcom 124
McCurdy, Samuel 69
    William 92
McCurry, Cazor 56
    Jacob 56,68
    William 54
McCurston, Jesser 111
    John 111
McDade, Edward 107
    John 128
McDaid, William 32
McDaniel, Alex 108
    Alfred 86,106
    Daniel 118
    David 13
    George 34
    Hugh 27
    James 16,25
    John 86,108
    Marshall 117
    Patrick 18
    Zachariah 133
McDate, John 128
McDill, Isaac 112
McDonald, Alexander 30,
    67
    Archibald 30
    Bartlett 78

Donald 30
Duncan 71
Eli 99
James 30,116
John 27,30,51,56,69,
  93,96,98,99
Jonathan 124
Joshua 17
William 100
McDonnell, Ignatius 122
McDougal, John 25
McDowell, Athan 57
Benjamin 57
Charles 63
Freeman 11
Hugh 125
James 134
John 57
Michat 62
Nathan A. 72
McDuffee, Duncan 98
McDuffie, Dugald 99
McDuffy, Dougle 49
Dugald 67
John 67
Malcolm 27
McEachern, Duncan 96
Lauchlin 96
Malcolm 96
McEacheron, Peter 93
McEachin, Gilbert 30
McEathan, Daniel 67
McEntire, James 133
William 133
McEntosh, George 54
McEustin, Robt. 111
McEwen, Daniel 93
John 30
William 93
McFalls, Daniel 57
James 134
McFalten, John 24
McFarland, James 67,138
John 17,56
Malcolm 98
Robert 128
Samuel 128
Thornton 32,107
William 105
McFarlin, Thornton 32,107
McFerson, Stephen 115
McGee, Blewford 62
Isham 101
Jesse 107
John 119
Tobias 96
McGee see Macgee
McGehee, Giliam 105
William 126
McGilvery, Malcolm 27
McGimpsey, John 139
McGinnis, James 53
McGlanklin, David 104
McGlaughlin, John 7
McGlaughlin see Maglauch-
  lin
McGlaulum, Luke 8
McGlawhorn, Turner 65
McGraw see McCraw
McGregor, Archibald 97
Duncan 67
McGridor, Alexander 20
McGruder, William 67
McGuffee, Abraham 136
Hardy 101
McGuin, Edward 133
McGuire, Hugh 25
John 6,117

Robert 128
Samuel 44
McHarney, James 74
McHenry, Enos 58
John 58
McIlie, Thomas 48
McIlwines, Reyney 26
McInnis, John 99
Kenneth 30
McInnish, Duncan 98
McIntire, James 133
Samuel 132
William 133
McIntyre, Archibald 96
Dugald 26
McInvail, Turner 63
McIver, Alexander 24
John 109
John, Jr. 98
Rober 98
McKackle, Allen 49
McKay, Alexander 31,67,
  115
Cornelius 95
Daniel 99
James 31
John 31,97
Neal, Jr. 128
Neal, Sr. 128
William 24
McKee, John 128
Robert 24
McKeithan, Gilbert 94
McKellan, Alexander 25
McKellar, John 25,30
McKellarand, Joseph 126
McKelroy, Thomas 85
McKelvia, William 125
McKennon, Angus 98
Neel 97
McKennoy, William 56
McKenny, John 16
McKenzie, Andrew 128
Hugh 97
McKey, James 41
Joel 58
Josiah 5
Thomas 75
McKimy, Andrew 135
McKinney, Benjamin 85
George 133
Jacob 133
James 82
McKinnon, Lauchlan 27
McKinnon see MacKinnon
McKinsey, Kenneth 49,57
McKinsie, Hector 49
Kenneth 30
James 24
McKinzie, Anguish 61
John 24
McKitchen, Dugald 24
McKnight, Hugh 43
James 128
Robert 125
McKoy, Elias 4
Lewis 11
Samuel 46
McLain, Charles 136
John 127
McLanchlin, Duncan
McLane, Alexander 98
John 98
McLastro, Younger 60
McLaughlin, Douglas 25
Duncan 98
James 45
James, Sr. 121

John 126
Samuel 121
McLean, Donald 27
Duncan 23,28,29
Hugh 97
McLelland, James 24
John 25
McLemore, Sugar 104
McLendon, Jesse 99
McLennan, Lochlin 30
McLeod, Alexander 29
Allen 98
Archibald 30
Daniel 97,98
John 27,30
Murdoch 25,97
McLeon, Hector 31
Neil 28
McLeran, Daniel 29
Neil 29
McLewinnen, John 95
McLiven, Braxton 62
McLon, Andrew 138
McLoud, Angus 30
Malcolm 97
McLoyd, Daniel 48
McLure, John 47
McMahan, James 127,137
McMahew, James 127
McMaster, Aaron 109
James 33
Rufus 109
McMasters, Rufus 110
McMath, James, Jr. 34
McMillan, Anguish 24
Archibald 67
Duncan 31,67
Ever 93
James 52,97
John 30,97
Neil 24,96,98
Randolph 93
Samuel 47
William 100
McMillion, William 60
McMin, Samuel 62
McMooney, Thomas 3
McMullin, Benjamin 59,138
Thomas 25
McMurray, Thomas 25
McNabb, Alex 67
McNair, Daniel 30
McNealey, Timothy 121
McNeel, Archibald 97
McNeill, Alex 97
Angus 97
Archibald 67,71
Daniel 97
Hector 25
John 30,96
Malcolm 27
Neil 24,25,67,97
Norman 25
William 97
McNer see Macner
McOnnel, William 68
McPhallair, Daniel 31
McPhattair, John 96
McPhaul, John 96
McPherson, Alexander 30
Hugh 97
James 109
Stephen 115
McQuain, John 99
McQueen, Angus 31
Hugh 96
McQuillan, Thomas 85
McRae, Alexander 30

Christopher 29
Daniel 31,99
Duncan 99
John 30,49
Jurguhard 29
Murdoc 25
Phillip 25
Thomas 47
McRaine, Malcom 97
McRannolds, Hugh 133
McRary see Macrary
McRee, David 127,128
James 96,128
McReel, Mashart 10
McReely, Thomas 56,69
McReley, Roderick 48
McRoy, Angus 128
McSween, Donald 30
Fenly 29
John 30
McTuller, Leven 77

- M -

Mabane, Gray 76
William 107
MacBeth, John 98
Macbau, Jason 13
MacDonald, John 98
MacFarland, Malcolm 98
Macgee, Archibald 98
MacKinnon, John 98
Mackney, Thomas 8
Mackoy, Samuel 46
MacMasters, Rufus 110
Macner, William 94
Macon, Gideon H. 104
William 119
Maconer, William 94
Macrary, John 120
Madaris, David 112
Madden, William 122
Maddux, Jesse 74
Mades, James 85
Madison, Payton 36,37
Madre, John 75
Madrew, Richard 74
Thomas, Jr. 74
Maga, Henry 38
Thomas 40
Mage, Calvin 13
Maglauchlin, John 126
Magleham, Arthur 87
Mahaley, Garret 51
Mahew, John 129
Mahoon, Henry 111
Mahow, James M. 10
Maiden, John 129
Mainard, George 15
Makins, Stephen 14
Malfraas, James 92
Mallard, Daniel 85
Elijah 15
George 94
Jacob 95
Shadrick 85
Mallery, William 60
Mallock, Samuel 30
Malone, Carter 37
John 33
Robert 111
Malpaas, William 92
Mammon, Solah 83
Man, Edward 81
Joseph 9
Manchy, Moses 15

Maner, Stephen 26
William 94
Manes, Richard 28
Mangham, William 114
Mangrum, Samuel 106
Mangum, Pleasant 36
Manly, Arthur 19
Frinifield 13
Mann, Claibourn 81
Clalon 22
Edward 81
German 81
Harmon 64
James 37
John 19,37,109,138
Joseph 9
Robert 37
William 104,106
Mannels, Jacob 26
Manner, Isaac 26
Manning, James 80
John 8,22
Joseph 72
Joshua 79
Marcum 38
Willoughby 22
Mannor, Jesse 26
Manor, John 16,27
Mansfield, Dachim 6
John 111
Manuel, Edmund 26
Jesse 96
Manus, Daniel 124
Mape, Daniel 124
Maples, Burwell 98
James 28
John 28
Nathan 28
Thomas 28
William 34
March, Abraham 122
Jacob 122
William 76
Marcomb, Nathan 32
Willie 107
Willis 107
Marden, Younge 131
Madre, Michael 121
Margan, Isaac 121
Mariner, Henry 81
Hezekiah 9
Lewis 16
Marit, Thomas 106
Markell, Peter 7
Marklan, David 45
Markland, John 123
Marknm, Thomas 74
Markum, John F. 5
Marlan, Robert 55
Marlin, Aaron 95
Elijah 120
Jos. 120
Marlow, Mark 129
William 129
Marquis, Ellis 57
Marmon, David 129
Thomas 129
Marriner, Benjamin 85
Marriott, Benjamin 101
Mars, Joshua S. 95
Levi S. 95
Marsh, Barnard 7
Grovesnor 38
Marshall, Eli 79
Hawkins 91
Henry 46
Humphrey 17
James 17,42

John 91
Martin W. 115
Matthew 115
Thomas 115
William 132
Martial, John 85
Thomas 85
Martin, Alexander 99
Benjamin 15
Burwell 89
Dempsey 83
Edward 49
George 50,108
Isaac 52
Jacob 136
James 29,46,52,54,61,
116
Jeremiah 56
John 27,28,51,52,56,
93,99,134
Joseph 114
Lewis 33
Richard 83
Robert 51
Samuel 42,65,114
Thomas 114
Valentine 132
William 38,46,48,105,
106
Zenas 38
Martinn, George 108
Masburn, James 16
Mash, John 116
William 116
Mashborn, Daniel 91
James 116
Mask, James 30
James G. 124
Pleason M. 98
Mason, Bennet 80
David 85
Isaac 30
James 19,36
John W. 110
Joseph 9
Lawrence 92
Peter 58
Phillip 6
Richard 47
Thomas 82
Wiley 111
William 16,129
William W. 100
Massengill, Reddick 81
Massey, Drury 25
Edward 40
Isaac 101
Jeptha 63
John B. 59
Nicholas 138
Reddick 109
Thomas H. 24
Master, John 53
Masters, David 68
George 46
James 84
William 51
Mastin, William B. 70
Maston, Matthias 115
Mathews see Matthews
Mathias, Jesse 76
Mathis, Aaron 101
Allen 133
Daniel 101
Thomas 60
Matison, Christopher 9
Matthews, Asa 97
Christopher 110

Dougald 27
Duncan 67
Ezekiel 120
Henry 15
Hugh 97
Isham 19
James 15,52
Jason 89
John 18,126,127
John J. 39
Jos. 108
Michael 94
Richard 94
Thomas 120
William 7,34
Willie 79
Matthias, Elisha 7
Matthis see Mathis
Mattocks, John 11
Maudlin, Benjamin 6
  Samuel 6
Maughon, John 78
Maulholland, James 128
Mauney, Isaac 130
  Peter 130
Mavey, Samuel J. 137
Maxfield, David 52
Maxlen, Clare 44
Maxwell, James 136
  John 129
May, Daniel 99
  Frederic 117
  Handy 29
  Jepthah 10
  Jos 10
  Lewis 39
  Powhattan 113
  Reuben 34,109
Maye, Joseph 40
Mayfield, Valentine 36
Maygeehee, William 126
Mayhew, William 128
Mayo, Allen 88
  Alvin 88
  Drury 89
  James 89
  John 3
  Lawrence 20
  Rowland 10
Mays, Levi 120
  William 48
Mayson, James 36
Mayton, John 114
Maze, Richard 62
Mazey, Ezekiel 34
Meador, Joel 100
  Levi 100
Meadors, Elias 66
Meadows, Daniel 106
  Elias 66
  James 36,37
  Joel 10
  Levi 100
  Riley 105
  Samuel 129
  Thomas 85
Means, James 125
Mears, Joel 86
  John 129
  William 38
Measles, William 13
Meazel, Aaron 21
  Jesse 21
  Seth 21
Mebane, Alexander 60
  Allan 107
  George 30,107
  John 60

William 32,107
Mecome, Elen 22
Mecory, Cornelius 4
Medcalf, Absalom 137
  David 100
Medders, James
Meddows, James 37
Medford, Daniel 22
  Ith 88
Medlin, Alexander 27
  James 104
  John 27
  Kinchen 63
Medlock, Charles 57
Medor, Levi 100
Meed, William 39
Meek, James 125
Meekins, William 82
Meeks, Simpson 88
Meggs, John 100
Meginess, John 129
  William 129
Meguire, John 6
Mekins, Nathaniel 49
Melone, Abraham 135
Meloney, Kenon 86
Melton, John 132
  Reuben 9,132
  William 132
Melvan, James 109
Melvin, Daniel 93
Menice, James 134
Menor, Fred 120
Mentith, James 125
Mercer, Cornelius 73
  Jeremiah, Jr. 72
  Miles 73
  Roding 4
  Thomas 4
  William 73
Meredith, Green 6
Merick, John 45
Merner, John 130
Merrell, Eli 57,136
  Laza 119
  Nimrod 58,136
  Samuel 11
Merrett, George 34
  John 50
Merrill see Merrell
Merrit see Merritt
Merritt, Benjamin 124
  Felix 95
  James 18,114
  John 104
  Thomas 79
  Wiley 95
Mersham, James 29
Merys, Gardner 53
Messenger, William 73
Messer, Burwell 99
  Ephraim 101
  Jeremiah 99
Messick, John 18
  Lean 18
Mestinghams, Tobias 127
Mewbern, George 72
Mhoon, John 77
Michael, David 123
Michaels, Thomas 134
Michel, John 69
Micks, Hardy 17
Middleton, George 40
  John 7,138
  Robert 112
Midgett, Sparrow 82
  Spencer 9
Migett, Richard 10

Migginson, John 30
Mikel, Jacob 118
Miles, Augustus 125
  James 108
  Jonathan 109
Milican, Lemuel 56
Milken, Christopher 127
Millar, Anthy N. 114
  Frederick 115
  Godfrey 115
  Harman 115
  Henry 116,118
  John 118
  Joseph 83
  Joshua 85
  Richard 92
Millard, Bennet 95
Miller, Abraham 118
  Charles 6,77
  Frederick 41,65
  Fulty 67
  George 68,121,127
  Henry 41,49,86
  Isaac 33
  Isaiah 67
  Jacob 45,54
  Jacob, Sr. 42
  James 29,86
  James B. 12
  John 54,119,123
  John, Jr. 95
  Jonathan 120
  Josiah 65
  Lewis 77
  Mertin 43
  Nathaniel 72
  Reuben 76
  Silas 11
  Solomon 43
  Thomas 48
  Tobias 128
  William 12,21,27
  William K. 77
Milliken, Samuel 119
Millington, T,omas 108
Mills, Britain 101
  Edward 61
  Ezekiel 33
  Fred, Jr. 11
  Frederick 11,91
  James 91,124
  John 119,120,124
  Naisby 87
  William 84,87
Milson, Edmund 91
  John 117
Milsaps, John 69
  Joseph 129,137
  William 46
Miltoe, Samuel 55
Milton, Henry 91
  Jeptha 50
  Jesse 54
  John 67
  Joseph 124
  Sterling 19
  William 55,98
Mims, Joseph 110
Mink, William 118
Minnis, Allen 59
  James 108
Minor, John 65
  Lazarus 36
Minshew, John 113
Minster, John 120
Minter, Abner 109
Minton, Jason 77
  Jesse 62

Valentine 79
Mints, Elisha 8
Mires, Conrad 122
  Ezekiel 129
  Henry 123
  Thomas 72
Mirow, Zedekiah 83
Miskingham, David 128
  Matthias 128
Mitch, Rheuben 90
Mitchell, Archibald 105
  Benjamin 16
  Cader 65
  Cullen 19
  Daniel 17,39
  David 111
  Edmond 37
  George 13
  Gilliam 106
  James G. 35
  Jesse 72
  John 4,17,37,90,127
  Joshua 85
  King 77
  Lemuel 23,80
  Reuben 101
  Robert 12
  Samuel 46,60
  Silas 64
  Thomas 3
  Watson 110
  William 16,91,129
  Zachariah 37
Mizells, George 77
  James 77
  Timothy 77
  Lawrence 77
Mnnden, William 74
Mobley, Lurrel 96
Mobly, William, Jr. 41
Mock, Peter 122
  Philip 123
Mode, Samuel 133
Moffet, Aaron 119
  Henry 120
  Jonathan 119
Molenby, Lelin 41
Molesby, John 41
Molton, James 130
Monet, Peter 61
Monford, James, Jr. 86
  James, Sr. 86
Mongar, Wilson 78
Mongus, William J. 41
Monroe, Colin 93
  Hugh 99
Monser, John 131
Montague, John 36
  Young 105
Monteath, Thomas 57
Montford, William 19
Montgomery, Abraham 111
  George 39
  John 111
  John C. 8
  Robert 76,126
  Samuel 39
Montgory, William 138
Moody, Alexander 41
  Benjamin 46
  John 46
  Thomas 134
  Thomas L. 39
Moon, John 77,89
  Joseph 46
Mooney, Arthur 94
  Christy 55
  Elias 82

William 93,94
Moor, William 49
Moorcy, John 109
Moore, Aaron 54,131
  Abijah 34
  Alexander 34,47,53,
    56
  Alfred 19,54,75,108,
    133
  Allen 76,87
  Anthony 104
  Archibald 55
  Augustin 87
  Barrwill 64
  Benjamin 25,92
  David 47,126
  Ebenezer 121
  Edward 27,63,111
  Eleon G. 50
  George 53,88,92,107
  Gideon 67
  Gregor 79
  Henry 88,95
  Icabod 87
  Jacob 87
  James 47,64,104,132
  Jesse 19
  John 25,29,37,39,92,
    98,127,132,135
  John, Jr. 19
  Jordan 16
  Josephus 88
  Lain 36
  Levi 47
  Lewis 25
  Mark 63,132
  Matthew 114
  Maurice 71
  May 64
  Moses 18,64,89
  Needham 25
  Radner 86
  Robinson 129
  Samuel 87
  Samuel, Jr. 17
  Tavner 137
  Thomas 32,57,64,82,
    108
  Walker 86
  William 17,19,32,49,
    86,119
  Williamson 111
Mooring, William 11
Mooss, Daniel 127
Morce, Isaac 100
Morefield, William 118
Morel, John 99
Moreland, Francis 51,117
  William M. 10
Morgain, Benjamin 7
Morgan, Andrew 84
  Benjamin 7,42
  Daniel 38
  Elias 112
  Ezekiel 129
  George 121
  Hardy 49,72
  Henry 22
  Hugh 75
  Isaac 121
  James 27,117,118,121
  Jesse 78,132
  John 91
  Joseph 50
  Joshua 51,78
  Keder 74
  Laban 26
  Nathan 120

Newit 20
Robert 113
Seth 77
Thomas 77
Valentine 40
William 21,49,51,100,
  117
Willis 75
Winkfield 105
Moring, Henry 86
Morisett, Phillip 4
  Tully 4
Morris, Benjamin 28
  David 21
  Eaton 79
  Elias 50
  Harvey 84
  Henry 7,36,79,132
  Isaac 32
  Jessy 89
  John 16,98
  Joshua 83
  Lawrence 116
  Leonard 37
  Nathan 21
  Solomon 48
  Thomas 10,83,89,105
  Thomas, Jr. 50
  William 74
Morrison, Andrew 45,46,47
  Angus 27
  Archibald 30
  Benjamin 25
  Daniel 53
  Everett 81
  Henry 128
  Isaac, Jr. 125
  James 20,126
  John 47,49,97,99,126
  Malcolm 40,99
  Neil 27,126
  Robert C. 49
  Thomas 47
  William 128
Morriss, Everett 81
  James 20
Morrow, Daniel 136
  John 61
  Joseph 58
Morse, Charles 9
  Isaac 100
  John 73
Morten, James 128
Morton, Joseph 85
  Stephen 49
  William 49,85
Mosely, Joshua 12
  William 12
Mosely see also Mosley
Moser, Frederick 108
  Henry 48
  Tobias 60
Moses, Peter 41
Mosley, Joshua 86
  William 86
Moss, James 44
  John 6,122
  Thomas 100
  Tully 6
  William 124
Mossman, Frederick 124
Mosteller, George 54
Mostinger, Daniel 123
Motholand, John 22
Mott, Benjamin 92
  Richbell 45
Motton, John 13
Mount, John, Jr. 41

Motthias, Jr. 41
  Pleasant 41
Mowrey, Peter 68
Moxley, Samuel 113
Moye, Franklin 87
  John 87
Mulder, George 29
  William 29
Mulford, John 93
Mulholland, David 47
Mulhollen, Henry 107
Mull, Peter 134
Mullen, John 127
  Nathaniel 79
Mullens, Jonathan 132
Muller, Oram 63
Mullin, William 12
Mullinax, Isaac 131
Mullins, John 23
  Thomas 34
Mullis, Francis 28
Mumford, Joseph 92
  Thomas 122
  William 11
Muncas, Elijah 50
  Joseph 50
Munden, Benjamin 6
  Elijah 5
  James 74
  William 5,74
Munholland, John 80
Munhollen, Hugh 30
  John 30
Munro, Neel 25
  Peter 25
Munroe, Daniel 99
  Peter 96
Munteeth, William 48
Murcheson, Angus 99
  William 28
Murder, Samuel 79
Murdock, David 11
  John 46
Murdough, John 77
Murdy, William 68
Murett, Joshua 16
Murphray, Martin 22
Murphree, William 104
Murphrey, Parker 59
Murphy, Alexander 71
  Cornelius 18
  Daniel 99,120
  Duncan 96
  James 23
  John 54,113
  Joseph 134
  Patrick 24
  William 117
Murrah, John 86
Murray, Andrew 108
  Bethuel 9
  Joseph 33
  Nathan 94
  Robert 12
  Walter 107
  William 137,138
Murrell, Isaac 129
  John 91
  Kinchen 19
Murrey, William H. 137
Murry, Coleman 59
  Jabes 133
  James H. 104
  Samuel J. 58
  Thomas 137
  William 58,110
Muse, Joshua 9
  Lewis 37

Richard 5
  Sampson 27
  Thomas 98
  William 85
Musgrove, John 13
Musick, Austin 133
  George 134
Muskram, Arthur 113
Musslewhite, Jesse 30
  Reuben 96
Myatt, Acril 101
Mydgett, Benjamin 81
  John 9
  Lewis 81
Myers, George 44,45
  Jacob 123
  John 115
  John, Sr. 44
  Michel 44
  Thomas 6
Myers see also Mires
Myre, Daniel 122
  Michael 122
  Philip 122
Myres, Arhus 100
Myrick, Azel 34
  Cornelius 34
  James 34
  James C. 67
  John 27
  Moses 98
  Owen F. 22,80

- N -

Nail, Alexander 62
Nailing, William 104
Nailor, Abram 26
  Jacob 123
Nance, Agrippy 36,104
  James, Jr. 63
  William 129
  William, Jr. 129
  Wyatt 100
Nancy, Nicholas 56,68
Nancy, James 132
Napper, Hugh 117
Nar, Edward 8
Nardike, Jonathan 53
Naresworthy, William 78
Narris, Samuel 102
Nash, George 100
  Josiah 5
  Stephen 29
  Wilson 72
  Wilson W. 5
Nawl, John 103
NayBo, Alex 108
NayUts, Alex 108
Neagle, John 53
Neal, Cudburth 23,80
  John 114
  Thomas 101
Neale, Abner 11
  Reuben 103
  Samuel 114
  Thomas 8
Neathery, Samuel 117
Needham, James 75
  Lot 74
  Samuel 74
Neel, Clayton 134
  Jacob 115
Neele, Andrew 47
  George 114
  James 47

Robert 114
Neeley, Samuel 125
Neil, Andrew 128
  Samuel 42
Neill, William 57
Nellsmall, Reddick 23
Nellum, David 37
Nelms, James 23,104
  John 103
  William 37,110
  Willis 35
Nelson, Abisha 85
  Abram 46
  Alexander 17
  Benjamin B. 111
  Caleb 87
  Charles 11
  Elijah 42,114
  Frost 122
  Jacob 114
  James 40
  Jesse 110
  John 138
  Jordan 87
  Naboth 87
  Samuel 60
  Thomas 33,85
  William 34,42,112
Nelums, William 37
Nesbet, Ross 61
Nesbitt, Alexander 62
Never, Eli 81
Nevill, Elijah 79
Nevin, Daniel 34
New, Gilbert 92
  John 93
  William 18
Newburb, George 72
Newby, Exum 6,16
  Mexum 75
Newcomb, Thomas 68
Neweam, Richard 132
Newel, Francis 69
Newell, Eli 69
  Hardy 60
  Jesse 60
  Thomas 60
Newit, William 49
Newman, Benjamin 131
  Thomas 23,80
  William 133
  Willis 60
Newsman, Thomas 80
Newsom, Benjamin 30
  Cordel 20
  Elijah 14
  Jacob 13
  John 20
  Joseph 13
  Riggan 30
  Samuel 117
  Seamore 20
  Willis 86
Newsum, Randolph 19
Newton, Aaron 116
  Hardy 17
  Henry 32
  Jacob 45
  James 56,69
  William 133
Niblick, Wilson 121
Nichilson, Abel 52
  Daniel 30
  Ephraim 52
  Nathan 6
  Thomas 19
  William 5
Nicholas, Neal 65

Samuel 91
Nichols, Alsey 63
　Amos 62
　David 5
　Eli 28
　Isaac 28
　Jeremiah 41
　John 32
　Joseph 56,67
　Kinchen 18
　Moses 12
　Wilie 63
　William 87
Nicholson, Guilford 19
　James 3,127
　John 24
　Samuel 73
　Wallis 18
Nickolas, Amos 107
　George 107
Nickolls, William 72
Nickols, Elisha 94
　Jeremiah 92
　Robert 92
　William S. 92
Nickolson, James 136
　John 98,112
　Nathaniel 103
　Peter 96
Nicolson, Jos. 119
Night, Elijah 42
　William 38
Nighton, James 111
　John 38
　Turner 38
Nillens, Curtis 95
Nilman, Wekins 55
Nipper, William 38
Nisler, David 127
Nixon, Delight 6
　James 92
　Richard 71
　William 92
Nixon see Noxon
Nobles, Eli 94
Noblet, John 34
Noles, David 16
None, John 48
Nooten, Aaron 116
Norbet, Henry 55
Norman, Aquilla 81
　Daniel 118
　Eliakim 8
　George 118
　Henry 82
　Isaac 116
　James 114
　John 54
　Thomas 20
　William 120
　William S. 125
Normand, Isham 38
　Westley 38
Norris, James 25
　John 111,117
　Niel 35,63
　Peyton 102
　Samuel 102
Norriss, James 94
　William 87
North, Danut 40
Northam, Eli 30
　James 3
Northcutt, James 79
Northern, Elijah 44
　Frederick 73
　James 73
　Walter 44

Northington, Allen 25
　Jesse 25
Norton, Berry 30
Norvil, James 89
Norwood, Burwell 78
　John 36,60,110
　Samuel 78
Norworthy, John 19
　Thomas 20
Nowell, John 21
Nowells, Luke 89
Noxon, Martin 72
Nuby, Exum 16
Nunby, Reuben 44
Nunly, Reuben 44
Nunn, Ilie 35
Nunnery, William 25
Nunon, Edward 41
Nusman, John 127
Nuthercut, William, Jr.
　　94
Nutt, Cader 35
　Elkhannon 63
　Robert 63

- O -

Oakley, McFarland 106
　Mark 107
　William 36
Oaks, Barnard 57
　John 45,57
　Lemuel 112
Oats, Jesse 67
　John 97,130
　Robert 53
O'Briant, Elizah 106
O'Brien, John 60
O'Bryan, Lewis 86
Ochiltree, Murdoch 97
O'Connor, Dennis 20
O'Daniel, Green 108
Odium, Theophilus 85
Oens, John 115
Ogborn, Nicholas 39
Oglesby, Archibald 134
　Thomas 68
　William 68,134
O'Kelly, Zenas 100
Oldham, Ephraim 110
Olery, Robert 25
Olington, James W. 41
Olive, James 35
　John 35,138
Oliver, Alexander 99
　Andrew 7
　Everet 78
　Francis 105
　Frederick 80
　George 53
　James 86
　John 132
　Josiah 106
　Lewis 17,91
　Thomas 51,110
　William 22,28,32,42,
　　53,80
Oman, James 91
O'Neal, Asa 82
　Frederick 15
　Henry M. 134
　John 31,95
　Micajah 103
　Michael 4
　Spencer 73
　Stephen 103

O'Neale, Levi 10
O'Neil, William 29
O'Neill, John F. 134
Onions, William 19,79
Orchillred, Murdock 25
Orion, John 27
Orman, Adam 48
　Jacob 98
　Samuel 48
Orme, William 91
Orneal, Michael 4
Orr, Luton 92
　Nathan 62
　Robert 136
Orsburn, Robert A. 125
Orton, James 45
Osborn, Jeremiah 136
Osbourn, Thomas 51
Osburn, Christopher 127
　John 39
　Joseph 15
　Robert A. 125
Osby, Meady 93
Ostien, Caleb 94
Otary, Starling 26
Outland, Thomas 90
Outlaw, David 65
　Jesse 15
　John 7
　Levi 65
　Noah 77
　Ralph 77
Overcast, Jacob 127
Overman, Reuben 6
　Samuel 5
Overstreet, James 18
　Moses 18
Overton, Elisha 76
　Jacob 76
　John 86
　John C. 113
Owen, Abraham 121
　Elijah 111
　Ezekial 121
　James 27,44
　Martin 122
　Thomas 122
Owenby, Arthur 56,58
　William 134
Owenly, John 55
Owens, Aaron 118
　Alfred 44
　Dempsey 88
　Ezekiel 95
　James 10,45,73
　John 56,115
　Joseph 98
　Joshua 58
　Levi 107
　Moses 111
　Raleigh 56
　Reuben 108
　Stephen 82
　Thomas 95,122
　William 56,104
Owensby, John 133
　Sims 133
Owerly, Arthur 68
Owmson, John Royals 96
Owrey, Michael 49
Oxendine, Charles 30

- P -

Pack, Austin 135
Padge, Silas 113

Padgett, Nehemiah 132
Page, Absolam 87
    Amos 111
    Bellentine 21
    Benjamin 119
    Burwell 88
    Joseph, Jr. 89
    Lawrence 89
    Owen 96
    Samuel 113
    William 27
Paget(t), Abraham 132
    David 92
    Lemuel 57
Paim, John 120
Pain, Benjamin 45
    John 120,123
    Joseph 6
    Solomon 37
    Thomas 119
    William 45
Paine, David 82
    Micajah 57
    Mitchel 9
    Robert 60
    Thomas 25
Painter, Leonard 55
    Wyatt 106
Paisley, Hezekiah 117
Palin, Thomas 74
Pall, Colin 49
Palmer, George 125
    John 58,137
Paquanet, Jacob 85
    John 85
Parham, Mathew 124
    Mitchel 135
    Thomas 64
Parish, Absolam 104
    Alexander 72
    Andrew M. 125
    Edward 9
    Frederic 80
    Hillsman 102
    James 107
    Joel 31,104
    John 50,113
    Jones 72
    Joseph 99
    Jyre 35
    Nicholas 47
    Noel 39
    Reuben 36,40
    Tyrel 64
    William G. 115
Park, James 45
Parke, George 126
Parker, Abram 7
    Allen 26,101,110
    Daniel 95
    Darius 77
    Elisha 7
    Francis 20
    Gabriel 12
    George 105
    Hardy 97
    Harrison 32,107
    Henry 12
    Ica 97
    James 4,8,46,47,76
    Jesse 64,76
    Jethro 18
    John 12,18,21,46,89,
        92,100,110,125
    Kindred 76
    Luke 7,27
    Michael 21
    Miles 7

Mills 79
Morris 20
Moses 67
Payton R. 95
Robert 7,76
Samuel 21,76
Solomon 136
Stephen 21
Theophilus 21
Thomas 4,112
Thomas B. 18
Willis 35
Zachariah 95
Zepheniah 95
Parkes, John, Sr. 125
    William 11
Park(e)s, Allen 35
    Benjamin 56
    David 108
    Hiram 38
    James 56,68
    James M. 62
    Jepthah 38
    John 12,51,116
    Jonathan 72
    Joseph 128
    Joshua 118
    Noah, Jr. 120
    Reuben 57
    Samuel 62,125
    William 36
Parmale, Timothy 83
Parmer, John 130
    William 17,140
Parnell, John 96
Parr, James 73
    Jesse 3
    Peter 73
Parram, Littleton 54
Parris, Peter 84
Parrish, James 68
Parrot, Charles 60
    John 106
Parson, James 123
Parsons, Richard 84
    Robert 39
    Thomas 124
Partin, Benjamin 79
    John 124
Paskill, John 36
Pass, James H. 11
Passenger, Methias 127
Passmoer, Enock 118
Pate, Bryan 86
    Charles 96
    Daniel 30
    Elias 30
    John 98
    Zachariah 12,96
Patilla, Edward 80
Patrick, Isaac 84
    Selby 7
Patridge, Jesse 34
Patten see Patton
Patterson, Archibald 24,97
    Berry 117
    David 60,115
    Edward 28
    Isaac 38,111
    James 54,131
    Joel 51
    John 43,99
    John, Jr. 102
    John S. 129
    Julius 115
    Malcomb 25,26
    Mathew 58
    Nathan 103

Peter 30
Robert 59,113
Samuel 78
Thomas 32
William 33
Wilson 39
Pattin see Patton
Pattison, Archibald 24
    Malcolm 25
Patton, Alex 108
    Alexander 32
    Bennet 107
    George 63
    John 137
    John M. 58,137
    Lewis 107
    M. Houston 37
Paul(l), Benjamin 79
    Irra 83
    William 116
Paxton, Richard 76
Payner, Samuel 73
    Peace, Henry 117
    James 63
    John T. 37
Peacock, Abraham 86
    Asa 33
    Isaac 83
    Jacob 103
    Jesse 14,90
    John 14
    Noah 14,90
    Simon 90
    Wiley 90
    William 121
Peal, Jesse 22,116
Peale, John 15
    Willis 103
Pealor, Anthony 121
    Jesse 121
Peane, Hardy 101
Pearce, Arthur 103
    Asa 100
    Ason 29
    Benjamin 18,94
    Ezekiel 68
    Isaac 8
    Isham 8
    Jehu 21
    Jesse 59
    Loverd 15
    Meredith 45
    Moses 29,100
    Pleasant 60
    Thomas 119
    William 29,75,119
    William A. 91
Pearson, Asey 97
    Edward 17
    Henry 23
    Jesse A. 43,71
    Joon 117
    Jos. 108
    Preston 35
    Samuel 35
    Stephen 102
    William 86
Peartree, John 9
Peary, Bryant 40
Peaster, William 76
Peck, Ezra 17
    John 122
    Louis F. 67
Peden, Amos 15
    John 15
Peddy, John 102
Peebles, Anderson 23
    John 79

Peed, Cyrus 54
Peel, Elisha 7
  Reddick 7
Peele, Joel 78
  John 64
  Lewis 89
Peetigrew, Ebenezer 81
Pegford, Wm. 18
Pegg, Jesse 40
  Joab 40
  John 40
  Martin 40
Pegram, John 112
Pelet, Amos 88
Pelon, Asa 75
Pelt, Jonathan 87
  Simon V. 125
  William 127
Pemberton, Edward 24
  John 62
  William 62
Pender, David 89
  James 64
  John 15
  William 15
Pendleton, Henry 75
Pendry, Jonathan 51
Penix, Thomas 111
Penland, Abraham 137
  George 138
  James 57
  Robert 138
Penly, Jonathan 135
Pennington, James 95
  Joshua 118
  William 110
Penny, Francis 61
  John 89
Pennywell, William 88
Peoples, Richard 126
Peppin, Banister 104
Perdue, Daniel A. 23,80
  Isham 79
  John 112
  Philemon 22,80
  Robert 118
  Rowland 36
Perkins, Alexander 63
  Charles 73
  George 73
  James 29,114
  Job 6
  John 57
  Jonathan 11
  Levi 53
  Linkford 84
  William 3
Perkinson, Valentine 81
Permerter, James 64
Perry, Albert 23
  Barnabas 107
  Bennet 24,101
  David 93
  Francis 125
  Jacob 7
  James 34,75
  John 80,101
  John C. 23
  Kader 74
  Micajah 22
  Noah 5
  Reuben 15
  Richard 118
  Simon 88
  Solomon 103
  William 108
  William C. 24
Persithe, Simuel 37

Pertilla, Edward 23
  William 23
Peters, Redding 11
Peterson, Aron 27
  Daniel 54
  Gabriel 95
  Jacob L. 68
  James 138
  Samuel 131
Petery, Henry 127
Petman, James 89
Pettes, John D.O.K. 61
Pettiford, Lervey 37
  Moses 36
Pettigor, Abraham 6
Pettigrew, Ebenezer
Petty, John 81,102
  William 116
Pew, Nathaniel 130
  Samuel 129
Pharis, Daniel 67
  Duncan 26
Phelps, Charles 81
  Darius 82
  Even 81
  Hezekiah 81
  Killion 61
  Lovet 46
  Thomas 123
  William 104
  Willoughby 81
Phifer, Mathias 121
Philips see Phillips
Phillippic, Leonard 113
Phillips, Aswell 137
  Benjamin 108
  Bennet 117
  Charles 9
  Curtis 12
  Dixon 102
  Edmond 117
  Enock 120
  Frederick 34,109
  Henry 13,98
  Isaac 15,108,114
  Jacob 29
  James 120
  Jeremiah 9
  Jesse 78
  John 27,47,57,86,96,
    122,126
  Joseph 7
  Kinchen 7
  Michel 5
  Peter 12
  Phillip 46
  Raiford 27
  Ransom 7
  Robert 84
  Spencer 12
  William 17,101
  Zacheriah 108
Philpot, Samuel 10
Phinney, Joseph 51
Phips, Isaac 15
Pickett, Jacob 92
  Joseph 18
  Walker 107
Pickhart, Elisha 108
  Jesse 108
Pickle, Henry 12
  Richard 12
Pickler, James 122
Pickolson, Mathew 88
Pierce, James 78
  John 33,123
  Peleg 17
  Whitmel 21

Piercy, Ephriam 59
Pigett, William 85
Pigg, William 51
Pilano, Richard 20
Pilcher, James 51
  John 117
Pilear, Jacob 67
Pilkington, Anthony 54
Pilley, John 83
Pindar, James 108
  Thomas 13
Piner, Josiah 17
Pinkham, Nathaniel 85
Pinkston, Morris 43
Pinner, Arthur 66
  James 17
Pinney, Isaac 103
Pipes, Hiram 117
Pipkin(s), Bryan 90
  Joseph 13
  Need 13
  William 13
Pippin, Breedlove 23
  Ethelred 59
  Lalathel 96
Pirant, William 48
Pitell, Benjamin 117
Pitle, Isaac 41
Pitman, Brittain 21
  Dempsey 30,79
  Jacob 31
  John 16,84
  Reuben 21
Pitt, Edmond R. 35
  Isaac V. 47
Pittard, Thomas 110
Pittcord, Kelan 42
Pittman, Brittain 21
  Dempsey 30,79
  Elijah 96
  Elijah V. 85
  Jacob 31
  Jesse 96
  John 16,84
  Joseph 89
  Michael 120
  Reuben 21
  Thomas 85
Pitts, Hardy 16,91
  John 79
  Philip 134
Piver, James 85
  Samuel 85
Pleasants, Joseph 104
Pledger, George W. 78
  Joseph 82
  William 78
Plemmons, Andrew 58
  John 58
  John, Jr. 58
Plot, Elias 53
Plumber, Samuel 24
Plummer, Aaron 93
  Edward 93
  James 62
Plunk, Jacob 130
Plunkett, John 99
  Richard D. 127
Poe, Hasten 108
Poindexter, Archer 51
  Francis A. 117
  William 114
Pollard, Equilla 11
  Hansford 114
  John 114
  Willie 101
Pollock, John 95
Polson, John 76

Polyard, Joseph 12
Ponder, Joseph 137
Pool, Elijah 132
  Farniford 86
  Hardy 102
  Howard 64
  James 103
  John 61
  Joshua 75
  Moses 86
  Patrick 60
  Phillip P. 36
  Samuel 93
  Theophilus 103
  William 48
Poole, Jacob 121
Pope, Archibald 89
  Barnaby 78
  Benjamin 27
  David 132
  Hardy 31
  Henry 26
  Jacob 99
  James 123
  Jesse 13
  John 27
  Juni 95
  Lewis 27
  Nathan 20
  Reuben 14
  Robin 26
  Samuel 90
  Stephen 95
  Thomas 31
  William 27,37
Poplin, George 124
  Jesse 125
  John 50
Porch, Bridgers 102
Porter, Alexander 135
  Banister 50
  Hartwell 26
  James 27,125
  John 19,26,56
  Jos. G. 113
  Josiah 28
  Matthew 96
  Michel 26
  Peter 101
  Ridley 14
  Robert 54
  Samuel 62
  Spencer 30
  Thomas 35
  William 56,62,68
Portis, Benjamin 21
  David 47
  Joseph 21
  Samuel 21
Portlook, Thomas 5
Portor see Porter
Poteet(e), James 137
  John 134,137
  William 57
Pott, Thomas 80
Potter, John 87
  Major 81
  Stephen 116
  William 50,68
Potts, Selathiel 12
  Thomas 80,117
Pouland, John 22
Pound(s), Leroy 99
  William 66
Powell, Allen 19
  Campbell 33
  Dempsey 92,96
  Eaton 19

  Elijah 134
  Irby 79
  Isaac 16
  Jacob 16
  James 23,80
  James, Jr. 79
  Jesse 64,65
  John 41,103,108,134
  Josiah 94
  Lewis 90,134
  Oliver 108
  Oran D. 80
  Ransom 19
  Robert 75
  Stephen 9,96
  Sterling 96
  Thomas 108
  William 23,80
Powers, Edmond 79
  Frederick 12
  Gambol 108
  Hardy 82
  James 114
  John 96,97,99
  Selby 9
Poyland, John 22
  Philip 78
Poyner, James 73
  Joel 3
  Joseph 3
  Samuel 122
Prater, John 114
Prather, John 43
  Thomas 46,56
Prator, Thomas 133
Pratt, Charles 36
  Hopkins 118
  Stephen 114
Prentiss, Reuben 85
Prescott, Jesse 85
  Moses 84
  Wilboga 85
Presnal(l), Abner 57
  William 119
Presnill, Enock 135
Preston, Robert 28
Prestwood, Augustine 137
Price, Abraham 110
  Absalom 10
  Ansel 101
  Benjamin 32
  Bud 15
  George 66
  Hardy B. 88
  Irvin, Jr. 103
  Isaac 62,125
  James 18
  Joel 20
  John 52,55,69,125
  Joseph 100
  Kerce 130
  Lewis 94
  Martin 102
  Rice 102
  Saul 122
  Stephen 103
  Sterling 107
  Thomas 21,102
  Wilie 103
  William 32,62,78,107,
    121
  William W. 111
Prichard see Pritchard
Prichet see Pritchett
Prickhard see Pritchard
Priddie, Benjamin 103
Priddy, John 42
  Pillis 42

Pride, John 35
Prifly, Valentine 48
Prigen, Peter 81
Prim, Andrew 125
Prince, David 100
  John 23
Pritchard, Alexander 111
  Elias 38
  Elisha 65
  Enoch 5
  Grandey 74
  Jarrot 125
  Peleg 74
  Thomas 74
Pritchett, Hugh 88
  Jesse 116
Privet(t), Erwin 36
  Israel 63
  Jacob 129
  Milus 46
  Richard 46
  Wallis 129
Privit see Privett
Prock, John 135
Proctor, Benjamin 129
  John 32,56,68
  Joseph 106
  Richard 129
  William 5
Prolst, Michel 54
Proxter, John 32
Pruden, Jacob 65
  Lodswick 65
Puckett, Hopni 80
  Isaac 50
Pue, Amos 74
  John 74
Pugh, Archibald 32
  Augustin 65
  Edward 4
  Frederick 19
  Henry 75
  Hinton 101
  Peter 74
Puiser, Jesse 83
Pullen, John 103
  William 103
Pulley, Jedemiah 101
Pulliam, Drury 106
  Drury A. 106
  William 104
Pullin, Rica 19
Pullum, John 37
Pully, Joseph 18
Pumm, Joshua 51
Pumphrey, John 10,62
Purdon, Elijah 42
Purify, Asa 11
  Thomas 12
Purnell, William 76
Purrell, Benjamin 66
  Fountain 113
Purser, Moses 126
Purson, John 134
Purvin, Jason 59
Purvins, Antheris 48
Purvis, John 34,108
  Lewis, Jr. 89
  Moses 77
  William 31
Pyland, Elisha 76
  Shedric 76
  William 76
Pyott, William 135
Pytent, Benjamin

- Q -

Quaits, Joseph 112
Quakenbush, Peter 109
Queen, John 135
Quick, John 99
Quidley, Bartlett 4
    John 4
    Joseph 4
Quin, Enock 94
    John 88
    Lofton 66
Quinby, Frederick 17
    Henry 17
    Jonas 26,96
    Joseph 17
Quinley, John 119
    Stephen 87
    William 87
Quinn, Morris 55

- R -

Rabourn, Reason 63
Baby, Peter 131
Radett, Asa 65
Radford, Jesse 59,137
Ragans, William 32
Ragen, Charles 51
Raglin, Evan 105
Ragon, Eli 118
Raiberry, James, Jr. 76
Raimer, Masbum 76
Rainer, David 96
    James 89,96
Raines, Hervey, Sr.
    John 117
    Oliver, Jr. 117
Rainey, Allen 79
    Henry 93
    Isaac 108
    James 107
    John 37,68
    Littleton 120
    Virgil M. 38,111
Rains, John 117
Rainwater, John 67
    Mathew 30
    Vincent 99
Rainy, Lewis 37
Raiuey, Virgil M. 38
Raleigh, James 8
Rampler, Jacob 56
Ramsay, Lewis 37
Ramsey, Allen L. 8
    John 65
    Lewis 37
    Mial 109
    Robert 53
Ramson, Baldy 38
Ramsour, David 62
    Henry 62
    John 119
Ranch, James 87
Rand, John 35
    Michael 19
    William 101
Randal, Blueford 133
    Elijah 84
    Thornton 133
Randels, James 128
Randle, Frederick 50
    Noah 124
Randolph, George 38
    John 137

Joseph 79
Kedar 87
Oney 111
Paul 20
Peter 23,80
Robert 111
William 111
Raney, James 107
Rankin, Alexander 130
    Robert 92
Ransom, Baldy 38
    Edward J. 81
    Lewis 136
Ranton, William 82
Rape, Samuel 126
Raper, Henry 5
    Lewis 50
Barden, John 112
Rary, Jacob 43
Rash, Luke 118
Ratcliff, James 92
    Jesse 29
    Jonathan 116
    Nathan 116
    Samuel 29
Ratiff, Jesse 29
Ratley, Josiah 31
Ratliff, Samuel 29
Ratts, Henry 44
Raugh, Jacob 54
Rawls, Abraham 88
    Reddick 88
    William 10
Rawson, Isaac 8
Rawts, William 10
Ray, Angus 25
    Cornelius 93
    David 106,108
    James, Jr. 32
    Jesse 108
    John 25,67,108
    Joseph 137
    Lylas 58
    Parrum 39
    Peyton 39
    Robert 102
    Skipwith
    Wilson 25
Ray see also Rea, Rhea,
    and Wray
Rayner, David 21
Rea, Joseph G. 8
    Will 48
Rea see also Ray
Reace, Daniel 106
Read, Abner 59
    Alexander 46
    David 64
    George 125
Reader, Thomas 56,69
Readit, William 81
Reak, Edward 126
Reaves, Arthur 64
    Jespry 123
    John 60
    Micajah 50
    Richard 50
    Samuel 102,120
    Thomas 120
    William 101
    William W. 104
Reavis, Jespry 123
Rector, Daniel 46
    John 46,47
Reddell, John 69
Reddic(k), James 21,100
    Jethro 76
    John 72

Josiah 77
Kader 7
Lemuel 7
Obadiah 6
Robert 7
Shedrack 114
Thomas 42,114
Timothy 87
William 81,101
Reddin, Levi 124
    William 31
Reddish, James 100.
    William 101
Redford, William 48
Redman, James 59
    William 55
Redmond, Maurice 87
Redwine, Daniel 50
Reece, Daniel 50
Reed, David 125
    George 58
    Henry 40
    Isaac 84
    Joseph 126
    Levi 61
    Robert 75
    Solomon 126
    William 126,130,132,
        134,135
Reeves, Arthur 35
    James 31,136
    Malley 137
    Reuben 110
    Samuel 25
    Stephen 13
Register, Burrell 95
    John 82
    Levi 95
    William 94
Reid, Andrew 135
    James 42
    John 33
Reider, George 134
Reinhart, Charles 62
Rell, John 115
    Thomas 115
Renair, John 122
Rench, James 96
Rener, Samuel 126
Renshaw, Andrew 46
    Thomas 121
Repton, Daniel N. 42
Revells, Arthur 35
    Ralph 30
    Samuel 27
Revenbark, William 92
Reves, Arthur 35
    James 136
Rew, Beverly 9
Reymer, Peter 130
Reynolds, Barajah 116
    Charles 124
    David 26
    Dudley 50
    Elijah 28
    Elsey 58
    James 85,129
    John 28,62
    Jonathan 50
    Nicholas 124
    Owen 26
    Perry G. 54
    Richard 28
    Robert 85
    Simon 26
    Whiting 26
    William 113
Rhadshaw, Thomas, Sr. 108

Rhea, Cilas 137
John 66
Thomas 72
Rhea see also Ray
Rhine, Adam 130
Jacob 130
John, Jr. 62
Solomon 130
Rhinehart, Jacob 49
Rhodes, Allen 110
Bryan 90
David 136
James 53
James, Jr. 16
John 20,65,129,130
Noah 60
Thomas 28,57
Westley 107
Rhodes see also Roads and
Rodes
Rhody, John 72
Rhom, Isaac 132
Rice, Baldy 40
Evan 24
Isaac 59
James 137
James B. 41
John 11,35,48,59,80
Peter 13
Samuel 43
Thomas 35,105
William 120
William H. 113
Rich, Daniel 126
Richards, Benjamin G. 23
Green 106
John 20
Thomas 78
William 22
Richardson, Drury 27
Ira 120
Isaac 34
Ivy 119
John 15,27
Levi 15
Mabry 14
Richard 119
Stephen 74
Thomas 26
William 15,16,113
William F. 34
Richerson, William 16
Richey, Adam 127
Richison, Isaac 34
Mabry 14
Rick, Willie 80
Rickets, Benjamin 58
Burret 135
Jonathan 34
Robert 56,68
William 57
Ricks, Duncan 80
Whitmell 80
Riddish, William 57
Riddle, Allen 110
Anarser 60
Stephen 42
Ridley, James 114
Riel, John 134
Rigdon, Walter 120
Riggins, Jacob 40
Moton 40
William 40
Riggs, David 91
Dempsey 74
George 32
Hugh 107
Isaac 17

John 66,106
Samuel 115
Silas 74
William 42
Right, Stephen 11
Rigsby, James 102
Thomas 118
William 63
Riks, John 18
Riley, John 92
Peter 121
Rimer, Jeremiah 37
Volentine 121
Rimon, Eli 136
Rine, David, Jr. 53
James 58
Rinehart, Christian 121
Riner, Robert 135
Ringstaff, James 98
William 106
Riples, Abraham 39
Ripple, Henry 115
Rippy, Jesse 132
John 132
Rising, James 93
Ritchey, Abraham 128
Ritchie, Michael 125
Ritengous, Daniel 127
Ritter, George 98
Jesse 67
John 12
Rivenbark, Benjamin 95
Rivers, William 100
Rivis, John 56
Roach, Anderson 34
James 55
Roads, Jesse 63
Randolph 46
William 101
Roads see also Rhodes
Roan(e), John 79,110
Willis 78
Robards, John 118
Robason, Thomas 83
Robberson, Doctor, G. 80
Robbins see Robins
Roberson, David 21,22
Nathaniel 105,109
Roberts, Azra 58
Charles 74
David 129,136
Francis 32
Henry 90
Isaac 73
James 136
James, Jr. 116
Jeremiah 106
John 36,107
John M. 72
Joseph 75
Mark 137
Martin 113
Obadiah 72
Robert 137
Stephen 51
Thomas 52,73,136,137
Thomas James 137
Warren 122
Wiley 35
William 135
Willis 6,107
Robertson, And. 113
Buck 23
Calvin 50
Celsby 43
David 51
Doctor G. 80
Doctor M. 22

Edward 137
Elisha 7
Enoch 64
Eps 43
G. 80
George 137
George W. 46
Hugh 123,145
Isaac 11,53
James 7,48,126
John 23,58,67,114,117
Joshua 11
Littleton B. 80
M. 22
Newman 36
Robert 103
Thomas 57,113
Timothy 7
Will 48
William 65
Robeson, Amos 130
Archibald 193
Collen 59
Elias 67
Henry 22
Jesse 4,10
John 93,133
Joseph 61,98
Nathaniel 33
Niel 17
Noah 22
Samuel 21,26,138
Thomas 83
William 30,92,93,98
Robinet(t), Allen 117
James 68
Robins, Alexander 33
Daniel 119,120
Enoch 82
Joel 66
John 120,124
Joseph 56
Josiah 8
Thomas 56
William 120
Robinson, Allen 85
Edward 79
George, Jr. 95
Israel 115
Jesse 73
Jonathan 131
Joshua, Jr. 88
Robert 69
William, Jr. 95
Robison, John 61
William, Jr. 53
Robling, Lewis 122
Rockell, Benjamin 92
Rockett, Alsey 63
Rockford, William 130
Roddick, Timothy 87
Roden, Upton 47
Rodes, Wilson 123
Rodes see also Rhodes
Rodford, Miles 90
Rodgers, George 109
William 76
Rodgers see also Rogers
Roe, James 92
Roe see also Row and Rowe
Roebuck, William 88
Roebuck see also Roubuck
Rogers, Benjamin 63,65
Crewry 14
David 58
Edmond 21
Elisha 27
Jacob 87

James 86,127
John 8,60
Joseph 37,47
Joseph, Jr. 128
Micajah 49
Nicholas 95
Ozni 127
Samuel 63
Stephen 58
William 21,120,138
Rogerson, Abel 6
John 21
John, Jr. 75
Josiah 88
Rolan, Abel 49
Isaac 39
Roll, John 83
William 65
Rollins, Miles 65
Richard 14
Rone, James 126
Rooker, John
Rooks, Job 13
Joseph 92
Timothy 92
Rorden, James 116
Jeremiah 116
Rose, Benjamin 52
Edward 82
Fracis 115
Joel 118
Philip 108
Sterling 52
Tompkins 80
William 120
William, Jr. 13
Roser, Arris 29
Roser see also Rosser
Roses, Jonathan 5
Ross, Alexander 61
Dennis 135
Duncan 37
George 132
James 43,48,112,127
John 29,135
John, Sr. 43
Leaven 60
Thomas 21,39
Rosser, Abel 29
Horatio 100
Rosson, Bennona 109
Ira 109
Rothwell, Jonathan 66
Rough, Philip 135
Roughton, Ozias 9
Roulac, John M. 81
Roundtree, Obed. 11
Rouse, David 15
John 98
Lewis 95
Row, Jacob 22
Rowbuck, John 21
Raleigh 21
Rowbuck see also Roebuck
Rowe, Henry 49
Rowe see also Roe
Rowell, Hermon 20
Rowland, Alfred 24
Joel 125
Mitchel 67
Rowling, Gardener 98
Rows, Thomas 86
Rowse, Burwell 13
Roy, Isaac 11
Royal(1), Hardy 27
Isom 96
John 96
Willis 27

Royer, Samuel 119
Royster, John 105
William 106
Rozwell, James 111
Rudaice, John 54
Rudasil see Rudisil
Rudd, Pleasant 38
Ricardo 9
Rudisil, Henry 53
John 43
Jonas 130
Rue, Hardy, Jr. 83
John 16
Ruffin, John 65
Joseph 89
Thomas 77,107
Whitmel 77
Rulland, Whitmel 19
Rumage, Mathew 28
Rumfelt, Ebner 130
Rumple, Philip 120
Rundles, Elsey 36
Runnels, Coleman 66
Runnion, James 59
Runnols, James 99
Runyan, Jeremiah 62
Rupard, Peter 61
Rush, James 25
Reuben 119
Zebedee 119
Rushing, John 29
Stephen 100
Rusley, Richard 15
Russ, David 96
George 93
William 9
Russand, James 61
Russel(1), Aaron 124
David 12
Elijah 17
Ezra 98
Isaick 121
Jarrett 124
John 106
John F. 99
Joseph 123
Levi 124
Louis 67
Major 50
Martin 124
Nevil 66
Robert 112
William 124
William, Sr. 123
Russon, John 29
Ruston, John 120
Ruth, James 133
James B. 35
Rutherford, John 58,119
Robert 35
Ruthoen, Daniel 97
Rutland, Johnston 65
Redden 65
Rutledge, John 117
Ryal, Parks 84
Tolson 12
Ryan, Hyram 52
John 50
Ryer, Charles 43
Ryke, Michel 33
Ryman, James 65
Ryno, Elisha 20
Ryolds, David 26
Owen 26
Whiting 26
Ryon, Elisha 20
Peter 26
William 26

- S -

Sadler, Henry 129
John 125
Richard 82
Thomas 129
Sailer, Mickael 115
St. George, John 18
Sale, John 52
Salenger, Reuben 18
Sales, Clemm 96
Salmon, John D. 115
Samuel 25
Salter, Edward T. 11
Henry 85
James 24
Joseph 61
Wallace 66
Sammons, James 120
Thomas 19
William 91
Sampson, Benjamin 106
Thomas 54
Sams, John 59
Samuel, Archibald 110
Harbert 110
Lewis 111
Rowzee 111
Sandeford, Elisha 104
Sandeford see also Sandiford
Sandefur, John, Jr. 19
Sandelin, Ezekiel 136
Sanderford, Noah 99
Sanderlin, Abner 4
Ezekiel 136
Ferebee 73
Josiah 74
Sanders, Benjamin 117
Britton 35
Elijah 62
John 66,105
Joseph 11
Larkin 107
Lemuel 76
Luke 111
Samuel 85
Seth 82
Sherrod 103
William 57,84,104
Sanderson, Amos 85
Joseph 4
Thomas 82
Sandiford, Charles 63
Sandiford see also Sandeford
Sandler, Trininger 4
William 94
Sanding, Elrey 17
Sandline, James 16
Sandy, Uriah 84
Saner, George 45
Sanford, Linas 53
Sap, Brummel 45
Sargent, Dempsey 110
James 55
Noah 132
Sarnot, John 89
Sasser, Frederick 28
John 13
Satterwhite, Anderson 105
Solomon 36
Sattonfield, Michael 131
Saulter, Henry 85
Saulter see also Salter
Saunders, Benjamin 19
Edward 6

Elisha 130
Hardy 16
James 17
Jesse 17
John 7
John, Jr. 16
Richard 92
Robert 18
Solomon 117
Savage, Charles 44
Hezekiah 75
James 34
John 34
William 20,89
Sawer, Henry 123
Sawyer, Archibald 5,45,73
Charles 3,73
Enoch 5
Freeman 74
Henry 123
Hollowell 3
Isaac 74
James 4,74
Joseph 3,73
Maxsey 74
Miles 84
Robert 74
Thomas 9
Willis 81
Wilson 82
Zephaniah 10,74
Sax, Joseph 9
Scales, Alfred 113
James H. 41
John 113
Scarboro, Edward 62
Scarborough, Benjamin 13
Isaac 89
James 94
Jesse 92
Miles 63
Samuel 124
Thomas 4
Willie 124
Scarlet(t), John 107
Lewis 33
Sceutill, Richard 136
Schoots, Bryant 64
Scoggin, Charles 55
John 55
Samuel 55
William 54
Scott(e), Benjamin 16,98
Charles 91
Cornelius 5
Daniel 42
David 16
Edward 5
Herbert 20
Hillery
Isaac 16
James 38
John 8,18,35,47
Larkin 45
Patrick 56
Reuben 20
Samuel 58
Stephen 5
Will 48
William 29,98,127
William A. 124
Wyett 49
Scruggs, Elias 133
Robert 133
Scull, John 8
Seabold, Ludwith 36
Seabrook, Daniel 82
Seagraves, William 124

Seagroves, Stephen 102
Seall, John 76
Seamon, Joseph 74
Searcy, Aron 25
Leml 97
Seares, William 36
Sears, Charles 72
Searsey, Samuel 25
Seaton, William W. 35
Seaward, John 83
Seawell, German 25
Jacob 26
Sebastian, Hezekiah 118
Sedberry, David 124
Sedford, William 63
Segimore, John 43
Seiter, Abraham 54
Andrew 54
Selah, Jesse 58
Selby, Burrige 10
Samuel 82
Sell, Jonathan 115
Sellars see Sellers
Sellers, Benjamin 14,66
Daniel 93
Duncan 92
Elisha 93
George 130
John 14,92
Richard 15
William 16,93
Semple, Samuel 63
Senter, Joseph 53
Sergant, Noah 132
Serjiner, Thomas 99
Serkin, John 41
Sessions, Isaiah 28
Sessoms, William 76
Sessums, Joseph 89
Settle, Josiah 113
Setton, Edward 37
Samuel 131
Sewell, Abram 27
Jacob 8
James 12
Jethro 8
William 76
Sewit, James 36
Sexton, Miller 35,64
Seth 102
Seymore, Peter 4
Shackleford, John 38
Shafer, John 131
Sham, Jepeth 53
Shamel, Jacob 115
Shamell, Peter 115
Shanklin, Robert 107
Shanks, Charles 33
Shannon, James 103
John 4
Nathan 4
Robert 48
Sharp(e), Amos 72
Benjamin 64
Cunningham 48
Durham 40
Eli 38
Fans 68
John 89,113
William 48
Willima 40
Sharpless, Thomas 17
Sharply, William 47
Shavener, John 82
Shaver, Frederick 38
Jacob 48,120
Shaw, Alexander 30
Colin 24

Daniel 24
Findlay 61
Henry 39
James 79,127
Jesse 112
John 24,25
John, Jr. 97
Jos. 112
Joseph 101
Joseph B. 60
Malcom 30
Robert 24
Simon 117
Simpson 31
Thomas 33
William 83
Shearer, Andrew 118
John 118
Shearod, John 76
Sheaver, Frederick 38
Sheerren, Elish 80
Sheets, David 123
Sheffield, Everitt 27
Nicholas 35
Shehorn, Morris 126
Shelby, Joseph 129
William 20,100,112,
125,126
Shelfer, John 86
Shelly, William 40
Shelton, Freeman 130
Lodeman 79
Menucan 53
Willis 18
Shelvey, William 125
Shemel, Henry 121
Shepard, Isham 98
James 107
John 91
Joseph 137
Larkin 117
Thomas 98
Shepherd, Andrew 62
Egbert 107
Henry 17,32
Josiah 30
Peter 136
Thomas 47
Wader 30
Woodham 18
Sheppard, Larkin 117
Shepperd, John 39
Joseph 59
Joshua 16
Sherod, Edward 64
Elisha 23
Gabriel 14
John M. 23
Selathiel 21
Sherrel, Colbert 53
Sherren, Elish 80
Lewis 23,80
William 23,80
Sherril, Alfred 13
John 36
Sherrin see Sherren
Sherwood, Edwin 88
Neil 8
Shewcraft, Silas 76
Shields, John 18
Shillington, John 61
Shine, Elias 131
Shiner, Aaron 64
Shines, William 11
Shinner, Benjamin 6
Shipman, Edward 58
Ship(p), Bartlett 114
John 3,50,68,84

Peter 19
Reading 10
William 114
Shipton, John 121
Shipwash, William 96
Shirley, David 86
Kelly 115
Michael 95
Shiver, Edward W. 91
Shivers, John 41
Shoaf, John 121
Shoemaker, John 52
Tarlton 61
Sholders, Cullen 77
Moses 92
Shook, George 131
Shoolders, Cullen 77
Shore, Henry 117
Ransome 118
Short, James 121
John 21
Jonathan 112
William 78,129
Shorter, John 4
Shorton, Owen 26
Shote, Man 136
Shoulse, Joseph 121
Shoup, Solomon 130
Shouse, Jacob 51
Shover, Jacob 120
Show, Colin 24
Shufford, John 131
Shufler, Philip 134
Shuford, Daniel 43
Daniel, Jr. 44
Shular, Abram 44
Adam 69
Shulleberger, John 130
Shurley, Michael 95
Shute, Henry 84
Sides, Michel 53
Levi 53
Moser 62
Sifford, Gatlip 53
George 53,69
John 53
William 53
Sikes, Abner 4
Alfred 93
Beattie 93
Britton 8
David 93
James 92
John 31
Matthew 92
Nathan 22
Sampson 22
William 29
Wilson 4
Sikes see also Sykes
Siler, Benjamin 98
Sills, John 79
Silver, Jacob 137
Silvers, James 44
Silverthorn, John 82
Silvey, Anthony 123
William 102
Simes, Thomas 57
Simmimer, James 48
Simmons, Anthony 72
Beverly 17
Everett 91
Jacob 49
John 66,85
Jos. 112
Joseph 17
Malachi 140
Mitchell 73

Peleg 9
Richard 91
Samuel 17
Sherrod 95
William 16,24,93,113
Simonds, James 65
John 27
Simons, Abraham 74
Henry E. 20
John 19
Robert 75
Simeon 16
Thomas 10
William 77,127
Simonton, Theophilus 46
Simpkins, Benjamin 14
Ephraim 11
Ezekiel 84
Thomas 14
Simpson, Charles 72
Francis 112
Frederick 7,92
Hardy 64
Isaac 91
Jacob 5
Jephthy 84
John 5,75
Levi 111
Moses 38
Robert H. 54
Sims, Harwell 102
Jacob 89,90
John 44
John, Jr. 41
Nathiel 48
Sinclair, Benjamin 29
John 67
John, Jr. 41
Orrin 29
Sincunger, Benjamin 44
Singenwinder, Henry 43
Singletary, Brayton 93
David 24
James 93
Samuel 93
William C. 24
Willis 93
Singleton, Phillip 37
Richard 89
Sterling 131
William 37,38,39
Singling, John H. 134
Sink, Christian 44
Jacob 68
Michael 122
Sisemore, Richard 134
Sisk, William 44
Sivels, James 9
Skeen, James 119
Skerd, Philip 130
Skider, James 45
Skidmore, Henry 111
Thomas 11
Skiles, John 59
Skinner, Charles W. 75
James 76
Ralph 79
Thomas 122
Skipper, John 90,133
Levi 13
Niram 66
Skittlethrop, Arthur 8
Edmund 8
Isaac 8
Skussing, Jacob 43
Slade, Benjamin 9
Jeremiah 18,71,83
Nathan 11

Uriah 83
Valentine 83
Slagle, John 62
Slaughter, Samuel 101
William 114
Slawson, David 101
Slay, Thomas 29
Sleatey, William 83
Sledge, Amos P. 22,80
Dilworth 24
Slightfoot, James 19
Slinkard, Andrew 129
Slismore, Jesse 86
John 86
Sloan, James 125
John 128
Thomas 61
William 34
Sluillei, Frederick 134
Small, Joseph, Jr. 72
Joshua 76
Nathan 74
Richard 96
Timothy 66
William 114
Smalley, John 135
Smallwood, William 50
Smart, Elisha 124,126
John 122
Joseph 55
Osborn 126
Smedick, Mark 82
Smipes, William 103
Smisson, Joshua 5
Smith Aaron 67
Abner 103
Abram 10
Alexander 8,47,101
Allen 10,84
Ambrose 17
Anderson 111
Arthur 45,93
Ausein 42
Bettie 79
Benjamin 10,75
Boswell 78
Bradley 5,73
Britain 78,101
Bryan 16
Burges 133
Cajer 136
Caleb 79
Cannon 10
Charles 27,36
Cornelius 44
Cudias 130
Daniel 34,38,49,67,
86,98,110,120
David 10,113,121
David, Jr. 129
Dawson 13
Duncan 28,97
Ebenezer 82
Edmond 121
Edward 86
Elam 14
Elijah 14,52,93
Elisha B. 124
George 16,31,34,45,
121
George D. 125
George T. 61
Giles 14
Henry 10,20,21,62,75,
101,110
Hezekiah 14
Inley 44
Isaac 119,129

Isaiah 28
Jacob 55,56,130
James 20,23,28,30,31,
   80,102,105,116,
   135
James, Jr. 116
James S. 136
Jasper 9
Jeremiah 90,133
Jesse 134
Joab 87
Job 84
Joel 42
Joel, Jr. 79
John 3,10,42,43,50,
   60,61,85,87,93,
   97,98,100,110,
   113,114,125,133,
   134,136
John A. 63
John B. 25
John S. 84
Jonathan 6,97
Joseph 90,107,108
Josiah 75
Kennedy 11
Landin 79
Larkin 102
Lennard 121
Lewis 16,103
Malcolm 97
Maurice 71
Michael 42
Moses 50
Nelson 5
Nicholas 87
Noah
Obed 92
Peter 79,110
Peter M. 43
Phillip 45
Reding 94
Robert 107,132
Reuben 124
Sampson 60
Samuel 10,11,26,75,
   135
Sandy 38,110
Simon 93
Simpson 31
Sparkman 87
Taylor 90
Thomas 1,7,24,44,61,
   99,113,114,130
Thomas, Sr. 72
William 16,17,21,31,
   39,42,48,49,85,
   93,97,98,109,110,
   117
William, Jr. 98
Willie 11
Wright 13
Zebediah 112
Smithall, George 121
Smitherman, John 33
Smithson, Joshua 5
   William 74
Smithwick, Joel 88
   John 21
   Luke 77
Smitteds, Conrad 43
Smoot, Hiram 117
   Thomas 122
Smothers, William 41
Smoyer, Jacob 62
Smythe, James 116
Snead, Hanly 30
Sneed, Edward 54

Hanly 30
Reuben 49
Snell, Hiram 8
   Rogers 8,81
Snelson, Thomas 136
Snider, George, Jr. 45
   Henry 120
   Jacob 123
   John 127
   William 3
Snider see also Snyder
Snipes, Robert 78
Snow, Hail 116
   John 68,115
   Levi 68
   Thomas 115,116
   William 43
Snowden, Isaac 73
   James 73
   Thaddeus 5
Snyder, John 31
   Joseph 8
Snyder see Also Snider
Sohlar, Archibald 134
Sollace, Joseph 95
Solomon, Bennet 125
   Drury 48
   Jeremiah 103
Solon, John 47
Somers, James 38
Sommerlin, Frederick 88
   Henry 95
Sorrals, William 134
Sorrat, William, Jr. 121
Sorrel(1), Jacob 102
   James 24
   Thomas 65
   William 65
Sorsby, Samuel 22
Sossiman, John 127
South, Nathan 15
Southam, John 116
   Joshua 42
Southerlin, John L. 20
Southward, William 106
Sowell, Isom 24
   Jethro 76
Sowens, Jacob 45
Spafford, Samuel 121
Spain, Frederick 64
   Littleton 104
   Taswell 104
Spainhour, David 114
   Henry 114
   Solomon 42
Sparger, Henry 50
Sparks, Elijah 132
   George 118
   James 40
   Joel 116
   John 118,123
   John, Jr. 68
   Jonathan 118
   Richard 46
   Solomon 68
   William 51,116
Sparrow, John 85
   Patrick 86
Spavey, Benjamin 126
Speak, John 44
   Samuel 116
Spear, Abner 19
   Arthur 19
   Jehu 36
   Noah 83
Spears, Willie M. 35
Speed, Benjamin 60
Speer, George 51

Samuel 51
Speight, Adam 54
   Christy 54
   Lemuel 13
   Noah 76
Spell, Lavis 26
Spelman, Davis 5
   John 117
   Samuel 5
   William 51
Spelman see Spillman
Spence, Arthur 3,73
   Daniel 74
   Henry 3
   Robert 5
   William 5,72
Spencer, Abraham 16
   Christopher 111
   Elijah 97
   Frisby 82
   John 56,66
   Selby 10,82
   William 124
   William B. 82
Spengler, Jacob 54
Spicer, James 98
   John 27
Spier, Christopher 101
   Miles 87
   Samuel 118
Spikes, William 84
Spillman, John 117
Spillman see Spellman
Spinks, Enock 119
   Garrat 33
   Raley 33
Spinner, Carney 82
Spires, James 7
   Joseph G. 127
Spivert, Robert 112
Spivey, James 11
   John 60
   Moses 7
   Richard 104
   Timothy 75
   William 34,58,76,136
Spivy, Caleb 13
Sponse, Christopher 42
Spoon, David 33
   George 108
   John, Jr. 39
   William 39
Sprat, William 132
Spright, James 7
   John 7
   William 7
Springle, William 83
Sprinkle, John 115
   Peter 117
Sprouts, Aron 39
Spruel(1), Samuel 88
   Uzziah 81
Spruill, Andrew 8
   Emai 9
   Joseph 8
   Uriah 9
Sprulin, Hugh 131
Spurgin, Samuel 45
Spyva, John 89
Squires, Dempsey 74
Stableford, William 12
Stackhouse, Thomas 32
Stacy, Elisha 133
Stadler, John 38
   Robert 38
Stafford, Adam 74,110
   Eli 111
   George 109

Markum 5
Stagg, James 107
Staley, Frederick 118
Stallings, John 64
  Lott 21
  Richard 22
  Simon 7
  Uriah 89
Stallions, Joseph 89
Stallons, Bryant 88
Stalls, James 21
Stamper, Jacob 52
  Robert 36
Stamy, John 131
Stanaland, Henry 93
  Peter 93
Stanback, John B. 78
Stancel, Nathan 15
Standen, William 6
Standford, William 57
Standing, John 6
Standly, Etheridge 4
  Nash 102
  Robert 36
Stanfield, Jeremiah 37
  John 37
  Joseph M. 106
  Josiah 38
  Major 111
Stanford, Jonathan 127
  Moses 48
  William 57
Stanley, Daniel 86
  Elisha 103
Stanly, Jacob 26
  James 17
  John 16
  William 114
Stansberry, Moses 117
Stansill, Godfrey 102
  John, Jr. 103
  Nathan 15
Stanton, George 59,137
  James 6
  John 75,137
Stanual, Allen 87
Staples, Abner 57
  Elijah 73
  John 57
Star, William H. 81
Starks, Asa 11
  John, Jr. 39
Starns, Daniel 68
  Jacob 48
  Nathaniel 126
Starnt, John 112
State, Abner 137
Staton, Bythel 26
  Frederick 26
Stator, Elisha 42
Stawls, Bond 88
Steadman, William 9,34
Steatman, William 9
Stedman, Charles, Jr. 117
Steed, Frederick 33
  Isham 33
  John 33
  Moses 124
  Thomas 117
Steedman, Thomas 134
Steel(e), James 126
  John 25,98,126,128
  Ninian 128
  Ninian, Sr. 47
  Robert G. 50
  Thomas 32
Steely, Enock 8
Steet, Simon 132

Stegall, Absolam 29
Stenkman, Lewis 17
Step, Reuben 58
Stephens, Arthur 107
  Benjamin 103
  Caleb 28,94
  Calloway 30
  Erwin 27
  George 112
  Hardy 26
  Izekiah 23
  James 25
  Joel 96
  Jones 97
  Joseph 28,84
  Levi 94
  Lorick 29
  Miles 34
  Moses H. 84
  Reuben 94
  Simon 109
  Thomas 26
  William 95
  William A. 40
  Zachariah 49
Stephenson, Benjamin 103
  Brittain 35
  Hugh 48
  John 17,36,37,75,104
  Joseph 17
  Mosey 47
  Uriah 4
  Walter 17
  William 53,103
Sterling, William 28
Sterns, Benjamin 46
Stevens, Bartley 15
  Edward 103
  James 25
  Joseph 23
Stevenson, James 15
Steward, Hugh 123
  John 124
Stewart, Alexander 126
  Allen 48
  Andrew 48
  Archibald 30
  Benjamin 23
  Charles 6,80,100
  Daniel 30,97
  David 61
  Dugald 67
  George 41
  James 97
  Jesse 41
  John 30,60,99
  John, Jr. 65
  Neil 96
  Ralph 128
  Robert S. 41
  William 96,107
Stife, Henry 42
Still, John 43,49
Stillar, Henry 120
Stillwell, Daniel 57
  Tillman 57
Stilwell, Elias 126
Stipp, Achillis 52
Stiriam, Elish 9
Stirran, Wallis 4
Stirwalt, Jacob 127
Stockard, John 32
Stocks, Cannon 11
  John 87
  Levi 11
Stockton, Thomas 132
Stoddard, Charles 23
Stofel, John 41

Stogner, John 30
Stokely, Buckner 92
  Harvey 74
Stoker, Richard 125
Stokes, Montford 71
  Moses 123
Stone, Asa 109
  Conway
  Ephraim 50
  Joseph 123
  MacKollach 103
  Tilmore 38
  William 43
Stoner, Jacob 44
  James 44
Storm, Charles 30
Story, David 38
  David W. 127
  George 58
  James, Sr. 127
  John 58
Stough, Jacob 69
Stout, Aron 34
  William 121
  Zachariah 123
Stoutenberg, John 44
Stover, Isaac 68
Stow, Benjamin 4
  Daniel 4
Strahorn, Samuel 32,107
Strain, David 107
Strange, James 91
Straughan, Guilford 110
Straughn, Larkin 34
  Samuel 92
Strawn, Marmon 112
Strayhorn, Samuel 32,107
Stredy, James 24
Street, William 132
Streeter, Isaac 30
Streets, William 94
Strickland, Alfred 81
  David 96
  Edward 81
  Elbert 96
  Gadi 97
  Jesse 27
  John 39
  Martin 96
  Nathan 96
  Reuben 80
  Silas 30
  Thomas 89
Stricklin, Micajah 63
Strickling, Benjamin 78
Strilling, James 13
Strond, Peter, Jr. 57
Strong, Hardiman 113
  Zach 113
Strope, John 115
Strother, Charles 29
  William H. 59
Stroud, David 57
  George 60
  Peter, Jr. 57
  Ransom 23
Struter, Willis 99
Stuart, James 94
  John 11,97
  Samuel 32
  Stephen 111
Stubbs, George 94
  William 94
Stublefield, Peter P. 111
Stud, Mark
Studard, Richard 116
Studer, Henry 136

Studivant, Daniel L. 79
    Joseph 19
    Joseph A. 79
    Thomas M. 110
    Whiles 19
Studman, Joseph 134
Stulland, Matthew 59
Stunford, Moses 48
Styers, John 115
Styson, James 85
Sudler, Henry 43
Suduth, James 113
Sugg, Rading 21
    Samuel 101
Suggs, Allgood 66
    Harbert 124
    Lewis 93
    Marsel 49
    Uriah 85
Suit, Riley 106
Suite, James 104
Suits, William 113
Sulivant, Neil 98
Sullivan, Dickson 95
    Felix 94
    George 61,112
    Isaac 30
    James 15
    John 66
    Levi 39
    Levin 39
    Samuel 131
    Thomas 122
    William 48
    Zachariah 19
Sumerlin, Benjamin 64
    Stuart 87
Summers, Charles 128
    George 68
    Jacob 62
    Thomas 117
    William 46
    Zera 40
Summey, Frederick 53
Summitt, Daniel 131
    Francis 131
Summon, Thomas 72
Summuns, Dixon 64
Sumner, Asa 16
    James 78
    Samuel 15
    William 7,128
Sumners, Solomon 128
Sumpter, John 135
Surls, John 102
    Raymond 12
Surrasy, Elijah 55
Surry, Thomas 73
Suthard, Arges 40
Sutherland, Jeremiah 17
    Roderick 31
Sutliff, John 51
Suttle, Benjamin 62
    Robert 56
Sutton, Campbell 42
    Coleby 55
    Edward 104
    John 136
    John, Jr. 134
    Joseph 5
    Nathaniel 92
    Thomas 95
    Whitfield 95
    William 86,129
    William, Jr. 134
    William R.
    Zachariah 8
Swafford, Enock 119

Nathan 119
William 119
Swain, Abraham 116
    Elakin 82
    James 88
    Jesse 42
    Joseph 82
    Joshua 9,82
    Levi 66
    Michael 51,113
    Nathan I. 8
    Simson 9
    Stephen 81
    William 9,88,113
Swan, James 7
    Jesse 122
Swann, James 111
    Jos. 111
    Jos., Jr. 111
    Thomas 111
Swean, Marmaduke 33
    Michael 120
Sweany, James 33
    Wilie 107
Sweat, Virtue 45
Sweedy, Thomas 82
Sweeney, William 123
Swenny, Edmond 51
Sweter, Benjamin 78
    Henry 78
Swift, Harroway 38
    Thomas 118
Swim, William 45
Swindell, John 82
    Zedekiah 82
Swing, Henry 39
Swink, Daniel 121
Swinson, Daniel 95
    John 94,95
Swivit, Harris 46
Swonner, James 83
    Jesse 83
Sydes, George 125
Syke, Ethelred 25
Sykes, Isham 79
    Jacob 79
Sykes see also Sikes

- T -

Taddis, Alexander 33
Tade, William 39
Tague, Michael 46
Tailor, William 75
Tallow, John 96
Tally, James 23
    Joel 23
    Thomas 23
Talton, Joshua 6
Tapley, Pleasant 43
    Robert 28
Tapp, Vinson 37
Tapping, Thomas 6
Tarkinton, Enos 8
    Starkey 9
    Zebedee 8
Tarlington, Israel 27
Tarlton, Thomas 6
Tart, James 96
    John 96
Tate, David 107
    George 31
    James 104
    James G. 36,37
    Joel 33
    William 39

William R. 31
Tatlock, James 75
Tatom, Edward 42
Tatum, Daniel 73
    Harbert 40
    Joseph 73
    Mixey 73
Taunt, Ervin 84
Taylor, Abraham 88,96
    Absolam 62
    Alexander 28
    Amos 30
    Archibald 28
    Arden 21
    Benjamin 3
    Cornelius 81
    David 124
    Edmond 47
    Edwin 12
    Elijah 91
    Elisha 88
    Fisher B. 39
    Fletcher 36
    George 45
    Henry 59
    Hiram 60
    Isaac 76,92,95,118
    Jacob 95
    James 41,89,96,124,
        132
    Jesse 90
    John 24,25,34,54,64,
        84,92,107,108,
        109,122
    John H. 41
    Jonathan 67
    Joseph B. 13,132
    Joshua, Jr. 89
    Josiah 3,86
    Kinchen 76
    Kinnon 13
    Mark 86
    Micajah 29
    Nathaniel M. 104
    Reuben 73,89
    Richard 93
    Samuel 67,83
    Saunders 100
    Sutton 112
    Thomas 15,45,137
    Valentine 131
    William 12,25,75,92,
        93,99,108,119,137
    Wilson 126
Taylous, John S. 49
Teachey, David 94
Teag, Michael 115
Teague, Isaac 98
    John 46,130
    Joseph 51
    Moses 123
Teal, Benjamin 29
    John, Jr. 87
    Micajah 88
Teasly, Daniel 51
Teat, James 21
Teats, Jacob 41
Teddar, Benjamin 109
Tedder, David D. 98
    James 34
    Sion 25
Tedrick, John 102
Telfair, Hugh 87
Tellers, Eldred 66
Telley, John 138
Telliton, William 83
Temple, Britton 5
    Henry 74

Templeton, James 46,47
   Joseph 47
   Robert 128
   Samuel 46,128
Tenneyhill, Zachariah 48
Tennison, David 21
Terrell, William 38
   William G. 77
Terry, John 100
   Thomas 105
   William 36
Tews, Blackman 27
Thack, James 75
   William 75
Thagard, John 25
Thalley, Caldwell 90
Tharington, Thomas 23
Theek, Daniel 108
Thespin, John 89
Thigpen, Gray 21
   Howell 21
   James, Jr. 21
   Jonathan 21
   Lemuel 94
   Reddin 64
Thomas, Alderson 11
   Andrew 39
   Benjamin 30,104,114
   Daniel 33
   David 64,67
   Elias 30
   Elijah 40
   Elisha 21
   George B. 24
   Henry 23,98
   Hilliard 89
   Jacob 60,121
   James 80,110
   James B. 128
   Jesse 41
   John 39,64,88,121
   John William 100
   Jonathan 89
   Lewis 98
   Martin 98
   Moses 28
   Nehemiah 33
   Robert 23
   Samuel 59
   Solomon 22,31,80
   Theophilus 21,64
   Thomas 32
   William 88,109,113
Thomason, Benjamin 60
   John 116
   William 83
Thompson, Alexander 12
   Anderson 108
   Andrew 133
   Bartholomew 73
   Benjamin 47
   Bryan 90
   Charles 91
   David 13,90
   Drury 80
   Duncan 98
   Edmund 20
   Elijah 116
   Everit 90
   Henderson 116
   Henry 126
   Isaac 121
   James 23,48,55,69,
     102,107,129,132
   James, Jr. 108
   John 13,31,32,78,90,
     111,116
   Joseph 133

Lemuel 30,33
Lewis 91
Nathan 16
Neil 27
Neill 97
Newcomb 107
Nicholas 111
Patrick 49
Robert 20,32,56
Samuel 63,133
Theophilis 32
William 3,49,60,103,
   120,133
Thorn, James 35
   William 75
Thorne, Jacob 54
   Thomas 8
Thornton, John 123
   Solomon 10
   Thomas 117
Thorp, Jesse 81
Threadgill, Gideon 99
   Homer 29
   Thomas C. 29
Thrower, John 19
Tidder, James 34
Tiley, Boston 109
Tilley, Edmond 118
   John 114
   Reuben 114
Tillingast, William 25
Tillman, David 50
Tilly, John 107
   Lewis 42
Tilman, John 86
   William 109
Times, Thomas M. 45
Timpleton, Robert 128
   Samuel 128
Tindal, James 90
Tindall, Charles 86
   James 29
Tiner, Laura 103
Tines, West 65
Tingle, James 11
   Major 11
Tinkle, John 43
Timmon, Thomas 107
Tipps, George 116
Tirrell, John 110
   Lewis 111
   Paul 111
   William 111
Tisdale, Eli 22
   Elisha 81
   Nathan 9,71
Tison, Charles 87
   Stephen 87
Titman, Peter 130
Tobin, James 112
Tod, Pleasant 113
Todd, Elijah 63
   Hugh 47
   James 69
   Levi 65
   William 72,101
Tolby, James 52
Toler, John 37
Toley, Charles 58
   Enos 13
   Isaiah 67
Toliver, William 118
Tolley, James 80
   Joel 80
   Thomas 80
Tolliver, William 52,118
Tollock, William 11
Tollor, John 138

Tolson, David 66
Tomberlin, Freeman 57
   Moses 126
Tomerlin, David 100
Tomison, Josiah 34
Tomlinson, Humphrey 129
   Perry 129
   William 68,125
Tompson, Moses 45
Tood, Henry 77
Tooke, Littleton 20
Tooley, Jeremiah 83
   Sheldon 82
Tore, Hezekiah 42
Torry, James 29
Towd, John 125
Townsell, James 125
Townsend, Eli 124
   Jesse 66
   John 96,124
   Luke 17
   Thomas 106
Townson, Aaron 131
Trackler, Lewis 52
Tragall, Solomon 100
Train, James 126
Trawick, Horney 96
Traxler, Peter 120
Tray, Abraham 131
Traywick, John 101
Trebble, 51
Treble, Benjamin 117
Trees, Jacob 68
Tribble, Abner 51,62
Triggler, Richard 22
Trill, Henry 32
Trip, Hardy 87
Triplett, George 57
   William 57
Tripp, Cullen 11
Trollinger, Adam 112
Trotman, Demsey 7
Trott, Murphy 85
Trout, John 54
Troutman, Demsey 4
   George 127
   Jacob 129
Troxler, Barney 108
   John 108
   Nickolas 108
   Peter 120
Troy, Abraham 131
   John B. 26
Trueblood, Joshua 74
Trull, Charles 100
   Solomon 28,100
   Thomas 100
   William 100
Trulman, Andrew 127
Trulove, Michena 72
Truss, Samuel 87
Trussel, Ezekiel 17
Trusty, Abram 50
   David 118
   Henry 52
   William 49
Trutman, George 127
Tucker, Aron 45
   Charles 116
   Daniel 53,105
   Edward 118
   Elijah 15,46
   Enoch 119
   Frederick 135
   Ira 95
   Jacob 128
   James 118
   Joab 81

John 53,112,114
Joseph 22
Lemuel 6
Lewis 80
Nathaniel 27
Thomas 129
William 129
William S. 114
Woody 22
Tulcher, Joseph 85
Tull, Arthur 86
Tumlinson, Enoch 40
Tunmire, Isaac 134
Turlly, David 133
Turnage, William 87
Turner, Alfred 74
Axum 99
Benjamin 82
Edward 65,118
George 131
Harrison 6,75
Isaac 87
James 33,74,79
James, Jr. 6,67
James, Sr. 6
Jesse 29,64,89
John 32,54
John, Jr. 103
John W. 95
Miles 5
Myles 6
Nathan 22
Sihon 39
Thomas 111
Urias 5
Washington 18,65
William 5,23,26,27,
135
Turnstall, Peyton 104
Peyton R. 79
Turrege, John 67
Turrell, Nathan 14
Turrentine, Robert 107
Tussell, Arthur 23
Tuter, George 126
Tutral, Matthew 108
Tutton, Person 13
Tweddy, William 6
Tweed, James 136
Twiddy, Isaac 6
James 75
Stephen 6
William 6
Twidwell, Obadiah 45
Twitty, Burford 60
Two, Daniel 26
Elias 26
Joseph 26
Landen 26
Twoney, Isaac 122
William 45
Tyler, Absalom 13
Lemuel 36
Tyner, Arthur 20
Tyrrell, Jephthah 101
Tyser, Frederic 117
Tyson, Amos 28
Hosea 83
Thomas 28

- U -

Umphreys, John 20
Underwood, David 27
Henry 34
James 111,114

John 28
Lemuel 34
Major 113
Moab 20
Nathan 40
Pendleton 58
Thomas 114,120
William 52,109,120
Upchurch, Berkely 104
Bentess 35
Burtess 35
James 104
Ruffin 110
Stephen 34
Upright, Peter 43
Upsom, James 32
Urry, Richard 49
Ussery, James 124
Samuel 105
Welcome 124
Utley, Alvin 35,64
Jacob 63
Little John 35
Utly, Burrel 134
Utzman, George 43
Jacob 43
John 43
Uutly, Sion 102
Uzzell, James 13

- V -

Valentine, James 20
Thomas 22,80
Vance, David 58,136
Vancy, Joel 62
Vanderpool, Isaac 51
John 118
Vandiford, William 99
Vandigriff, Jacob 103
John 100
Vanhook, Isaac 37
Vann, Eli 21
Vannay, Joel 117
Vannoy, Andrew 117
John 51
Vanover, William 118
Vanpelt, John 11
Vanter, Bradford 42
Vanzant, Isaac 62
Vardell, Holowell 5
Varnell, Benjamin 64
Varner, Wm. 119
Varnum, Francis F. 31
Vaughan, Benjamin 20
Caswell 106
Gideon 101
Hilary 76
Isaac 30
James 19,113
John 18,63,76
Kinchen 39
Lemuel 20
Peyton 54
Vaughn see Vaughan
Vause, William 86
Veark, John 68
Vendrick, Jesse 11
Venters, Francis 17
Peter 91
Samuel 11
Venzant, Jacob 132
Vermilion, Jesse 40
Verner, William 62
Vernon, Elisha 42
Green 113

John D. 113
Josiah 113
Richard 42
Samuel 113
Verval, Henry 61
Vest, Peter 117
Vestal, David 34
Isaac 117
William 120
Vick, Arthur 76
Benjamin 79
Joseph 80
Moses 126
Richard 79
Samuel 80
Vickers, Charles 117
John 54
William 55
Vincent, Jacob 103
James 24
Oran 35
Vines, John 10
Samuel 10
Thomas 10,66
Vins, Lat. 64
Vinson, Groves 126
Isaac 33
John 76
Laban 79
Nehemiah 20
Reuben 28
Warren 79
Voun, William 135

- W -

Waddy, James 37
Wade, Caleb 66
Downey 106
Eliza 66
Isaac 85
James 16,23,95
Jan. 78
Seth 33
Wadkins, Alfred 92
Isaiah 55
Wadsworth, Barney 11
Wafer, William 137
Waff, George 72
Waggerman, Christian 115
Waggoner, Jacob 40
John 56
Valentine 40
Wah, Samuel 47
Wailes, Isaac 129
Waite, Valentine 4
Wakefield, John 57
Wakins, William 29
Walden, Drew 20
Jesse 74
John 28
Walder, Amos 15
Waldriss, Elis 136
William 135
Waldrop, Ezekiel 55
Walford, James 12
Walk, Jonathan 44
Walker, Amos J. 94
Andrew 47,69,125,127
Aron 39
Bird 37
Burk 107
Daniel 106
Edward 98
Elijah 134
Green

Jacob 14
James 18,39,41,43,48,
  102,113
James, Sr. 81
John 55,92,96,98,125,
  134
John F. 77
Jones 103
Lewis 97
Martin 81
Matthew 24,111
Owen 115
Reuben 134
Richard 116
Solomon 37
Tandy 35
Thomas 23,80,107,115
William 39,47,53,56,
  80
Zachariah 69
Wall, Abraham 78
Absolam 99,113
David 22
James 113
John, Jr. 41
Micajah 101
Peter 40
William 113
Wallace, Andrew 15
David 66
David A. 85
John 87
John E. 78
Jonathan 10
Matthew 47
Robert 16
William 99,132
Wallen
Waller, George 121
Henry 88
Joseph 95
Wales, Ruel 128
Wallis, John 31
Joseph 85,126
Mathew J. 125
Walls, Burges 104
Kinchen 128
Walsh, Jonathan 118
William 118
Walston, Amburrus 3
Amos 88
Waltan, John 65
Walten, John B. 20
Walter, Charles 49
Henry 64
John B. 20
Paul 127
Peter 127
Walters, Alexander 104
Dawson 31
Isaac 12
John 31
Joseph 30,66
Lewis 117
Mills 8
Nathaniel 12
William 31
Walton, Herman 12
John 35
Lewis 119
Thomas 60
Thomas J. 102
William 7,75
Wamble, James 34
Wamick, Peter 39
Wammot, Thomas 41
Wamock, David 132
Thomas 132

Ward, Amos 110
Barnabas 75
Benjamin 17,36
Charles 37,131
Charleston 72
Conrade 131
Elijah 39,67
Fountain 87
George 65
Hardy 60
James 6,21,109,132
Jasper 77
Jesse 6
John 7,93,102,131
Joshua 108
Josiah 72,91
Lewis 58
Micajah 7
Minos 119
Nathaniel 35,36,94
Richard 22
Robert 94
Robertson 64
Samuel 122
Solomon 39
Thomas 19,28,99,106,
  108
Thomas A. 50
William 9,12,42
Wardlow, James 41
William 41
Ware, Joseph 90
Robert 38,111
Warford, Joseph 44
Warley, Elijah 28
Warlic, David 131
Warlow, James 57
Warner, Herbert 79
Jeremiah 10
Warr, Lemuel 78
Warrels, William 104
Warren, Daniel 83
James 44,120
John 31
Joshua 20
Kalib 21
Lewis 84
Peter 106
Robert 20
Samuel 78
Timothy 110
Warrick, Hardy 96
Warturs, Jesse 90
Warwick, George 26
James 20
John 19,28,103
Wasburn, John 56
Wasden, James 86
Wasdon, Daniel 12
John 90
Washam, Alexander 48
Washbam, Jesse 68
Washington, George 11
Jeremiah 11
Woodson 104
Wasnor, John 121
Waters, Charles 10
Frederick 10
James 83
Jeremiah 86
John 56
Jonathan 10
Nias 96
Reason 40
Waterson, Benjamin 54
Watington, Armstead 37
Watkins, Benjamin 99
Edward 117

Isaac 22,80
James 29
Moses 99
Needham 95
Reece 40
Watman, Daniel 57
Watson, Alexander 38,93
Allen 102
Daniel 30,132
David 12
Frederick 83
Hugh 132
Isaac 28
James 48,96
John 7,17,35,50,77,
  138
Michael 90
Richard 96
Robert 40
Stott 20
Thomas 138
William 39,55,97,103,
  113,138
Willie 18
Watts, Alexander 128
Andrew 47
Ewell 104
Robert 54
Waugh, David 62
William P. 62
Wauley, Sampson 10
Waworth, Daniel 45
Wayne, William
Weab, John 121
Weaks, Hewet 125
John 85
Weant, Jacob 121
Wear, Joseph 131
Weather, Isom 55
Weatherington, Jesse 84
Southey 12
Weatherly, Henry 112
Weathers, Edward 36
Weaver, Cannon 30
Isaac 118
James 108,136
Jared 60
Jethro 64
John 8,63,120
John, Jr. 58
Mark 118
Moses 21
Timothy 109
Webb, Benjamin 137
Caleb 46
Darlin 133
Dempsey 75
Floyd 114
George 7
James 108
Jeremiah 132
John 29,108
John, Jr. 99
Laban 59
Lewis 127
Moses 6
Reuben 57
Robert 132
Samuel 124
Thomas 6
William 89
Webster, Charles 108
James 113
John 113
Pleasant 113
Wilson 4
Wedenton, Cirus 127
Weeks, Archibald 55

Joseph W. 75
Purry 75
Samuel 6
Weer, David 123
John 123
Samuel 45
William 45
Wehunt, Michel 137
Weir, Howard 48
Welborn, Henry 52
John 44
Moses 123
Moses, Jr. 123
William 45,119
Welch, David 6
David, Jr. 76
James 58,127,138
John 116,138
Michel 34
Turner 46
William 42,58,114
Weldon, Samuel 79
Thomas 79
Well, Andrew 46
Wellbourn, Samuel 62
Wellons, Jesse 14
Wells, Anderson 130
Henry 91
John 108
Joshua 134
Miles K. 99
Stephen 108
Welsh, James 138
John 138
Richard 99
Wemack, Wiley 64
Wenters, William 134
Wessen, Abner 55
West, Alexander 135
Benjamin 58
Charles 55
Isaac 9,38
John 9,65,122
Jonathan 45,53
Joseph 108
Mathew 125
Nimrod 6
Noel 102
Robert 47
Stephen 89
Thomas L. 77
William 16,19,29,84
William M. 59
Westbrook, John 86
Thomas 42
Uriah 96
Westmoreland, Peterson
128
Rhoda 128
Robert 47
Thomas 41,115
Weston, Henry 133
Isaac 15
Thomas 8
Wetherby, Peter 39
Wetherford, Hiram 38
Wetherly, Allen 62
Isaac 61
Isaiah 61
Wethersby, Shadrack 93
Wever, James 136
Weymire, Rhudolph 33
Whaer, Joseph 80
Whaley, Rigdon 90
Whally, Willoughby 73
Wharton, Evan 61
John 60,66
William 21

Wheatley, John 21
Wheedleton, Elijah 84
Wheeler, Ezekiel 104
James 78
Jesse 53
Nathaniel 18
Samuel 106
Sion 78
Wheless, Archibald 22
Elijah 80
Whidbee, George P. 6
Whidler, Benjamin 72
Whiley, Jeremiah 128
Joab 26
Whilly, Elias 26
Whirly, Pleasant 133
Whisanhunt, Henry 60
Whitaker, Isaac 116
James 18
Jesse 116
Nathaniel 63
Peter 121
William 116
Willis 63,101
Wilson C. 18
Whitamore, John
Whitbee, George P. 6
James 9
Whitby, Samuel 14
White, Alexander 73
Cader 65
Daniel 5,23,74,80
David 24,77,127
Edward 22
Elisha 57
Frederick 3
George 5,77
Hardy 65
Henry 133
Isaac 77,84,112
James 11,16,28,73,
100,110,129
James L. 18
John 26,27,28,32,74,
75,123,125,133
John, Jr. 3,75
Joshua 3
Marshal 89
Michael 47
Moses 132
Perry 89
Peter 77
Reuben 57,100
Richard 50,64
Shadrack 39
Stephen 89
Thomas 57,81,104,119
Whitmel 77
William 9,36,37,64,
75,93,95
William M. 100
Worley 87
Whitehall, Thomas 4
Whitehead, Abner 12
Anderson 107
James 88,107
John 34,115
Joseph 22,110
Nathaniel 110
Whitehouse, Alexander 5
Whitehurst, Enoch 72
Hilery 83
Samuel 72
William 87
Whitener, Daniel, Jr. 54
Whiteside, Joseph 125
Whitesides, William 132
Whitfield, Arch D. 81

Guilford 22
Hatch 12
John 12
Needham 12
William W. 76
Whitford, Will 84
Whithead see Whitehead
Whitheral, James, Jr. 3
Whitley, Eunuch 103
George 76,125
John 83
Whitlock, Bowen 51
John 116
Whitly, Thomas 64
Whitney, David 27
Dempsey 39
Ebenezer 39
Whitsell, Jacob 108
Whittenburg, Daniel 135
Whittington, Nehemiah 113
Richard 15
Whitworth, Archibald 40
John 131
William 113
Whorton see Wharton
Wiat, James 49
John 48
Wiatt, Abraham 53
Aron 51
William 44
Wichel, Jacob 3
Wichidht, John 24
Wicker, Benjamin 28
Mathew 28
Robert 104
Wier, David 54
Wiggins, Anthony 65
Edmund 79
Elijah 22
Harrel 104
Henry 8
Isaac 65
James 104
John 12,104
Joseph 12
Robert 12
Thomas, Jr. 89
William 100
Wiggs, Abner 13
Raiford 90
Wilborn, John 44
Wilcox, Archibald 83
James 96
John 85
William 86
Wilcoxen, Elijah 67
Samuel 52
Squire 52
Wild, Henry 58,134
John 59
John J. 59
Wilder, Abram 66
Jesse 91
John 72
Malachi 17
Myles 72
Samson 72
Samuel, Jr. 103
Wilds, Henry 134
Wiley, Charles 81
David 60
Hugh 47
Isaac 48
Josiah 60
Samuel 48
Wilker, Jacob 38
Wilkerson, John 30,100,
106

Jonathan 125
Jos. 109
Wilkes, Henry 65
  James 65
  John 65
  Rheuben 65
Wilkey, William 133
Wilkins, Alfred 101
  George 42
  James 132
  John 30
  Lemuel 19
  Richard 108
  Robert 95
  Thomas 42
  Wil. 65
Wilkinson, Jacob 83
  John 25,61,67,128
  Joseph 32
  Kinchen 98
  Micajah 14
  Neill 97
  Oden 9
  Osborn 126
  Richard 25
  Thomas 25
  Timothy 26
  Willie 20
  Zachariah 82
Wilks, Elijah 97
  Kinchen 77
Willard, Allen 51
Willey, William 18
  Even S. 127
Williams, Aaron 112
  Absolam 40
  Alexander 14
  Anson 75
  Anthony 8
  Benjamin 28,69,76
  Benjamin B. 77
  Bennet 29
  Britain 137
  Bryant 16
  Burwell 109
  Byrd 95
  Caleb 134
  Charles 96,130
  D. G. 23
  Daniel 30,76
  David 76,101
  Edward 44
  Elbert 110
  Elijah 33,64
  Enoch 33,136
  Ephraim 51
  Frederick 75
  Garrat 86
  George 91,100,119
  Green 106
  Guilford 79
  Hardy 76
  Henry 17,83,110,120,
    129
  Hill 17
  Howard 132
  Isaac 5,54,74,100
  Isom 69
  Jacob 3,45,63
  James 30,39,74,76,89,
    101,129,138
  Jesse 30
  Joel 100,133,135
  John 22,29,38,44,55,
    73,74,80,119,134
  John C. 21
  John M. 19
  Joseph 79,86,125

Laban 26
Lewis 95
Littleberry 35
Manassah 95
Matthew 12
Matthias 52,60
Miles 74,76
Nathan 95
Nathaniel 104
Newbern 28
Peter 5
Richard 113
Robert 15,37,53
Robert B. 101
Samuel 22,44,81,87,
  130
Simon 101
Stephen 15,100,122
Theophilus 16,94
Thomas 20,55,64,101,
  108,110,124
Tully 6
William 8,12,17,41,
  60,64,84,116,137
William, Sr. 64
Willie 59
Willis 100
Zachariah 27
Williamson, Anthony 92
  Henry 73
  James 16,26
  Kinchen 23,80
  Lois 67
  Samuel 82
  Stephen 103
  Thomas 81
  Urban 16
  William 120
Williavy, Anderson 60
Willie, Andrew 116
Williford, Isaac 77
  Jonas 89
  William 96
Willins, William 102
Willis, Augustus 79
  Benjamin 66
  Cason 66
  Elijah 110
  Elisha 33
  Hardy 11
  Henry 111
  Jacob 133
  James 4
  Joseph 56,69,85,132,
    134
  Littleton 85
  Moab 96
  Philip 44
  Reubin 85
  Royal 31
  Samuel 31
  Stephen 109
  Thomas 66,121
  Washington 85
  Williams 130
  Wilson 110
  Zachariah 66
Willls, Lewis 79
Willoughby, John 87
  Willie 76
Wills, Francis 6
  John 17
  Lewis 79
Willson, Joseph 134
Willy, John 40
Wilmoth, Gabriel 133
Wilsen, Levi 118
Wilson, Abner 56,69

Amous 112
Andrew 136
Benjamin 57,125
Caleb 3
Charles 56
David B. 47
Demsey 4,17
Dennis 100
Edmond 78
Edward 40
George 33,65,122
Henry 110,111,112
Hugh 126
Isaac 6,65,95
James 31,44,88,96,
  108,125,133
James, Jr. 77
John 31,33,39,48,54,
  94,107,113,121,
  124,126,128
John, Jr. 94,125
Levi 118
Lodwick B. 40
Luke 56
Matthew 136
Maxwell 39
Meskick 94
Peaton 32
Philip 59
Richard 32
Robert 36,38,54,76,
  96,113,136
Samon 39
Samuel 110,113
Shadrick 94
Silas 54,65
Stogdel 135
Thomas 96,137
William 13,27,56,58,
  68,106,107,112,
  134,136
William J. 129
Willis 4
Wimberly, Abram 29
  Fred 65
  Lewis 77
Wimborne, Stephen 20
Winborne, Lemuel 78
Winburn, Benjamin 65
Winchester, William 40
Windley, Israel 83
  Moses 9,82
  Wyriott 82
Winecoff, David 127
Wines, William 49
Winetuter, John 28
Winfield, John 9
  Thomas 10
Winflet, Levi 90
Winfrey, Isaac 116
Wingate, Jesse 17
  John 75
  Needam 129
  William 7
Winkfield, Freeman 99
Winklar, Peter 122
Winkler, Henry 134
  Matthew 135
Winningham, Abel 33
  Adam 33
Winslow, Joseph 72
Winson, Elisha 131
  Nimrod 131
Winstead, Samuel 106
Winston, Jesse 103
  Joseph, Jr. 71,139
  Moses 36

Wintosh, Alexander 47

John 47
William 47
Wiot, James 49
Wisdom, Bird 111
Wise, Benjamin 57
    Thomas 104
    William 16
Wiseman, James 44,121
    Thismothy 122
    Wilson 44
Wisenghunt, Michael 134
    Peter 134
Wishon, Leonard 128
Wistt, John T. C. 35
Witcher, Ephraim 67
Withellene, George 43
Witheral, James, Jr. 3
Witherell, Raiford, S. 31
Witherington, James 8
    Thomas 86
Witherly, James 39
Wodel, Richard 90
Woldrige, Joseph 41
Woldson, Luke 133
Wolf, Jacob 114
Wolfington, Isaac 112
Wollard, David 64
    John 83
    Nathaniel 21
    Silas 21
Wolles, William, Jr. 125
Wollington, John 41
Womack, James 122
    Rora 110
    Wiley 35
Womble, Jacob 110
    Neal 102
    Tyson 109
Womouth, Washington 105
Wood, Augustus 22
    Daniel
    Green 24
    Hardy 16
    Henry 123
    Hugh 32
    Isaac 106
    James 10,16,31,59,79,
        137
    Jaret 44
    John 32,33,43,92
    John, Jr. 123
    John C. 77
    Jonathan 85
    Joseph 133
    Josiah 20
    Newton 100
    Reddick 6
    Richard 36
    Robert 43,48,113
    Robert B. 49
    Samuel 21,37
    Simeon 78
    Stephen 51
    Thomas 118
    Truth 120
    Vincent 132
    William 29,55,93
    Young 96
Woodall, Absolam 14
    Alexander 103
    John 103
    William 126
Woodard, Caleb 4,19,72
    Christopher 35,101
    Henry 10
    James 14
    Jethro 72
    John 128

Joseph 35,102
Micajah 15
Nathaniel 83
Peter 14
William 102
Willis 15
Woodburn, Robert 60
Wooders, Chesley 40
Woodle, Luke 30
Woodley, Eli 81
    John 75
    Thomas 5,6
    William 8
Woodruff, John 19
Woods, Henry 96
    James 107
    John 84,107,111
    John L. 106
    Thomas 107
    William 32,107
    Zadock 11
Woody, John 107
Wooldrige, Aurelua 42
Wooten, Abraham 51
    Benjamin 16
    Ephraim 64,88
    Henry 89
    John 12
    Thomas B. 28
    William 133
Word, Elisha 121
Worhine, William 29
Workman, Henry 56,69,121,
    133
    Richard 108
    Thomas 44
    William 44,108
Worlaw, Michael 123
Worman, Joseph T. 78
Wormington, John 119
Worrell, Dempsey 94
    James 76
    Jesse 90
    Ransom 80
    Richard 90
Worsham, Henry 106
Worsley, Pitman 20
Wortham, Benjamin H. 36,
    37
Worthington, Jacob 33
Wortman, John 122
Wortrind, Westly 29
Wray, John 111
    Skipworth 41
Wren, Allen 23
    Boen 81
    John 119
    Joseph 23
Wrier, James 56
Wright, Benjamin 119
    Cader 73
    Charles 73
    Cornelius 74
    Fedding 41
    George 114
    Henry 10
    Henry H. 74
    John 42,131
    John, Sr. 19
    John H. 73
    John J. 113
    John M. 17
    Jonathan 3
    Joseph 128,136
    Levi 74
    Richard 23
    Seth 73
    Sharp 79

Solomon 57
Wrightet, Frances 39
Writentt, Thomas 4
Wyatt, John C. 71
Wyles, Lewis 117
Wyne, Henry 59
Wynens, John 125
Wynn, Archills 40
    Ezekiel 99
    John 9
    Peter 82
Wynne, Hicks 103
Wynns, Ann 125
    David 88
    George 88
    Henry 88
    William 8,76
Wyse, Morris 13
Wyuns, Benjamin 76

- Y -

Yancey, Charles 105
Yandles, Jesse 48
Yarborough, Alex 121
    Archibald 59
    Frederick 25
    John 123
    Moses 124
    Washington 79
Yarrell, Thomas 41
Yates, Alsey 101
    Clifford 42
    Edward 114
    Malcolm 67
    William 102
Yaudles, David B. 126
    Samuel 126
Yaw, Andrew 127
Yealock, Robert 111
Yeargan, Donas 64
Yeargin, Patterson 107
Yeargon, Doran 119
    Thomas 119
Yeats, William 76
Yerby, William 126
Yoakley, Andrew 68
York, Abner 128
    Adam 119
    Edward 90
    Jabaz 119
    Nathan 34
    William 60,112,133
Yost, John 120
Young, An'd 134
    Francis 55,68
    James 40,42,79
    John 46,63,68,106
    Jos. 104
    Joshua 81
    Mathew 61
    Nathan 26
    Robert 42
    Samuel 68
    William 114

- Z -

Zaloe, Jonathan 77
Zickler, Abraham 120
Zimmerman, Christopher 42
    John 62
    Joseph 42
Zimmerson, Christian 123
Zink, George 123
Ziveley, James 44